A HISTORY OF
CHELTENHAM

A HISTORY OF
CHELTENHAM

BY

GWEN HART

LEICESTER UNIVERSITY PRESS

1965

PRINTED IN GREAT BRITAIN
AT THE UNIVERSITY PRESS, OXFORD
BY VIVIAN RIDLER
PRINTER TO THE UNIVERSITY
FOR LEICESTER UNIVERSITY PRESS

TO

ISABELLE POSNETTE

WHOSE GENEROSITY MADE POSSIBLE

THE PUBLICATION OF THIS BOOK

The town of Cheltenham is and time out of mind
hath been an ancient borough and market town.

WILLIAM NORWOOD, A.D. 1600

PREFACE

THE first recorded attempt to write a history of Cheltenham was made by John Prinn shortly before the discovery
of the medicinal properties of the waters and the development of the Spa. All that survives is a description of the town
written by his own hand on the front pages of the Cheltenham
Court Book for the year 1692. He begins:

Cheltenham, alias Chilteham alias Cheltham, is a Towne situated
on ye north side of a small purling Silver Stream or Rivulet called
Chilt. . . . It is an ancient Market Towne . . . which is one Street
continued with the buildings on each side for a full mile in length.
. . . Albeit not a Corporation, yet it is a very ancient Burrough
abounding in Sundry Priviledges. . . .

Nearly a century and a half later, John Goding wrote his
History of Cheltenham. The town was still not incorporated
and was governed by a body of Commissioners, although it
was by that time a parliamentary borough of over 40,000
inhabitants. Since the publication of his book in 1863, no other
history of the town has been completed.

The rapid growth of the Spa had led to the publication of
a number of guide-books—valuable for the facts they gave
of the contemporary scene but not always accurate in their
references to the earlier history of the town. Goding took
much of his material from these publications and often repeated
their inaccuracies, but he also carried out considerable research
in other directions. He was interested not only in the glories
of the Spa, but in social conditions, political parties, and problems of local government in the immediate past. He availed
himself of the personal memories of his contemporaries and of
the survivors of an earlier generation. His work as Assistant-
Overseer of the Poor gave him access to documents dealing with
the administration of the Poor Law, and as an active member
of the Vestry, the old Vestry Records were available to him.
He was also deeply interested in the medieval background
of the 'ancient Burrough', and devoted a section of his book

to such information as he could obtain about its manorial
organization. Although he was untrained (and sometimes
unreliable) as an historian, he was the only writer of his generation in Cheltenham who realized the importance of the sources
then available: the Cheltenham Court Books, the old Vestry
Books, and the collection of documents made in the eighteenth
century by John Prinn. Unfortunately, the Prinn collection
has been widely dispersed since that time and most of the
Cheltenham items cannot be traced. An early eighteenth-
century Vestry Book from which John Goding quoted has
also disappeared in recent years. His work, however, is a most
valuable source book to which I am deeply indebted.

In the years since its publication, local interest in the history
of the town has by no means waned. Considerable research
has been carried out, much of which has been recorded in
articles published in the *Transactions of the Bristol and
Gloucestershire Archaeological Society*, the *Proceedings of the
Cotteswold Naturalists Field Club*, the *Gloucestershire Notes &
Queries*, and the *Victoria County History of Gloucestershire*,
Vol. II. To the contributors of these articles I should also like
to acknowledge my debt.

To these earlier sources I have been able to add the Minute
Books of the Town Commissioners (covering the years 1786–
1852). Local government in the ancient borough of Cheltenham
was for centuries carried out very largely by the courts and
officials of the lord of the manor. When this system of manorial
jurisdiction broke down in the eighteenth century, Cheltenham
—like many other growing towns—obtained Acts of Parliament
under which bodies of Commissioners were appointed to carry
out specific duties of local government. The recovery of the
Minute Books has made it possible to follow the work of these
Commissioners from the early days of the Spa until the first
elected body took office in 1852, and so to complete the story
of how the Saxon settlement on the Chelt developed through
varying stages, as a royal and ecclesiastically owned manor, a
market town, a centre for the production of malt and tobacco,
a famous Spa (set in the fine architecture of a Regency town),
and a great educational centre, until by royal charter in 1876
it became an incorporated borough with a Mayor and Council.

Lastly, I have tried to give unity to the story by setting it where possible against the background of English history of which it is part. One value of local history, in addition to the interest of those immediately concerned, is that it shows the detailed working of the great national processes. Conversely, no community develops in complete isolation from the nation to which it belongs. 'What is local is also national.'

GWEN HART

Cheltenham, 1965

ACKNOWLEDGEMENTS

I AM most deeply indebted to Professor H. P. R. Finberg who very kindly read the first draft of the book and gave me valuable criticism and advice. I have received generous help, over a long period, from Mr. Irvine Gray, the Records Officer for the County of Gloucester, from the Assistant Archivist Mr. Brian Smith, and his predecessor, Mr. A. T. Gaydon. I have to thank Mr. H. G. Fletcher, Librarian and Curator of the Cheltenham Public Library and Art Gallery, for making available to me at all times the resources of the Local Collection and for permission to reproduce pictures in the Art Gallery. I should like at the same time to acknowledge the courteous help which I have received from the staff of the Library and Art Gallery. Mr. F. D. Littlewood, the Town Clerk of Cheltenham, allowed me to make a thorough examination of the minute books of the Town Commissioners. To him and to Mr. Richard Board, the Deputy Town Clerk, I am grateful for the interest which they have shown in the progress of this book.

I have also to thank the President and Fellows of St. John's College, Oxford, for permission to consult documents in their possession relating to Pate's Grammar School and Almshouse; Mr. Guy Whinyates of Buckfast, Devonshire, for allowing me to print extracts from the diaries and papers of his family; the late Mr. Leslie Bayley for giving me access to some of the Hughes papers in his possession; and Dr. A. Goldfoot for supplying information from documents concerned with the early history of the Jewish synagogue in Cheltenham.

I should like to express my gratitude to Dr. Helen Cam for her kindness in answering so fully my numerous queries; to Miss Ruth Butler, from whose notes for her article on the social and economic history in the *Victoria County History of Gloucestershire* (Vol. II) I first became aware of the wealth of documents available for the study of medieval Cheltenham; to Dr. Alwyn Ruddock for throwing light on some dark places in the Tudor scene; and to Mr. William Dreghorn for his help in connexion with the map of the Hundred of Cheltenham.

I also wish to acknowledge with gratitude the considerable help—in ways too numerous to mention—which I have received from two friends, Mrs. Leila Hoskins and Miss Nancy Stevens.

Most of all I thank my husband, not only for compiling the Index, but for his constant encouragement and help during the writing of this book, of which indeed he was the instigator.

GWEN HART

CONTENTS

ILLUSTRATIONS

MAPS

ABBREVIATIONS

BM	British Museum
CPL	Cheltenham Public Library
GCL	Gloucester City Library
GRO	Gloucester Records Office
PRO	Public Record Office
Cal. Pat. Rolls	*Calendar of Patent Rolls*
TBGAS	*Transactions of the Bristol and Gloucestershire Archaeological Society*
VCH	*Victoria County History for Gloucestershire,* Vol. II
Goding	*Norman's History of Cheltenham* by John Goding (1863)
Griffith	Griffith, J. K. *A General Cheltenham Guide* (1816)
	Griffith, S. Y. *A Historical Description of Cheltenham* (1826)
	Griffith, S. Y. *A History of Cheltenham and its Vicinity* (1838)
Fosbroke	Fosbroke, T. D. *A Picturesque and Topographical Account of Cheltenham and its Vicinity, which includes a Medical History of the Waters by Dr. John Fosbroke* (1826)

I

THE BEGINNINGS

WHEN in the eighteenth century the discovery of the Spa waters brought fame to Cheltenham, it already had a long history as a market town. Leland called it Cheltenham Street—a name which appeared again on an early nineteenth-century map of north Gloucestershire. The old name shows that Cheltenham, like Winchcombe, Northleach, and other Cotswold towns of Saxon origin, consisted for many centuries of one long street—the present High Street which is still the main artery of the town—with paths or lanes leading out of it on either side. One such path led (as it does today) to St. Mary's Church, where traces of Norman work may still be seen. The field on the south-west of the church, which is now bounded by Royal Crescent, was called within living memory Church Meadow; it is almost certainly part of the holding recorded in the Domesday Survey as that of Reinbald the Priest. The Promenade nearby is built on land marked on a plan of 1818 as the Lord's Meadow—part of the demesne of the medieval lords of the manor which is also mentioned in the Survey.

A much older landmark—a small barrow or knap—was still in existence in the early nineteenth century and is commemorated in the name of Knapp Road near St. James's Railway Station. This barrow is a reminder that Cheltenham is situated in a part of England almost as famous for its barrows and ancient landmarks as Salisbury Plain. Within a radius of ten miles from the centre of the town there are some of the most important prehistoric remains in the Cotswolds.[1] To the south-west, towards Gloucester, is Hucclecote, unique as a site where excavations have revealed relics which span the ages between Palaeolithic occupation and the building of a Roman villa. To the south is the Leckhampton Hill Camp with an adjoining round barrow, and further round the hill among the smaller

barrows is the spot where the famous Birdlip Mirror was discovered nearly a century ago. The long barrow at the Crippetts
is even nearer.

On the north are the earthworks on Cleeve, the unexcavated
hill camp on Nottingham Hill and the well-known long barrow
of Belas Knap with its unusual orientation. One of the round
barrows on the nearer side of Cleeve Hill formed part of the
medieval boundary of the old Hundred of Cheltenham. This
ancient boundary mark, known for centuries as 'the Stones on
Northfield' was excavated in 1925, but unfortunately the bones
and pottery sherds have since been lost so that it is now impossible to assign any date to its construction. Many small barrows
have been destroyed in the farming and building operations of
the last hundred and fifty years—a fate which befell the round
barrow near the centre of Cheltenham. Although the late
O. G. S. Crawford and many others have tried without success
to find specific details of this barrow, there can be no reasonable
doubt of its existence and of its destruction in 1846 when the
Great Western Railway station was completed. Goding, writing from first-hand evidence supplied by the older generation
of his time, states that the opening of the barrow in 1832
revealed three large upright stones and a massive capstone
which was later used as part of a cider press at Knapp House.

A few prehistoric relics have been found within the town
—a polished celt in 1910, a Neolithic axehead in 1930, another in
1939, and in the same year a bronze spear. A recent excavation
in the Sandy Lane area has revealed sherds of Iron Age
pottery. It is therefore possible that men of the Neolithic,
Bronze, and Iron Age cultures traversed the land in their
journeys from hill to hill, but there is no evidence of their
settlement in the area now covered by the town.

It is also unlikely that Cheltenham was in existence in
Roman times. Within almost the same ten mile radius there
are the Roman villas at Winchcombe, Witcombe, Whittington,
Withington, and Chedworth. Cirencester, the second largest
town in Roman Britain, lies only twelve miles away, and
Gloucester is much nearer. There is an interesting theory
that the Cheltenham terrain is part of the land which was
centuriated—that is, assigned to Roman soldiers of the military

settlement at Gloucester; there is, however, little evidence in support of this.[2] Many Roman coins have been dug up in the town, particularly during the great building operations in the early nineteenth century. These have been found in the High Street near the 'Plough' (1816)—a large number in the Bath Road near Thirlestaine House (1818) and others in 1848 when the present Hales Road was made. Goding himself had collected eighty-three such coins during excavations for building purposes in various parts of the town. The coins were reputed to be from the reigns of Roman emperors from the time of Claudius to that of Valens. Unfortunately they all passed into private collections and no accurate account of their numbers has survived. More recently occasional finds have been reported, but these amount only to five coins in the last fifty years. Romano-British skeletons have also been found during the last few years in the Naunton Park area. It is, however, unlikely that there was any permanent settlement until Saxon times.

The name Cheltenham is of Saxon origin—Chelt meaning a height or cliff and ham a settlement.[3] The name of the River Chelt is undoubtedly a back formation, the use of which was not known before the sixteenth century. The Chelt has been identified by Dr. Finberg as the stream called Arle—mentioned in a Saxon charter in 1065.[4] The first documentary reference to Cheltenham itself occurs earlier in an account of the Council of Cloveshoe held in 803, by which time the main Anglo-Saxon kingdoms had already taken shape, and Christianity had been established with an organized church in all of them.

In Gloucestershire it appears that the first conquest was made by the West Saxons, following the defeat of the British kings of Bath, Gloucester, and Cirencester at Deorham in 577 by the West Saxon Caewlin. It is known, however, from Bede's History and other sources,[5] that there was an early settlement of people known as Hwicce, of mixed Anglian and Saxon origin, in a territory which included most of Worcestershire, Gloucestershire, and west Warwickshire. Whether in its early stages this territory was or was not ruled by the West Saxons, it passed to the overlordship of the Mercians with the victory of Penda at Cirencester in 628. The Cheltenham area was thus part of the kingdom of Mercia, of which Winchcombe was for a short time the capital. Later the struggle with the Danes in the time of King Alfred ended in the overlordship of Wessex and led eventually to the unification of England.

In the early stages of its conquest by the Mercians the land of the Hwicce was ruled by the sub-kings, Eanhere, Eanfrith, Osric, Oshere, and others. These sub-kings seem to have played a great part in the spreading of Christianity and the organization of the church in Gloucestershire. The bishopric of Worcester, in which diocese Cheltenham remained until the Reformation, was established for the Hwicce about the year 680 by Theodore of Tarsus, Archbishop of Canterbury and 'perhaps the greatest prince of the Church in all English history' (Trevelyan). Shortly afterwards Osric of the Hwicce founded the Abbey of Gloucester and it is possible that the Abbeys of Pershore and Tewkesbury were founded within the next forty years.

By the beginning of the ninth century a number of small monasteries—or mission stations—had been founded at various places in Gloucestershire. Among these communities there were Beckford, Cleeve, Deerhurst, Cheltenham, and, most important of all, Winchcombe, which later became a great medieval abbey. At the Council of Cloveshoe (803) a dispute was settled between the Bishops of Worcester and Hereford, each of whom claimed the revenues of a monastery at Cheltenham.[6] The statement that the Bishop of Worcester had been drawing these revenues for the previous thirty years shows that it must have been in existence at least by 773. No further records of this monastery have been found. It has been assumed that (like so many others) it was destroyed by the Danes who were at Gloucester in 877 before their defeat by Alfred at Ethandune, and that it was not refounded. There is a long-standing tradition that it was located in the Cambray area. When John Prinn wrote in 1692 'Anciently there was a Priory within the Towne . . .', he gave as its exact site a house which fronted the High Street between the present Barclays Bank and the entrance to Cambray, which was at that time the property of the Cheltenham rectory.

It has been pointed out, however, by Stenton and others that a religious community which was described in the eighth century as a monastery did not necessarily mean that its members were monks, since the term was often used at that time for 'a church served by a group of clergy sharing a communal life'. It is therefore probable that the Cheltenham monastery was in reality a minster—a mother church—which in this sense has had a continuous existence from the eighth century to the present day, and that like many other ancient parish churches it 'represents a monastery which has disappeared without trace'. The details given in Domesday Book —that the church in Cheltenham held 1½ hides (more than usual for the ordinary parish church with a single priest) and the reference to priests in the plural, add support to this point of view. It should be noted also that the earliest known references to the chapels at Leckhampton and Charlton Kings make them subject to the mother church at Cheltenham. However, the change of ownership at some unknown date from that of the Bishop of Worcester in 773 to that of Reinbald at the time of the Domesday Survey raises some difficulties.

From the time of the Council of Cloveshoe there is no other known reference to Cheltenham until the record made in the Domesday Survey of 1086. During the intervening centuries, however, there were three outstanding lines of national development which affected Cheltenham. First, the smaller kingdoms were forced gradually under the power of the ruling house of Wessex—from which our present Queen is descended—and in this way there developed a united England under one monarchy. By the time of Edward the Confessor, Cheltenham was the property of the King. How far back this royal ownership began, whether with the Kings of the Hwicce or of the Mercians, is not known.

Secondly, during these years the boundaries of our counties and their subdivisions, the hundreds, were being slowly established. The origin of both shire and hundred is obscure, but by the middle of the eleventh century both were in existence, with shire moots and hundred moots and their officials for the administration of justice and the collection of taxes. The Worcester monk Hemming writes that Eadric Streona, first under Ethelred the Unready and then under Canute, 'joined district to district at his will,' and in this way the former independent county of Wincelcumbshire (Winchcombe) which included Cheltenham, became part of the county of Gloucestershire.

Lastly, by imperceptible stages the system of landowning, with its grouping of social classes which we associate with Feudalism was taking shape. The unit of landownership became in the course of time the manor, and though boroughs, vills and hamlets grew up, most of these were also for many centuries either manors or parts of manors and subject to the authority of the lord of the manor concerned. Some royal or otherwise important manors such as Cheltenham gave their name to the hundred. The description of Cheltenham which is given in Domesday Book concerns therefore the manor of Cheltenham itself and the smaller manors which were also contained in the Cheltenham hundred, and from this description we are able to form our first impression of Cheltenham as it was at the time of the Norman Conquest.

The decision to collect the information for what was later known as Domesday Book was first taken only a few miles from Cheltenham. It was at Gloucester according to the Anglo-Saxon Chronicle that William the Conqueror took counsel with the Witan in 1085 and decided to order a survey of the whole country. Gloucester was at this time one of three centres of government in the kingdom. William is said to have worn his crown three times a year when he was in England—'at Easter he bore it in Winchester, at Pentecost at Westminster, at Midwinter at Gloucester; and there were with him all the rich men from over all England—Archbishops and Bishops, Abbots and Earls, Thanes and Knights.'[7] Gloucester was important also because it was a bulwark against the attacks of the Welsh which constituted a serious threat to the peace of the kingdom.

The Domesday Survey was carried out mainly because William I for various reasons found it essential in 1085 to know the full resources of his kingdom. His object therefore was to obtain a detailed evaluation of all his own landed property and that of his tenants-in-chief. For this purpose commissioners were sent into each English county, with the exception of those in the north, and there they were to question on oath 'the

Sheriffs, all the barons and freemen, and of the whole hundred the priests, bailiffs, and six villeins of each vill'.[8] They were to find out the value, size, resources, ownership and other details of each manor at three given dates: in 1066, at the time when the king granted the manor to its present owner, and at the time of the inquiry. Thus the manor was taken as the unit of property, but the unit of inquiry within each county was the hundred. It seems likely, however, that the information thus collected was returned by the Commissioners to the Treasury at Winchester not as a statement from each separate hundred, but in some form which approximated more nearly to the arrangement in the Survey of the tenants-in-chief and their manors in the county.[9]

Charles Taylor, in his *Analysis of the Domesday Survey of Gloucestershire*, writes that in view of the grouping of the hundreds in the lists of properties of various owners, the centres where the commissioners collected their evidence in this county were probably Gloucester, Winchcombe, Tewkesbury, and Bristol. He also suggests that some of the spellings recall the Cotswold pronunciation which persists to this day. For example, Udecestre' for Woodchester shows that 'a wood was an, ood eight centuries ago'.

The final summary of all the information which the commissioners collected was recorded in Latin in two books, the first of which, with the owners' names shown in red ink and place names indicated by a red line, contains the survey of Gloucestershire. This opens with an account of the city of Gloucester and of the land between the Usk and the Wye (Caerleon). The borough of Winchcombe is next mentioned, giving some indication of its importance at the time; and level with this is a list of the owners *in capite* (tenants-in-chief) of whom the King was the first. Under the heading of *Terra Regis* the first entry deals with Cheltenham:

Terra Regis King Edward held Chinteneha. There were eight hides and a half. One hide and a half belong to the Church: Reinbaldus holds it. There were three plough teams in demesne and twenty villani and ten bordarii and seven servi, with eighteen plough teams. The priests have two plough teams. There were two mills of 11s. 8d. To this Manor King William's Steward added two bordarii and four villani and three mills. Of these two are the King's; the third is the Steward's; and there is one plough team more. In the time of King Edward it paid £9. 5s. and three thousand loaves for the dogs. Now it pays £20 and twenty cows and twenty hogs, and 16s. instead of the bread.

We have here the first actual description of Cheltenham, written nearly nine centuries ago, when it was one of the eleven estates in Gloucestershire owned directly by the King. It gives a very incomplete picture since it was compiled purely for purposes of assessment, and unfortunately the terms used cannot be defined with any accuracy. The area of the hide seems to have varied. According to Taylor it averaged in Gloucestershire from 250 to 300 acres. It is, however, generally accepted that the number of hides given in Domesday Book refers to the amount of the taxable land rather than to a definite acreage. The plough team is usually regarded as consisting of eight oxen which were capable of keeping under cultivation about 120 acres. On this assumption Taylor calculates that the area cultivated in Cheltenham by the twenty-four plough teams mentioned would be roughly 2,880 acres. This area probably included Arle, Alstone, and Sandford which were mentioned as tithings in the earliest surviving Cheltenham court rolls. They were also the sites of medieval mills, and as mill sites rarely change, three of the five mills recorded must almost certainly have been in these areas. One of the remaining two was undoubtedly the main Cheltenham mill in Cambray, and the fifth may have been the second mill at Alstone, or it may have been in Charlton Kings—another area which was not mentioned by name in the Survey but is generally thought to have been included in the manor of Cheltenham at this time.[10] On the other hand, Swindon (belonging to the Prior of St. Oswald's, Gloucester), Prestbury (to the Bishop of Hereford), and Leckhampton (to Leuric) are recorded as separate manors in the hundred of Cheltenham. From the fact that, according to Taylor's calculations, only 7,270 acres of this hundred could be cultivated by the number of plough teams recorded, and that the male population for this area is given as 114, it would appear that almost half of the hundred was not under cultivation at this time.

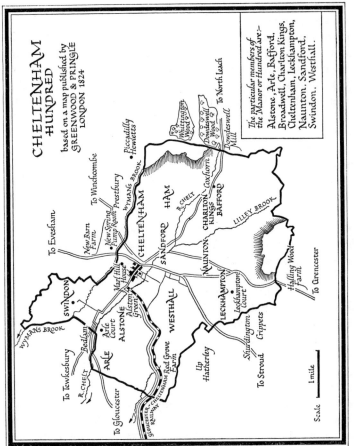

CHELTENHAM
HUNDRED

based on a map published by
GREENWOOD & PRINGLE
LONDON 1824

The particular members of
the Manor or Hundred are:—
Alstone, Arle, Bafford,
Broadwell, Charlton Kings,
Cheltenham, Leckhampton,
Naunton, Sandford,
Swindon, Westhall.

To Evesham

To Winchcombe

New Barn Farm

New Spring Prestbury
Pump Room

WYMANS BROOK

Piccadilly Howletts

Whittington Wood

Dowdeswell Wood

To North Leach

Dowdeswell Mill

CHELTENHAM

SANDFORD HAM

R. CHELT

CHARLTON Coxhorn
KINGS
BAFFORD

LILLEY BROOK

Marl Hill House

Alstone Green

NAUNTON

Halling Wood Farm

To Gloucester

To Tewkesbury

R. CHELT

Bedlam

ARLE

Arle Court

ALSTONE

SWINDON

WYMANS BROOK

WESTHALL

Red Grove Farm

Up Hatherley

LECKHAMPTON

Leckhampton Court

Shurdington Crippets

To Stroud

To Cirencester

GLOUCESTER & CHELTENHAM RAILWAY

Scale   1 mile

FIG. 1

There were two small manors in Leckhampton. One was held in the time of King Edward by Osgot and under King William by Leuric; the other by Brictric and Ordric jointly under Edward, and by Brictric for the later part of William's reign. Taylor suggests that in the Survey the manor of Lechetone (held by Humphrey the Cook) was wrongly placed in the Hundred of Slaughter and was in fact part of Leckhampton in Cheltenham. As this Lechetone belonged in the time of King Edward to Ordric, the theory may be correct. It is borne out by a reference in the cartulary of Cirencester Abbey to the tithes due from Geoffrey the Cook to the priest of Leckhampton (1162), and there is a later record (1226) in the Book of Fees that Leckhampton was at that time held 'by serjeanty of the King's Cook'. Since land held in serjeanty was usually granted by the King for some personal service, the reference to Humphrey the Cook seems to indicate preparation of food or lodging for William I when he was on his way to Gloucester.

The payments in food date back to an earlier time when it was customary for the King and his Court to move from one royal manor to another and to live on the produce of each in turn. The reference to the bread for the dogs suggests a connexion with royal hunting, but despite strong local tradition there is no direct evidence that either Edward the Confessor or William I ever hunted in the woods of Charlton or Leckhampton.

It is difficult to attempt any calculation of the total population of the Cheltenham of the Domesday Survey since apart from the slaves the numbers given possibly refer only to those holding tenancies, that is heads of households. The slaves could still be bought and sold and transferred at the will of their owners, unlike the villeins and the bordars. Maitland,[11] in discussing these last two groups, suggests that the difference between them was economic rather than legal, the average holding for a villanus being about 30 acres, and for a bordarius 5 acres. Taylor, on the other hand, says that in Gloucestershire the average holding of the villanus was the equivalent of 80 acres, and of the bordarius 30 acres. The difference between these two estimates confirms Maitland's statement that the whole question is 'sadly obscure'. More recent research has not removed the obscurities and Stenton writes that the meaning of these terms still remains 'the central problem of Domesday study'.

The Domesday Survey is not concerned with recording the details of the parish churches, but the essential facts emerge that a church existed in Cheltenham at the time and that it was generously endowed with 1½ hides of land and held by Reinbald. It is unlikely that the latter was one of the priests in residence, since he held at least sixteen other livings.[12] He also held the office of Chancellor under King William and was Dean of a College of Secular Canons at Cirencester, which was later refounded as a house of Augustinian Canons in Cirencester Abbey. Nearly five centuries later Leland the Antiquarian visited this abbey and noted the tomb of Reinbald and its epitaph:

> Hic jacet Reinbaldus Presbyter
> quondam hujus Ecclesiae decanus et tempore
> Edwardi Regis Angliae cancellarius.

This tomb was destroyed with the abbey itself at the time of the dissolution of the monasteries. Extracts from the cartulary of the abbey make it clear that Reinbald was regarded as an honoured founder whose anniversary was celebrated each year by the monks with much feasting. He may well have been Norman and have come to England with Edward the Confessor. In his office as Chancellor he was able to accumulate considerable property, and he was a great pluralist.

Reinbald's lands passed on his death to his college at Cirencester, and were part of the endowment assigned by Henry I to the new abbey in the charter of 1133. This endowment included 'the Church of Cheltenham, with the land thereof and the mill, and the Chapels, and all other appurtenances to the said Church belonging'.[13] Thus for the succeeding four centuries the Church of Cheltenham belonged to Cirencester Abbey, until with other properties it was confiscated by the Crown when the monasteries were dissolved in 1539.

Much of this property can be identified from later surveys.[14] It included what were known as Church Meadow and Cambray Field which were used for centuries as farm land, until

Joseph Pitt bought the rectory in 1799 and immediately resold them for building sites. Shortly afterwards Royal Crescent was erected on part of Church Meadow, and on the Cambray Field were built Watson's Theatre, Cambray House, Wellington Mansion, and Georgiana Cottage—with their historic associations for Cheltenham—which have long since disappeared. For a short time Cambray was the most fashionable quarter of Cheltenham, where the exiled French royal family, the Duke of Wellington, Lord Byron, Charles James Fox and many other distinguished visitors found temporary residence. The mill pond of the old Cambray mill may still be seen on the bank of the Chelt as it flows through Sandford Park.

One other site mentioned in the Domesday Survey remained virtually unchanged until the early nineteenth century. At that time the middle section of the present Promenade still kept the name of Lord's Meadow, by which it was known when it was part of the demesne—the private property of the lord of the manor. On the site of this meadow there now stand the magnificent block of Regency Villas which house the Municipal Offices, and the colourful shops of the Promenade.

II

THE MEDIEVAL OWNERS OF
CHELTENHAM

LITTLE or nothing is known of Cheltenham during the next two reigns after the making of the Domesday Survey, although William Rufus was frequently in Gloucester where on one occasion he summoned King Malcolm of Scotland to do homage to him and where in the same year he appointed Anselm to the long vacant See of Canterbury. It is likely, therefore, that in his reign 'the Court still sojourned every Christmas at Gloucester and halted at Cheltenham on the way'.[1] Henry I, on the other hand, seems to have spent far less time in this city than his father or his brother. The only known link between Henry and Cheltenham is the already mentioned grant of Reinbald's possessions to the Abbey of Cirencester.

In the civil war which broke out after Henry I's death between his daughter Matilda and his nephew King Stephen, Gloucestershire was deeply involved. Milo, known as the constable of England as well as of Gloucester Castle and sheriff of the county, was one of Matilda's main supporters, and for some years the city of Gloucester was the chief centre of resistance to Stephen. It was from Gloucester that Milo led his troops to pillage Worcester.

Matilda's forces at one time seized and then imprisoned Stephen in Gloucester Castle, while Matilda herself entered London and claimed the Crown. After four years of fighting, however, she was obliged to leave the country to Stephen. During the short time when she considered herself to be Queen she made Milo Earl of Hereford and gave him certain Crown lands which included Cheltenham. He in turn granted part of the manor of Cheltenham to Walter de Ashley, who is later described as holding 'four librates of land as tenant in chief in the King's Manor of Cheltenham by gift of Count Milo'.[2]

In this way the semi-independent little manor of Ashley (part of Charlton Kings) came into existence. Its court leet was still held within living memory.

Milo's army had been stiffened with Welsh mercenaries and Stephen had brought hired Flemish troops into the county, so that on both sides there were lawless self-seekers who maintained their food supplies by plundering, and seized goods and property by means of torture and murder. The suffering of the people in Gloucestershire as in other parts of the country was terrible and the weakness of King Stephen after his final victory enabled many of his barons to continue their oppression. Four miles from Cheltenham, under the brow of Cleeve Hill, is the beautiful little Norman church of St. James (Postlip). It was built at this time by William de Solers, because he was 'moved by the tears and supplications of his tenants, who were waylaid and plundered as they tried to make their way to Winchcombe Church'.[3] Cheltenham probably suffered less than Winchcombe, since in 1177 it was assessed by the Justices-in-Eyre for Danegeld at £5, whereas Winchcombe which had not yet recovered from the civil war paid only £2. 13s.[4]

Henry II put down the lawlessness with a firm hand. In his reign Milo's sons Roger (Earl of Hereford) and Walter were successively sheriffs of Gloucestershire and Roger retained most of Milo's lands, including 'Cheltenham and its appurtenances'. Later these lands passed to Milo's daughter Margaret and her husband Humphrey de Bohun, who called himself Earl of Hereford. King John confirmed him in this earldom in return for the surrender of Roger's lands, and in this way the property of Cheltenham returned to the Crown.[5]

There is evidence in the cartulary of Cirencester Abbey that the medieval tithings of Arle, Alstone, and Naunton—not named in Domesday Book—were already in existence at this time. Arle is mentioned as early as 1143 when Roger of Hereford confirmed a gift of land made by Walter de Brussels to the church in Cheltenham, in return for the provision of a service three days a week in his chapel at Arle; Alston is mentioned in a later deed of gift (c. 1223) in which Walter of Naunton is one of the witnesses.

From the same cartulary we learn that there was a chapel

at Leckhampton in 1162, when a dispute between its priest Henry and the canons of Cirencester Abbey was settled before Archbishop Thomas à Becket, and confirmation was given that the chapel and tithes belonged to the Cheltenham Church. The chapel at Charlton Kings, which was consecrated by the Bishop of Hereford in 1187 at the request of Abbot Richard of Cirencester, also formed part of the property of the church in Cheltenham. The abbey's ownership of this property was confirmed three times in the reign of John, and in the last of these confirmations the revenues were appropriated by the Bishop of Worcester to the canons 'to support their hospitality and maintain their sick brethren, saving the support of two chaplains to serve the Church in Cheltenham'.

King John must have known Gloucester well. He imprisoned his wife Isabella of Angoulême in its castle and during his long contest with the barons he was often in the city both before and after the signing of Magna Carta. He died soon after the barons had called in the French to help to depose him, and it was in the Abbey Church in Gloucester—now the cathedral —that his nine-year-old son was crowned as Henry III.

Early in Henry's reign Justices-in-Eyre were sent for the first time for seven years to Gloucestershire to deal with cases of civil law and with the crime and lawlessness which had for so long gone unpunished during the civil war and the oppression of the foreign sheriffs appointed by John. By good fortune the records of their work have survived and a famous transcript was made by Maitland[6] in which the number of cases of homicide which the justices dealt with in 1221 is given as 250. Exactly how the trials took place is not known, but every hundred in the county had to send a jury of twelve men to make a statement of the crime committed since the last Eyre and wherever possible to present the criminals concerned. They were accompanied by four men and the reeve from each of the little townships in the hundred. The men of Cheltenham must have found an imposing assembly at Gloucester, where six of the King's judges held their court—the forerunner of our present assizes—in the presence of the earl marshal, the sheriff, the bishop of the diocese, and very probably the abbots of most of the monasteries in the same area. These twelve men from each hundred were often called as witnesses, so that their function was by no means always that of a jury of today. The method of deciding guilt seems to have varied from trial by ordeal—then recently denounced by the Lateran Council—to that of trial by combat and that of reliance on the evidence of sworn jurors. The list of criminals shows that the hundred of Cheltenham did not escape the general lawlessness of the period. With the names of the criminals and their victims we meet for the first time some of the actual inhabitants.

John of Brockhampton killed Christine of Arle and fled to the Church and escaped. No one else is suspected. Let him be found and outlawed. He had no chattels to confiscate. This happened in time of war. Although the deed was not done by soldiers it was not considered murder because of the war.

Two unknown men were found killed in the fields at Ham. It is not known who they were, or who killed them. William le Messer found them, but he is dead. Verdict: two murders.

In Cheltenham, criminals came to the house of Hugo, and killed him and Matilda his wife and John his son and Julia his daughter. It is not known who did this. Englishry was claimed.[7] Verdict: murder. . . .

A certain unknown woman was killed in the sheepfold beyond Prestbury. It is not known who did this. Verdict: murder.

John, son of Abraham of Charlton, fled into the Church and admitted he was a robber and agreed to leave the country as an outlaw.

William de Fonte and Alexander his son are suspected of the death of a certain merchant who was a guest in the house of William, and who was seen to go in there but he never came out alive. They came to defend themselves and refused to stand their trial. The Jury say that Alexander and Agnes his mother killed this merchant and took his belt containing 15 marks and that William consented to the robbery. The townships of Charlton, Leckhampton and Ham say the same thing because they know that the merchant was in the house and was taken away dead. It was ordered at first that William should be kept in prison but later that he should be released (on bail?). The others to remain in prison.[8]

It will be seen that a surprising number of criminals were not caught. In the case of those who were caught and convicted, the most common penalties were confiscation of goods and outlawry. For the whole county very few hangings are recorded. Judged by the summary of fines at the end of the record, the hundred of Cheltenham seems to have had a smaller number of crimes to answer for than many of the other hundreds in the county, but there is a sinister note about a gallows privately erected by the Bishop of Hereford, who owned the manor of Prestbury: 'Giles de Braose (former bishop) erected gallows in the common pasture of Wynesdon belonging to the Lord King, and Hugo Foliot (his successor) deprived the King of that land by reason of the gallows. Judgment: Let the (present) bishop be sent for that he may answer for this.'

Some fifty years later it is recorded in the Cheltenham hundred roll that this field has remained in possession of the Bishop of Hereford. The site of the gallows has not been identified but on Dalrymple's map of 1806 the lane leading from Cheltenham to Prestbury is marked as Gallows Lane. This name may, however, be derived from that of the Gallows Oak marked on the same map at the corner of Old Bath Road.

It is likely that good order was soon restored in Cheltenham because five years later Henry III made a grant[9] of the hundred and the manor for four years to the inhabitants themselves, for an annual rent of £64. At the same time he gave them the right—which had the most far-reaching results for the future of Cheltenham—to hold 'one market each week on Thursday and one Fair each year to last for three days—on the eve of St. James day, on St. James day and on the day following'. The King's writ to the sheriff runs:

Know ye that we have granted to the men of Cheltenham our Manor of Cheltenham . . . and that neither you nor your bailiffs are to have right of entry there, except for pleas of the Crown and for holding views of frank-pledge,[10] neither are you to levy any fines or other money, but you are to permit the aforesaid men to hold the aforesaid manor and hundred and to hold the aforesaid Market and Fair.

The importance of this writ (1226) cannot be over-estimated since it marks the beginning of the market which was to provide for centuries part of the income of the inhabitants. The fair continued late into the nineteenth century, and market day in

Cheltenham is still Thursday, as it has been for a period of nearly eight hundred years.

If Henry had granted this lease for the whole period of his reign, Cheltenham might have developed as an incorporated borough centuries before this actually happened. The lease was renewed in 1332 for ten years, and in 1336 he granted 'the town of Cheltenham' with other properties to his wife Eleanor of Provence for her life, as part of her dower.[11] By 1244 it had been leased to the Bishop of Hereford, but as he was overseas when the lease ran out he was allowed to hold it until his return. During his tenure he planted a number of fruit trees and when in 1247 Henry granted Cheltenham to the Norman Abbey of Fécamp in exchange for its English coastal possessions, King Henry ordered the abbot to allow the fruit to be gathered for the bishop. Apparently difficulties arose and the King then sent a writ to the sheriff commanding him to see that the bishop's bailiff should be allowed to enter and take the fruit.[12] With this deed of gift to the great abbey in Normandy there began a new phase in the history of Cheltenham and a long period of monastic ownership which only ended with Henry VIII's dissolution of the monasteries.

There were in Gloucestershire at this time a number of religious houses which belonged to monasteries in Normandy—generally as a result of gifts from early Norman kings or their barons—and known as alien houses. Among these were Beckford, Deerhurst, Brimpsfield, and Newent. Other Norman monasteries had been granted secular properties in England. Of these the Abbey of Fécamp had perhaps the oldest English associations, having received from Canute a considerable grant of land in Sussex which included Rye and Winchelsea. During the reign of Edward the Confessor the contemporary Abbot of Fécamp was making his monastery a centre of cultural and architectural influence throughout Normandy. Edward, whose Norman mother was born in Fécamp, was almost wholly Norman in his sympathies and more monkish than regal in outlook. He not only founded our own Westminster Abbey but confirmed and increased Canute's grant of English land to the Abbey of Fécamp. In his devotion to the cause of monasticism, he had included in his charter of endowment rights of jurisdiction so complete that in their English properties the abbots were virtually free from the customary royal authority exercised over lords of the manor. These rights were maintained with little dispute throughout the reigns of those English kings who were also Dukes of Normandy. Under William I two English bishoprics were held by monks from Fécamp, one of whom, Remigius, was the Commissioner who probably came to Gloucestershire to carry out the Domesday Survey, while other Fécamp monks became heads of English abbeys. When, however, King John lost Normandy to the French, a difficult situation arose through the abbey holding a commanding position on both sides of the English Channel, and for the next two centuries it has been said 'Fécamp's relations with its English estates are inseparable from the larger context of Anglo-French diplomacy and war'.[13] When it became necessary for reasons of defence that the Cinque ports should be in English hands, Henry III by a deed of exchange (1247) revoked the earlier gift of Rye and Winchelsea and in their place granted to the Abbey of Fécamp properties which included Cheltenham, with the same complete authority over these which the abbot had formerly held in the two Cinque ports.[14] These powers were so great that for the next three centuries the hundred and manor were known as the Liberty of Cheltenham, since the owners were freed to a considerable extent from the control of the Crown exercised in many other manors.

The terms of Henry III's charter were unusually explicit:

Whereas the consideration of the safety of the realm has shewn that the towns of Winchelsea and Rye which are called the nobler members of the Cinque Ports cannot be held by the Abbot and monks of Fécamp, who are not able to fortify them without danger to the realm in time of war, the King now revokes by the counsel of the great men of the realm and with the goodwill of the said Abbot and monks, the gift of the said towns . . . and in exchange for the land so resumed, the King gives to the said Abbot and monks the Manor of Cheltenham, Co. Gloucester with the Hundred, the Manor of Slaughter and the Hundred of Salmondsbury in the same county and the Manor of Navenby, Co. Lincoln, to be held of the King as they held the aforesaid towns by gift of St. Edward and the subsequent confirmation of King William and King Henry . . . with all royal liberties, customs, justice of all matters arising in their lands, nor shall any intermeddle with their authority . . . and if anyone shall presume to act against this grant, he shall forfeit £100 of gold to the Treasury.

In order further to reassure the abbot, King Henry in the same year issued a reminder to his justices of his grant to the abbot and an instruction that when they were in circuit in Gloucestershire they were to guard the rights of the abbot and his monks in Cheltenham and Slaughter as they would those of the King himself. On the other hand, if the new owners needed help, Henry gave instructions that they might call in one of the King's Justices to act with their own.[15]

One of the first tasks of Edward I on his accession in 1272 was to restore the power of the Crown after its weakness during the recent civil wars. All over the country, landowners had taken the opportunity to increase whatever legitimate authority they had in the manorial courts. In some cases, as had happened earlier in Prestbury, they had put up gallows illegally; in others they had encroached on Crown lands and taken free warren for themselves. Some had resisted the sheriff when acting on his lawful business in the shire or hundred. Not only the barons but the sheriffs themselves and other local officials of the Crown had been guilty during these troubled years of corrupt practices and mal-administration; of collecting money for the King and retaining it for themselves; of receiving bribes for conniving at the escape of prisoners, and of wrongful arrest of others.

Early in his reign Edward came to Gloucester to deal with a Welsh rising. He then turned his attention to the restoration of the royal authority throughout the kingdom. For this he needed more exact information than was immediately available, and in order to gain it he used the procedure already adopted for the Domesday Survey—and fairly common in the interval since then—of holding an inquiry or inquest, and requiring answers to a list of pre-arranged questions, county by county, throughout the kingdom. Within each county, evidence was collected from the sworn testimony of twelve men from each hundred. The rolls of parchment on which the King's Commissioners or their clerks wrote this information were there-

fore known as the Hundred Rolls. They were also called the
Ragman Rolls because of the row of dangling seals—one for
each juror in the hundred—which hung from them. Many of
these rolls have been lost and others have become illegible
through wear and tear. Those which survive provide so much
valuable information that they may be said to offer 'a bird's eye
view of local government all over England in the reign of
Edward I'.[16] The Hundred Roll for Cheltenham is not among
those which have been printed by the Records Commission,
no doubt because parts of it are damaged. Fortunately, however, a considerable part is still legible.[17]

The names of the twelve jurors who gave evidence on oath
included John of Arle, Walter Sturmey, Thomas de la Forde,
Walter of Ham, John of Oakley, John and Richard of Naunton,
and John Wyberd of Leckhampton, showing that most of the
component parts of the hundred were represented. The thirty-
nine questions submitted to these jurors were mainly concerned
with the ownership of the hundred and its value, and with
searching out whether tenants or others had usurped royal
authority or acquired land illegally. From the answers—subscribed in the Hundred Roll—it is clear that the Abbey of
Fécamp has maintained its rights of jurisdiction. 'The King
has no Manor in his hand in the Liberty of Cheltenham' the
jurors state, and the abbot and the monks hold it with 'all the
privileges which belong to a royal manor'. They also say that
the abbots of Circencester and Llanthony have extended their
holdings within the manor by purchase and gifts and have
evaded their service to the Cheltenham courts, and that the
Abbot of Hailes has illegally erected a gallows near Slaughter.
On the other hand, in the roll of the neighbouring hundred
of Gretistan (Winchcombe) it is recorded that the jurors complained that 'the Liberties of Cheltenham, Slaughter and
Salmonsbury (the property of Fécamp Abbey) hinder common
justice and undermine the royal authority, because they obey
neither the itinerant justices nor the King's servants'. There
can be no doubt that at this time monastic authority was very
strong in this part of Gloucestershire.

By the Statute of Gloucester (1278) a further inquiry was
ordered into the private jurisdictions of which information had

been collected in the Hundred Rolls. All landowners claiming rights of this kind were expected to appear before the Justices-in-Eyre to show by what warrant (Quo Warranto) they held them. Thus 'the Abbot of Fécamp was summoned to reply to the Lord King and to show by what warrant he claimed to hold the Manor and the Hundred of Cheltenham. And the Abbot through his attorney came and said that because of the exchange of Manors made by Henry III the Abbot held the rights in Cheltenham already mentioned'.[18] At the same inquiry the Abbot of Cirencester claimed view of frank-pledge in his property of the Cheltenham Church lands (from the original endowment), and said that he used the pillory and tumbril (judicalia) of the King's bailiff in Cheltenham. Presumably he was referring to the bailiff of Fécamp, who held virtually royal jurisdiction and rights in Cheltenham. A more precise definition of these rights was given in Edward III's confirmation of the grant to Fécamp Abbey of the Cheltenham property in 1367: '. . . That the Abbots should have there—view of frank-pledge of all tenants, cognisance of all pleas as well of the Crown as of common pleas, their own gallows and gaols to be delivered of all homicides and others by their own bailiffs. . . .'[19]

Despite their great powers, the Abbots of Fécamp left no lasting mark on Cheltenham, from which they derived considerable revenue. It is unlikely that the abbots visited their Gloucestershire estates, but undoubtedly some of the monks came to Cheltenham—probably to arrange for the transport of revenue. There is a reference in the accounts of bailiff Thomas Best (1345–6) to provender for the horses of brother Peter le Val. Shortly before this it is recorded in the cartulary of Cirencester Abbey that brother Vigo—the general bailiff of all the Fécamp properties in England—was present in his Abbot's Court in Cheltenham, when he settled a dispute between the Abbot of Cirencester and a tenant.

This traffic was inevitably interrupted during the wars with France. Two years before Edward III took Calais, he confiscated all the English properties of Fécamp Abbey.[20] These were restored (with confirmation of rights) when he made peace in 1361; they were confiscated again when Richard II[21] was at war with France and restored later in the same reign.

A few years before the death of Henry IV an English force burnt the town of Fécamp and finally—the year before Henry V began his attack on France—the English properties of all foreign abbeys were transferred to the Crown by an Act of Parliament (1414). In this way the long connexion of Fécamp with Cheltenham came to an end.

In place of the remote figures of the former abbots, the new owners on whom Henry V conferred the property were his aunt—Elizabeth of Huntingdon—and her second husband Sir John Cornwall, later Lord Fanhope. Sir John has been described as a 'hard headed shrewd financier', because he made large sums of money from the ransoms of French prisoners taken at the Battle of Agincourt—where he himself captured Louis de Bourbon.[22]

The grant of Cheltenham and the other properties of alien priories to Elizabeth and her husband was only for the period of their lives, since Henry V had already ear-marked the revenues as part of the endowment of the new convent which he proceeded to build at Twickenham. At the outset of his reign he had sought and gained the support of the Church for his war with France, and he seems to have had a genuinely religious side to his nature. Perhaps because his sister Philippa was married to the King of Sweden, he became interested in the monastic ideals of St. Bridget of Sweden, and in the year of Agincourt he founded 'the Monastery of St. Saviour and St. Bridget of Syon, of the order of St. Augustine', named after the Holy Mount.[23] Provision was made for 60 sisters and 25 men, including 13 priests, 4 deacons, and 8 laymen, among whom were 4 Swedish nuns and 2 Swedish monks. For building the convent he granted 1,000 marks in gold and he provided an annuity of another 1,000 marks until the revenues from endowments of property should reach that amount. Chief among these endowments were the confiscated possessions from alien priories, including Cheltenham and Slaughter after the tenancy of Elizabeth Huntingdon and her husband ended.

And so Cheltenham passed once more into the ownership of a great abbey. The terms of Henry V's grant were extremely generous. He not only confirmed the rights held by the previous owners of the manors concerned but he exempted the new owner—the Convent of Syon—from the obligation to pay most of the taxes due to the Crown.

In 1423 Henry VI ratified his father's grant to Syon but omitted the clauses which exempted it from taxation—tenths, fifteenths and tallage. He later gave it another charter which contains, in the highly specialized medieval vocabulary which had been developed for use in the complicated legal and judicial machinery of the period, the most complete account of the powers held by the Abbess:

And that the aforesaid Abbess and Convent and their successors shall have . . . their thrice weekly court before their stewards or bailiffs . . . and likewise may hold there all manner of pleas of account, debt, trespasses, assault . . . and shall cause the persons against whom the like complaints in the courts aforesaid shall be prosecuted . . . to be arrested and to be committed and retained in prison . . . and to terminate pleas by their own judgements and executions in like manner as the pleas in our royal courts are decided.

And that no sheriff or officer or minister of the Crown shall . . . arrest or take any of the people or tenants of the Abbess by any writ, mandate or warrant wheresoever they shall be found, but the same shall be sent to the Abbess to cause execution.

That no escheator, sheriff, bailiff or any other officer of the Crown may enter in the lands . . . aforesaid.

That the Abbess shall have and hold assize of bread and beer and other victuals and measures and weights . . . with all profits arising therefrom, with soc and sac, treasure-trove, deodands, wreck of the sea . . . and gallows, pillory, tumbril in whatsoever place shall seem meet for the punishment of malefactors.

These extraordinary powers were held by the Convent of Syon for more than a hundred years and were confirmed once more in the charter given by Edward IV. By reason of its endowments Syon was one of the richest abbeys in England and as such was one of the first of the larger abbeys to be dissolved by Henry VIII, at which time the hundred and manor of Cheltenham became once more Crown property (1539).

III

THE LIBERTY OF CHELTENHAM

FOR our knowledge of what was happening in Cheltenham during three centuries under monastic ownership we are largely dependent on the records left by those important medieval officials the stewards and bailiffs of the manor, since it was not until Edward IV came marching down the Old Bath Road on his way to the Bloody Meadow at Tewkesbury that Cheltenham was again involved directly in the main stream of national history. In the court rolls, however, and in the bailiffs' accounts and the surveys and rentals of the manor, details are given which reveal many aspects of life in medieval Cheltenham. These documents—worn and discoloured with age and in places smudged and indecipherable—date from the reign of Edward III.

The court rolls are records of the courts held by the lord of the manor,[1] and their importance lies in the fact that the scope of the work of these courts was extremely wide. They not only dealt with crimes but with some of the work now carried out by various local government bodies which then did not exist, and with the enforcement of the customary labour services and payments due to the lord from his tenants. They therefore played a most important part in the lives of the inhabitants, for whom compulsory attendance was in most cases part of their obligations as tenants. They were usually presided over by the steward—often a man of considerable rank—since in Liberties such as Cheltenham, where the visits of monastic owners must have been infrequent, he was the actual representative of the lord of the manor and was responsible for the administration of the whole property. He was also responsible for the safe keeping of the records of the court, which were written by clerks provided for the purpose. In the case of Cheltenham, the later court books (from 1555 to the nineteenth century) were still in the possession of the

steward of the manor until 1956, when they were transferred
on loan to the Gloucester Records Office. The salaries of the
medieval steward and the clerk, together with the price of the
parchment used, were recorded by the bailiff in his accounts:
'And in fees of Robert Clynton the Steward 50/- a year;
Walter French bailiff 40/- a year; John Fayreforth clerk 20/-
a year; John Chiltenham under bailiff and warner 3/4 a year;
Nicholas Baker cryer and catchpoll 3/4 a year ... and in parchment bought for the Court Rolls, Sessions and Extract 2/-'
(1421).

The bailiff was the important official who was concerned
with the actual day-to-day farm work on the demesne land
of the lord of the manor. Either he or the reeve superintended
the labour services of the tenants. He was also required as part
of his duties to keep detailed accounts of all the revenue and
expenditure of the manor. These included the payments and
rents due to the lord from the tenants and the expenditure on
wages, food allowances, tools, journeys connected with
manorial business, and labour and materials for the maintenance of the Hall or Court House in which it was customary for
him to have his own quarters in the absence of a resident lord.
The steward also, who was generally non-resident, was often
accommodated in this house when he arrived to carry out his
duties, and it is possible that in Cheltenham as in many other
manors the actual courts were held in this hall.

The descriptions given in the court rolls are not easily
understood without some knowledge of the medieval system
under which the manorial courts all over England carried out
their functions. While it is dangerous to generalize about this
system, since each area seems to have developed its own
variations, it is safe to say that in most parts of the country
the chief court was that held twice a year in each hundred and
called the Great Tourn to distinguish it from the less important 'three weeks' hundred court; and that within the hundred
each manor might also have a separate court.[2]

Each vill or township in the hundred sent the reeve and
four jurors to this important half-yearly hundred court, where
in most cases the sheriff was in charge as the official representative of the King. A bailiff, appointed by the sheriff, worked

under him; but if, as in the Liberty of Cheltenham, the hundred
was privately owned, the owner himself appointed the bailiff.
Either the sheriff or the bailiff then held a 'view of frank-pledge'
and dealt with all matters concerned with writs of the
Crown and with money disputes involving amounts of less than
£2, and with the collection of money due to the King. On the
judicial side he was responsible for passing on to the King's
Justices those criminals whose offences were too serious to be
tried in the hundred court. View of frank-pledge was held to
see that every male over twelve years of age was placed in a
small group known as a tithing, as a member of which he took
an oath to be loyal to the King and to keep the laws. If one of
its members committed a crime and was not brought to justice
the whole tithing was held responsible and fined. Each man in
the tithing paid his penny, and these tithe pence (often called
cert money) together with other payments and fines made the
ownership of the hundred courts very profitable. In the Cheltenham hundred courts criminals who would in other courts
have been taken to await the King's justices when they held
their sessions or assizes in Gloucester, were tried before a
special session of judges appointed by the owner.

Within each hundred the various manors were often in
separate ownership, and the lord of the manor (while himself
owing suit of court to the owner of the hundred) held his own
court. In theory these courts were also distinguished by the
name of court baron when attended by free tenants and hall-
motes when held for the villeins, but in practice many medieval
court rolls show little distinction of this kind, and in the
course of time the term court baron came to be used by the
court lawyers for courts dealing with property and inheritance,
and the court leet for those dealing with other matters such
as petty crime and regulations and orders affecting the general
welfare.

In the Liberty of Cheltenham the difference between the
types of medieval courts is even less clear than in many other
places because the hundred and most of its component parts
were held by the same privileged owner and therefore it was
administered as a whole and not as a group of separate manors.
Among the sixty Cheltenham court rolls which are now

in the Public Record Office, fifteen are records of the half-yearly hundred courts with view of frank-pledge, and thirty-six of the 'three weeks' hundred court; the remaining rolls are estreats or records of special sessions presided over by the judges appointed by the owners.

It is important to realize that all the inhabitants of the Liberty, whether villeins or freeholders, were in one sense tenants of the lord. At the Domesday Survey the inhabitants of Cheltenham were classified as villani and bordarii—both of which classes were bound to render certain labour services on the demesne land of the lord. Under what circumstances a group of freehold tenants and burgesses came into existence in Cheltenham it is impossible to say,[3] but by the reign of Edward III, from which time written records of the courts survive, there appear to have been four types of tenants. These were freemen who paid a relief or fine when they inherited land; burgesses who held a burgage tenancy in the borough of Cheltenham, and whose obligations were similar to those of free tenants, except that they were exempt from all labour services; villeins who held their land in base tenure by labour obligations and were later called customary tenants or copyholders; and tenants in demesne, that is those to whom—from comparatively early times—parts of the demesne land (the private property of the lord of the manor) were let at a money rent. Such tenants in demesne might also be either copyholders or free tenants or burghers.

The first matter to be recorded in the rolls of the three-weekly hundred courts was the list of essoins—the names of those whose excuses for non-attendance had been accepted. It would appear that even powerful tenants were not exempt, when summoned to attend. Thus in 1333 the Prior of Llanthony who owned land in Arle (Redgrove) and the Giffards of Leckhampton, had in each case two draught animals confiscated; while a poorer man lost two geese for the same offence.[4]

After the excuses had been dealt with in this three-weekly court the officials and tithingmen from the various parts of the hundred brought forward matters concerned with their own area. At the head of these was the bailiff of the borough, followed by the tithingmen from the vill of Cheltenham and from the tithings of Arle, Alstone, Sandford, Westhall, Naunton, Charlton, and Bafford. In the half-yearly court and view of frank-pledge the tithingmen from Leckhampton and Ashley were also present. Prestbury, which was placed in the hundred of Cheltenham in Domesday Book, was by the end of the Middle Ages included in the hundred of Tewkesbury. I have been unable to find any record of when or why this happened.

The early distinction between the borough and the vill of Cheltenham—in so small an area—seems curious. There is no mention of burgesses in Henry III's grant of a market and fair to 'the men of Cheltenham', but in the tax list of 1307 'it appears as an urban community',[5] and in the lists of 1313 and 1336 as a borough. By the time of the first surviving court rolls (1332–3) the bailiff of the borough emerges as a recognized official. By what stages this development took place during the intervening years it is impossible to say. Undoubtedly the grant of a market gave it a considerable impetus. It is certain that the growing community would need craftsmen and tradesmen, and that these would be freed from their labour services so that they could follow their occupations, paying to the lord of the manor a rent instead of labour for their burgage tenancies. It should be noted, however, that in Cheltenham it was in the hundred court that the bailiff of the borough presented all cases concerned with the borough. For centuries there is no record of any separate court in which he might have exercised jurisdiction, until the long existence of the court of Pie Powder is revealed in the complaint[6] about the contemporary bailiff of the borough made in the court of Exchequer at the end of Elizabeth's reign. According to William Norwood—at that time lord of the manor—the town of Cheltenham 'time out of mind hath been an ancient borough and market town', in which 'by all the time wherein the memory of man is not to the contrary, a Court of Pie Powder hath been held, at the direction of the High Bailiff and the Steward of the Manor . . . and never taken by any Bailiff of the Borough', until William Stroude claimed that right in 1600. Since the borough was a part of the 'Hundred and the Manor of Cheltenham'—a Liberty in which the owner had more than ordinary powers—it would seem that this indissoluble connexion prevented it from becoming detached and independent (cf. Chapter V). It should therefore be stressed that for many centuries the unit of local government was the area of the whole hundred, in which it is virtually impossible to assess the exact powers of the bailiff of the borough. To the Abbots of Fécamp and their successors, their property here meant not merely the borough with its market and long street but the far wider extent of the hundred. Since the tithingmen met in the courts at such frequent intervals it is clear that there was constant traffic and intercourse between the inhabitants of the outlying hamlets and tithings which with the little borough made up the medieval Liberty of Cheltenham.

Apart from the differences already mentioned, the early Cheltenham Rolls do not show any clearly marked distinction in the scope of matters dealt with by the two courts. The tithing-men 'presented' cases of disputes, theft, trespass, actions against the common welfare (such as the fouling of the water-supply or the sale of short-weight bread or bad ale), and matters concerned with property transactions.

Many of the offences presented were concerned with assault and battery when the accused had 'drawn blood' from his victim or opponent. Any witnesses of the action were expected to join in the hue and cry and assist in catching the offender. If they failed to do this they too were fined and the whole tithing was also liable to a fine unless the offender was brought to court. The usual penalty in such cases was also a fine. A similar procedure was carried out in cases of burglary.

Whereas it was presented at the last Court that one Amicia . . . feloniously broke into the house of Agnes the Millward at Charlton and carried away goods and chattels worth 10/-, and the aforesaid Agnes raised the hue and cry upon her. . . . Information was given that John Abraham seized her but let her go and she fled to the Church, wherefore the bailiff was to make the aforesaid John Abraham appear at the Court and the twelve jurors to enquire into the matter.[7]

This affair dragged on through several courts; eventually John Abraham was acquitted of negligence, and as Amicia was not caught the whole tithing was fined 1s.

The greatest number of cases were perhaps offences connected with brewing and baking. If the owner of the manor held the assize of ale, no brewing could take place without his licence, for which in the borough of Cheltenham the brewer paid 1*d*. annually, and outside in other parts of the hundred 3*d*. Standards of quality and price were laid down and deviation from these was reported to the court and dealt with by fine. These cases were so frequent and continued for so many centuries that the fines exacted brought a steady income to the owners, and evidently came to be regarded as something in the nature of an additional licence fee—at the expense of the consumer. For this reason there seems to have been no determined attempt to prevent the breach of the assize of ale. In each tithing there was an ale-taster, who was usually elected to this office. 'John Myles—chosen for the assize of beer at Alston, and sworn for the third time'.[8]

In some parts of England the tenants were compelled to have their corn ground in the mills of the lord of the manor. In Cheltenham these mills appear to have been sublet to millers who then made their own charge. Cases of exorbitant charges were almost as common as those concerned with the sale of bread or ale, and similar fines were imposed.

Another frequent offence was that of trespassing. In the medieval system of farming, the fields were inclosed only for the period from the sowing of the seed until the end of the harvest, and were thrown open as common pasturage for the rest of the year. Within these 'common fields' the tenants' holdings, all sown with the same crop, were in scattered strips separated only by balks or mounds, and it could not have been easy to prevent beasts from straying or to prove the ownership of those which did damage to corn or pasture. Thus Walter de Northfield was brought to court because four of his oxen were found in the lord's corn (1334).[9] The beasts which were caught were placed in the pound (for centuries this was in Henrietta Street near the present Fleece Hotel) and only released after the payment of fines. From time to time tenants were dealt with for planting crops contrary to the arrangements made for all the common (or open) fields. Thus John le Rok and Simon Hawthorn—'because they sowed in a field not to be sown this year'—were fined 2*d*. and 4*d*. each,[10] and Walter Brand was fined 6*d.* 'because he put his meadow into fences, whereas there was to be no fenced pasture this year'.

There was also considerable temptation to poach in the woods and rabbit warrens. The fines for these offences, though comparatively heavy, seem mild in comparison with the brutal punishments inflicted for similar offences in the eighteenth century: 'Robert de Bradenstock (and other jurors when sworn) say by their oath that Adam Prive hunted in the Lord's warren and fished in his pond. He is adjudged in mercy—and the tithing man and the whole tithing, for concealment of the same are . . . fined 6*d.* . . .'[11]

There must have been occasions when the bailiff did not find it easy to collect the fines which had been imposed in the court. Thus Thomas Rolf was 'distrained for falsely defaming the bailiff and officers of the Lord when exacting a fine from him' (1334).[12]

While the lord of the manor drew considerable income through his courts from the fines collected, he was at the same time carrying out his own duties of maintaining order and enforcing the laws of the King. This is shown in the case reported in 1334 of a breach of the almost contemporary statute of Winchester which provided for the keeping of watch and ward:[13]

It has been established by inquisition that the Constables of the Peace and Watchmen according to the Statute of Winchester . . . have not kept their office of summoning the Watch . . . and other things which pertain to it . . . also that the townships of Cheltenham, Arle, Alston, Westhall . . . Charlton, Leckhampton and Swindon have not kept watch according to the said Statute.

This seems to show a somewhat wholesale neglect of this statute and an attempt to enforce what was undoubtedly a difficult task.

A very large part of the business of the courts concerned the landlord and tenant relationship which existed between the lord of the manor and its inhabitants all of whom, whether free or villeins, held their land from him in return for customary services or payments such as heriots, fines, and reliefs. In this way villeins (holders of land in base tenure) became known later as copyholders because their title to their land was by the record or copy of the Court Roll. This recording of payments in the court books was to continue until the distinction between copyhold and freehold land was removed by Act of Parliament in 1925. As late as 1920 there were people in Cheltenham paying heriots and such dues to the steward of the lord of the manor.

In strict theory the villeins, whose persons as well as property belonged in one sense to the lord,[14] could not sell or let their holdings or bequeath them by will to their heirs. In practice it was customary in Cheltenham and most other parts of England, after the land of a dead villein had been surrendered to the lord, and a heriot paid, for his heir to succeed to the holding on payment of a fine. If, however, a villein wished to transfer his property, he might from early times in Cheltenham obtain a licence from the lord, provided that the transaction was entered in the court roll, and the customary fine paid: 'John le Kynge comes into Court and alienates by the Lord's licence to Robert the Lorimer of Prestbury 2 plots of land.' On the other hand, a freeman or a burgage tenant could sell freely, although the act of sale had also to be entered in the Court Roll: 'John of Hasfield and Agness his wife granted in Court to Thomas Coke and Alice his wife one burgage. . . .'[15]

The actual condition of labour services and payments due from the villeins in Cheltenham in return for their holdings can be discovered, however, not in the court rolls, but in two other sets of records which have survived—the Ministers Accounts (or Compoti) and the Rentals and Surveys.

In one of the earliest surviving surveys of property in the manor[16] (probably made in the middle years of Henry VI's reign) a list is given of 359 Cheltenham tenants with their holdings and the annual rents paid for these. Among them were 130 burgage tenants, some of whom, however, held only a half or a third or a quarter of a burgage. Annual rents varied for a full burgage from 1s. to 2s. 6d.

There were also 142 copyhold tenancies and in these the labour services due from each holding (and their value) were given as well as the rents. Thus Richard Greene had one toft and half a virgate for which he paid 4s. annually in rent and owed the following services—stated to be worth 2s. 1d.—to the lady of the manor.

Harrowing	1 day in summer
”	1 day in winter
Hoeing	1 day
Mowing	1 day with one man
Lifting the hay	1 day
He had to find one man for cocking the hay	1 day
He did 3 bedripes with one man at his own cost	3 days in autumn

If he sold a horse within the manor he and the buyer paid the lady of the manor 2d. He could not arrange marriages for his sons or daughters without licence (and payment of merchet). He gave pannage for his pigs—usually 1d. for full-grown pigs and ½d. for piglets—for their right to feed in the woods. His best beast was given as a heriot at his death and his heir paid relief before obtaining the holding. In case of an arrest he had to guard the prisoner for a day and night from sunrise on the first day to sunset on the second.

The amount of land held by copyholders varied from one virgate (approximately 30 acres, but sometimes more and sometimes less) to that of a mere toft. Their rents ranged from 9s. to 2d. a year, in addition to which some of the tenants in Arle paid three hens and a cock each year. There was a similar variation in the amount of the customary labour services due from each villein.

A few of the tenants in Arle, Bafford, and Charlton had to pay tallage, from which it may be presumed that the majority did not pay. In many manors this payment of tallage—a sum of money raised at the will of the lord—was a heavy burden, and it is therefore probable that the villeins of Cheltenham were less liable to oppression than many of their contemporaries. This may have been due to the fact that Cheltenham was originally 'ancient demesne', where the inhabitants as tenants of the Crown were generally more free than those on manors in private ownership. Certainly the value of heriots taken during these years—usually the best beast—was considerably less in Cheltenham than in some other places where the widow might have to surrender to the lord on the death of her husband most of the livestock and household goods. It is worth noting also that the labour services which are shown in this survey are less specified than those exacted from his tenants at an earlier period by the Abbot of Gloucester, as recorded in the cartulary of that abbey. Refusal to carry out these labour services was dealt with in the manor courts. Thus in 1334 Walter de Northfield was fined because 'he had not come to the Lord's works as he was summoned to do'.

The names of four tenants mentioned in this survey have survived as the present place-names of Monkscroft, Fiddler's Green, Hesters Way, and Bayshill. Richard Munke, William Fidler, and William Herte had holdings in Arle; Matilda Bayse —a freeholder—owned over sixty acres in Alston for which she paid 9s. a year, and was obliged, when called upon, to deliver letters and briefs for the lord of the manor.

It should be noticed that the value of Richard Greene's copyhold services was calculated at 2s. 1d.—the amount he would pay in work-silver to the lady if he were allowed to withhold his labour. From the reign of Henry V the bailiffs' accounts include the item of £10. 0s. 6¾d. for 'works and customs of divers tenants', in lieu of services, showing how the process of commuting services for money payments or rents had developed by that time.

This process had been in operation in Cheltenham at least as early as the reign of Edward III, when the bailiff included in his accounts an item: 6 days' ploughing sold for 6d., 18 days' harrowing sold for 1s. 6d., and 18 days' weeding for 9d. In the same accounts he also notes wages paid for similar work— for grinding and winnowing barley at 1½d. a quarter and for 8 days' ditching at 1½d. a day. Craftsmen were already earning relatively higher wages than labourers on the land. Thus a thatcher at this time was paid 2d. a day for mending the roof of a barn, and the boy helping him 1d. The process of commutation was accelerated in many parts of England by the Black Death (1349) which caused so many deaths that there was a great scarcity of labour. The Statute of Labourers (1351) was an attempt to restrict the inevitable rise in wages. Unfortunately, no Cheltenham court rolls have survived from the plague

years, so that there is no evidence as to how far the town was
affected, but it is known that both Gloucester and Hailes which
were not far away suffered heavily. There was, however, a
marked rise in wages—some of which were doubled within the
next fifty years. The thatcher's wage of 2d. in the early years of
Edward II was 4d. in 1389.[17]

Various authorities claim that wages in England increased
more than prices in the years between the Black Death and the
economic depression of the period of inclosures under the
Tudors. In Cheltenham there was a most determined attempt
to check the rise in both prices and wages. Two special Sessions
of Justices were held—in the last year of Henry V and the
first year of his successor—to deal with tradesmen who charged
too much for their goods, and with workmen who demanded
higher wages.[18] The fact that these special courts were generally
summoned to deal with serious criminal cases shows how
seriously these offences were regarded by the owners of the
manor. It was in these sessions, when the lord through
his own judges exercised full authority over his tenants, that
the Liberty of Cheltenham differed from many other manors,
and whereas it was in general unlawful for any lord of the
manor, even if he held the right of gallows, to hang criminals
except in the presence of the King's Coroner, in Cheltenham the
lord had his own coroner for this purpose.[19] The fact that
Edward I and Edward III from time to time ordered the inquiries (already mentioned) into the origin of legality of these
powers shows that the Crown did not lightly relinquish its
authority in such Liberties, and in later reigns the owners of
Cheltenham had still to carry out certain legal formalities before
exercising their rights. Thus in the first year of Henry VI's
reign the bailiff (Walter French) entered in his accounts the
expenses 'calculated for riding to Gloucester to the Assizes and
Sessions of the Lord King for claiming the Liberties of the
Lordship of Cheltenham, three times this year, 2/-'.[20]

From the heading of the records we are reminded that the
holding of these sessions was a special privilege belonging to
the owners of the Liberty: 'Cheltenham, Session of the Peace
held there by virtue of the Liberty, before Robert Cireston,
Robert Clynton, Walter Peion, Justices of John Cornwall,

Knight, and Elizabeth his wife, Countess of Huntingdon—farmers of the Lord King of all the lands and possessions of the Abbot of Fécamp in England—in the presence of the Lord.'

There follow the names of twelve jurors, and then a list of tradesmen and craftsmen who had sold goods or labour at prices in excess of what was apparently recognized as a fair price, and the names of men to whom these were sold. The list included eleven butchers, who had sold meat at prices varying in excess from 7*d.* to 1*s.* 8*d.*; three ostlers for selling fodder for horses at an excess of 6*d.*; one man selling fish and four bakers selling bread at the same excess; nine weavers charging 6*d.* in excess for their work, and one labourer for selling corn in winter at 6*d.* in excess.

At the court held the next year these same profiteers were fined, each one having to find a surety for the payment of his fine. The fines ranged from 6*d.* to 1*s.* 8*d.*, and the total paid was 17*s.* 6*d.* This seems to have been a serious attempt to keep down costs by controlling prices and wages. Whatever the immediate effect may have been, we know from later court rolls that in the long run it was unsuccessful, since butchers, bakers, weavers and others were constantly being fined in succeeding centuries for charging prices in excess of what was generally regarded as reasonable and just.

The shortage or the expense of labour at this time is suggested by such items recorded by the bailiff as 'rent of a certain pasture in Okeley Grove let to save tree cutting—10/-', and from the fact that a considerable amount of demesne land within the precincts of the manor grounds was let instead of being directly cultivated by the lord of the manor. Thus in 1421 £13. 2*s.* 6*d.* was received 'in issues of demesne arable land and meadows per year granted to divers tenants,' and of this 13*s.* 4*d.* was received for the rent of meadow 'within the Lord's inclosure'.[21]

An item in the same account which runs '. . . and 2/- for new rent of John Purs for curtilage new made on the Lord's land next the horse pool and extending to the doors of the Court', reminds us that one of the main features of medieval Cheltenham which has long disappeared was the Manor House or Court. There can be no doubt that this was built on some part of the site now occupied by St. Matthew's Church and the Police Station, and that its grounds—which included the Court close and the lord's meadow—stretched as far as the present Plough Hotel on the east and the churchyard on the north. It is probable that within this Manor House the chief bailiff of Fécamp's English possessions, and later the steward of Sir John Cornwall, presided over their courts.

The many references to its repair and upkeep show its importance in the life of the medieval manor. Whether it was built within a walled inclosure is not clear from such references as '80 feet of crestes for saving and keeping the wall of the Manor—8/-'. The inner walls and the roof needed frequent repair. There is a charge of 1s. 2d. 'for making and repairing broken walls of hall'. A detailed account is given of the cost of re-roofing the kitchen and repairing the owner's quarters. The last item—one cementer to repair foundations—is significant.[22]

The roof had to be mended again and again—in the reigns of Henry IV, Henry V, and Henry VI. Finally a new 'Halle and Crosse-chamber' within the site of the manor were built in 1459.[23] The actual cost of the new hall is noted to the last penny. Among the items recorded are: carpenters' wages £14. 2s. 0½d., sawyers' wages £18. 0s. 5d., labourers' wages £4. 7s. 6½d., tyler's wages £2. 13s. 0d., dauber's wages £1. 18s. 10d., timber £39. 10s. 0d., nails 12s. 5½d., crestes (tiles?) 9s. 8d., straw 1s. 6d.

There are many references to the lord's close. Wages are noted 'for the carriage of thorns and for making of hedges for closing the Lord's close, and for cutting and carrying of hay'. It is mentioned separately from the lord's meadow, where 'making hay and carrying it' cost 1s. in wages.

The most vivid local scene which can be gathered from these records is that of Oakley, the woods of which play a great part in the economy of the manor. Much trouble and expense was involved in keeping these woods inclosed. In Richard II's reign the wages of two men 'working six days to enclose the grove at Okeley' are recorded, and there are several similar entries, and others which show the extent of the work there. 'Five men cutting wood in Okeley Woods, paid 1s. 8d. a day and 1d. for their drink.'[24] A significant entry in Henry V's reign gives the total amount taken from the sale of wood for the year as £13. 5s. 6d. Some of this would be derived from small items: willow branches from Arle (48s.), and from Sandford (1s. 6d.); alder from Alstone Moor (48s.); but the greater part came from the sale of oaks in Oakley Wood.

It was from Oakley that timber was brought 'to make a tumbril for the neighbourhood and a stall for the Market', at a cost of 8d. for carriage and 1s. 10d. for carpenter's wages.[25] Where the tumbrill—a ducking stool—was placed we do not know; it was used to punish dishonest tradesmen as well as scolding women, though there is no known record of its use.

The firewood which was prepared in anticipation of a visit from the lord was cut at Oakley. In the reign of Richard II we have the entry: 'for cutting and splitting firewood against the coming of the Lord; one man's wages for $7\frac{1}{2}$ days, 1s. $10\frac{1}{2}d$.', from which it may be inferred that the coming of the lord was a great occasion.

It is possible that the lord referred to was Simon of Burley, to whom Richard II had granted the custody of the English properties of Fécamp Abbey which were 'in the King's hand on account of the war with France . . . and during the schism between Pope Urban and the Anti-Pope'.[26] The abbots of Fécamp sent monks to keep an eye on their Cheltenham property, but no details of their sojourn there have so far come to light. It is not until Elizabeth of Huntingdon and her second husband—Sir John Cornwall—took possession of the manor that the actual personalities of the owners emerge. Some of their letters, filed by careful bailiffs with receipts and other accounts, give us details of their tastes and activities. Both had a great liking for lampreys taken from the Severn. A letter from Elizabeth to her 'treasurer et bon ami' bailiff Will Goderich runs: 'Dere and welbeloved frende y grete yow wel often tymes praying yow yif ther be ayny lampreys at Clowcestr that ye wol sende unto me 300 and this letter shal be your warant praying yow hertly that ye wol do beside your devoir to resceyve us the rentes now att this Estri. (Written at Steventon the XXVI day of February—1419–1420).' This is one of many references [27] to money spent by the bailiff on lampreys 'for the Lady' and sometimes for Sir John, and on the expenses of

sending them to Cheltenham or Ampthill. A typical item runs:
'And for 6 lampreys bought for the Lord 22/-. And in carriage
of them from Gloucester to Cheltenham 4*d.*, and in linen cloth
for the same 3½*d.*'

There are several letters from Sir John to bailiff Walter
French asking him to inquire for a good horse. On one occasion
the bailiff approached the Abbot of Winchcombe, from whom
a horse was bought for £5. A few years later another was
bought from the Prior of Deerhurst for £7. 6*s.* 8*d.* There are
also what appear to be heavy bills for sadlery which was sometimes purchased in London.

Although Elizabeth and her husband did not live permanently in Cheltenham, Sir John at least visited it from time
to time. He was present, as we have seen, at the sessions for
the trial of the men who demanded excessive prices and wages.
The expenses of such a visit appear to have been heavy. On one
occasion £9. 15*s.* 0*d.* is recorded as the cost of the lord's visit
of three days (1428–9).

During the last years of Sir John Cornwall's ownership
Cheltenham was already declining in prosperity, perhaps
because of the heavy taxation which was caused by the long-
drawn-out war with France. This is suggested by an Act of
Parliament passed in 1441 for the relief of 'all cities and towns
desolate or wasted or overcharged', in which Cheltenham was
included with Scarborough, Andover, Headington and other
towns where the payment of taxes pressed heavily. By this Act
'the lay people of Cheltenham were to be quit and discharged
from the payment of fifteenths and tenths'. Nothing is known
of the immediate causes or working of this Act.

Sir John died shortly after the passing of the Act and the
Abbess of Syon then came into possession of the lands granted
to her convent by Henry V. From now onwards there are items
in the bailiffs' accounts of the expenses to and from Syon and
of payment made to the treasuresses—the nuns who acted as
bursars within the convent. There is no record that either the
Lady Abbess or any of her nuns ever visited Cheltenham. By
the rules of their order they were confined to an almost silent
régime and there was no need for them to come in person
because their convent had a highly organized central staff of

laymen—a chief steward, a steward of the hospice, a general receiver, and an auditor. In Cheltenham they had two chief stewards, each paid £3. 6s. 8d. a year, a steward of the court (£1. 6s. 8d.), and a high bailiff (£2. 13s. 4d.). It is therefore likely that the expenses of administration were higher than at the time when Sir John Cornwall was owner.[28]

There is evidence which suggests difficulties in the collection of payments due from the tenants and others. One example of this concerns the widow of William Giffard of Leckhampton, who on remarriage moved to Bristol.[29] The bailiff records two journeys there and back to collect 25s. as a heriot and the following year the debt is still outstanding; and there were also considerable amounts of money which the bailiffs failed to collect at the time they were due.

Another example of this independent attitude was the refusal of the tenants (in base tenure) to pay the full amount of the £10. 0s. 6¾d., already mentioned as the amount of work silver due to be collected from them annually in lieu of labour service. Bailiff Walter French reveals in his accounts (1452) that 'divers discords exactions and demands' have arisen among the tenants who are only willing to pay £6. 3s. 4d. as work silver instead of the annual amount of £10. 0s. 6¾d., which has been customary for many years. In the same year the dispute between the abbess and her tenants was finally settled when both sides agreed that Ralph Boteler of Sudeley should be called in to arbitrate between them.[30] The bailiff notes the expenses of the Lord of Sudeley when he came over from Winchcombe to Cheltenham with twenty-four men and horses—'for to hold a colloquy between the Lady Abbess and her tenants by base tenure in Cheltenham on divers urgent matters, with three other arbiters and their horses, staying three days'; and of another visit by Lord Sudeley of five days with forty-six men and horses to hold a session to make 'a perpetual concord of peace between the Lady Abbess and her tenants'—all of which cost £9. 18s. 0d.

The award—made in the presence of the Prior of Deerhurst, Thomas Boteler (Knight), William Tracey, and William Giffard—reduced the annual amount to be paid by the tenants to £6. 13s. 4d. The abbess accepted this decision, provided that they paid this sum each year 'justly and perfectly for their labour and customs'. It appears to have been a considerable victory for the tenants. Unfortunately, no other details are known of what may have been a seven-year fight.

These difficulties may be one of the reasons for the sub-letting of the properties of Cheltenham and Slaughter. For a short period there was a frequent change of lessees which in itself was not likely to increase the efficiency of administration. Among these were Ralph Boteler of Sudeley, Thomas Asplyn, the Abbot of Llanthony, and the Abbot of Winchcombe, who held the property for two years (1464–5).

Ralph Boteler was perhaps the most interesting personality connected with Cheltenham in the Middle Ages. He had various offices under Henry V and Henry VI, and for a short time was Governor of Calais. He went to France with Humphrey Duke of Gloucester to negotiate the Treaty of Troyes, and later accompanied John Duke of Bedford at the time of the trial of Joan of Arc. He is credited with a great naval victory over the French, from the spoils of which he rebuilt Sudeley Castle and found the money to pay for part of the new church at Winchcombe. He seems to have been a great builder and it is possible that it was he who built in Cheltenham the new 'Halle and Crosse-chamber' already mentioned. He lost his wealth, however, and his beautiful castle, through loyalty to the Lancastrian cause in the Wars of the Roses.

Cheltenham was not directly involved in these wars, but indirectly the effect was a further decline in prosperity. By the end of Edward IV's reign the bailiffs' accounts reveal a decline in land values.[31] The rents of the lord's close have dropped from 26s. 8d. to 24s., and part of the Marsh from 15s. to 5s. A cottage in Westhall has been vacant for nine years, and two burgage holdings for the same period, while in various other properties the bailiff notes that he is unable to collect rents.

The records of tolls of the market reveal also that there must have been a steady decline in the business and trade involved. In the reign of Edward III it is recorded that 60s. was paid for 'the farm of tolls for the market'; in the first year of Henry VI's reign the tolls are valued at 25s. 1d., later in the reign at 29s. 4d., and in 1466 at 6s. 8d.[32]

During these two centuries Cheltenham, like other medieval manors, was very largely self-supporting, providing for its own needs in respect of food, fuel, clothing, and house-building. Thatchers, slaters, carpenters, weavers, bakers, brewers, millers, and other craftsmen—whose work was essential in an economy which was mainly self-contained—figure in the records. There is a reference in Henry V's reign to a fulling mill[33] at Cudnall 'which has lately fallen into disuse and by assent of all it is let by copy of Court Roll for term of his life to Robert and Joan Walker . . .' and Robert is to rebuild it 'with two stockes called walking stockes and the Lord's bailiff is to find the timber . . .'. Fulling is also mentioned in an early record of Edward III's reign, and weavers were included among those who were tried before the Sessions for demanding extortionate wages. There is no proof, however, that Cheltenham was an important centre of weaving, and although wool must have been sold in Cheltenham market, no such fortunes appear to have been made there as those of the merchants in the wool towns of Northleach and Chipping Campden.

With the decline of the market, agriculture was probably the main source of livelihood. Many of the tenants were occupied almost entirely on the land, and if they no longer gave direct labour services to the lord of the manor, they were still required to do their share in the repair of the roads and bridges and in the maintenance of public order. Thus the tithing man of Leckhampton reported that a ditch at Collumstreete was flooded and the whole tithing was ordered to amend it.[34] By another order, in Henry VIII's reign, all residents in Westhall were required 'to help break stones and repair the highway at Westhall and to stone the bridge and make it fit for the King's lieges to cross without damage to body and goods', subject to penalties of 5s. for everyone who owned a plough and 3s. for the others, in case of negligence.[35]

The medieval system of farming required a high degree of co-operation between the tenants since their holdings in the open fields were all planted with the same crop—or all left fallow—according to the agreed rotation on a three-yearly basis, and after the completion of the harvest were thrown open as common pasture. The later court rolls of this period record penalties for tenants who put in more cattle than they were entitled to do from the size of their holdings or before the harvest was gathered in, and of others, who were not even tenants, bringing cattle for pasturage. In Henry VIII's reign a court order was made forbidding anyone to put sheep[36] in the common pasture at Charlton Kings unless he was a tenant there, while another order forbade anyone in Arle to pasture his beasts in the common fields there before St. Martin's Day, or to ring his pigs before All Saints' Day, and the penalty for infringement was 3s. 4d.

The picture of daily life in medieval Cheltenham which emerges from the court rolls shows an agricultural and in many respects a primitive society. It was, however, regulated by a highly developed system of law and order, the maintenance of which was to some extent a common responsibility. Men ploughed and sowed and reaped according to the seasons; some of them trespassed and poached and robbed one another; they sometimes cheated in the quality of the goods they made and in the prices they charged; they often neglected the cutting of hedges and the cleansing of the ditches, the mending of roads and the repair of bridges; and for these and other misdemeanors they answered in the courts of the lords of the manor.

There was of course a different side of life from that which was presented in the court rolls. The customary or copyhold tenants—some of whom had several holdings of thirty acres—were apparently in a position to insist on a reduction of the original payments due to the lady of the manor in lieu of labour services (1452). This independent attitude may have been due to the fact that by this time the more prosperous copyhold tenants (as well as burgage and free tenants) were already obtaining additional copyhold land when it became available through the failure of heirs or for other reasons. In this way much copyhold property was passing into the hands of a new yeoman class very far removed from the villeins who had given labour services to the owner of the manor in return for their holdings. Thus by the end of Henry VII's reign there were prosperous farmers and craftsmen able and willing to buy land which came into the market, and in connexion with this there was enough legal business carried on in the area to support several attorneys. John Greville, writing to Sir Edward Tame in 1501, recommends that either Richard Machyn or John Chadwill should act on his behalf in the Court of the Abbess of Syon in Cheltenham.[37] Richard Machyn held considerable property in the town at this time, and he included in his will (1509), in addition to his Cheltenham possessions, the furnishings of his room in London where he also conducted business. On the other hand, the poorer tenants, whose holdings varied from less than half an acre to six or seven acres, could doubtless earn wages for themselves as labourers in a community where inclosure and sheep farming had not as yet created large numbers of landless and unemployed men. It is significant that when William Greville of Arle ordered in his will (1513) that the proceeds from the sale of a thousand sheep should be used for the repair of the highway between Cheltenham and Gloucester, these animals were not from his Cheltenham estates.

Arle Court,[38] of which all that remains is a few beams and bricks incorporated into the present Arle Court Farm, had at this time passed by the marriage of the heiress of the de Arle family to Robert Greville of Charlton Kings, from whom it was purchased by his brother, William Greville. These two were descended from William Greville of Chipping Campden—'the flower of the Wool Merchants of all England'.

On his brass memorial in the chancel of the parish church William Greville of Arle is described as a judge of the court of Common Pleas. It is by no means certain that he was buried nearby, since in his will—a most interesting document which reveals a kindly and pleasant personality—he directed that his body should be buried 'in such holy Church or Churchyard where Almighty God shall please to provide', and at the same time he left money for the provision of a vault in Winchcombe Abbey. He also directed that at the time of his interment 'there be plenteous vitayll provided for poore men, and for others as little as convenient may be . . .'. Of the three sons depicted in the memorial none survived him, and his estate at Arle passed to his daughter Margaret Lygon.

Another famous medieval family—the Giffards of Leck-hampton—came to an end in the male line during the reign of Henry VII, when the heiress Eleanor Giffard married John Norwood. His descendants of that name held the estate until the beginning of the nineteenth century.

It should be emphasized that the Grevilles of Arle and Charlton Kings and the Norwoods of Leckhampton owed suit to the lord of the manor of Cheltenham—to whom they paid an annual rent. Ashley (Charlton Kings), however, was a semi-independent manor; this was made clear in the Act of 1625 (cf. Chapter VII).

There was, however, another authority and another system of interests which greatly affected the lives of the inhabitants of Cheltenham—that of the Church. When a man died at this time, his heir paid not only a heriot of the best beast or its equivalent to the lord of the manor; he also gave the second best beast to the priest; and while every tenant paid reliefs and rents to the lord he also paid (and often unwillingly) his tithes to the Church. In addition to his enforced attendance at the manorial courts, he might also be summoned before the Consistory court of the diocese if he committed adultery,[39] slandered his neighbour, or failed to pay his tithes, and after his death his will was proved before the same court.

The administration of the parish church of Cheltenham and its property seems to have been entirely separate from that of the manor, since it was owned by the Abbey of Cirencester and was probably an example of a Liberty within a Liberty. Certainly the abbot held his own view of frank-pledge for the little group of tenants on this property, and if he was on occasion fined for not attending the Cheltenham courts, this was probably in respect of small amounts of manorial land which had been acquired (after Henry I's original grant) by purchase or gift (cf. Chapter II), and which were therefore held on the usual conditions.

There is little evidence to show how the abbey administered the church and its property in Cheltenham. The disputes recorded in the cartulary over the title to the vicarage, between Randulf the priest and Reginald the chaplain, and later between

Reginald and the abbot (1174–1195) ended as explained in
Chapter II in the final appropriation of the revenues to the
abbey, provided that out of these it maintained two chaplains to
serve the church (1216). Dr. Ross has pointed out in his pre-
face to the cartulary that during these forty years 'The incumbency of Cheltenham had engaged the attentions of no less than
four popes, two archbishops, and several bishops, abbots and
priors, acting either in their ordinary capacity or as papal
judges-delegate',[40] but he is unable to throw any light on the
question as to whether the canons in person served the church
in Cheltenham. There is, however, a statement in the Worcester
Diocesan Records that when the bishop made his visitation
of the abbey in 1378, he found among other disorders that the
conduct of some of the canons had given rise to serious scandal,
and that among these was the keeper of the parish church of
Cheltenham, who was to be deprived of his office.[41] Despite
the lack of any direct evidence, it has generally been assumed
that the tombs set in the north wall of the church, which resemble
some tombs in Tewkesbury Abbey, were made for canons who
had served the church.

At the time when Henry VIII dissolved the monasteries and
confiscated their property, the canons of Cirencester had leased
their estates in Cheltenham for an annual rent of £74.[42]
Although little is known of their earlier administration of these
estates, they were of course responsible for the fabric of the
church, which they altered and enlarged, century after century,
until it became the church we know today.

The oldest parts—the west wall of the nave and the piers
which support the arches under the tower—are late Norman,
probably contemporary with the building of Cirencester
Abbey. The lower stage of the tower and its windows, immediately above the roofs of the main building, are Early
English. The spire, the arcades of the nave and the tombs
of the unknown built into the wall of the north aisle were
probably built in the early fourteenth century, and many
of the windows, particularly the rose window in the north
aisle, are beautiful examples of the decorated period. The north
porch was completed later in the perpendicular style.

In the late Middle Ages two chantries were established

within the church, with endowments to support two priests to say masses in perpetuity for the souls of their founders and all Christian souls. The rose or wheel window—sometimes called St. Catherine's window because she suffered martyrdom on the wheel—may have been connected with the chantry of St. Catherine, the founder of which is unknown. The chantry of St. Mary was endowed by Walter French[43] who as bailiff kept the accounts of the manor for many years. In his will, proved in 1476, he directed that certain rents from his properties should be applied 'to the maintenance of two chaplains to celebrate in the service of St. Mary in the Parish Church and in the Church at Charlton Kings'.

From the will of Richard Machyn (1509) we learn more details of the interior of the church. He directed that his body should be buried there 'before the image of St. Christopher, St. Erasmus interceding for him'. He gave to the high altar 'for tythes forgotten' 20d., to every light in the church 20d., to the building of the middle aisle of the said church ten marks (£6. 13s. 4d.). He also directed that his best horse should be sold and if it fetched more than eight marks the residue was to be given to burning a light before the image of St. Erasmus—'I will that a taper of 7 lbs. of wax shall be made to burn before the said image.' The fact that both St. Christopher and St. Erasmus were patron saints of travellers suggests that the monks (or their officials) who made the hazardous journey from Fécamp to Cheltenham may have been responsible for the placing of these statues in the church.

In two other contemporary wills there are references to the parish church. John Greenhill, who was also bailiff to the Abbess of Syon, left five marks towards 'the reparations of the Church', which seem to be still in progress. Another gift came from the wealthy William Greville of Arle who left property for an endowment called the Holy Bread, which provided 25s. a year for the distribution of bread to the poor.

Neither the chantry endowments nor the money for the Holy Bread were left in the possession of the church for many years, since Henry VIII, shortly after dissolving the monasteries, turned his attention to chantry property. Most of this was confiscated in the next reign. In Cheltenham, however, it was restored by Elizabeth I as the main endowment of Pate's Grammar School.

By this time the great Convent of Syon had been dissolved and the nuns dispersed, and the Abbey of Cirencester had been virtually razed to the ground. The dissolution of the monasteries was thus for Cheltenham the end of an epoch.

THE EFFECTS OF THE REFORMATION IN CHELTENHAM

AFTER his failure to obtain papal sanction for the annulment of his marriage to Catherine of Aragon, Henry VIII began a systematic attack on the authority of the Pope and the wealth of the Church in England. Among the measures taken was the suppression of monasteries and other religious houses, of which in Gloucestershire alone there were forty-three at this time.

The first of the larger establishments to fall was the Monastery and Convent of Syon (1539). One of its monks—the great scholar Richard Reynolds—had already been hanged for refusing to accept Henry's claim to be Supreme Head of the Church of England. A second reason for its suppression was the attraction of its great wealth. In the survey ordered by Henry in 1535 (and known as the Valor Ecclesiasticus), the net annual income of Syon is given as £1,731. 8s. 4¼d., which included £79. 1s. 8d. for the Manor of Cheltenham.

After the suppression, all this property was confiscated by the Crown. Its former owners were then ejected and pensioned with amounts which varied from £200 a year for the abbess and £100 for the prioress, to £10 and £6 for the nuns.[1]

The Manor of Cheltenham was then leased by the Crown to Lord Andrew Wyndsor[2]—the brother of the prioress. It reverted to the Crown in the reign of Edward VI, and according to the court rolls of that reign was administered by Thomas Dutton—'overseer of the said King for his county of Gloucester'. Under Mary it was leased for a short time to Roger Lygon of Arle Court and his wife—Catherine Buckler. Their tomb may be seen in the Lady Chapel of Fairford Church. Roger Lygon was probably the grandson of William Greville, whose memorial in the parish church has already been mentioned; Catherine, whose first husband was the grandson of

Edmund Tame of Fairford, was thus connected with another famous wool family of the Cotswolds. In Elizabeth's reign the lessee of the manor was Sir John Woolley, and from 1589 until the lease from the Crown ran out, William Norwood of Leckhampton, whose name is still preserved in the 'Norwood Arms' and whose descendants are represented by the present Trye family. A part of his home at Leckhampton Court remains today in its original setting, with the tree-lined walk to the nearby church in which he and other members of his family were buried. He was virtually the first resident lord of the manor, and from his lawsuits with the Crown and his difficulties with the bailiff of the borough, more is known of him than of any of his predecessors.

The suppression of Cirencester Abbey followed a year after that of Syon. Its buildings were ruthlessly and almost completely destroyed. There were, however, no martyrs since all the canons accepted the Royal Supremacy. The property and the pensions were less than those of Syon, but from the terms of the abbot's will it appears that he was able to live comfortably in his retirement. One of the ejected canons became parish priest in Cirencester, and another—Richard Lane—was probably the Reynaldo Lane who was curate in Cheltenham in 1540.[3]

Among the property confiscated by the Crown from this abbey was the rectory of Cheltenham. Details of its value were given in the Valor Ecclesiasticus:[4]

Cheltenham. To wit, a charge consisting of the rent of the site of the rectory there with all the tithes pertaining to the said rectory, together with the demesne land and with the rent of a mill and other tenements of the demesne there let to Thomas Pakker by indenture at a lump rent

£73. 13. 4d.

Fines derived from a View of frankpledge held there annually

3. 8d.

£73. 17. 0d.

From which the following deductions are made:
Assignment of the aforesaid rent paid annually into the hands of the chief cook of the aforesaid monastery for

the food of the brethren, and afterwards charged to the aforesaid office of master cook	£64.	0.	0.
Payment of rent to the heirs of William Compton, Knight, for water rights for the aforesaid mill		1.	0.
	£64.	1.	0.
The clear yearly value is	9.	16.	0.

Thus immediately before its suppression the abbey had let the whole of the Cheltenham church properties and transferred most of the rent directly to the head cook to spend on food, leaving a mere £9. 16s. 0d. for salaries and other expenses in Cheltenham. If the church was served by the canons of the abbey, the smallness of the amount would be comprehensible, but it seems probable that for the most part the chaplains were salaried. Cheltenham therefore may well have been one of the many medieval churches appropriated to monasteries where the priests in charge received an annual salary of less than £10. The poverty of these parish priests had long been regarded as a serious problem.

After its confiscation the rectory of Cheltenham, like the manor, was granted by the Crown to a series of lessees—among the most important of whom was Sir Francis Bacon—until it was finally bought outright by the wealthy London merchant Sir Baptist Hicks in 1612.[5]

There is evidence that the church itself and the parishioners were neglected during part of this period. It is recorded in the Gloucester Diocesan Records in 1563,[6] when the property was let to Sir Henry Jerningham and by him sublet or 'farmed' to Thomas Higgs, that 'the Churchwardens and Parishioners present that the Chancel of their Church is in Ruins and Decay . . . which the farmer Thomas Higgs ought to repair . . . and that the Fortieth which ought to be given to the Poor is not so given and distributed'.

Shortly before his death Henry VIII had made plans for confiscating still more ecclesiastical property, particularly the endowments of the chantries which had been established to maintain prayers in perpetuity for the souls of the founders.

The government of Edward VI decided to continue this policy and in 1548 sent six commissioners to assess the endowments in Gloucestershire.[7] The chantry certificates which they subsequently issued included details of the two Cheltenham chantries of St. Mary and St. Katherine, and gave the number of communicants (houseling people) in the parish as 600.

The Parish of Cheltenham within the Deanery of Winchcombe where are houseling people 600.

Our Lady's Service
founded by diverse persons not known and the lands . . . from which hath been a priest maintained at the altar of Our Lady in the said Parish Church praying for the souls of the Founders and all Christian Souls.

Sir Thomas Ball . . . aged 54, having no other living than the said service, which is worth yearly £4.

The lands and tenements of yearly value	£6.	10.	8d.
In reprises are paid yearly		19.	2d.
And so remaineth clear by each year	£5.	11.	6d.
Ornaments thereunto belonging valued		13.	5d.
Plate and Jewels		None	

Thomas Ball had been granted a pension of £3. 6s. 8d. as a former monk of Tewkesbury Abbey. The body of John Ball his predecessor as chantry priest and probably his brother, lies in the old porch of the parish church of Cheltenham, where he asked that three priests should bury him 'in accordance with laudable custom and receive 8d. everyone for their labours'. Of his few small possessions he left 16d. and his best sheet to his confessor, his bedstead and a sheet to one of the witnesses of his will, his best shirt and 6d. to Elizabeth Mason, and his fustian doublet to his clerk.

St. Katherine's Service is also described:

The foundation thereof unknown, but the lands . . . were given by divers persons . . . whereof there hath been a priest maintained and kept singing at the altar of St. Katherine within the said Parish Church for the souls of the founders . . . and all Christian souls

Sir Edward Grove incumbent there, aged 60 years,
having no other living than in the said service,
which is yearly £5. 0. 0d.
The lands and tenements belonging to the same
are of the yearly value of £6. 16. 10d.
Whereof in reprises yearly 19. 2d.
And so remaineth clear £5. 17. 8d-
Ornaments thereunto belonging 10. 2d.
Plate and Jewels None

On a second visit the commissioners recorded that the
priest, Sir Edward Grove, 'was charged by special Covenant
between the parishioners of the said town of Cheltenham and
himself always to teach their children, which town is a market
town and much youth within the same, near whereunto is no
school kept'. The commissioners therefore recommended 'the
same to be a meet place to establish some teacher and erect a
Grammar School, so it might stand with the King's Majesty's
pleasure'.

This recommendation must have been accepted in principle,
for although the property of both the chantries and of William
Greville's endowment for buying bread for the poor were
confiscated by the Crown, the annual salary of £5 was paid to
Edward Grove for the rest of the reign of Edward VI. Its
payment is thus recorded: 'Paid to Sir Edward Grove, schoolmaster of a certain Grammar School of the foundation of the
Chantry of St. Katherine in the parish of Cheltenham . . . for
his wages £5.'[8] There is no record of this payment after the
first years of Mary's reign, but in 1574 Queen Elizabeth granted
the property of these chantries to one of the former Commissioners, Richard Pate of Minsterworth, to enable him to
carry out his intention of maintaining a free Grammar School
for Cheltenham.

Richard Pate (born 1516) was for some years Member of
Parliament for Gloucester and Recorder of that city, in the
cathedral of which he is buried.[9] Little is known of his early
life. He was probably related to Bishop Richard Pate of
Worcester and was almost certainly the son of Walter Pate
of Cheltenham, where his wife's father Thomas Lane, his
brother William, and his nephew Richard held considerable

property. It is possible—though by no means certain—that his own education began in the little school kept by the chantry priest Edward Grove, or his predecessor, before he went to the college of Corpus Christi at Oxford when he was a youth of sixteen. In 1541 he was admitted at Lincoln's Inn and was later called to the Bar. In 1586 he endowed his old college with some of the chantry property which he had purchased and with that already granted to him by Elizabeth in 1574, on condition that three-quarters of the income should be used by the college 'for the perpetual maintenance and foundation of a free Grammar School at Cheltenham . . . for the exercise of Grammar and other liberal arts and science there . . . and also a Hospital or Almshouse for six old poor people, of whom two were to be women'.[10]

The only school fees demanded were 4d. on entrance from the sons of those in the parish and 8d. from others, but any scholar who absented himself for more than four days, 'especially in time of harvest', had to be readmitted and his entrance fee paid again. This money was to be spent on books 'to be tied with little chains' so that they could not be taken away.

At least four of the fifty scholars (who were to be considered the minimum number for which the endowment provided) were to be taught Latin and Greek; at least five were to be taught enough Latin to enable them to translate their native tongue into it; and at least eighteen were to be given some teaching in Latin. Presumably Richard Pate knew the capabilities and interests of the boys likely to come to his school and he did not expect too many of them to be turned into learned classical scholars. He knew also the strong counter-attractions which might lure them from school in time of harvest. The master of the school, who 'must be a Master of Arts', was to receive an annual salary of £16 and to have the use of a schoolhouse and also the profit of the pasture adjoining the schoolhouse and 'pasture for one cow in the fields of Cheltenham as a thing belonging to the burgage ground whereon the schoolhouse is builded'.

The original Grammar School was built on part of the site of the present school in the High Street. By the early nineteenth century the Fellows of Corpus Christi had evaded the spirit of the original endowment to such an extent that a suit was successfully brought against them in Chancery,[11] as a result of which they were compelled to apply to the school and the Almshouse the original proportion of the revenue to which these institutions were entitled. Later, after many vicissitudes, it was decided to build a new school, but a part of Richard Pate's own building remained in use until 1886 (cf. Chapter XX).

The Almshouse was built on the north side of the High Street—opposite Rodney Road. When Goding wrote his *History of Cheltenham* there were people living who remembered it and described it to him. It consisted of a stone house with a chapel attached to it, a courtyard with grass in front, and a garden, pasture, and orchard at the back, reaching to Albion Street—altogether a pleasant place. By the regrettable arrangement sanctioned under the Inclosure Act of 1801, the Fellows of Corpus Christi allowed the building and site to be sold, using part of the money to build the much smaller house that still exists in Albion Street (cf. Chapter XX). The original endowment provided for an income of 1s. a week to each of the six inmates, with an additional quarterly allowance of 4d. and sufficient black cloth for gowns. A separate room and a separate patch of garden was also included, so that by the standards of later centuries the provision was generous.

It has been estimated that during the twelve years after Henry VIII began the confiscation of Church property, one-sixth of all the land in England changed hands and passed from the Church by way of gift, lease, or sale into secular control. Cheltenham was thus a typical example of this change. Not all the confiscated property, however, passed into secular hands. One of the first local effects of the suppression was the creation of the new diocese of Gloucester with the church of the former abbey as its cathedral, and the former Abbot of Tewkesbury as its first bishop. Thus from 1541 Cheltenham ceased to be in the diocese of Worcester, where for four years it had been under the jurisdiction of Bishop Latimer.

Confiscation and transference of monastic and chantry property was, however, only one stage in the national movement from which, by the end of Elizabeth's reign, there emerged what we now know as the Church of England. On the accession of Edward VI the strongly Protestant group which had been held in check by his father gained power and began to effect doctrinal changes in the services of the Church. Acts of Uniformity enforced the use of the Book of Common Prayer compiled in English by Cranmer; and the use of the Bible in English, already sanctioned by Henry VIII, was continued. Henry had also agreed somewhat reluctantly to the destruction of relics. The best known of these in Gloucestershire was the 'Blood of Hailes'—for the removal and analysis of which Bishop Latimer himself was chiefly responsible.

Extremists in various parts of the country broke up the images of the Virgin and the saints, whitewashed many wall-paintings, and destroyed tombs which had become shrines where gifts and prayers were offered. We do not know if the ex-monk Reynaldo Lane exercised a moderating influence in Cheltenham, or indeed how long he remained as one of the curates of the church, but in 1548, after the confiscation by the Crown of all chantry property, the former chantry priests Edward Grove and Thomas Ball, who had thus lost their occupation, became curates. In 1551, in the course of Bishop Hooper's visitation, the clergy of the diocese of Gloucester were questioned as to their knowledge of the Lord's Prayer, the Ten Commandments, the tenets of the Christian faith, and their sources. Stephen Poole was curate of Cheltenham at this time but unfortunately he had been examined before, and so we do not know whether he reached the standards required by his bishop. Hooper preferred 'an honest table decently covered' to an altar and ordered the removal of roods, screens, and shrines, and the defacing of wall-painting and images. Since Bishop Hooper found time to meet most of the clergy in his diocese, it is certain that his injunctions were at least known in Cheltenham. The destruction of the images of St. Christopher and St. Erasmus, the defacing of the 'stone altar of high antiquity . . . and the wall-painting'[12] uncovered in the chancel in 1807 were in direct line with these injunctions.

No accounts have survived of how the parishioners of Cheltenham reacted to these changes, but there is a tantalizing

reference in the record of a suit in the[13] Gloucester Consistory
court (1554) which shows that Cranmer's second Prayer Book
was a matter of some parochial interest. Katherine Sturmey—
giving evidence that one woman had slandered another on the
way home from church—deposed 'that three or four years past,
betwixt summer and corn harvest . . . coming on a Sunday
from Cheltenham Parish Church from Evensong . . . talking
of many things including the English service...'. Unfortunately
the rest of her evidence concerns the slander and not the new
Prayer Book.

With the accession of Queen Mary the old Latin service was
restored and the counter-attack began against the Reformers.
Papal authority was restored and the law for the burning of
heretics enforced, although Parliament would not agree to
the restoration of the recently confiscated Church property.
During her short reign of five years, three hundred heretics
were burnt at the stake, of whom fifty were women. Among
the victims were the two former bishops who had held authority
over Cheltenham. The seventy-year-old Latimer was burnt with
Ridley at Oxford, and John Hooper, after a year's imprisonment in London, was brought back to Gloucester to be burnt
as 'an obstinate heretic'.

It is probable that there were men from Cheltenham among
the seven thousand who watched Hooper die in the flames at
Gloucester. Cheltenham's victim, however, was not burnt in
his own town but in Salisbury. Foxe refers to a wandering
preacher who came into Gloucestershire and later returned with
two of his converts (William Cobberley and his wife Alice)
to Salisbury. There, after aggressively interrupting the Service
of the Mass, they were arrested, charged with heresy, and
condemned to be burnt; but Alice recanted and returned
home. Foxe's statement is corroborated by entries in the Cheltenham court rolls where it is recorded (17 April 1556) 'that
John Cobberley who held one messuage and fourteen acres of
land [in Westhall] was lately attainted and burnt for diverse
heresies and false opinions in Salisbury . . . whereby his
messuage and lands are seized into the Lord's hands'. A
query is raised in the margin as to whether his goods were
forfeit to the lord of the manor, but when, two years later,

Alice remarried, she and her second husband successfully claimed the inheritance.

On the accession of Elizabeth, papal authority was again repudiated and by the Act of Supremacy the Queen was declared 'Supreme Governor of the Church of England'. The use of Cranmer's second Book of Common Prayer was again enforced in all churches and regular attendance at services was ordered by the Act of Uniformity. As the reign continued, these Acts were challenged by both Roman Catholics and Puritans. For the first twelve years, however, the penalties exacted from those who did not conform generally took the form of fines or loss of office, but the situation changed with the promulgation of the Papal Bull of 1570, in which Pope Pius V excommunicated Elizabeth, deposed her from the throne, and released her subjects from their allegiance. As a result penalties against Roman Catholics were increased, and those found guilty of being implicated in plots against the Queen, and militant missionaries such as the Jesuits, suffered extreme and barbarously cruel punishments for treason. Puritans also, if they actively opposed the Queen's supremacy in the Church, were liable to the death penalty, although they were more often pilloried or imprisoned.

In the attempt to discover the recusants the Privy Council demanded from the bishop of every diocese the names of those who had failed to attend the services of the Church as ordered by the Act of Uniformity. The lists which were submitted by Bishop Richard Cheyney in 1577 for the diocese of Gloucester are recorded in State Papers of Elizabeth's reign.[14] Only three names from Cheltenham are included in these lists: Henry Hatheway and his wife, and William Norwood of Leckhampton—probably the lessee of the manor during the last years of the reign. In the City of Gloucester there were fifteen recusants, but in Winchcombe only two. Unfortunately, Bishop Cheyney did not indicate whether these were Roman Catholic or Puritan. The smallness of the numbers, however, and of the few Cheltenham cases of failure to attend the Communion Service (which were dealt with in the Consistory court) bears out later evidence that the Elizabethan Church settlement was generally accepted without serious opposition in Cheltenham. It is likely that Richard Pate had considerable influence in the town, and he was both by conviction and as a lay member of the Court of High Commission a strong supporter of this settlement.

During the later years of the reign the Perpetual Curate, as the incumbent of the parish church was to be called for the next three centuries, was William Panton of happy memory. He 'discharged his office for above thirty years with the good liking of all his parishioners', despite the fact that, according to the report of his bishop, he was 'a sufficient scholar, but no preacher'.[15] The earliest surviving parish register dates from 1558, but is almost certainly a copy of the original and made by William Panton who continued to keep the registers until his death in 1624. In the first Register it is recorded that on April 28th 1572, 'the first stone of the schoole howse was laide'. This is the first known reference to the building of the grammar school.

The neighbouring town of Winchcombe suffered a permanent loss from the suppression of its abbey, around which so much of its life and trade had revolved. Queen Elizabeth on the first of her visits there (1564) was petitioned to grant a charter allowing an additional annual fair, because 'the said borough appeared to be fallen into so great ruin and decay, that its inhabitants were not able to support and repair it, for the great poverty that reigned among them . . .'.

It is unlikely that Cheltenham was affected in the same way. The Convent of Syon had been a remote landlord, administering its property by means of stewards, or sub-letting it to secular tenants. The great power held by the distant monastic owners over the Liberty had undoubtedly hindered municipal development, but this disadvantage was counterbalanced by the fact that neither the Convent of Syon nor subsequent lessees under the Crown carried out any large-scale inclosure of land such as brought suffering to many other parts of England. There is no evidence that any lasting or substantial damage occurred to the inhabitants as a result of the permanent change from monastic to secular ownership. The catastrophic rise in rents described by Bishop Latimer in his famous sermon given before King Edward VI did not occur in Cheltenham.

This is shown clearly by the statement of John Norden, who made a survey of the manor for King James I, that the rights of the owner and the profits accruing to him from the tenants had seriously declined under Crown ownership.

The chief means of livelihood in Cheltenham during this period were agriculture, the market, and—towards the end of Elizabeth's reign—brewing.

The developments which followed the main national trends during the period—attempts at inclosure, the struggle between officials of the manor and the borough and between the Crown and the lord of the manor—are described in the next chapter.

V

'A LONGE TOWNE HAVYNGE A MARKET'

SHORTLY before the dissolution of the monasteries, John Leland (who carried out considerable antiquarian research for Henry VIII) set out on his travels to find material for a topographical account of England and Wales. In the course of his journeys he came to Cheltenham, which he described in his itinerary: 'a longe towne havynge a Market. There is a brook on the South Syde of the Towne.' Later he included it among the market towns in the Vale and gave the alternative name of Cheltenham Street. In another chapter he stated that 'from Southam to Cheltenham market is five miles'. Leland must therefore have considered that the market had considerable local importance.

There are other indications that the market played an important part in the economy of the town. A Market-house and Booth Hall are mentioned in the court books of this period, and at the end of Elizabeth's reign there is evidence that a court of Pie Powder (a court which dealt exclusively with disputes connected with the market) had been in existence for many centuries.

From the reign of Mary Tudor the records of the courts of the lord of the manor were entered in books, instead of on rolls, and from the references in these court books[1] it is possible to find many details of the appearance of the Street at this time. Thus it is recorded (April 1556) that 'the tenement between the Booth Hall and the Lord's Prison and the High Cross, and the said prison itself with two chambers are part of the Lord's demesne'. The Booth Hall was probably used at this time for the holding of the courts and public business and as an additional Market-house. The High Cross was clearly not the cross which stands in the churchyard today, but another—since destroyed—in the Street itself, near to the present Promenade.[2] The Booth Hall and a small prison behind it were still in existence in the High Street in the latter part of the eighteenth century,[3] in front of what is now the 'Eight Bells', and it is likely that the site at least was unchanged from the reign of Mary and perhaps earlier. A few years later there is a reference to the Market-house (October 1559): 'The tithing-man of Cheltenham presents that Richard Machyn has blocked three lanes with a door, which lanes lie next to the High Crosse and Market House.'

If the site of this Market-house was the same as the one erected in 1655,[4] it was a free-standing building in the Street itself and opposite the present 'Plough'. This inn, or one of the same name, was already in existence. It was referred to in a cross-suit (already mentioned) before the Gloucester Consistory court, where two women accused each other of slander, and one accused the other of loitering outside the 'Plough' and lying in wait for her husband.

The Court House and the Close were let on lease for a number of years.[5] Near it was a church house—which was used for the church ales and other functions for raising funds for the poor, until the Puritan reaction against these had set in.[6] On the north side of the Street, stretching from the present Pittville to the back of Swindon Road, was the common known as the Marsh where the master of the Grammar School could keep his one cow because of his burgage holding.

The maintenance and repair of the Street was the responsibility of those who lived in it. A typical court order (April 1558) laid down that each inhabitant should make up the paving in the Street to a width of two yards, and another (April 1565) that the Street should be cleansed weekly (on Wednesdays). Another order (March 1562), that no one was 'to wash clothes within twelve feet of the common pump in the lower part of the town', shows that means were taken to prevent the pollution of the town well. There were also orders (1597–8) forbidding curriers and tanners from putting their skins in the river or letting water from lime- or tan-pits run into it.

The great importance of cleansing the Street was fully recognized, and there are frequent references to the use of the water from the Chelt, a portion of which was deflected at Cambray Mill and allowed to flow from the mill pond down the

Street several times a week. Thus the court ordered (April 1560) that the miller Richard Pate should 'allow the water to flow at his mill through a board with three holes continually and once in the week the whole stream, so that the common stream may be used according to the ancient custom'.

The next year the mill had been sublet and another court order runs: 'That Edward Barthiam tenant of Cambray Mill shall have a sluice in the lower end of his pound in the place accustomed with three holes through which the water may run 3 days a week. One hole to be bored with a yoke and the second with an inch auger, and the third with a $\frac{3}{4}$ inch auger' (October 1561).

Six years later another order was made that Edward Barthiam shall not 'grind away the water at the Mill but that the pound may be so full that the water shall run over at the holes in the sluice three days a week [on pain of penalty of 100s.] and that the bailiff of the borough shall see this order to be kept and that weekly 2 burgesses shall go with him to inspect the same. The days when holes shall run shall be Sunday, Tuesday and Thursday' (September 1567).

Much later in the reign (April 1597) Richard Trinder was fined 40s. for not allowing the water to flow down the Street 'according to the custom which hath ever been used beyond the memory of man' and threatened with heavier penalties if he failed to obey the order. The Cambray mill-pond still remains in its original position with the walls of the mill-house forming two sides of the enclosure which is here referred to as the pound.

There is a curious record of another difficulty encountered in the Street at this time (1576). 'It is ordered that any man that will keep a mastiff dog or bitch that he shall keep him muzzled or tied up, for there cannot go into the streets neither man, woman nor child nor beast nor pig without hurt or danger of life . . . and therefore desiring you Mr. Steward to see some good order to be taken therein, or else there is no man nor beast can escape but shall be devoured with these mastiffs that be in the Town of Cheltenham.' Dogs and other animals were prohibited in the streets of some other towns at this time on grounds of cleanliness, but the reason given here is unusual.

The functions of the courts seem to have changed little

since the days when the Abbess of Syon owned the manor.
All matters concerning the sale, leasing, or inheritance of
property were recorded; view of frank-pledge was still held;
petty crime was still 'presented' and the penalties recorded;
disputes concerning farming operations and other matters
were settled; regulations for the sale of food as well as for the
cleansing and paving of the Street were laid down.

There are fewer records of cases of tenants 'drawing blood'
from each other, perhaps because such cases were dealt with
more frequently by the increasingly important justices of the
peace. It is recorded (1567) that ale-house keepers gave bonds
for their good conduct before two justices of the peace—
William Lygon and William Badger (who were also respectively
the Bailiff of the Liberty and the High Steward). Ale-tasters
(October 1556) were to assess ale at 4d. the gallon; each brewer
was to sell ale both inside and outside his house at 1d. the wine
quart (on pain of penalty of 40s.); and every wine- and ale-
house keeper was to provide lodgings when required for
travellers on foot as well as for those on horseback. 'Common
tipplers', however, were fined from 4d. to 6d. for each offence.
It was forbidden by law at this time to hold back grain in order
to command a better price, and a man was fined 40s. at the
same court 'as an engrosser of merchandise who keeps barley
and malt'. Six years later there was an order that the Bailiff of
the Liberty should check once a week the weight of bread sold,
and once a month should test the quality of ale (September
1564). The sale of unwholesome meat was punished with a
fine of 6s. 8d. (October 1597).

There is ample evidence that the main source of livelihood
was still agriculture, based on mixed farming rather than on
any form of specialization. Bequests of barley appear frequently
in the wills of the period, and barley and oats are included as
part of the tithes due to the owner of the Rectory. Various
orders in the court books indicate the importance of sheep in
the economy of the town. 'No one shall erect a sheep pen in
Well Lane on pain of payment of 20/- for each on market days'
(April 1565). Well Lane was known during the eighteenth
century as Fleece Lane and was used for the sale of cattle on
market days. It has since been renamed Henrietta Street.

The nation-wide trend towards inclosure of common and common fields was seen also in Cheltenham, although it was not necessarily caused by intensive sheep-farming. In Mary's reign nine wealthy tenants—mainly of Ham and Charlton Kings—were presented for having 'unjustly inclosed diverse parcels of land and holding them in severalty ... excluding the Lord's tenants from their common'. They were ordered to throw open the fields concerned from the end of autumn to the beginning of February following, but from later evidence it seems that some of them maintained their inclosures.

An almost complete record of the inclosure movement in Charlton Kings was written into the court books by John Stubbes—an attorney—who was appointed under-steward of the manor by William Norwood and was himself a copyholder in Charlton Kings. His account[7] begins with the statement that 'heretofore' (in the Middle Ages) the land of all the tenants in Charlton Kings was always thrown open as common pasture at stated times of the year—from hay harvest if pasture land, and corn harvest if arable—until Candlemas (2 February); and for the whole year if (as happened every three years) it was lying fallow. He and many others objected to this ancient custom because it led to more cattle being allowed into the fields than was considered to be good farming. He then refers to an earlier agreement (court books, 6 May 1556) whereby every tenant, whether freeholder or copyholder, should take up and inclose one acre for every ten acres he held in Charlton Kings and keep it inclosed for the whole of the year. The actual measurement was to be carried out by seven men appointed by the courts of Cheltenham and Charlton Kings. It appears from this that the inclosure definitely concerned the tenants' holdings and not the common lands or waste.

This arrangement, however, was not considered satisfactory by the majority of the tenants who at the end of three years pulled up the hedges and let their cattle run on the lands which had been inclosed. Whereupon, wrote Stubbes, 'many quarrels and suits of law were moved and stirred up between the said inhabitants both at common law and before the Court of the Marches of Wales'.

This last-mentioned court appointed as commissioners

William Lygon and William Read who investigated what had happened and issued an order (1564) that all tenants in Charlton Kings could 'inclose and keep in severalty [separately] three acres for every 20 acres they owned—for the period of their lives and twelve years afterwards'. A list of the names of the tenants concerned is given with the measurement and position of the land which they might inclose—amounting to a total of 291 acres. At the court held in Cheltenham in 1566 an order was made that hedges should be planted to inclose the specified lands, and one tenant who had persisted in putting his beasts in a field which was thus inclosed was fined 23s. 1d. After this some of the wealthier tenants of Charlton Kings became so hopeful that 'many did hedge up their grounds . . . having procured the consent and furtherance of Mr. Norwood the Farmer of the Manor of Cheltenham, on their behalf', but 'by the frowardness and obstinacy of some of the tenants, the said inclosed grounds were again layd open, without any hope of ever obtaining . . . that they should be kept in several . . . and thus the commons began to be more disorderly used than in any former tymes had byn accustomed'. The tenants of Ham and Northfield having securely hedged their own ground proceeded to run their cattle on the nearby lands of tenants in Charlton Kings during the time when the fields were thrown open, 'in a most unreasonable and unconscionable manner, under colour of having some ground in Cudnall fields lying open. . . . All the neighbouring townes [townships] about did put their cattell into the common fields of Charlton and did buy ricks of hay of purpose to winter greate flocks of sheepe there (so careless is everyone to the common good) . . . and besydes, this unreasonable kind of common did draw many who had stocks of money, to hire houses in Charlton in hopes of keeping their sheepe and horses upon the common grounds, and within a short time by the rotting of their sheepe they did lie upon the charge of the parish.'

In Arle, where the inclosure of tenants' holdings in the common fields was also proceeding, there seems to have been little of the resistance which was put up by the inhabitants of Charlton Kings. It is recorded in the court books (April 1597) that 'At this Court the Lord by his Steward with the assent and consent of all the tenants of Arle and Alston hath granted licence unto Arnold Lygon Esq. . . . to enclose and keep in several all that ground called Grovefield in Arle and during all such time [of inclosing] he shall forbear to enter common with the tenants of Arle and Alstone otherwise than to drive his sheep to the fold . . .'.

It would appear from these separately made arrangements for Charlton Kings, Arle, and Alstone, that each of the tithings or divisions of the hundred made its own regulations for the management of its fields, subject to the consent of the lord of the manor. In the succeeding reigns the common fields of Charlton, and of Arle and Alston, Naunton and Sandford, and the Cheltenham fields figure largely in the court books. There is little evidence that inclosure took place on any large scale in the Cheltenham fields—to the north of the town—but it is clear that before the end of Elizabeth's reign the inconvenience of the medieval custom of throwing open all the fields after harvest was increasingly realized. It was partly overcome by a series of agreements arranged by Stubbes in the next reign.

Before this time, however, steps were taken to prevent the intrusion of strangers into the hundred who were not self-supporting and might qualify for poor relief under the Poor Law policy of Elizabeth's government. Thus a court order in 1597 states that 'no one in Charlton Kings shall receive a subtenant who has not inhabited there for three years'. Two years later it was ordered that 'if any one let a cottage to a stranger to inhabit as sub-tenant contrary to ordinance', he should be bound in recognizances before a justice of the Queen to indemnify the parish for the family's support (October 1599).

Poverty elsewhere was more often caused by deprivation of rights in the common fields than by the fields being left open, and it is apparent that the conditions in Cheltenham continued to attract poor people from outside the town. There is further evidence of this in the next reign: 'Whereas Cheltenham and Charlton Kings have been burdened by the receipt of inmates and strangers within the past three years—every landlord is to give security for discharge of the town for liability for them—or remove them by Michaelmas next on pain of 20/- . . . . All strangers are to give security or go' (April 1616).

There are various references to the working of the remedial laws passed by Elizabeth's Parliaments to deal with the vagrancy and unemployment which arose when sheep-farming and inclosures—among other reasons—deprived many of the poor of work and land. Thus in March 1599, Robert Symone was presented at the court because he employed Richard Lawrence as a weaver when the latter had not finished his seven years' apprenticeship in accordance with the order made in the Statute of Apprentices (1563); and early in James I's reign there is a case reported of cottages being built without the four acres of land required by the Elizabethan statute passed in an attempt to hinder the growth of a class of landless labourers.

As part of the policy of tightening central control carried out by Elizabeth's government, there was a movement to challenge the powers of lords of the manor where they conflicted or competed with the local government authorities responsible directly or indirectly to the Crown. It was perhaps for this reason that in 1598 William Norwood was summoned to appear before the court of Exchequer to show by what warrant he claimed the powers and privileges listed in the indictment.[8] His defence was that all the powers he was accused of using illegally against the Queen's interests had been granted and confirmed to the Abbess of Syon and that after the confiscation of the monastic property these powers had reverted to the Crown and had subsequently been granted with the manor to Roger Lygon and his wife Catherine, and on their decease to John Woolley, from whom he himself held it for the last period of the lease. His evidence satisfied the Attorney-General and the suit against him was dropped so that in theory he retained the many privileges originally granted to the lords of the Liberty—of keeping out sheriffs and other officers of the Crown and appointing his own justices, with the right 'to erect gallows, pillory and tumbril for the punishment of malefactors' and to collect fines and other amercements from his courts, which in some other manors went to the Crown. It is, however, doubtful whether he exercised the greater part of these privileges. From Stubbes's accounts of his own lawsuits it is evident that these were tried at the Assizes and not by justices of the lord of the manor, and there are references to his meeting the sheriff's men in Cheltenham itself. It is unlikely that Norwood used the gallows, but there is a later reference in the court books to the setting up of the tumbril or ducking-stool. It was reported (April 1616) by the constable of Cheltenham that 'a gumstool or tumbril is already made ready to be set up, if there were a place convenient appointed for the same'. An order was then made that it was to be set up within one month at a place to be appointed by the steward.

There were, however, other threats to the powers of the lords of the manor besides those from the Crown. All over England at this time—and it would seem particularly in Gloucestershire—there was a growing spirit of independence in the towns. In many cases they succeeded in overthrowing the authority of the lord of the manor and managing their own affairs, being either completely incorporated, as at Tewkesbury and Chipping Campden (1605), or virtually independent, as at Northleach and Stow-on-the-Wold. In Cheltenham an instance of the same spirit of independence occurred in 1598 when the bailiff of the borough insisted on conducting the affairs of the court of Pie Powder on his own authority.

Pie Powder was a court set up to deal with cases arising during the holding of a market or fair. Its name was derived from a corruption of the French *pieds-poudrés*—the dusty feet of the market-place. It is known that many market towns held such courts for the duration of their fairs, but actual records of them are scarce, and this is the first known reference to a court so named in Cheltenham. Since the position in Cheltenham, as has already been explained, differed from that of many other places owing to the fact that the hundred and the manor had for many centuries been in the same ownership, the distinction between the jurisdiction of the hundred court and the other manorial courts is not always clear. Even the court of Pie Powder may at some earlier time have been fused with these courts but, whatever the earlier position, it is clear that in 1600 the bailiff of the borough—with the full support of his fellow townsmen—was determined to assert his right to hold this court, and that he did this with a noisy truculence which produced a strong protest from the lord of the manor, and an appeal from him to the court of Exchequer.[9]

In most humble manner-wise sheweth and complaineth William Norwood, farmer and tenant of the Manor and Hundred of Cheltenham, whereof the town of Cheltenham is and time out of mind hath been an ancient borough and market town belonging unto and part of the said Manor—the said town and certain parishes adjoining it are and time out of mind have been a Hundred exempted from the ordinary powers of the officers of the County of Gloucester ... and that in the same Manor and town hath been, by all the time whereof the memory of man is not to the contrary, a Court of Pie Powder, taken before the High Bailiff of the same Manor, the High and Low Bailiff of Cheltenham, and his steward, to hear and determine all manner of actions and debts and other personal claims to any sum whatever ... which Court hath been always held and kept from time to time at the appointment and direction and pleasure of the said High Bailiff, who hath always been accepted, taken and reputed to be the Chief Judge of the said Court. ...

William Norwood goes on to say that the burgesses, about forty in number, have always attended the court when called by the High Bailiff as 'parcel of their service incident to and belonging to their burgage tenures'. He therefore begs their Lordships of the Exchequer to deal with one William Stroude who was:

nominated, elected, chosen and sworn before the High Bailiff and his steward, at the Court Leet, to be Bailiff of the Borough. ... The said William, about last April, combined ... with other burgesses, to defame, disgrace and overthrow the said Court of Pie Powder, and thereupon the said William Stroude did insolently and arrogantly give out among the burgesses that he was Chief Judge and said that the Court belonged to them and that the Queen's Majesty nor her farmer nor their officers had not anything to do there ... and came upon a summons given by the said High Bailiff to the Court of Pie Powder held within the borough on the 23rd April and there offered to take his place and sit before and above the Steward of the said Court. ... Being denied, and requested to take his place as his predecessor, he utterly denied so to do, and thereupon offered with force and violence to pull up the said steward forth from his place, and did swear in very brutish and outrageous manner, by the Lord's blood and divers other blasphemous oaths that he would not sit in the Court and do any service there unless he might sit in the steward's place, and commanded the Crier to end and adjourn the said Court and persuaded the burgesses there present to arise forth of the said Court . . . and the said Stroude departed from Court in very contemptuous and proud manner, to the bad example of others.

At a similar court held in the following month, William Stroude insisted on sitting above the High Steward, and refused to move when ordered—the other burgesses encouraging him 'to continue in the same place always before used by the High Bailiff, and never before taken by any Bailiff of the Borough'.

William Norwood therefore asked that writs of subpoena should be issued against William Stroude. No record has been found of any action taken in the matter by the court of the Exchequer. As the court had before it at this time a number of cases arising out of customs governing the inheritance of property in Cheltenham, and as William Norwood's lease had only a few more years to run, it is possible that the Crown was already contemplating an inquiry into the whole situation there. William Stroude was, however, fined in the Cheltenham hundred court 21s., because he—'a principal officer—departed from the Court of Pie Powder on the 22nd of May last year and refused to execute his office' (October 1599).

There is evidence, however, that the bailiffs of the borough maintained their claims. Seventeen years later, John Norden, the famous topographer, carried out an inquiry into the position of several royal manors, and in the summary which he made, he says of Cheltenham: 'Court of Pie Powder: this may be kept by the Bailiff of the Borough and two Burgesses sitting with him', and that 'the Lord's Bailiff of the Hundred is excluded from the Borough'.[10]

It would appear from these statements that the bailiff of the borough and the burgesses won complete control of the court of Pie Powder and that they had a great deal of independence—as is also shown by the issue of by-laws by the bailiff in 1595[11] and later—in the administration of the borough. There was also another reason for the importance of the bailiff of the borough given in Norden's Inquiry—that no sale or transfer of burgage property within the borough could take place except in his presence in the court; details of such transactions continue to be recorded in the court books until the beginning of the eighteenth century.

It is, therefore, all the more puzzling that as the years went on Cheltenham did not develop as an incorporated borough. On the contrary, the bailiff's powers seem to have lapsed or to have been absorbed by the justices of the peace and later by the commissioners appointed under the 1786 Act, and Cheltenham was not incorporated as a borough until 1876. The reason may have been the almost indissoluble connexion of the borough with the hundred. The bailiff or steward of the hundred, appointed by the lord of the manor, was still supreme in the hundred court, meeting twice a year, and in the three-weekly court. Indeed, the bailiff of the borough was himself 'presented' in the hundred court on various occasions—once for 'using illicit games' (March 1600) and later, in 1629, for not maintaining the shooting butts in Cheltenham.

The reference to illicit games reminds us of the Tudor policy of encouraging activities such as archery and artillery practice which would be of service in time of war and prohibiting some other forms of recreation. Thus by an Act of Henry VIII (1542) no artificer, apprentice, or labourer was allowed to play dice, cards, tennis, quoiting, or bowls except at Christmas-time or with the consent of his master. There was apparently great difficulty in enforcing the Act and maintaining the shooting butts, except in times of extreme danger, such as that caused by the threat of the Spanish Armada.

In this connexion there was a firm belief in Gloucestershire that the plans of Philip II of Spain included a special instruction to destroy the Forest of Dean because of the importance of its timber in the construction of English ships. There was therefore a lively fear that the Severn estuary might be one of the main areas threatened by the attack. It thus became the duty of Lord Chandos of Sudeley as Lord-Lieutenant of the County to arrange for the call-up of the train-bands. Unfortunately a contemporary document giving the names of 'all able men in the county meet for Her Majesty's service in the War', which was formerly in the archives of Gloucester City Council, cannot now be traced.[12] It also gave details of the system to be adopted for the lighting of the beacons in case news of the arrival of the Armada had to be flashed onwards to the next county. The main Gloucester beacon fire stood waiting to be lighted on Robinswood Hill where communication was to be maintained with the men in charge of similar beacons on Cleeve Hill (part of which was included in the hundred of Cheltenham) and Bredon Hill near Tewkesbury. A little hut was to be set up on Robinswood Hill for the Gloucester watchmen, who were to be 'two of the ablest men of every parish', serving a day and a night each. They were to appoint two other men to serve under them as runners from parish to parish and to give warning all over the hundred, and were also to have a horse in readiness for the same purpose. If the beacons at Cheltenham or Tewkesbury were lighted, they were first to find out the reason why and then to ride back to the Mayor of Gloucester, without whose order the Robinswood Hill beacon was not to be fired. Unfortunately we do not know whether on that fateful summer night in 1588 the fire blazed forth on Cleeve Hill to spread the message that the Armada had been sighted.

Apart from threats from Spain, there was another cause of mortal fear during the last period of Elizabeth's reign. 'From plague, pestilence, and famine, Good Lord deliver us' runs the Litany which was composed to meet the needs of this time. Plague seems to have been endemic, but there were at least two outstandingly serious epidemics which affected the whole country. One of these occurred during the year 1592–3. It is known that Tewkesbury, Gloucester, Worcester and other neighbouring towns were badly infected, and there can be little doubt that it reached Cheltenham. The mortality figures from the parish register are extremely high for the ten years between 1587 and 1597, in which year there were four times as many burials as baptisms. Many of the regulations for maintaining cleanliness in the town were in the nature of preventive measures, and fear must have been constant, as is indicated by a reference in the court books early in the next reign (1611). It had been reported to the bailiff that one Guy Dobbins, accompanied by a few noisy labourers and artificers, was marching up and down the Street beating a drum and calling the people to come to see a play at the 'Crown'. The bailiff sent an immediate order for them to disperse and finally went himself to enforce his order, because the neighbouring towns of Tewkesbury and Tredington were infected with the plague, the town of Cheltenham itself 'much suspected', and he feared that 'by drawing company together' it might spread. Fines amounting to 30s. were subsequently imposed on the little group.

One of the main ways by which plague was brought into the town was through the market which probably supplied mainly the area in the immediate vicinity—as far afield as Southam, Andoversford, Withington, Whittington, and the villages on the way to Gloucester—although Leland gave the mileage from Hailes and Southam but not from Gloucester. He writes: 'The road all the way from Cheltenham to Gloucester and thence to Tewkesbury . . . very foule to travel in. I passed two or three small lakes betwixt Cheltenham and Gloucester.' William Greville, as we have seen, left money in his will (1513) for the repair of this road, and Richard Pate in his grant for the endowment of the Grammar School laid down that any surplus money should be devoted partly to the distribution of bread to the poor on Good Friday mornings, partly 'upon poor maidens' marriages' and partly 'on the reparation of the high-way between Cheltenham and Gloucester'. This road, however, continued to be notoriously bad until the end of the eighteenth century, and this was one cause of the isolation of many of the inhabitants of Cheltenham.

This isolation should not, however, be over-emphasized. William Greville of Arle was, as we have seen, a judge of the court of Common Pleas and Richard Pate was a distinguished servant of the Crown. Elizabeth Baghott (the lessee of the Cheltenham rectory) is mentioned with some frequency in the court books of the last years of Elizabeth's reign, sometimes for neglecting hedges and ditches, but more often in cases of disputes with her neighbours. Before her first marriage to Thomas Higgs she was Elizabeth Stephens of Eastington, in which place her family had acquired prosperity in the cloth trade. Her nephew was Attorney-General to Prince Henry— the eldest son of James I. Charles Cox, whose lease of land is recorded in the court book (1601), is described as 'of Clifford's Inn and Gentleman of the Great Key', while a similar record in the same book describes William Higgs (of the Charl-ton Kings family of that name) as 'gent. mercer and citizen of

London', on the occasion of his purchase of land from Thomas Packer. The Packer family at this time included Ludovic, who was commemorated in St. Mary's Church by a tablet which ran 'Ludovic Packer, gent. gave in 1603, the third bell to this parish'; Ludovic's brother, the prosperous John of Alston; his cousin Toby, in whose name a writ in Chancery was obtained against the owners of the Rectory; and Alexander, the owner of Ham and other property within the hundred. Two close relatives of the Cheltenham family of Packers—the brothers John [13] and Thomas Packer—held high office under James I as Clerks of the Privy Seal. John was sent on a mission to Bohemia in 1610 and (in the light of surviving letters from Frederick of Bohemia) it is possible that he may have had some part with the preliminary negotiations for the marriage of King James's daughter Elizabeth to that king. He was later Secretary to the Duke of Buckingham and as such had considerable influence, some of which he exercised on behalf of the parishioners of Cheltenham and Charlton Kings in their long struggle to force the lessee of the Rectory to pay reasonable salaries to the ministers of the two churches. These activities were for the most part, however, concerned with the next reign and will be dealt with in a later chapter.

VI

CHELTENHAM IN THE REIGN OF
JAMES I

AT the time of the accession of James I, William Norwood
was still lessee and farmer of the manor; his son Henry
—a barrister with a practice in London—was steward,
and the under-steward was the attorney John Stubbes to whom
we are greatly indebted for the records which he preserved
with the court books.

In addition to these records there are other new sources of
information available for this period. Among the most valuable
is the book *Men and Armour*, compiled in 1608 by John Smyth
when he was steward to the Earl of Berkeley. In this he collected the names of all able-bodied men fit for military service
in Gloucestershire, giving the lists for each hundred in the
county, with its tithings and hamlets. Another important
source is John Norden's Survey of the Manor (1617) carried
out for King James or Prince Charles after William Norwood's
lease had run out and the manor of Cheltenham had reverted to
the Crown.[1] When the information from these two sources is
considered in conjunction with that given in the already mentioned account by John Stubbes of the attempts to inclose the
common fields, the whole system of manorial organization
becomes much clearer. At the same time the orders recorded
in the court books illustrate the connexion between the
activities of the farmers and burgesses in a closely knit community which was still largely dependent on the authority of
the owner of the manor; and yet another aspect of contemporary life is revealed in Stubbes's account of the parishioners'
struggle with Mrs. Baghott and her sons—the lessees of the
rectory.

Men and Armour was compiled to assist the Earl of Berkeley
who had succeeded Lord Chandos as Lord Lieutenant of the
County. The long war with Spain had ended in 1604, but fear

of invasion remained. The Lord Lieutenant was responsible for maintaining the train-bands in readiness in the event of rebellion or invasion. He was also required to raise an additional number of 'pressed' men if an army should be needed to serve abroad, since the train-bands were not expected to leave the country.[2] In this book John Smyth codified the able-bodied men of each hundred according to age groups: round about twenty years old, up to forty, and over forty; and according to stature, as to whether they were most fitted to carry a musket, a caliver, a pike, or 'of mean stature, fit only to be a pioneer'. He also gave the amount of armour which each division of the hundred of Cheltenham was able to provide: Leckhampton—one corslet and one caliver, with the furnishing; Charlton Kings—two corslets with the furnishing; Westall and Sandford—one corslet with the furnishing; Arle —armour not before mentioned; Swindon—one corslet, one musket, and one caliver; the borough of Cheltenham and the tithing—four corslets and two muskets.

In the borough, however, he records that 'Elizabeth Badger, widow, and Thomas Machin, gent. had each one corslet', while Thomas Gough had one corslet, one musket, and two halberds; and that there were two additional calivers in the possession of William Gregory and Walter Lane of Arle.

Fortunately John Smyth not only gave the names and capabilities of those fit for service; he also noted whether they were already in the train-bands, whether they were prosperous enough to pay the subsidy, and in most cases he included occupations of the men whose names he recorded. Since his lists include only the able-bodied, they do not, of course, provide a complete statement of the numbers engaged in the various occupations.

The results of an analysis of the names given for the borough of Cheltenham, and for Leckhampton, Charlton Kings, Swindon, Arle, Alstone, Sandford, and Westall, are, however, of great interest. Among 351 names we find the following occupations: 40 husbandmen, 38 yeomen, 50 labourers, making a total of 128 men mainly engaged in agriculture, in addition to 28 servants—some of whom were also concerned with farm work; 13 shoemakers, 13 tailors, 12 maltsters (and 1 cooper), 12 weavers, 8 carpenters, 6 butchers, 6 tanners, 4 bakers, 1 chandler, 1 smith, 1 scrivener, 1 wheeler (wheelwright).

If these figures are representative, the inhabitants lived very largely by their fields, their markets, and their malt. The large number of tailors, shoemakers, and tanners could only have been kept occupied by making goods for the customers who came in from the surrounding neighbourhood to the market and bought their clothes, shoes, leather goods, and cloth at the same time.

In this connexion, the jurors giving evidence for Norden's Survey say:

> There is a market holden within the Borough upon Thursday every week in the year unless it happens on some great Festival day, and then it is put over to some other day. . . . And there are two fairs kept yearly within the said town, the one on Ascension Day and the other on St. James Day, unless it happen to fall on a Sunday, and then it is put over to Monday. And the profits of the tolls of the said markets and fairs and of the standings and stallage the High Bailiff of the Manor and Libertie or his assignees taketh to his or their uses, which profits are yearly worth, as they conjecture £6. 13. 4d. or thereabouts. . . . There are two Market houses within the Towne which standeth in the streets of Cheltenham.

It is probable that with the increase in local trade the Booth Hall mentioned in the reign of Mary Tudor had been converted into this second Market-house mentioned here for the first time.

No doubt at this market a great deal of beer would be needed, and there is every indication that malting was an important industry and remained so for at least a century, until the Royal Well provided another type of profitable drink. Frequent references in the court books point to the great fear of fire breaking out during the making of malt.

> Every maltster within the town of Cheltenham shall pay and provide before Whitsontyde next one or more buckets of leather, to be ready in their houses against any casualty of fire, and that every other able inhabitant of the towne shall pay all such sums of money as the constables and churchwardens, or the more part of them, shall tax upon them for buying and making sufficient ladders, rooches and other small hooks to be necessarily used at time of

need . . . upon paine that every person making default or refusing
to pay his several taxation, shall forfeit 6/6d. [April 1615].

Another significant order was made in the same court: 'No
maltster or other person within the Hundred shall dry any malt
on the Sabbath or in night time after 9 of the clock in winter,
10 of the clock in summer, on pain of penalty of 20/-.' The
following year the order about the provision of buckets was
repeated, with the proviso that they should be inspected by the
bailiff (April 1616). Nineteen years later, those who concealed
their buckets were to be liable to a fine of 20s.

The malting industry must have fluctuated considerably.
During the famine years of 1587, 1609, and 1622 all grain was
scarce in Gloucestershire. Every attempt was made at this time
by the central and local authorities to cut down the making
and consumption of malt in order to save barley for bread.
In 1612 the Assize Justices ordered that there should be only
one ale-house to a village and two to a market town, but
how far this order was enforced in Cheltenham it is impossible
to say.

The barley used for the malt was grown locally in the common fields and the court orders regulating the conditions under
which the malt was made were contemporary with other orders
dealing with the management of the open fields. John Stubbes's
account of his first attempts to keep his holdings in Charlton
Kings inclosed throughout the year has already been mentioned.
In his capacity as under-steward of the manor he was responsible for some years for keeping the records of the courts, and
he included in his own account[3] many details of the courts orders
which particularly concerned his attempts to make regulations
for the common fields in Charlton Kings. Thus in 1609 (April)
an order was made that for one year no one should keep more
than 30 sheep, 6 beasts, and 2 horses in the common fields for
every 20 acres of his holding, although beasts and horses might
be interchanged for sheep. 'If any will keep sheep only, it
amounteth by stynt unto 70 for 20 acres', and a penalty of
3s. 4d. was to be paid for every additional beast and 12d. for
every additional sheep above the number specified. A few
months later, with the concurrence of William Norwood, his

son Henry Norwood (the high steward), and Giles Greville (lord of the manor of Ashley), another court order was made whereby all inhabitants in Charlton Kings were to be permitted to inclose their fields 'except arable land in the common fields', and no one but the owner was to put any beasts on the land inclosed. On the other hand, any common pasturage claimed was to be lessened in proportion to the amount inclosed.

There must have been considerable opposition to this order because, immediately after it was made, a number of tenants caused the foreman of the jury of the Cheltenham court to inform the High Steward: 'We do repeal all the orders made for Cheltenham . . . and for Charlton.' Stubbes claimed that this repeal was made without the knowledge and consent of the majority of those present in the court, and the High Steward thereupon ordered the suppression of the record of the repeal.

'Then', wrote Stubbes, 'we thought the victory had been won and we laboured to keep our grounds accordingly . . . although our hedges were daily thrown open, yet we made them up again.' Many of Stubbes's own hedges were broken down but 'none durst do it openly'. At last he discovered that the culprit was his neighbour Walter Higgs, and having secured witnesses he brought an action against him in the court of King's Bench for trespass, won his case, and was awarded costs. Higgs promised to pay the latter without further compulsion but was prevented by his relative—the formidable Mrs. Baghott (Badger). Stubbes writes: 'Presently I went to Cheltenham, being Thursday (Market Day) and finding the Sheriff's men there, and seeing Walter Higgs go into a house to measure corn, I delivered them the writ, who went after him and took him into execution.'

Mrs. Baghott, however, was not prepared to agree that rights of common should be lost so easily, and she instigated a neighbour, Mrs. Elizabeth Greville, described by Stubbes as 'a sole widow woman indeed but exceeding rich and a great usurer and not unfit for law', to put her oxen into Stubbes's inclosures. On hearing of this he rode off to Cheltenham to report the matter to the bailiff of the hundred, and then on to Leckhampton Court to consult William Norwood. But 'finding them both from home', he returned to the inclosed field and with two of his servants impounded the oxen. Mrs. Greville then appealed to the hundred court for their return, lost her case, and immediately brought a suit against Stubbes in the court of Chancery, claiming common right in the open fields '. . . . every two years . . . from after the end of corn harvest . . until Candlemass . . . and every third year, when the same fields have been used to be fresh and fallow . . . all the year until the same fields be sowed again'.

In his defence Stubbes quoted the previous orders (permitting inclosure) made in the Cheltenham court, and stated that he had sent a copy to the minister 'to be published in Charlton Church according to ancient usage' and that very few tenants had dissented and none of those with 'the larger holdings'. Stubbes's account reveals extreme dissatisfaction with the corrupt and dilatory practice of the court of Chancery —a feeling which apparently was widely prevalent at the time.[4] Even Mrs. Greville grew weary of the delays and finally 'sent to Mr. Norwood to make an end of it'.

William Norwood then asked to hear the case for and against inclosures, and afterwards arranged a meeting of tenants at Charlton church 'in order to settle the controversy if he could by any means'. To this meeting he came very early in the morning for a preliminary conference with Stubbes and a few others. Stubbes was prepared with a list of proposals, since, as he told Henry Norwood, 'unless we have the same in writing . . . we should have many words and no deeds'. When the other tenants arrived and William Norwood was about to address them, his son presented Stubbes's list, to which he then assented. The forty-one tenants assembled there also agreed and appended their signatures.

Stubbes's proposals were prefaced with a restatement of the orders permitting inclosures:

Whereas the most of the tenants of Charlton Kings want severals [separate] grounds for the keeping of their plough cattle and milch kine for the necessary maintenance of their tillage . . . notwithstanding these orders some of the inhabitants have in contempt broken open the said inclosures and put their cattle there, whereby many strifes, contentions and lawsuits have happened, it hath therefore pleased Mr. Norwood to vouchsafe to come himself in person to treat of a charitable end of such controversies. . . .

The main points to which they agreed were: That it should be lawful for all tenants in Charlton Kings to keep any of their land inclosed at all times of the year; that hedges were to be maintained by those who inclosed their land; that all existing roads and paths must be kept open despite inclosures; and that the number of beasts allowed on uninclosed grounds should be severely restricted according to the amount of land owned. 'None shall keepe above the number of 3 beasts, one horse and ten sheep for every 20 acres that he owns and after that rate for a more or less quantity of ground.'

Despite the tenants' agreement, the court, while accepting the proposals for inclosure, made an order increasing the number of animals permitted in uninclosed land to 4 beasts, 2 horses, and 20 sheep for the same 20 acres, stating specifically that 5 beasts = 20 sheep and that 1 horse = 6 sheep. Overseers of the fields were appointed for the following year to see that this order was carried out, and no cattle were to be put in the stubble fields until the date decided by the overseers had been published in Charlton Church.

As a result of this settlement a considerable amount of land in the common fields may have been permanently inclosed, but the fact that an arrangement was made for the number of animals allowed pasture after the gathering of harvest indicates that much arable land at least was left open for a considerable part of the year.

Stubbes's account concludes with the statement that there was little further trouble over the inclosures, although Mrs. Baghott and others did not at first inclose their land because they hoped to get the orders reversed when William Norwood's lease of the manor ran out. Mrs. Baghott, who held a lease of the impropriation of Cheltenham church, revenged herself on Stubbes as the instigator of the movement by bringing a suit against him in the Consistory court at Gloucester for non-payment of tithes.

One of the services rendered by Stubbes at this time is that he preserved a copy of the massive Report on the Manor of Cheltenham—drawn up on the King's order by the famous topographer John Norden and his son in 1617—a report almost as valuable for Cheltenham history as the Domesday Survey itself.

James I had found that rents and other fixed payments on his royal manors were not always consistent with rising costs, and that in many cases the tenants had increased both their holdings and their independence of former obligations at the expense of the owners. He therefore instituted a series of inquiries into the exact state of affairs in a number of Crown properties. Among these was the manor of Cheltenham which he bestowed on his son Charles after the lease of William Norwood had ended (1616).[5]

In addition to the main report, John Norden, who was at this time Surveyor to the Crown, drew up the already mentioned[6] summary of his preliminary inquiries. This gives information about Cheltenham which is not repeated in the final report. Norden is clearly of the opinion that the great powers of the lord of the manor have sadly dwindled and 'have been and are daily infringed', and that copyholders are able to conceal and keep back much of their rent. He thinks the manor needs 'totally reforming' before anything further is done by the Crown, 'the reasons being manifest and the probability of profit plain'.

The methods adopted by John Norden resemble those used for the Domesday Survey. Thirty-two men, including freeholders and copyholders chosen from the whole hundred, were nominated as jurors and sworn on oath to answer truthfully the questions put to them. Among these are the names of the more important tenants—Richard Pate, John Packer, Christopher Merrett, William Whithorn of Charlton Kings, Robert Machin, Thomas Ashmeade, William Gregory, John Sturmey, and a number of others who made their mark instead of writing their signatures. The thirty questions submitted to the jurors covered every aspect of the manor—from its area and boundaries, its courts and their officials, its tenants and their holdings, its ancient customs, the value of the church living, woods, common land, fisheries—even to 'park of deer, warren of conies and banne of swans'—and the trout and eels in the Chelt.

Taking these questions in order, the jurors first gave the geographical boundaries of the manor:

to the first article they say that the compass, extent and circuit of the Manor namely the Hundred beginneth at Barbridge North West and thence extendeth to Hawling Mill and from thence to Swindon Brook, and thence to Rye Hedge and from thence to Mantle Meadow, and from thence to Swindon's Gate, to Monie Hill and from thence to Cheltenham Brook, and thence extending along the said Brook to Cake Bridge, and from thence to Bouncer's Gate and so to Hewletts, and from thence to the stones on Northfield Hill. . . .

As many of the place-names mentioned have now disappeared, it is not possible to trace all the boundaries, but some of the names are still familiar today: the Hyde, the Hewletts, Cakebridge, Bouncer's Lane, and the round barrow at Northfield on Cleeve Hill. Barbridge has been identified as a place near the present Arle Court in the Gloucester Road.

The jurors were next asked to define the manor, the hundred, and the borough. This somewhat baffling task, in which the distinctions to us seem so involved, did not defeat them.

They believe that the Hundred within which the Manor lyeth doth belong to the Manor as a thing annexed . . . but not otherwise, for that the Hundred can stand without the Manor being a Libertie of larger extent and differing nature. Howbeit the Manor and Hundred have anciently and by all times been used and enjoyed by the name of the Manor with the Hundred of Cheltenham, and so many Courts have been so called, and the parishes, villages, hamlets and tythings which do lye within and do suit unto the Hundred Court are the parishes of Cheltenham, Leckhampton, Swindon, the Tythings of Cheltenham, Charlton, Ashley, Bafford, Westhall, Naunton, Sandford, Alstone, Arle and Brodewell, which pay their common fines at 2 Leets and tything silver or cert money. . . . And there is also a Three Weeks Court which ought to be kept from three weeks to three weeks, and is so kept for the most part.

They go on to define the borough:

They believe there is a Charter whereby the Town of Cheltenham was created a Borough, but how ancient they know not, and they believe that the Borough of Cheltenham is not parcel of the Manor but is holden of the same, for that all Burgage holders do pay their rents and reliefs to the Lord of the Manor, and whether the said Borough hath been from time to time confirmed by former

Kings they know not, but they know that the same hath been in the time of King James that now is and before the time of Elizabeth the Queen always allowed and taken to be a Borough. . . . They cannot precisely set down the boundaries of the Borough because other lands lye dispersedly and intermixed with the burgage tenements of which the Borough consisted, but they say that in their lists of Borough tenants it may be seen how far the burgage extendeth.

After this there follows a complete list of all the tenants, the amount of their property and of their payments due to the lord of the manor for each holding. The total of 233 tenancies is made up of 65 freehold, 66 burgage, 89 copyhold, and 13 holdings of demesne property leased for a term of years. The numbers do not represent the actual number of tenants because in some cases, as with Richard Pate and the Packer family, land was held in all four categories, while the Ashmeads, the Higgs, the Sturmeys, the Machins, and the Gregory family held copyhold with either burgage or freehold land.

From the recorded payments it is possible to assess the difference between the four types of tenure. Apparently the freeholder paid a yearly rent to the lord of the manor and was obliged to attend the courts; also on his death the heir paid a relief. Thus at the head of the list of freeholders comes William Norwood, Esq.—no longer the lessee of the manor: 'William Norwood, Esq., freely by charter, to him and his heirs, the Manor of Leckhampton and Brodewell. Rent 15/- a year; suit of Court; one year's rent as relief.' Giles Greville for the 'manor of Ashley, alias Charlton Kings', owed suit of court fealty and relief, and paid a rent of 2/8 a year.

A typical burgage tenant or burgess also paid rent, attended the courts, and from his heir a similar relief was due. There was, however, one important difference, since burgage property could only be bought or sold legally in the lord's court in the presence of the bailiff of the borough.

William Stroude, probably the bailiff already mentioned, held: '1 Burgage with dwelling house, garden and backside (one acre). Rent 12d; suit of Court; relief.'

From copyholders, however, more payments were due in compensation for the original labour services which had been performed in the Middle Ages. Richard Pate, gent., paid for one of his holdings of copyhold property: 5s. 4d. rent, 14d. works, 4d. common fines, 1d. Peter's Pence; his best beast as heriot; fine of double rent on death or termination of tenancy.

The common fine referred to in the survey was another name for the tithing or cert money—originally paid at view of frank-pledge by every male of twelve years old as a member of the tithing. It was still collected at one of the half-yearly courts by the bailiff of the hundred. The works money represents the money paid to release the tenant from his works or service to the lord of the manor. Once at least, on the occasion when Ralf Boteler had arbitrated, the tenants had asserted their independence and insisted on the reduction of the amount. Apparently they were equally tenacious of their rights at this time. The jurors stated clearly that the sons and daughters and widows of copyholders might marry without the lord's permission, and

that no service workes to their knowledge are to be done, for that they are, as they suppose, discharged by paying their work silver. And that no cocks, hens or eggs are to be paid, and that no customary tenant or freeholder ought to carry writs and letters which the Lord hath occasion to send.

Demesne land—that is, land privately owned by the lord of the manor—was now let for a term of years (unspecified) to thirteen tenants, called here 'tenentes terrarum dominicalium pro terminis annorum'. Richard Gough was tenant of '1 ancient house called the Court House and the close adjoining'. For this and other demesne lands in Whaddon, in the common fields of Cheltenham, in Arle and Alstone, he paid an annual rent of £5. 6s. 8d. The Lord's Close, divided into three parts, was let to Henry Mayles. This is almost certainly the Lord's Meadow, part of which is marked in a plan of 1818, and which is called in an eighteenth-century lease the Lord's Close. In a survey of demesne lands made in 1634 Richard Gough was still the tenant of the 'Court House, orchard, gardens, and close . . . close on backside . . . with garden (?) shooting upon the Churchyard stile . . . and Laverham Meadow'. In a slightly later survey (1648) the tenant was Peter Oviatt—the second husband of Richard Gough's widow.

Demesne land and freehold were apparently interspersed with copyhold in the common fields, of which the greater number in Cheltenham itself were still thrown open for common pasture from the end of harvest to spring sowing.

The freeholders, burgage tenants, and copyholders were, of course, tenants only in the sense that they made fixed yearly payments and accepted certain obligations to the lord of the manor. Otherwise they were landowners free to buy, to sell, to let their holdings, and to leave them to their heirs according to the custom of the manor.

The copyhold land had originally been held by those who rendered labour services to the lord of the manor. Norden's survey shows that much of it had passed from its original owners into the hands of wealthy freeholders. The most striking example of this was Richard Pate—nephew of the founder of the Grammar School. He held copyhold land in Charlton Kings, Alstone, Arle, Westhall, Naunton, Sandford, as well as freehold property in Charlton Kings and Cheltenham fields, a house and two acres on burgage tenure in the borough, and 13½ acres of demesne land on lease. It is not surprising that he applied for a coat of arms! This, however, was refused, and he is included in a list of those not entitled to this honour 'not being gentlemen'.[7]

The family of Packer also had wide holdings of freehold and copyhold land. Alexander Packer held most of Ham, Warden's Hill, and the Reddings. John Packer, yeoman, had land in Alston, and was sufficiently well off to pay the subsidy. Robert Packer had two large holdings known as Compton's Manor and Power's Manor. Tobias and Ludovic Packer probably lived in the borough and had substantial property there.

On the other hand, the names of the fifty labourers and the twenty-eight servants listed in *Men and Armour* do not appear to be among the tenants mentioned in Norden's Report.[8] They were part of the landless class which was then increasing in numbers. This class is mentioned directly by the jurors in reply to a question on encroachment: 'the eight or nine cottages or hovels built upon the highway or waste by certain poor men by licence of the Lord and allowance of the Justice of the Peace'. There are also references in the court books to these labourers and to the vagrants from other parishes. Thus a court order (April 1615) ran:

> Every householder within the town of Cheltenham (excepting only poor day labourers and other poor persons) shall pay yearly towards the hire and maintenance of a beadle to punish vagrants and others according to Statute . . . such sum of money as shall be levied upon them by the constables and churchwardens . . . not exceeding 6d per annum . . . upon penalty for every householder who refuses, for every refusal 1/11d.

In Cheltenham there was indeed very little common land in the sense of actual waste which was free to all. It may be conjectured therefore that the greatest threat to the independence of the poorer people was not so much the inclosure of common land as that of the open or common fields, and the growing tendency towards speculation in copyhold land, with the resulting temptation to small copyholders to sell their holdings. Thus, in reply to searching questions put by John Norden on the matter of common land, the jurors stated:

> The Commons are two in Charlton Kings called Hartinghill and Ravensgate (both 50 acres) lying on the sides of two high hills in barren places, whereof the tenants of Charlton Kings are the only Commoners. Other Commons they [the jurors] know not—other than the ordinary high passages and lanes.

The large area of marshy land on the north side of the High Street covering some of the present area of Pittville, St. Paul's, and the back of Swindon Road was used as common pasturage by the burgage tenants only.

> They also hold to them and their heirs . . . one Marsh called the Lower Marsh containing . . . 20 acres wherein every burgage holder for a whole hath pasture for two beasts and for half a burgage one beast . . . and according to that rate and not otherwise, for which they pay no rent other than they pay for their Burgage holds. The said Burgesses do likewise hold another Marsh called the Lady Marsh containing by estimation 12 acres wherein they have pasture for their beasts in manner . . . as aforesaid. And do pay yearly to the Lord of the Manor for the said Marsh 11/8. And that a Beast's pasture is there worth 4d or 6d.

There were many questions concerning the woods, fisheries,

and hunting rights, to which the jurors replied: 'That there was never any park of deer, warren of conies or banne of swans in the Manor . . . that the Lord had the liberty of fishing and fowling on the Manor . . . and there is a small brook [the Chelt] which doth yield both Trout and Eels, and one wood called Ocley [Oakley].'

They also stated that there were 'two market houses within the Towne of Cheltenham which standeth on the streets . . . for the market people's uses, and there is a house called by the name of a Church house—the greatest part of which stands in the Churchyard where heretofore the parishioners did meet, but it is now in the occupation of two poor people . . . which were put in by the parishioners who took upon them the disposing thereof, but by what right they know not'.

This church house was undoubtedly where the church ales and other festivities for the raising of money for the poor had been held. The fact that these had been discontinued seems to point to the growth of Puritanism in Cheltenham itself although these activities were still continued in Charlton Kings, where, in 1624, the dismissed minister Robert Walker complained of 'maypoles on Whitsunday and Church Ales on the Lord's Day with dancing in time of prayer'.[9] The jurors described the value of the church: 'There is an impropriate parsonage worth £300 per annum, and one chapel in Charlton Kings which is belonging to the impropriation and it is in use. There is no Vicarage to their knowledge.'

Among their replies concerning the ancient customs of the manor, the jurors explain that the heirs of freeholders and burgesses inherit according to common law from father to son, but the lands of copyholders (customary tenants in base tenure) 'descend to youngest sons and in default thereof to their youngest daughters and in default thereof to their youngest sisters, according to the custom of the Manor'. This custom is clearly Borough-English and was altered in the 1625 Act so that the inheritance of copyholders passed in the same way as that of the other tenants. The jurors insisted, however, that copyholders did not forfeit their holding by reason of treason, felony, murder, or outlawry, nor by letting their tenements decay, nor by selling timber. Thus Norden's earlier statement about the lost powers of the lord of the manor is confirmed.

One other item makes it clear that rights of medieval lords to appoint their own justices and to be entirely independent of the sheriffs' jurisdiction have completely lapsed '. . . And for amerciaments levied on the tenants . . . and for not appearing at the Assize and Sessions, and for misdemeanours estreated under green wax, the Sheriffs of the County for the time being useth [are accustomed] to levy the amerciaments . . . and to whom in right they ought to belong they [the jurors] know not'.

'Many other customs of the said Manor there are . . .', said the jurors, 'but presently they do not remember them'! The said customs before mentioned, however, 'have ever been past the memory of man used and confirmed by their long continuance the beginning whereof is unknown. And they ought not to pay anything for brewing of beer or ale'! It is not clear whether this last defiant statement refers to an attempt made within the hundred to prevent this, or whether it is concerned with regulations recently made by the Justices in Assize in their efforts to reduce general consumption of malt in the county when grain was scarce.

It is probable that Norden's survey was ordered by the Crown as a kind of valuation, necessary before a future sale. It was followed shortly afterwards by an Act of Parliament which, by clarifying still further the rights of the tenants and their exact obligations to the lord of the manor, made it easier to effect such a sale. In 1628 the manor was purchased outright by John Dutton of Sherborne, in the possession of whose family it was to remain for over two centuries, and with this purchase the long connexion of the manor with the Crown came to an end.

VII

THE MANOR AND THE CHURCH IN THE TIME OF CHARLES I

THE preliminary steps leading to the Cheltenham Act of 1625 are described in detail by John Stubbes. He tells us that the copyholders of Cheltenham petitioned Prince Charles for leave to bring in a Bill to remove 'inconvenient customs', in return for the sum of £1,200, of which £300 was to be paid at once and the remainder in quarterly instalments. At the same time the copyholders of Charlton Kings were to pay their own lord of the manor—Giles Greville—£326[1] for the same privileges.

It is highly probable that Stubbes was himself the instigator of the proceedings, in which he was appointed to act as attorney. 'That we have constituted and appointed our trusty and well-beloved John Stubbes as our true and lawful attorney and by these presents give him full power to present a Bill in Parliament' runs the deed which is signed by Richard Pate, Richard Bannister, and Ludovic Packer. Among the thirty-six witnesses occur the names of Toby Packer, William Whithorn, Richard Wager, and John Mason.

The opening paragraph of the Act explained clearly that it was passed for the advantage of both the lord of the manor and the tenants, because so much trouble and expense had been caused in recent lawsuits that the manor 'had yielded little profit to either'. The Act, therefore, legalized an agreement made between the copyholders of Cheltenham on the one hand and the lord of the manor, Charles, Prince of Wales, on the other; and between the copyholders of the Manor of Ashley on the one hand and Giles Greville, Esq., lord of the said Manor of Ashley (Charlton Kings). The terms were brief and explicit. The customary tenants, or copyholders, in Cheltenham and Charlton Kings were to hold their lands 'by copy of court roll, suit of court and yearly rents, works silver, Peter's-pence and bederipe[2] money to be paid annually and respectively, double the rents only being payable by not adding thereunto the work, reap money and other payments'. A fixed heriot of 30s. was payable on the death of the tenant, and if the holdings were divided, only a proportionate amount of the 30s. was to be paid from each section. The sale or lease of land, if carried out in open court or before two copyholders, was legalized by the payment 'of one year's ancient rent' of the land sold, and again, if the holding had been divided, of a proportionate amount of the rent.

The remaining clauses of the Act dealt with the system of inheritance. The system of Borough-English was discarded and lands were to descend to male heirs in fee simple, according to common law. Failing male heirs, the eldest female heir should succeed. Widows were entitled to 'freebench' of one-third of their husband's holding, and if a woman owning copyhold property died, her husband could not in marrying again convey the land from her natural heirs. A woman who agreed to the sale of any part of her husband's copyhold land could not claim one-third of that part if left a widow, and, by inference, if she had not agreed to such a sale, she could claim a third part, and therefore a husband could not dispose of copyhold land without his wife's agreement. This led to a long-drawn-out case in the first half of the nineteenth century when Colonel Riddell, long separated from his wife, and considered to be a bachelor, sold property of which his widow later successfully claimed her share. Under this Act the lord of the manor and the tenants managed their property transactions as long as copyhold tenure existed. In the nineteenth century, by which time the administrative and legal powers of the manorial courts were no longer enforced, the court books became merely records of change of ownership of property and of the fines and heriots paid. The Act was of inestimable value to the Cheltenham tenants. Twice at least in the nineteenth century, when lords of the manor tried to extend their financial claims—in 1853 and 1863—they were defeated by the clearly stated terms of tenure as laid down in the Act.

Three years after the passing of the Act, the Manor of Cheltenham was purchased from King Charles by John Dutton of Sherborne for £1,200. At the time of the purchase the thirty-five-year-old John Dutton was already a wealthy land-owner. According to a contemporary legend his father could ride all the sixteen miles from Sherborne to Cheltenham without moving off his own land. Sherborne itself, near Northleach and the clear stream of the Windrush, remains today one of the loveliest of Cotswold villages. In the Middle Ages it had been the most valuable of the properties of Winchcombe Abbey —where the large flocks of sheep from all the Cotswold manors were driven for the annual shearing and where the abbot and his monks kept festival after the bagging of the wool for the merchants.[3]

The new lord of the manor of Cheltenham was known both to his contemporaries and his descendants as Crump Dutton[4] because he was hunchbacked. He had graduated as a Bachelor of Arts at Oxford and at some time later was a member of the Middle Temple; he was described by Anthony à Wood as 'a learned prudent man and as one of the richest, so one of the meekest men in England . . .'. This description of his prudence is not borne out by the stories of his gambling tendencies, which were apparently so strong that on one occasion he pledged Sherborne itself, and the estate was only saved by the butler, who on hearing the players call out 'Sherborne's up', carried off his master and locked him up until the others had left. This episode, however, may well have occurred in his early life, since he inherited Sherborne when he was only twenty years old. The purchase of the manor of Cheltenham coincided with the beginnings of Charles I's attempt to rule without Parliament (1629–40) which was one of the main causes of the Civil War. In this war Crump Dutton, although crippled, took an active part, and Cheltenham, as his pro-perty, was also involved.

Almost contemporary with the change of ownership of the manor was the sale of the impropriation of the churches of Charlton Kings and Cheltenham, which had been let by the Crown to a series of lessees from the time of its confiscation by Henry VIII. The new owner of the Rectory was Sir Baptist Hicks, a wealthy London merchant who had been able to advance money to King James I which he badly needed. The

Cheltenham rectory was one of several impropriations sold by the Crown at this time to contractors, but in 1612 it was transferred from these by a formal grant made by King James[5] '... of our Rectory and Church at Cheltenham, our Chapel at Charlton Kings ... and our Church at Campden ... to Baptist Hicks who has well and truly paid large sums at the receipt of our Exchequer ...'. A list of the property concerned was included in the grant and must for the main part have been the property (excluding Chipping Campden) originally bestowed on Cirencester Abbey by Henry I—the nucleus of which was the land recorded in the Domesday Book as belonging to Reinbald. A much more detailed inventory was given in a Survey made in 1632 of the Cheltenham rectory property.[6] This mentions 'a fair parsonage house accommodated with outhouses, a large barn, oxhouse, stables and beyond these a fair court with a large pond in it, a garden and a little orchard ... of 1 acre, one other large orchard 2 acres 3 roods; one meadow ... beyond the Church commonly called the Church mead; one meadow in severall [inclosed] with a fishpond in it adjoining the site of the Rectory called Cambray Meadow'. The total amount of land which made up the church property, including arable meadow and pasture was given as 224 acres.

The sale of the impropriation to Sir Baptist Hicks did not have any immediate effect on the Cheltenham rectory because one of the leases granted by Queen Elizabeth to Sir Francis Bacon (1598) had not yet run out. Sir Francis paid an annual rent of £75 to the Crown and by the terms of the lease was bound to keep the chancel in repair and to provide at his own charge two chaplains and two deacons, the bread and wine for the communion service, bell ropes, and straw. He, however, continued to sub-let the property, on the same terms, to a member of the Higgs family which had held it since the early days of Elizabeth's reign (cf. Chapter IV). It is probable that the negligent Thomas Higgs, of whom the parishioners complained in 1561, remained in actual possession of the revenues of the rectory for the remainder of his life. His widow or daughter-in-law, who by a second marriage became Mrs. Elizabeth Baghott (Badger), was the opponent of Stubbes in the matter of inclosures at Charlton Kings.

She and her sons John and Thomas Higgs continued as sub-tenants of the property under Sir Francis Bacon, whose covenants with the Crown in connexion with the maintenance of the ministers and all other matters they were bound to honour. The refusal of Mrs. Baghott to carry out these covenants caused a long-drawn-out struggle with the parishioners in which John Stubbes took an active part. We are indebted to him for a full account of the events of these years recorded in the court books.[7] 'In my little book', he wrote, 'I have restored all the passages of this business, so that posterity may hereafter know. . . .'

According to this record there were almost 2,000 communicants in the two parishes of Cheltenham and Charlton Kings, and the annual income of the rectory was £400. Mrs. Baghott, however, paid the two ministers only £10 a year each and the lay deacons 26s. 8d. For this salary the parishioners were unable to get 'learned men' as their ministers, and in 1609 Stubbes laid the matter before Dr. Parry, the Bishop of Gloucester. The Bishop came to preach in Cheltenham and 'persuaded Mrs. Baghott by all possible means to give unto the preaching ministers sufficient stipends according to the good intention of the said Covenants, but his Lordship could not win her, either by fair means or threats, to increase the said stipends; whereupon my Lord Bishop on the parishioners' behalf petitioned the Lord Treasurer to nominate two Chaplains since Covenants by lease had been broken'.

As a result of this petition the Lord Treasurer (Robert Cecil, Lord Salisbury) wrote a remarkably conciliatory letter to Mrs. Baghott, pointing out that although the stipends she allowed to the ministers were 'to the scandall of the Church of God and the defrauding of his Majesty's subjects of the spiritual food of their souls', he would not call her to strict account for breach of covenant but merely require her to 'reform the abuse by appointing two sufficient preachers' at a competent stipend. Failure to carry out this instruction would be met with an order 'to repair unto me to the Court to show what reason you have to continue such an abuse', and he signed his letter 'Your loving friend R. Salisbury' (1610).

Mrs. Baghott seems to have been somewhat shaken by this

letter and to have asked her nephew Thomas Stephens, who was Attorney-General to Prince Henry (the eldest son of James I), to intervene on her behalf, especially as the Bishop of Gloucester was chaplain to the same Prince. She was doubly fortunate, however, in that the bishop was shortly afterwards translated to the see of Worcester and that Lord Salisbury died at the same time, so that no immediate steps were taken against her. Thomas Stephens promised on her behalf that after she had discharged certain debts an allowance of £20 a year should be made to each of the ministers. By 1620, however, he admitted that 'he could not procure her to give to the said Ministers any increase of their stipends'. Sir Baptist Hicks, the impropriator, also tried unsuccessfully to make her pay the additional salary.

The parishioners next sent a petition to Sir Francis Bacon—now Lord Verulam—who by this time had become Lord Chancellor. They complained that his lessee Mrs. Baghott allowed no money for deacons or for the bread and wine for communion, and paid only £15 a year each to two 'reading Curates'.

The Lord Chancellor took the petition seriously and wrote to warn Mrs. Baghott of the penalties for breach of covenant and to require her 'to reform the said abuses by allowing to two such discreet Chaplains as shall be nominated by His Majesty a sum of £40 a year each . . . so there be no further cause of complaint . . .'.

Immediately afterwards, however, the Lord Chancellor was deprived of his office and Mrs. Baghott took no further notice of his warning. It seems likely that she herself died at this time, since the parishioners next petitioned King James, asking that her sons John and Thomas Higgs should be made to fulfil the covenants of the lease. The King referred the matter back to the Bishop of Gloucester (Dr. Miles Smith), which action did not please the petitioners since 'they had heard that the Bishop did give but small stipends to his own curates of parsonages which he held in commendam . . . and therefore they did not trouble his Lordship' with the petition.

In the meantime the Higgs brothers sought the interest of the King's favourite, the Duke of Buckingham, through his friend Endymion Porter. The parishioners, however, also had friends at Court in John and Thomas Packer, relatives of the Cheltenham family of Packers, who were described by Stubbes as 'Clerks of his Majesty's Privy Seal in London', and they were asked to state the parishioners' side of the dispute. As a result an agreement was signed (based on the decision made by Endymion Porter) by which the Higgs brothers were to pay a total of £80 a year for the two stipends, but they were first to be allowed five years' grace to enable them to settle their debts, during which they were to pay only £55 annually.

The situation was further complicated by the actions of one of the ministers concerned. In Cheltenham William Panton—now an old man—was still the well-loved curate. But in Charlton Kings the parishioners had only agreed to the appointment of Robert Walker as a temporary measure and on condition that he promised to vacate his position when the stipend was raised and so make way for 'a more learned preacher'. Unfortunately, when under the terms of his agreement he was asked to leave, he 'straitwayes underhand did inform the Bishop, Sir Baptist Hicks, Mr. John Packer and many others that the parishioners did most unconscionably go about to deprive him of his meanes of livelihood and replace him without any just cause. Whereupon', writes Stubbes, 'Sir Baptist Hicks did tax me for unkindness towards our minister and the Lord Bishop did ask Mr. Norwood what Mr. Grevill and I were about. . . .'

Robert Walker also wrote a long letter of complaint to John Packer in London. He was told firmly in reply that the increase in the stipend was intended to be 'for a worthy preacher and a very good scholar—at least a Master of Arts' and that as there was small hope of his fulfilling these qualifications he should use the next six months to find another post.

The parishioners were also incensed with Walker because he was content to accept the original low stipend still paid by the Higgs brothers in flagrant violation of their agreement made under the Endymion Porter award. As a proof of their dislike, eighty-seven of them signed a petition to the bishop asking for the removal of Walker 'as very unfit for us and very defective . . . in his duty, giving content to none!' Walker, however, 'got to Gloucester on foot' to support his case 'before we could get there on horseback', writes Stubbes, but the bishop decided to remove him 'in respect of his promise and for that he is not capable of his place being no Master of Arts', suggesting at the same time that some provision should be made for him until he could find other employment. The parishioners refused to advance any money for this purpose (since they thought that such provision should come from arrears of payment) and Walker refused to leave.

In this deadlock it appeared that the two Higgs would continue to keep back the agreed increase in the stipends. The parishioners of the two parishes therefore brought a suit in the court of Chancery, in the name of Toby Packer, for the enforcement of the full payment of the stipends, and the brothers were ordered by a decree of the court (1624) to pay the full amount of the stipends.

In the meantime the Bishop of Gloucester had appointed Richard Brookes, B.D., Fellow of Trinity College, Oxford, to the benefice of Charlton Kings, considered vacant after the dismissal of Robert Walker. When Brookes arrived in the church he was prevented by Walker from taking the service. 'So', writes Stubbes, 'the next Sunday we caused the door of the church to be kept locked until the coming of Mr. Brookes, at which time Mr. Walker being there . . . with some of Mr. Higgs' men, he offered to thrust into the church before Mr. Brookes. . . . Then I willed him to desist . . . and told him plainly that he should never more serve in this church, unless he could recover it by course of law . . . after which he departed and never offered to intrude himself again into this church.'

He did, however, apply to Sir Baptist Hicks for the benefice of Cheltenham, vacant by the death of the minister William Panton, but the Bishop of Gloucester, shortly before his own death, had already licensed Dr. English for this office.

Sir Baptist Hicks claimed that the right of appointment belonged to him, but John Packer, on behalf of the parishioners, took Counsel's opinion and was informed that until the forty years' lease ran out the right of nomination still lay with the Crown, and therefore in this case with the bishop. Meanwhile the Higgs family had found in the bishop's appointment of

Dr. English a new excuse for not paying the full stipends. There followed a succession of petitions and lawsuits. Finally, sixteen years after the parishioners had begun their proceedings against Mrs. Baghott, the Higgs family were compelled to pay the full stipends of £40 annually 'in good gold as well as the costs of the law suit of 1625'.

Shortly afterwards the Higgs's lease ran out and Sir Baptist Hicks then took over the right of appointment of ministers in addition to the impropriation which he already held. In 1629 he delegated the right of nomination of the two ministers to Jesus College, Oxford, under specified conditions. Their stipends were to remain at £40 a year each; they must be Masters of Arts of two years' standing and unmarried, and they must not hold any other benefice. The impropriation passed before the end of the century to the Earl of Essex (Capel) from whose family it was purchased by Joseph Pitt in 1800.[8] The advowson, however, remained with the Fellows of Jesus College, Oxford, until they exchanged it for that of the living of Bagenden held by Joseph Pitt (1812), so that he then held both the impropriation and the right of presentation. By this time he had sold most of the church land for building purposes, with the exception of that bought by the Vestry to extend the church yard. In 1843 his heirs sold the remaining property (the chancel, the chancel pews, and the impropriation itself) to a firm of solicitors. In 1861 the Reverend Edward Walker, who was then the incumbent, bought it for the parish, and with this purchase ceased to be Perpetual Curate and became the first Rector.

Sir Baptist Hicks made no further attempt to displace Dr. English, who remained as Curate in Cheltenham until he was sequestered by the Puritans in 1646. In the intervening years he accepted two additional and more lucrative benefices[9] and was appointed a prebendary of Gloucester Cathedral.

The city of Gloucester under Bishop Miles Smith—one of the translators of the Authorized Version of the Bible—became increasingly Puritan, but when William Laud was appointed as Dean in 1616 he issued injunctions with the object of checking these Puritan tendencies. He moved from Gloucester shortly before the appointment of Dr. English to the Cheltenham church and within a few years had become Bishop of London, and then Archbishop of Canterbury. He left at Gloucester a small group of cathedral clergy devoted to his ideals, to whom Dr. English soon gravitated. Dr. Miles Smith was succeeded as bishop by Dr. Goodman, whose views were almost completely opposed to those of his predecessor. He was considered by many to be a Roman Catholic,[10] and was a determined opponent of the Puritans. When in 1640 Charles was at last compelled to summon a Parliament, a group of Puritan clergy, who had been suspended by Dr. Goodman, took an active part in an attempt to elect a member for the county who would 'hold the King's nose to the grindstone and ruin the Church'. In a letter describing this election, Dr. English is mentioned as one of the anti-Puritan clergy.[11]

Neither he nor Dr. Goodman could have foreseen how soon the situation would be reversed. Dr. Goodman was arrested and tried at the same time as Laud, and although he was released after two years' imprisonment, the Civil War broke out soon after his return to Gloucester. His palace was then sacked, and he fled to Wales. In the following year Dr. English —as he recorded in the memorial in Cheltenham church to his wife—suffered 'eighteen weeks of close confinement'.

The sad memoriall of John English, Dr in Divinitie,
to Jane, his most deare wife, davghter to the H[le]
Eliz[th], Lady Sandys, Baronesse de la Vine, Comit, Sovthton,
from whom hee was divorced by 18 weeks close imprisonm[t],
which soone after cavsed her death on Avg: 8th, 1643;
& to Marie, his 2[d] davghter, who deceased Oct[r] 25 followin.

By this time the war between King and Parliament had already been waged for three years, and the lord of the manor of Cheltenham had become deeply involved.

VIII

CHELTENHAM DURING THE CIVIL WAR

THE attempts of Charles I to obtain money from his subjects by unconstitutional methods were strongly resisted in Gloucestershire. When in 1626 the justices of the peace were instructed to collect a benevolence or free gift, 'one unanimous answer was received from those they approached . . . that they humbly submitted themselves and their estates to be disposed of by his Majesty *by way of Parliament* . . .'.[1] In the following year the pretence of a free gift was abandoned and a forced loan was demanded. John Dutton, the lord of the manor of Cheltenham, who had been M.P. for the county in 1625, was among those imprisoned for his refusal to act as one of the commissioners to make the collection of the loan, and there is a family tradition that Dutton was later imprisoned in Gloucester gaol for his refusal to pay Ship Money.[2] He was by temperament, however, a moderate man, and when in 1640 he was elected to what proved to be the Long Parliament, he evidently disliked the extreme views which were being expressed by many of his fellow members, particularly those who were strongly Puritan.

His own county of Gloucester was one of those which petitioned for the abolition of Episcopacy, and in the subsequent debate in the Commons on the Bill to suppress the bishops, one member from Gloucester city proposed the confiscation of the revenues of the Dean and Chapter of the Cathedral and their transfer 'to other godly, pious and charitable uses . . .'.[3] Anthony à Wood described Dutton at this time: 'He was one of the Knights . . . to sit in the said Parliament, but being frighted thence by the tumults which came up to the Parliament door, as other Royalists were, he conveyed himself privately to Oxon, and sate there'—presumably with the King's forces.

The Civil War may be said to have begun when Charles left

London and set up his headquarters at Nottingham. One of his strongest supporters at this time was the Lord Lieutenant of Gloucestershire—the young Lord Chandos of Sudeley (Winchcombe). In Cheltenham the lord of the manor was now a Royalist, and so were Conway Whithorn and John Stubbes of Charlton Kings. Henry Norwood of Leckhampton (the grandson—but not the heir—of William Norwood), William Lawrence of Shurdington, the Hicks family of Chipping Campden; and the great house of Berkeley also supported Charles. On the other hand, the port of Bristol was at first held for Parliament, and Cirencester and Gloucester were strongly parliamentarian. Gloucester—important for many reasons—barred the way across the Severn between royalist South Wales and the King's headquarters at Oxford.

By 1643, however, the forces of Charles held Plymouth, Bristol, and Tewkesbury, and as a result of royalist victories, most of the north. Despite this Charles hesitated to march on London without taking Gloucester. His demand for its surrender was met with a firm refusal and he therefore began the siege of the city. Parliament too realized its importance. 'The city of London . . . cannot be long in safety if Gloucester be lost.'

Gloucester then 'did stand without help and hope'. Its successful resistance was made possible by the skill of Colonel Massey and the heroism of its citizens—among whom even women and children helped to plug the holes made in the walls by the bombardment. In the meantime Parliament—after tremendous efforts—had raised an army of 15,000 men (including the London train-bands) and sent it under the Earl of Essex to relieve the city. Charles dispatched Rupert to intercept this army, but beyond a skirmish near Stow-on-the-Wold —which caused Rupert to swear that all the Roundheads in England had come—there was no opposition. On the evening of 4 September, Essex reached Cleeve Hill, and on his arrival discharged four pieces of ordnance to warn Gloucester of his approach. The vanguard of his army reached Prestbury, hungry and soaked to the skin and harassed by enemy skirmishers. The rearguard, unable in the darkness to get their guns down the steep slopes of Cleeve, spent the night on the hill during a storm so severe that 'divers of their horses died'.[4] The next day they came down the hill and advanced through Southam and Prestbury into Cheltenham, where there was still resistance. Essex 'was fain to fight for his quarters and beat the enemy out of it at a market town called Cheltenham'.[5]

He spent the next three days resting his men in Cheltenham despite another attack from the enemy. There was now no need for haste. The firing of his guns from Cleeve had not only encouraged the citizens of Gloucester—it caused Charles to order the siege to be abandoned. The order came just in time to save the city, now down to its last two barrels of gunpowder.

In the meantime, Charles moved sadly away to Painswick, where he spent one unhappy night, and then returned to Sudeley. There was little chance now of carrying out the original plan of a march on London unless the army of Essex could be prevented from returning to protect the city. Rupert was out watching with his men on the hills, hoping to intercept Essex. Charles, on the other hand, seemed at first lethargic and content to remain inactive at Sudeley. Essex moved to Tewkesbury and Upton where he made a pretence of planning to cross the Severn; then by a forced march through Cheltenham during the night he entered Cirencester, took the sleeping Royalists by surprise, and collected all the provisions necessary for his army. From there he moved to Newbury and after an indecisive battle was able to continue without further hindrance to the capital. Charles's plan to regain London had then to be abandoned.

Colonel Massey, left in Gloucester with little money and with food supplies disorganized, raided the surrounding royalist strongholds. In November he planned to attack Cheltenham, seize the rents due to be paid by the tenants to John Dutton, and carry away food supplies and other necessary goods in carts which he sent on ahead. Lord Chandos, hearing of his plan, came over from Sudeley with 100 foot and 120 horse, defeated the raiders, and saved the property of Cheltenham, getting back almost unharmed despite a counterattack in Prestbury. Although the troops on both sides were still engaged in pursuit and retreat on the line of the hills from

Sudeley to Broadway, and although Sudeley was retaken by Waller for Parliament, Cheltenham seems to have escaped any further attack.

John Dutton was at this time a colonel in the King's army and had taken part in the siege of Gloucester, for which action Parliament 'disenabled and discharged him from being any longer a member of the House [of Commons]'.[6] He was apparently taken prisoner at Gloucester and shortly afterwards the Governor was ordered to send him to Westminster. At some time later he returned to Oxford and was said to have drafted the terms of the King's surrender of that city to Sir Thomas Fairfax (1646).

After this surrender, which marks the end of the first Civil War and the complete defeat of the King, John Dutton was one of many Royalists who were willing to compound for confiscated estates by paying the heavy fine demanded by Parliament—in his case amounting to £5,216. He claimed in the petition for his estates that the King's troops on their return from Edgehill in 1642 had forced his hand by threatening to burn down Sherborne House unless he joined them on their way to Oxford; and as he was never an entirely whole-hearted supporter of the King, it seems likely that this was true.

During the next ten years a curiously unexpected friendship, of which the origin is obscure, developed between John Dutton and Oliver Cromwell. In 1656 the Lord Protector wrote of Dutton that 'this gentleman hath given so many real testimonies of his affection to the Government and to my person in particular, so constantly for so many years past, that no man I know in England hath done more . . .'. In the same year John Dutton received a warrant from Cromwell allowing him to hunt in the forest of Wychwood and to take deer from it. With these deer he stocked the Lodge Park which he formed by inclosing land at Sherborne. Here he replaced the old monastic building[7] with a noble new house and a hunting lodge designed by Inigo Jones. In the mile-long paddock in front of the hunting lodge the deer were used for coursing greyhounds and were allowed to escape after the race through a trap-door at the end of the paddock.

His devotion to the cause of the Commonwealth is further

shown by the fact that he disinherited the heirs of his daughter
Lucy who as a very strong Royalist had given hospitality to
King Charles at Coberley. In his will he left his estate to his
young nephew William Dutton and at the same time appointed
Cromwell as guardian during his minority. He also referred
in this document to 'the discourses' he had had with Cromwell
on future marriage arrangements for his nephew and hoped
that 'when he shall come to ripeness of age, a marriage may
be solemnised between my said nephew William Dutton and
the Lady Frances Cromwell . . . which I much desire and (if it
take effect) shall account as a blessing from God'.

This marriage, however, did not take place because the
beautiful Frances Cromwell had set her affections on another
man.

William Dutton was, however, brought up in Cromwell's
own household for the next two years where his tutor was the
poet Andrew Marvell. Cromwell's letter, written at the time
of John Dutton's death to his widow, indicates the degree
of friendship between the two men:[8]

Dear Madam,

I wish to comfort you after your great loss of your noble husband,
my very good friend, and shall be ready in what will be in my way
upon all occasions to serve you. . . .

Your assured friend
Oliver P.

John Dutton's epitaph may still be read on the memorial
tablet which was transferred to the present Sherborne Church:

. . . a person of sharp understanding and clear judgment, very
capable of those eminent services for his country which he under-
went as Knight of ye shire in several parliaments and as deputy-
Lieutenant.

One who was master of a large fortune and owner of a mind equal
to it: noted for his great hospitality farr and neer and his charitable
relief of ye poor.

His memory is honoured by ye best and his loss lamented by ye
least.

Henry Norwood of Leckhampton, who like John Dutton
had joined the forces of the King on the outbreak of war, left

England for Holland in 1648[9] but returned to London in the following year and paid a fine of £15. He then decided, with two friends, to seek his fortune in Virginia, where the governor, Sir William Berkeley, was his second cousin. His subsequent account of the journey—*Voyage to Virginia*—better known today in the annals of Virginia than in those of his own country, described the unbelievable horrors of shipwrecks and starvation. Eventually he received from the exiled King the office of Treasurer in the Colony of Virginia, from which he drew the full income for the next nineteen years. He was back in England, however, in 1653 where he was twice arrested and spent two years as a prisoner in the Tower. On the restoration of Charles II he became in turn deputy-governor of Dunkirk, a member of the expedition which captured New Amsterdam, (New York) and commander of a regiment in Tangier. Pepys records that 'Major Norwood was with us . . . in Mr. Coventry's chamber in St. James, where we all met for a venison party' (November 1662). Two later references in the Diary show the friendship which existed between the two men, although Pepys strongly disapproved of Norwood's behaviour to the Mayor of Tangier—in 'the most proud, carping insolent . . . style I ever saw in my life'. After his many adventures Norwood returned to England, purchased the family estate at Leckhampton from his cousin, and settled there. Among his subsequent activities he became Mayor of Gloucester and later Member of Parliament for that city.

John Stubbes, whose records written into the court books have been so freely quoted in earlier chapters, was probably too old for active service, but the fact that he was among those to whom Charles applied for a loan in 1643 shows that he was a trusted supporter of the royalist cause. '. . . We do . . . desire you forthwith to lend us twenty pounds, or the value thereof in plate . . . and to pay or deliver the same within seven days after the receipt [of this letter] to the High Sheriff of the County . . . who is forthwith to return and pay the same at Corpus Christi College, Oxford.'[10]

On the death of John Dutton the manor of Cheltenham passed with other estates to his nephew, William Dutton, whose ownership thus began during the last years of the

Commonwealth when the former authority of manorial lords was replaced to a considerable extent by such instruments of the central government as the Major Generals. The court books which have survived from this period are almost entirely records of property transactions—a fact which may indicate that the powers of the courts of the manor were largely in abeyance. It is possible, however, that other records were kept which were lost during the general upheaval of the Civil War. Certainly, constables of the hundred still carried on some of their duties, and as in Cheltenham these officials were appointed in the manor courts it is probable that the courts still continued, but with considerably depleted powers.

Nothing is known of how Cheltenham reacted to the various experiments in government which were carried out when Cromwell was in power. It is tempting to suppose that the Major-General and his troops who were in charge of the west country (1655) made small impression on the farmers and malt-makers of the little market town. The independent attitude shown by these during the contemporary development of tobacco-growing lends colour to this supposition.

There is, however, some evidence of how the church in Cheltenham was affected during the period. The offices of bishops, deans, and chapters were abolished in the year of the outbreak of the war. Shortly afterwards the Scots demanded as the price of their help to the Parliament that a form of Presbyterianism should be established in England. For this purpose an ordinance was issued by which a service book known as the Directory was to be used instead of the Book of Common Prayer, and Presbyters and Elders were to be elected to replace the episcopal form of church government. But after the Scots had returned home there seems to have been very little attempt to enforce this ordinance, especially as powerful elements in the newly created army were Independent and strongly opposed to the authoritarian claims of the Presbyterians. In the virtual anarchy which developed in the churches as a result of this split, many forms of worship must have been practised, including perhaps the continued use of the Book of Common Prayer. The cause of the imprisonment of Dr. English in 1643 is not known. It is as likely to have resulted from some direct act of partisanship with the Royalists as from the tenacity of his religious principles, since he was not sequestered from his office until 1646, and then on the ground that, contrary both to the terms of his appointment as curate of Cheltenham as well as to a recent ordinance, he held other benefices. If, however, he was allowed to keep the more lucrative office, it seems strange that on his death in 1647 he should have been buried in Cheltenham.[11]

He was followed in quick succession by Benjamin Bourne and William Snow,[12] about whom little is known, but presumably they were Puritans. John Cooper, described as 'an able preaching Minister',[13] was appointed in 1650 at an increased salary of £60 a year. He had earlier succeeded the Unitarian John Biddle as Master of the Crypt School at Gloucester, from which it has been assumed that he also held Socinian views, but of this there is no proof.

'Cheltenham is a Market Towne . . . about 350 familyes there', is the description given at the time of Cooper's appointment, from which it appears that the Civil War had left little effect on the town, which again suffered less than its neighbours. In Gloucester the famous siege meant destruction of property and complete disorganization of trade. Winchcombe was twice occupied, and its famous castle was 'slighted' and the walls razed almost to the ground by order of Parliament, so that it was mainly unoccupied for two hundred years. In Cheltenham there was little direct interference with the main sources of livelihood, and it was indeed during this period that a new source developed in the growing of tobacco, which was to be of considerable importance to the town.

IX

THE COMMONWEALTH AND AFTER

FOR nearly half a century tobacco was cultivated in Gloucestershire on a scale large enough to threaten the prosperity of Virginian growers. Their protests were emphasized later by the Bristol merchants who feared a decrease in their carrying trade, while the central government objected to the loss sustained by the lessening of customs duties levied on Virginian tobacco. Against opposition from all three sources, the growers persisted in planting their fields with the forbidden plant and later in smuggling the dried tobacco on to the London market, despite royal proclamations, orders of the Privy Council, Acts of Parliament, and finally troops of horse and of the Life Guards. Fuller[1] tells us that 'tobacco was first planted in England about Winchcombe, and many got estates thereby, notwithstanding the great care and cost in planting, replanting, transplanting, watering, snailing, suckering, topping, cropping, sweating, drying, making and rowling it'. One of the growers, giving evidence on the matter in the reign of James I, stated that 'he did betake himself unto the County of Gloucester where poor folk do much abound, and there in one year planted so much tobacco as the poor had from the work of that year's crop £1,500 or upwards'.[2]

According to local tradition, tobacco-growing was introduced into the county by Sir Walter Raleigh through his connexion with Brockhampton. Whether this was true or not, John Stratford, a burgess in London, returned in 1622 to his former home at Farmcote and there in the fields above Hailes Abbey,[3] then in the possession of his relatives the Hoby family, he grew tobacco very profitably although he lost money later. In Winchcombe itself the land near the present hospital is known to have been a tobacco field. The exact location of the plantations in Cheltenham is not known but a report from William King (sent by the Privy Council in 1634 to enforce the uprooting of illegally planted crops) states that the inhabitants of the towns of Winchcombe, Cheltenham, Tewkesbury, Gotherington, Arle, and Charlton Kings 'have at the time great store of tobacco growing contrary to His Majesty's proclamation'.⁴

James I described tobacco-smoking as 'a custom loathsome to the eye, harmful to the brain and dangerous to the lungs'. At the beginning of his reign he added 6s. 8d. to the 2d. per lb. duty which had been imposed on imported tobacco in the last year of Elizabeth's reign. Despite his hatred of the practice of smoking, he soon realized the value to the customs of the importation of tobacco. As this heavy duty encouraged smuggling he reduced it to 1s., which was later raised to 2s.

The first imported tobacco was mostly brought from Spanish-owned Trinidad, but before the end of the reign the recently founded colony of Virginia was competing so successfully that one of James's last Acts (1625) was to forbid the importation of any tobacco except that from Virginia and Bermuda. By this time, however, the heavy duty and the high prices induced competition from growers at home. James tried to prevent this by a proclamation making its cultivation here illegal (1619). Despite the proclamation, the area of cultivation increased so rapidly in Gloucestershire that in 1627 the government of Charles I decided on direct action. The already mentioned messenger William King was sent to seize the tobacco and to order the growers to appear before the Privy Council.⁵ In Winchcombe the Council's warrants were torn up and although a serjeant-at-arms was sent to bring the Winchcombe bailiffs before the Council, there is no record that they went. Another Royal proclamation (1631) ordering the sheriffs to destroy local crops seems to have had little effect, and again the Privy Council sent a special envoy who complained to them 'that the said offenders and divers others have gathered their said tobacco and daily bring it to London by secret ways, and do usually sell it for Virginia and Bermuda tobacco . . .'.

The Council by this time was sufficiently angry to direct an order to the justices of the peace, laying on them the obligation of making the constables destroy the tobacco crops.

We could not have believed that after so many commands by

His Majesty and his Royal Father of blessed memory . . . any man could have presumed to have planted or maintained any English tobacco, until we have been lately informed that . . . in the County of Gloucester there is great quantity of English tobacco planted and continued contrary to these strict prohibitions.

It is probable that the justices of the peace, if not actually engaged as growers, were receiving indirect benefits from the trade, since they apparently did so little to carry out the order that three years later the Privy Council again sent William King to the county to insist on the destruction of the crop. In both Winchcombe and Cheltenham, the people defended their crops with violence. Further appeals from the Council to the justices of the peace proved useless and riots followed every attempt at destruction.

During the Civil War neither the King nor Parliament had time to harry the tobacco growers, although the armies of both sides must many times have looked across the fields planted with the forbidden crops as they rode down from the hills into Winchcombe, Cheltenham, and Gloucester. It was not until the war ended and Cromwell was in power that the matter was raised again by the merchants. In 1652 the Long Parliament passed an Act prohibiting the cultivation of English tobacco. This so alarmed local growers that they sent the following petition to the Council of State:[6]

To ye Parliament

The humble petition and cries of many landowners and labourers at Cheltenham and Winchcomb in ye County of Gloucester.

Humbly complaininge, sheweth unto your most excellent Majesty and Parliament, your obedient and faithful subjects, the growers and commonalty, of ye towns of Cheltenham and Winchcomb: that your petitioners have for many years past grown in ye common fields ye weed called tobacco, and pray that your Highnesse and Parliament will permitt them through your Council to practice the same, as their crops will be perilled and lost and it will be to ye ruin of very many labourers: our crops thereof growing and grown also into decay, with many other inconveniences, in tender considera-tion thereof, may it please your Majesty's Hon. Counsell, according to the necessity of ye cause, and your said obedient subjects, and all

the countries thereabout, shall accordingly pray for your Highnesse and Parliament.
Cheltenham, May 1652.

The petition met with some sympathy and another Act was passed allowing the planters 'to enjoy the English tobacco by them planted this year only without interruption', and so to escape the heartbreak of seeing their carefully tended plants uprooted. At the same time, 3*d*. a lb. duty was to be paid on this crop. However, the people of Gloucestershire had no intention of giving up their lucrative occupation when the year's grace was over, and so the planting continued. In 1655, Cromwell, now Lord Protector, decided that the earlier Act should be enforced. A letter sent to the mayor and justices of peace of the city of Gloucester ordered them to make this decision known to the people concerned in the county. The warning was ignored and the struggle began once more. In the last months of Cromwell's life a troop of horse, commanded by Cornet Joyce, marched out of Gloucester to destroy the tobacco about Winchcombe and Cheltenham. 'The County did rise on them—about 500 or 600—threatening to kill them, horse and men, so that they were constrained to depart.' What actually happened is described by an eyewitness in a letter[7] to one of the commissioners entrusted with the destruction of the tobacco crops:

Our hopeful proceedings are clouded, for this morning, I got together 36 horse, and went to Cheltenham early, and found an armed multitude guarding the tobacco field. We broke through them and went into the town, but found no peace officer, but a rabble of men and women, calling for blood for the tobacco, so that, had there been any action, blood would have been spilt. The soldiers stood firm, and with cocked pistols bade the multitude disperse, but they would not, and 200 more came from Winchcombe.
. . . Ten men could not in four days destroy the good tobacco about Cheltenham. The cornet would not act, and some of the county troops are dealers and planters. I was forced to retreat. The Justices of the Peace rather hinder than help us. The soldiers say, if this be suffered, farewell all levies and taxes, and farewell the Virginia trade for tobacco. . . .

It seems unlikely that this resistance would have been

permitted to pass without reprisals if Cromwell had lived, but no action was taken in the unsettled state of government during the interregnum that followed his death.

Almost immediately after the restoration of Charles II an Act was passed ordering all tobacco plants in England to be uprooted, and a fine of 40s. per rood planted was to be exacted. This order was carried out by the High Sheriff, Sir Humphrey Hooke, but apparently the fields were replanted, since Pepys states in his *Diary* (1667) that the Life Guards were sent to Winchcombe 'to spoil the tobacco there which the people do plant contrary to law, and always have done—although under force and danger of having it destroyed, yet will continue to plant it'. This is probably the incident referred to in 1666 in a letter to Lord Herbert of Raglan complaining that 'the inhabitants of Winchcombe and Cheltenham were gathering themselves together in a riotous and tumultuous manner and did not only offer violence but had like to have slain the sheriff . . .'.[8]

The plantations, however, were doomed. The fall in the prices of Virginian tobacco probably made it not worth while to risk the planting of continually uprooted crops. It is worth noting, however, that as late as 1691 Richard Teale—a miller of Cheltenham—demanded recompense from the Government for a small field of tobacco destroyed by the King's officers, which he had planted 'in ignorance of the law'![9]

Both Winchcombe and Cheltenham must have been severely affected when the growing ended. In the long run Winchcombe —described by Pepys' cousin as 'a miserable, poor place'— again suffered more than Cheltenham, where there were still two important sources of revenue besides farming—the market and the malting industry. Goding estimated that in the early eighteenth century at least a quarter of the property in the town was rated as malt-houses, and Sir Robert Atkyns in his *History of Gloucestershire* (1712) wrote: 'Cheltenham is a market town and derives a considerable trade in making malt. . . .'

By the end of the Civil War one of the market-houses mentioned in Norden's Survey was dilapidated. Christopher

Bayley, the master of the Grammar School, left £80 in his will for the provision of a new market-house for the sale of corn.[10] His executors petitioned John Dutton as lord of the manor 'for license to erect and build a market for the said use . . . and with a convenient room over the same for a wool market, and for keeping Court Leets . . . and for other public uses of the inhabitants of the said Town' (1655). They also asked that he would 'assign some convenient place . . . in or near where the old market-house before it was taken down did stand'. John Dutton's consent was recorded in the court books and the new market-house was then erected as a free-standing building near the centre of the Street itself, between Winchcombe Street and the Plough Inn. It was built of stone with stone pillars and survived, with the earlier market-house (which was almost certainly the old Booth Hall), until it was pulled down in 1786. The first Cheltenham guide-book had stated five years earlier that 'at present the Street is greatly encumbered with certain old coarse buildings supported on stone pillars . . . called the Corn Market and the Butter Cross'.

Farming operations continued in the common fields with apparently little change in methods. In Queen Anne's reign the boundaries between tenants' holdings seem to have been neglected. A court[11] order of 1710 runs: 'We do continue an order that Thomas White of Cheltenham do keep his mound in good repair, between John Ellis his football land and Thomas White, upon pain of six shillings and eightpence for default.' Another order recorded in the same court shows that the fields were still thrown open for cattle after the harvest: 'We do order that no sheep be kept in Cheltenham fields until harvest be ended in all the said fields upon pain of thirty-nine shillings for default; and we do also order that there shall not be any pigs kept within the said fields upon the same penalty.' In 1694 several men were presented at the court for 'keeping grey-hounds to destroy the game', and others 'for destroying the fishing within the said Manor'. The harsh penalties of the game laws had yet to be enforced. A keen eye was also kept on the use of common land: 'We do present Robert Maunsell for keeping horses in the common in Charlton Kings, where he had no right.'

Unfortunately, the only court books which survive from the period of the Commonwealth and the later Stuarts deal mainly with property transactions; but there can be little doubt that the powers of manorial courts declined during these years, and by the time of William and Mary many of the tenants were avoiding attendance at the courts by paying fines. The orders were concerned with maintaining the cleanliness of the Street, with the cutting of overhanging hedges and the scouring of ditches, the upkeep of the market-house as already mentioned, and the repair of the prison. 'Item, that the prison commonly called or known by the name of the Blind House in Cheltenham aforesaid be amended and repaired (the same being out of repair and dangerous to passengers that go along thereby) . . .' (1692).

The difficulty of forcing the millers at Cambray to allow sufficient water from the Chelt to flow from their mill pond down the Street was one of the recurring problems of the courts during the seventeenth and eighteenth centuries. When the current was slow the watercourse through the Street became foul with mud and slime, and there were frequent orders in the court books for the cleansing of this course by those whose houses were nearest to it. As early as 1626 four surveyors of the river were appointed with the other officials of the court leet, but their appointment seems to have lapsed after a few years and the surveyors of the highways were left to deal with the difficulties. There were large stepping-stones near the 'Plough' and later near the 'Fleece', and there were also two plank bridges to enable the inhabitants on the north side of the town to cross to the church. These, however, appear to have sunk in the mud from time to time. A court order was made in 1628 'for a bridge now to go to the church gate and the same should be made with an open ford and planks across'. Five years later another order runs: 'That the bridge at the great gate of the church shall be taken up and made with a fair ford of stones, and the bridge at the little gate to the church shall be taken up and a ford of stone to be made there and a convenient stone to be set over it for the passage of the people to church which we conceive should be done at the expense of the Vill . . .' and that 'the two bailiffs of the borough shall continue as before as viewers of the said watercourse, but we suppose that the whole current from the great church gate unto the house of Edmund —— is as yet too high for the rest above but we cannot judge of that until the other part first named is amended, for we do also conceive that all the whole work will be vain to be amended unless the filthy place of mud and mire which is against the house of William Mills be sufficiently scoured and pitched with stone for the passage of water'.

In a court held in 1692 it is recorded that 'we do continue an order that Thomas Humphris the miller and his tenant shall twice a week turn down the mill water into the common channel of the Street of Cheltenham'. This is the same order which had been fruitlessly continued from the late Middle Ages until the watercourse was diverted in 1786.

An order to the constable of Swindon to repair the stocks (1697) shows that the courts still had some responsibility for maintaining stocks and probably whipping-posts, but by this time the orders for their use came from the justices of the peace on whom the duty of maintaining public order and morality was increasingly laid. They judged cases of serious crime in Quarter Sessions or transferred them to the Assize courts. Lesser crimes and misdemeanours which for centuries had been handled by the manorial courts were now dealt with in Petty Sessions. The appointment of the officials of the Vestry —the general body of the ratepayers in each parish—had to be confirmed by the justices, and in this way they supervised the administration of the Poor Law through the overseers of the poor, and of the repair of the roads through the surveyors of the highways. The summons to meet the justices was issued in the formal and dignified language of the law, but the actual meetings were often held in the back parlour of a convenient inn. Thus in 1729 Thomas Ashmead, high constable of Cheltenham, sends an order[12] to the parish constable of Charlton Kings:

By virtue of a warrant to me directed, these are in His Majesty's name to require you to summon the Surveyors of the Highways of your parish to appear before His Majesty's Justices of the Peace for the County at the Pelican Inn in Cheltenham the 18th of this instant by two of the clock, and there be examined on oath touching the execution of their office and the condition of their Highway and to bring a list of those who have neglected their duty to the Highways,[13] and you are to be then and there present to make a return of this your warrant, hereof fail not. . . .

Among the administrative powers of the magistrates was that of fixing wages for the county and enforcing their payment. An order made at the Easter Quarter Sessions (1732) in Gloucester runs:

We do hereby direct and order that no person or persons within this county presume to give or receive respectively any greater rates than are hereby assessed. And . . . take notice that every master that shall directly or indirectly give any greater wages than herein assessed is to suffer imprisonment by the space of ten days without bail and to forfeit £5. And every workman, labourer, servant, etc., that shall take wages contrary to his assessment, is to suffer imprisonment . . . for one and twenty days, without bail.

One of the magistrates responsible for such matters in Cheltenham was the Reverend Francis Welles of Prestbury. He wrote a diary, of which unfortunately only excerpts have survived;[14] but these give a remarkably vivid account of his wide powers. In dealing with petty crime he records in 1714 that he ordered William Lyes 'convicted by his own confession of stealing wood from Mr. Baghott, to pay 2/- or be whipped', and Jane Clements to be whipped for hedge-breaking and stealing wood. Another woman was placed in the stocks for profanely cursing, and two others for 'haunting alehouses with lewd fellows'. In 1716 he granted a warrant to John Prinn (the steward of the manor) against two former overseers of the poor in Cheltenham for giving poor relief during their term of office 'without a badge'. This referred to a recently passed Act by which every person receiving poor relief from the parish, and his wife and children, should 'upon the shoulder of the right sleeve of the upper garment—in an open and visible manner wear such a badge . . . a large Roman P. together with the first letter of the name of the Parish . . . in red or blue cloth, as by the Churchwardens and Overseers of the Poor it shall be appointed'. Many of his orders concern the putative fathers of illegitimate children—to force them to pay weekly amounts to the parish for the expenses of their upbringing and future apprenticeship; others provide for the removal of intrusive paupers to their original place of settlement.

From time to time the Cheltenham market and fairs were the background for the crimes recorded by Welles. Thus in 1730 'Clare, a collar maker, was sued for the murder of one Wain by the blow of a whip at Troy Mill, as they were coming home from Cheltenham Fair on St. James's Day, and found guilty of manslaughter', and later a man was committed to the Sessions for 'stealing three hats from Edward Deakins of Evesham at Cheltenham New Market'. In 1730 he records what may well be the last case of using the threat of pressing a man to death if he refused to plead. 'Soloman Geary, accused of house-breaking, refused to plead until terrified by the Sheriff bringing in a carpenter to measure the body to make an engine to press him, he relented. . . . He was reprieved.'

The harshness of Welles's orders were probably more characteristic of the period than of the man himself. He was extremely angry when some young officers enlisted a Cheltenham man who was too drunk to know what he was doing, and insisted on the man's release because 'that was such treatment as could not be endured by Englishmen, who always gloried in their liberties and the excellence of their Constitution'.

Welles had been sworn in as justice of the peace three months after the death of Queen Anne, and although there was little immediate opposition to the accession of George of Hanover, it was thought necessary in Cheltenham, as in other parts of the country, for the principal inhabitants to take an oath of allegiance to the new king. It is recorded in the Gloucester Sessions Order Book (1715) that Henry Mease (the curate of Cheltenham), Thomas Ballinger (master of the Grammar School), Jeremiah Brett (the usher), Joseph Brock and Giles Head (high constables), and David Mitchell, gentleman, took this oath. Francis Welles writes in his diary that at this time he committed Mary Careless to appear at Quarter Sessions for saying twice 'that King George was a Papist dog' and Mary Hills for answering 'No, he was a Presbyterian'. This is one of the few recorded references to the

existence of Nonconformists in the town at this time. Archbishop Sheldon's religious census, taken in 1676, had given
the figures for the parish of Cheltenham, but without the
names of the sects concerned:

Conformists	1,068
Nonconformists	97
Papists	4

John Cooper was ejected from his office as minister of the
parish church after the Act of Uniformity (1662), and replaced
by the Episcopalian, Bowen. Goding claims that Cooper then
became minister to a Unitarian group, but there is no evidence
of the existence of such a group in the town before the nineteenth century. The first organized body of Nonconformists
was probably the Quakers, but this was only a few years ahead
of the Baptists. The first Anabaptist house to be registered at
Quarter Sessions for meetings in Cheltenham was dated 1698,[15]
but since Nonconformists as well as Catholics suffered persecution under the laws of Charles II, until the Toleration Act
of 1689 brought them some relief, it may well be that there were
underground meetings before that date.

More information is available about the Quakers—the
Society of Friends. The first references to them in Cheltenham
appear in their Quarterly Meeting Records[16] for 1670 and 1673,
when the Friends of Stoke Orchard were asked to bring a contribution for the use of the Cheltenham Friends, while at a
meeting held at Nailsworth to consider the sufferings of
Friends, Cheltenham was represented by Daniel Hayward.
Goding states that there was no persecution in Cheltenham,
but unfortunately the records of the Friends disprove this.
Thomas Mason, a hosier, was committed for trial in 1684 for
being at a religious assembly and for refusing to enter into
a recognisance to attend at the Sessions, and in the same year
Daniel Hayward and Thomas Allen (both collar-makers),
Richard Rogers (a weaver), Margaret Skinner, Eleanor Jefferies, and Elizabeth Jefferies were also committed for attending
their own services. The exact penalties are not given, but in the
following year Elizabeth Baker and Elizabeth Sandford were
actually committed to prison for the same offence and John

Hayward was fined for refusing to pay towards the repair of the parish church.

In other cases there was distraint of goods. 'The aforesaid Chancellor [of the Diocese] came with officers into the house of Richard Skinner and seized all the goods in his house with respect to some fine for being at meetings'. These goods were redeemed for £15 by a friendly neighbour, but shortly afterwards

ye said Chancellor wending to Cheltenham again, and ye said Richard Skinner seeing him and doubting he would come and pick the box again, therefore, he having therein about £3. o. od, thought good . . . to take it out; soon after came Mr. Chancellor and ye box he fingers, wherein he finds but 22/-, put there through custom and forgetfulness . . . which not being sufficient to satisfy the active priest and unjust Justice, he therefore took away two or three panns of brass [not valued]. This also upon ye aforesaid fine, nothing else being charged against him. . . .

The main persecution seems to have ended with the passing of the Toleration Act (1689) and early in 1696 the Quakers were making plans for building a meeting-house. The land for this was provided by Elizabeth Sandford and the transfer is recorded in the Cheltenham court book (27 October 1701)—to William Mason, John Pumphry, John Drewett—'to the only intent and purpose that a Quakers' Meeting House can be erected and built'. At a quarterly meeting at Gloucester the following year two of the Cheltenham Quakers who explained that they could not raise enough money to complete the building were granted £20. In 1703 the new meeting-house was licensed for worship, and shortly afterwards land was acquired for a burial ground in Grove Street. This meeting-house was used by Quakers until 1836, when it was replaced by a larger building adjoining the original site (and now the property of St. Mary's College) in Manchester Street. William Mason, the son of Thomas Mason and one of the trustees for the original building, was also a hosier. He was apparently prosperous, since before he died, he owned the Bayshill estate, including the Well which was to bring fame to Cheltenham.

By a fortunate coincidence two almost contemporary

accounts are available of the town as it was at the time of the discovery of the healing properties of the well. Sir Robert Atkyns[17] (1712) describes it as a market town with a good trade in malt: 'The parish is ten miles in compass and consists of good Pasture and Arable.' He estimates the total number of houses in the parish as 321, with 1,500 inhabitants, in addition to 102 houses and 550 inhabitants in Charlton Kings and 30 houses and 120 inhabitants in Leckhampton.

A little earlier John Prinn, the steward of the manor, recorded at the beginning of the court book, for the keeping of which he was responsible,[18] his account of the town 'situated on the eastern side of one of the most fertile valleys in ye world, and an ancient Market Town. . . . Its soil is sandy and very natural for carrets, cabbages and turnips—inasmuch as the whole neighbourhood is annually furnished with these for sundry miles around from this towne which is one Street continued with the buildings on each side for a full half mile.' He describes the church, the Grammar School, the Almshouse, and the two market-houses, and he also states that the site of the farm at Cambray—the Parsonage House which was described in the Survey of Rectory property (1632)—was that of the original eighth-century priory.

He does not include in his account the old Court House, although it was still in existence. By this time, however, it was no longer part of the demesne rented by a tenant. It had become the property of Richard Wills, a Cheltenham maltster.[19] In 1706 Wills sold to Andrew Green of Ledbury '. . . all that messuage with the appurtenances . . . called the Court House, and all that close of land lying on the South Site thereof called the Court House Close, and all the orchards, gardens, courtyards and backsides to the said messuage which lie together and extend from the Churchyard on the North, and ground called Church Meadow and land beyond on the East—and a little lane [presumably St. George's Place] on the West . . .'. This is the last known reference to the old Court House, but some thirty years later the Great House was erected on or near the site, so that presumably it was pulled down shortly after this sale. Atkyns mentions one other good house, belonging to Mr. Mitchell. This was the property known as Powers Court—

which was separated from Cambray Farm by the lane now known as Rodney Road.

In this little community of farmers and maltsters, hosiers, mercers, and shopkeepers, John Prinn (of the Inner Temple) was probably the dominant personality. He appears to have been the son of William Prinn whose name is included in the list of those paying the hearth tax in 1676[20] and who was buried near the chancel of St. Mary's Church in 1680. His position as steward to the non-resident owner of the manor gave him considerable influence, and his wide legal practice—he was solicitor to the Duttons at Sherborne and to Sir Berkeley Guise at Rendcombe—gave him enough money to buy the estate of Charlton Park and the Manor of Ashley (Charlton Kings). Like the former steward, John Stubbes, he left records which he thought would be useful to later generations and he made a collection of documents which had an antiquarian interest in his own time, but which have for the most part been dispersed since the nineteenth century. In his meticulously neat handwriting he not only recorded all the property trans-actions concerned with the manor but made an index of earlier transactions. He went to considerable trouble to rescue court books which had been lost, and in this way preserved a most valuable sequence of records of the town. Thus in one of the court books for the reign of James I it is recorded in his hand-writing, 'I found this book in the custody of Dr. Kear's sister in Cheltenham', and in the volume which covers part of the Civil War he wrote, 'This book and another—to the year 1656 —I had of Mr. John Careless of Gloucester—for which I agreed to give him and did give him 43 shillings of my own money and his clerk 2/6d, besides 2/-d spent on obtaining them . . . all of which must be allowed by the next succeeding Steward.'[21]

John Prinn died in 1735. His position as steward of the manor and his estate of Charlton Park passed to his son Wil-liam. Within three years a still more dominant personality— Henry Skillicorne—had settled in Cheltenham and was already planning the Long Walk and the buildings of the first Spa, which were to change so dramatically the destiny of the town.

X

THE BEGINNINGS OF THE SPA

IN a field at the back of the Chelt, and on, or near, the site of
the present Princess Hall in the Cheltenham Ladies' College,
there was a spring which flowed through the thick clay
of Bayshill and left a deposit of salts. The purgative properties
of the water from this spring had been known to the inhabitants
for a long time, since the observant Doctor Lucas, who analysed
it at the beginning of its fame, wrote that 'he had seen old men
drink Cheltenham water by the quart without number, or
experiencing any ill effect from so strange a practice, which
they had accustomed themselves to on certain days and holi-
days for upwards of thirty years, without having any disorder,
but because they thought it wholesome to cleanse their bodies;
therefore observed no rule but to drink it till the water passed
clean through them'.[1]

The well which was sunk near this spring was to become
known later as the Royal Old Well—the first and for nearly
a century the only Spa in Cheltenham. According to a popular
legend, the properties of the well were discovered in 1718 when
it was noticed that pigeons flocked to peck at the deposit of
salts nearby. For this reason these birds were later adopted as
part of the coat of arms of the town. By this time, William
Mason—the owner of the well—had retired to Bristol, probably to be near his son Joseph who was a merchant in that city.
There his daughter Elizabeth met the Manxman Henry Skillicorne—a former privateer and a merchant captain in the
service of the Elton family of Bristol. Their subsequent marriage was to have far-reaching effects on the destiny of
Cheltenham.[2]

In the meantime the well was left open for a few years so
that people in the neighbourhood might benefit from it. The
practice of drinking waters impregnated with natural salts was
already fashionable; Bath, Clifton, Tonbridge, and other spas

were flourishing. Rumours of the virtues of the Cheltenham waters soon spread and it was found necessary to enclose the well. Henceforth the waters were for sale not only on the site but in bottles which could be obtained as far afield as London, Bristol, Gloucester, and Worcester; a great deal of counterfeit water was also sold under its name. What finally set the seal on the value of Cheltenham waters was a statement in Dr. Short's *History of Mineral Waters* (1740) that on analysis they were superior to any in the country. Two years before this, however, Henry Skillicorne had moved from Bristol to Cheltenham where he acquired, partly through his wife's inheritance and partly by purchase from the other heirs, most of the Bayshill property. The longest epitaph on the walls of the parish church gives us a life history of this extraordinarily able man. He was 'tall, erect, robust, active', and after trading 'in the Mediterranean, the Morea, Turkey, Spain, Portugal, Venice, Philadelphia, Boston and Holland . . . doing business in seven tongues', finally settled in Cheltenham and was the main agent in the development of the early eighteenth-century Spa, and 'lived and died an honest man'.

Henry Skillicorne first deepened the well and instituted a pumping system. He then built a square brick structure over the well, resting on four brick pillars with a pigeon at each corner; on the west side he built a small ballroom where those drinking the waters could congregate, with a billiard-room above it. His attention was next turned to the making of a suitable approach to the new Spa which was at this time located in an open field.

His many travels had given him a much wider knowledge of the world than that of the little community in which he now found himself, and he must have been aware of contemporary ideas of landscape gardening—the use of trees, water, and gentle slopes for the creation of vistas to please the eye. Either he or his friend Narbonne Berkeley (later Lord Botetourt) planned the approach which later became the celebrated Well Walk. This was an avenue with a double row of elm trees on each side—leading from a rustic bridge across the Chelt to the well and continuing with elm and lime trees some distance beyond it. Attempts were made to include the Church Meadow in the avenue, but when these failed a winding path across it was gravelled and the vista of the church itself seemed to form part of the whole plan. In the course of the next century many of the nobility and most distinguished people in England and many from other countries were to walk under the trees in this famous avenue.

Skillicorne's diary is no longer available, but Goding was able to quote extracts:

In the winter of 1739 I made the upper walk, planted elms and lime to the number of 37, and made a new orchard adjoining. The winter 1740 I made the lower walk, planted 96 elms, at the expense of £56. Had that summer 414 subscribers at the Wells at 12d per piece. Built a yard round it, and 18 little houses. The summer 1740 proving very dry, I had 46 of the trees dead; set 44 in the room of the 46 dead the summer before, and had that summer 674 subscribers at the Wells at 12d per piece. The Summer 1741, proving very dry, 30 trees died . . . which I planted again. In 1742 built another room two storeys high; this year had but one tree dead, which I have planted. Had this season 667 subscribers.[3]

Two early drawings of Cheltenham made at this period have survived. The first shows a delightful scene of the avenue of recently planted saplings and the little Spa, against the background of hills, with no buildings to impede the distant view of Leckhampton Church and Manor House. It may have been drawn from a position in a house newly occupied by Lady Stapleton and known for the next hundred years as the Great House.[4] This was set in a large garden within a grove of trees on the site of the present St. Matthew's Church—where formerly the old Court House had stood—and when a few years later it became Mrs. Field's boarding-house it was often called Grove House. The second drawing (made in 1748 by Thomas Robins) shows the Great House itself, the church and Church Meadow, the Long Walk and the Spa, and in the background the Street.

Skillicorne's diary gives a list of annual visitors to his well. There were 644 in 1743, and 655 in 1748. The *Morning Post* of 1743 also reports that 600 people of 'great fortune and gentility' were in the Spa, with a long list of their titles. *The*

General Advertiser (15 June 1751) reports that 'on Thursday last Mr. Handel arrived in Town from Cheltenham Wells . . .'.

For the entertainment of these visitors there were the country pastimes of cock-fighting and bull-baiting with dogs in the Street. Cudgel matches were held outside the 'Plough': 'He that breaks the most heads in these bouts and comes off clear, to receive a good hat and a guinea in money.'

In one of the lanes leading from the High Street[5] a very small malt-house had been converted into a primitive theatre. It was here that the young Sarah Siddons appeared in *Venice Preserved* and so moved some members of the audience that they reported her performance to David Garrick. Shortly afterwards she began her famous career on the London stage. Travelling companies moving between Stratford and Warwick also played in the little Cheltenham theatre. There were balls and card parties and billiards in the newly built rooms at the Spa, and bowls on the green at the back of the 'Plough'. 'There is a great appearance of gentry at the Balls every Monday and Thursday and at the Card Assemblies every Tuesday, Wednesday, Friday and Saturday' (*Gloucester Journal*, 25 July 1758).

In the midst of these gaieties came a more serious note. Both George Whitefield and John Wesley visited the town.[6] In 1739 Whitefield was refused the use of the parish church, but he preached to nearly 2,000 people on the large bowling-green of the 'Plough'. 'Many were convicted of sin . . . some were so filled with the Holy Ghost that they were unable to support themselves under it.' In 1757, again unable to get into the Cheltenham church he preached from a tombstone in the churchyard. 'A singular spectacle it was—the closed church, the graves covered with thousands of people . . . some sobbed deeply; others wept silently. . . .' John Wesley did not visit Cheltenham until 1766 when he preached an open-air sermon to a large crowd. Later in the year he preached in the little chapel in Albion Street—built originally by Presbyterians, and destined later to play an important part among the Cheltenham Radicals as the Mechanics Institute. His efforts were opposed by both the Baptist minister and the curate of the parish church during his visit in 1768, but four years later he preached from the old Market-house opposite the 'Plough' to a very large audience.

The early Methodists, however, did not have the same success in Cheltenham as in Gotherington and Winchcombe, and their later visits were disappointing.

During the middle years of the century there seems to have been a slump in the number of visitors. Goding shows from the rating lists that the lessee of the well—Thomas Hughes—was exempted in 1757 from payment of rates on the well, and that in 1763 twenty-four out of the three hundred dwellings were untenanted. The second *Guide Book* issued by Simon Moreau in 1783 refers to 'the neglected state of the place for the last thirty years'.

There were various reasons for the so-called neglect. Visitors may have been frightened by outbreaks of smallpox. Goding quotes from the statements published in the journals of nearby towns: 'We whose names are underwritten, the Churchwardens and Overseers of Cheltenham, do certify that the town of Cheltenham in Gloucestershire is now and has been for six weeks past free from smallpox' (1757). Unfortunately this state of affairs was only temporary; the next year the church-wardens, overseers, and high constables of Cheltenham gave a warning 'that any person or persons presuming to bring sufferers to the town will be prosecuted, the small-pox being greatly upon the decline in the town, and must in a short time be entirely over, *there being but few remaining to have it*'!

In these early years the journey to Cheltenham from London entailed great difficulty. The first recorded coach to make the journey from Gloucester to London was the 'Gloucester Flying Machine' which took three days. For many years there was no direct coach service from London to Cheltenham. Passengers took the Gloucester coach and either found a conveyance from Gloucester to Cheltenham or got off at Frog Mill Inn, near Andoversford, and came on by post-chaise. Of course wealthy people—as, for example, Lord Chesterfield—travelled in their own carriages.

By 1770 the actual time was reduced to twenty-six hours directly from Cheltenham, but the journey was still an arduous one. William Winterbotham, ancestor of a famous Chelten-ham family (and himself a well-known Nonconformist minister in Plymouth who suffered two years' imprisonment for his religious and political opinions) describes among other aspects of life in Cheltenham the old coach itself.

Cheltenham, at the time of my leaving it (1773), was properly speaking little more than a good farming village, though undoubtedly designated a market town. Its waters had indeed obtained considerable celebrity, but there was professedly only one lodging-house for visitors. There were, however, two good inns, at both of which in the season a few families and individuals took up temporary residence. Our stage coach, the 'Old Hereford' which, with six horses, accomplished the journey to London in twenty-six hours, astounded the inhabitants by the celerity of its movement. Few of them, however, aspired to the honour of visiting the Metropolis in a coach, and those who did contented themselves with a place in an enormous basket which was attached to the hinder part of the body.

The third reason for the decline of visitors was the shortage of lodgings as suggested above, and the frequent lack of comfort in those available was certainly no inducement to travellers. There is indeed evidence that the inhabitants themselves were not anxious to attract visitors to the town. The main agents of eighteenth-century development—like those of the nineteenth century—were new-comers: the Manxman Henry Skillicorne, William Miller from London, and later Thomas Hughes from Monmouthshire.

Henry Skillicorne lived for twenty-five years in the town of his adoption. They were probably happy years, since, according to the account given on his memorial tablet, he was 'grave without austerity, and of a cheerful conversation without levity'. With 'conduct ingenious and manners attentive' he presided over the Long Walk; and he also served for two periods as churchwarden and was an active member of the Vestry. His son William continued his father's policy of developing the Spa. In 1776 he added the Long Room on the east side of the Pump. This was so much more convenient for parties and balls that the first room was soon converted into private dwellings. His partner in this was William Miller, who became lessee of the Spa. By this time the number of visitors was again increasing. One of these visitors complained in a letter to the *Morning Post* (1780), which was reprinted in the first *Guide Book*:

> The town of Cheltenham . . . would in all probability have remained unnoticed 'till the end of time', had not the Spa attracted the attention of the public. This seems to be the general opinion of the inhabitants, if we may judge from the little pains they have taken to decorate or improve themselves or their habitations. They likewise seem displeased that chance should have brought them to public notice, by their constant opposition to every improvement for the convenience and accommodation of those who visit them. This narrow-minded mode of thinking, we may naturally conclude, leads them on to insolence and imposition. Thus emerging as they are from a state of obscurity did they possess the understanding of rational creatures, we might expect to see attention and care to discover the favours of the public; but this seems to be distant from their ideas; and those whose health necessarily obliges them to go there must think themselves highly indebted to the public spirit of Mr. Miller of London, for the great exertion of his fortune and abilities, to render the place in the least sufferable.

This letter shows a Londoner's reaction to the natural independence of the countryman, and the complete lack of servility among the inhabitants of the little town. It is possible also that the astute Miller instigated this letter for purposes of advertisement.

Despite such criticism, the number of visitors continued to increase, and this encouraged Simon Moreau, a well-known figure in Bath, to come to Cheltenham for the summer season and act as self-appointed Master of Ceremonies. His position was at first strongly resented both by William Miller and Mrs. Field—the proprietor of the Great House, by whom the following doggerel was probably inspired.

> In short, I'm unable our pleasure to draw
> Good breeding and sense were our guide and our law,
> Without form we were gay—good humour went round,
> And mirth with contentment, Society crowned;
> But lately an ape in the shape of a Beau
> By the outlandish name of Simon Moreau
> Has officiously come at the balls to preside,
> To preserve etiquette, and pay homage to Pride.

Some use there may be in this creature 'tis true
Their way to the temple the ladies to show;
But I still must lament that such forms should efface
The native politeness and ease of the place.[7]

In the Torrington diaries there is a first-hand account of the treatment Moreau received from Miller and Mrs. Field. The author of these diaries—the Honourable John Byng—first came to Cheltenham in 1781. He described how after dining at the 'Swan' he settled at Grove House (the Great House) in 'the best lodgings in the town, comfortable, neat, spacious . . . and overlooking lovely meadows'. He found the town divided into two factions. The most powerful, headed by Miller and Mrs. Field, was strongly opposed to Simon Moreau; the other, headed by Mrs. Jones of the Town Rooms[8] and including most of the visitors, supported him.

I have heard both parties [writes Byng], and liking neither the character nor the manners of my hostess Mrs. Field, am inclined to yield subjection to Mr. Moreau, who is to be sure only self-elected and never was properly crowned here; at Bath, indeed, he has the honour to be *arbiter elegantiarum* to the Corporation. If he continues to behave with decency, I hope he may preside, as such a character seems necessary . . . and his opponents seem guided by ill humour and self-interest.

Some weeks later he writes:

Mr. Miller of the Long Room continued his impertinence and tyranny to Mr. and Mrs. Moreau by refusing them the waters (tho' Mrs. C's mangy dog drank of it constantly), and by turning his subscription book out of the Room. I hate oppression; and as this is particularly against the sense of the company, Moreau should be supported. After dinner, at the Walks this affair was canvas'd and some gentlemen meeting in Mrs. Field's room (from which they have absented themselves on this account) determin'd not to subscribe to Mrs. Field's room, unless Mr. Moreau's book was suffer'd to be there; especially as the lodgers of her house, if supporters of Moreau were to be refused the water. We sent to Mr. Miller, who return'd this polite answer, 'That anyone who wanted him, might call on him.' Accordingly—a deputation of four gentlemen waited upon the great man, who at first was very violent, refused to have connection with Moreau etc. etc; but at last all was compromised, and by a shaking of hands, a kind of peace was established:

poor Moreau was in agonies of joy, and at his return home, fell into hysteric fits.

After this incident the opposition apparently died down, and Moreau seems to have been an active and efficient Master of Ceremonies. The first *Guide Book to Cheltenham* had appeared in London in 1781; two years later Moreau issued his own *Guide Book*, which was to reappear in succeeding editions until 1806. From Byng's diaries and from these early *Guide Books* we have a glimpse of life in the town as it was in the years immediately preceding the visit of King George III. At this time visitors came mainly in the summer, and as it was usual to drink the waters before breakfast, entertainments were adapted for early risers:

This public breakfasting is at the Long Room every morning at 10 a.m. during the season, each person pays one shilling. The balls begin every Monday at 8 in the evening and Country dancing closes them at 11. Each person who drinks tea or a dish of chocolate pays sixpence—ladies who dance excepted, the gentlemen their partners paying for them.[9]

There was music every morning at the well from 8 until 10 for a subscription of 5s. and cards and public tea at Mrs. Field's every evening, a cotillion ball every Thursday, and another ball every Monday which might be more properly called 'the Minuet rather than the Dress Ball, for etiquette of dress is not required here, no public place being so free from disagreeable restraints as this'.

Another Cheltenham personality who comes to life in the pages of Byng's diaries is the Reverend Hugh Hughes,[10] at this time incumbent of the parish church. One of Byng's greatest pleasures was a game of dumbo whist and he seems to have found in Hughes a congenial companion. On one occasion he records that after watching the first minuet of the season danced at the Pump Room, he 'played two rubbers of whist and won £2. 12. 6. from the Vicar, whose stipend is £40 a year'.

Byng tells us later how he himself attended Divine Service

as irreligiously perform'd as at most other places. The inhabitants are of different sects which is owing to the want of discipline in the Church of England, where the people would flock were pluralities abolished and more spiritual comfort to be had, which not being the case, the Religious fly to other persuasions. The Vicar of this place must be a Welshman from Jesus College, Oxon, and his stipend is £40 a year; which is considerably augmented by the present incumbent by subscriptions and his skill at whist.

Undoubtedly the Quakers and the Baptists had a fairly strong following; and there was the nucleus of a Wesleyan congregation. In spite of this, however, the congregation of St. Mary's had increased to such an extent that a petition was sent to the Bishop of Gloucester for permission to erect a gallery over the north aisle of the church, 'otherwise our families and lodgers cannot be accommodated with the convenience of hearing the word of God'.

Byng seems to have disliked Cheltenham. He resented the high prices he was charged for everything, complaining that even salmon was 7d. and 8d. a pound. He did not care much for the company, 'widows wanting husbands, old men wanting health, and misses wanting partners'. He was bored with the small talk over the evening tea-tables, and sarcastic about the cotillion ball which 'from want of skill ended in country dances'. He described his daily routine at the beginning of the summer season:

We have risen early commonly by seven o'clock, at eight have crossed the meadows to the Pump Room, there passed an hour in walking and taking two glasses of water; . . . and from that time until dinner at 3 o'clock I am out seeking new rides; we pass another hour in the evening at the Wells, and to bed early after our strawberries or some light repast. . . . But the Balls have now begun and the Players from Tewkesbury open their Theatre on Saturday next. . . .

His dislike of Cheltenham was mitigated by his enjoyment of the surrounding countryside. In the evenings he liked walking through the hay fields along the banks of the Chelt and watching the trout, or riding round the Marsh—'the Rotten Row of the place'. He also much enjoyed, apart from the extreme difficulty of bad roads, exploring further afield— around Leckhampton and past the 'well-looking seat of Mr. Laurence at Shurdington' to Whittington and back past Mr. Baghott's house at Northfield (the Hewletts) and over

Cleeve to Winchcombe—a 'mean dirty Market Town'—to Sudeley Castle.

His visit coincided with that of Lord Fauconberg, for whom William Skillicorne was at this time building on Bayshill a house which later became famous as the temporary residence of King George III. In the usual Cheltenham fashion, the bricks for this were made in a brick-kiln erected on the site, so that the smell of burning bricks reached the visitors at the well. Byng showed great interest in the new house, and tried to persuade Lord Fauconberg that with so much land available there was no need, as in London, for underground kitchens. If Byng's advice had been followed and a fashion for ground-floor kitchens begun in Cheltenham, generations of domestic servants would have had reason to thank him!

When Byng paid a second visit to Cheltenham three years later he noted rather sadly the changes which had occurred in the interval. A new theatre had been built by John Boles Watson in York Passage and the new elegant Assembly Rooms erected by Thomas Hughes had replaced the old ball-room kept by Mrs. Jones.

These new Assembly Rooms were the cause of a sharp collision between William Miller and Thomas Hughes. The latter came to Cheltenham in 1749[11] and was articled for five years at a fee of 150 guineas to John de la Bere (the steward of the manor) with whom he lived in the 'elegant house' in the High Street, the site of which is now occupied by the premises of Messrs. Woolworth. After his marriage with a wealthy heiress of the Bridges family he set up his own practice as a solicitor and bought for his residence the old Powers Court house and estate. This gave him a large area of land stretching from the High Street along the west side of the present Rodney Road to Oriel Terrace and included 'a walled garden, a moat, orchard and fishponds, a meadow called Claypits, courtyard, barn, stables, cow house and dove house . . . together with the Ball Room and its garden . . .'. On the site of this primitive old ballroom he planned to erect his new Assembly Rooms. Miller complained that only recently he had himself rebuilt the Upper Rooms[12] which would be adversely affected by competition from the new Rooms. A war of handbills followed. Hughes explained that his plans had been made some years before 'and an eminent architect from London, Mr. Holland, took a survey of the land', but that proceedings were held up by the opposition of the tenant of the old ball-room. The next tenant, Henry Rooke, was only too happy to have an entirely new ball-room, and so despite the ill will of William Miller, the beautiful new Assembly Rooms, presumably designed by Henry Holland himself, were built, and in this way the corner of the old Powers Court estate became for a century a famous centre for Cheltenham's most fashionable assemblies.[13] A surviving water-colour of the interior of Henry Holland's ball-room gives some idea of the elegance of the new Rooms with which neither the Long Room at the Old Well nor the rooms in the Great House could compete.

Most certainly the new Rooms were not in keeping with Christopher Bayley's rural Market-house which stood in the Street only a few yards away on the opposite side of the stream. The distaste which the aristocrat Byng felt for the recent changes was not shared by those who were interested in developing the Spa. Further changes were foreshadowed in the first *Guide Book*: 'At present the Street is greatly encumbered with certain old coarse buildings supported on stout pillars; these are called the Corn Market and the Butter Cross . . . another below them neither has nor merits a name. A little further down is a kind of cage or prison, built of stone, and not unsuitably decorated with an inscription in front, "Do well, and fear not". It is to be hoped that objects so very unsightly will soon be moved.'

Many of the desired changes, however, could not be carried out either privately or under the weakened jurisdiction of the manorial courts. There was therefore a demand that an Act of Parliament should be obtained by which a new authority could be set up. It seems likely that this course of action was initiated by those whose business interests were concerned—such as Thomas Hughes, William Miller, Henry Rooke, John de la Bere and his son whose lands were later sold to Henry Thompson and the Earl of Suffolk, and developed as the Montpellier and Lansdown estates. John de la Bere—a member of the Southam family of that name—was one of the several attorneys who served Cheltenham as stewards of the manor. Unlike his predecessors, he left no written records of his achievements but he undoubtedly played an important part in local affairs, especially as he was the only justice of the peace who lived in the town. His contemporary reputation is indicated by a former tablet in the parish church which ran:

> To preserve the memory of those whose excellences will never be forgotten, this marble records the names of John de la Bere, Esq. who died Jan. 12th 1795.
>
> Also of the Reverend John de la Bere his only son, who died at Burford 1810.

On the other hand, some of the inhabitants, whose identities unfortunately cannot be traced, strongly opposed such a policy of change. The following notice was inserted in the *Gloucester Journal* (25 February 1786).

> Whereas a report has been artfully and industriously propagated in order to prejudice the minds and alarm the apprehension of some of the inhabitants with respect to the Bill which is intended to be brought before Parliament . . . this notice is therefore given so that such of the inhabitants may rest assured that the scope and purport of the said Bill is only for the paving, cleaning and lighting of the town, and for removing certain buildings called the Market House, Butter Cross and Dungeon, and no private building whatsoever.

All objections were, however, overruled and later in the same year an Act was obtained, the importance of which it is impossible to over-estimate. It was the first of a series which helped to change the virtually rural community of the old market borough into a paradise for speculators and entrepreneurs—mainly new-comers—who in the course of the next half-century planned and built the beautiful Regency town which was to attract visitors from so many parts of the world. By this first Act a body of fifty-eight Commissioners was appointed with powers which were to be extended by three succeeding Acts under which the new Cheltenham took shape.

The first efforts of the new Commissioners were directed to removing the old picturesque obstructions from the Street. The filling-in of the channel of the stream was completed;

the Market-house pulled down and its site laid into the Street; a foot pavement four and a half feet wide was laid down, and a hundred and twenty lamps were provided. These alterations were completed in time for the arrival of the most important visitors the town had yet received. Two years later, on the advice of the doctors and perhaps influenced by Lord Fauconberg (one of his gentlemen-in-waiting), King George III with Queen Charlotte and three of their daughters spent five weeks in Cheltenham.

INTERLUDE: THE ROYAL VISIT

T HE royal visit to Cheltenham has a twofold importance.
First, it attracted a large number of people, both at the
time of the visit and for many years afterwards, and this
gave an impetus to the growth of the town. It also made
Cheltenham for a few short weeks the focus of the fashionable
world, so that it figures at great length in the columns of the
Gentleman's Magazine and the *Morning Post* and in the works
of Peter Pindar.

'The Cheltenham cap—the Cheltenham bonnet—the Cheltenham buttons—the Cheltenham buckles—all the fashions
are completely Cheltenhamised', says the *Morning Post*. In the
language of London journalists the Well Walk was glorified
as the Mall, and the underpaid curate was magnified into the
rector. From these sources there emerges a much more intimate
picture of life in the town than would otherwise have survived.
The diary of Fanny Burney, who came in attendance on Queen
Charlotte, contains a delightful account of what she is pleased
to call the Cheltenham episode, when for five weeks the royal
family were in residence in Lord Fauconberg's recently built
house on Bayshill:

I must now tell you the party. Their Majesties; the Princesses
Royal, Augusta and Elizabeth; Lady Weymouth, Mr. Fairly,
Colonel Gwynn, Miss Planta, and a person you have sometimes
met. Pages for King, Queen and Princesses, Wardrobe-women for
ditto, and footmen for all.

A smaller party for a royal excursion cannot well be imagined.
How we shall all manage Heaven knows. Miss Planta and myself are
allowed no maid; the house would not hold one.

When we arrived at Cheltenham, which is almost all one street,
extremely long, clean and well paved, we had to turn out of the
public way about a quarter of a mile, to proceed to Fauconberg
Hall, which my Lord Fauconberg has lent for the King's use during
his stay at this place.

It is, indeed, situated on a most sweet spot, surrounded with lofty hills beautifully variegated, and bounded, for the principal object, with the hills of Malvern. . . .

When we have mounted the gradual ascent on which the house stands, the crowd all around it was as one head! We stopped within twenty yards of the door, uncertain how to proceed. All the Royals were at the windows; and to pass this multitude—to wade through it, rather—was a most disagreeable operation. However, we had no choice: we therefore got out, and leaving the wardrobe-women to find their way to the back-door, Miss Planta and I glided on to the front one, where we saw the two gentlemen, and where, as soon as we got up the steps, we encountered the King. He inquired most graciously concerning our journey; and Lady Weymouth came downstairs to summon me to the Queen, who was in excellent spirits and said she would show me her room.

'This, ma'am!' cried I, as I entered it—'Is *this* little room for Your Majesty?' 'Oh stay', cried she, laughing, 'till you see your own before you call it little!' Soon after, she sent me upstairs for that purpose; and then, to be sure, I began to think less diminutively of that I had just quitted. Mine, with one window, had just space to crowd in a bed, a chest of drawers and three small chairs. . . .

On the ground floor there is one large and very pleasant room, which is made the dining-parlour. The King and Royal Family also breakfast in it, by themselves, except the Lady-in-Waiting, Lady Weymouth. They sup there also, in the same manner. The gentlemen only *dine* with them, I find. They are to breakfast with us, to drink tea where they will, and to sup—where they can; and I rather fancy, from what I have yet seen, it will be commonly with good Duke Humphrey.

A small, but very neat dressing-room for His Majesty is on the other side the hall, and my little parlour is the third and only other room on the ground-floor: so you will not think our Monarch, his Consort and offspring, take up too much of the land called their own! . . .

On the first-floor is the Queen's drawing room in which she is obliged to dress and to undress because she has no toilette apartment. Who after that can repine at any inconvenience here for the household?

Here, after breakfast, she sits with her daughters and her lady, and Lady Courtown, who, with her Lord, is lodged in the town of Cheltenham. And here they drink tea and live till supper-time.

Over the King's dressing-room is his bedroom, and over my

store-room is the bedroom of the Princess Royal. And here ends the first floor.

The second is divided and sub-divided into bedrooms, which are thus occupied:—Princess Augusta and Princess Elizabeth sleep in two beds, in the largest room. Lady Weymouth occupies that next in size; Miss Planta and myself have two little rooms, built over the King's bedroom; and Mrs. Sandys and Miss Macentomb, and Lady Weymouth's maid, have the rest.

This is the whole house!

Not a man but the King sleeps in it!

The King kept a reasonably strict routine during his stay, reaching the well at six o'clock on most mornings to drink his first glass of water. The Queen and the princesses usually accompanied him at this early hour and walked with him under the elms until the party returned to breakfast at half-past seven. Much of the day was spent in walking or riding; dinner was between four and five, and at seven o'clock they appeared again in the Walks or paid calls on their friends staying in the town. On three occasions they visited the little theatre. Sometimes they watched their servants playing cricket in the field near Fauconberg House, since King George, afraid that they would not have enough exercise, had sent for cricket bats and balls for them.

On Sundays Their Majesties attended morning service at the parish church. On their first appearance the Bishop of Gloucester was there to receive them and to preach the sermon; but the choir was so overawed that 'they had not resolution enough to perform'. At this time there was no organ in the church—the first organ was installed in 1810—but before the following Sunday 'a very good bassoon' was obtained, and with this support the choir 'performed "How pleasant are thy dwellings" in a style superior to anything which could be expected'.

King George genuinely liked the simplicity of his surroundings and found great pleasure in walking about the town attended only by his two little dogs. He talked without restraint to people of all ranks whom he met, thus showing—as was remarked in a contemporary journal—'a confidence and condescension that would have made even rebels loyal'.

A King who had earned the nickname of Farmer George,

and who once interpolated in the gracious Speech from the Throne the words 'Gentlemen, you will be pleased that fat stock prices have risen', was not likely to neglect the opportunities which his visit to Cheltenham afforded him of learning something of the condition of agriculture and the price of livestock in the west of England. Many stories are told which illustrate this interest.

One day His Majesty rode over to Birdlip, wearing his greatcoat, the weather being rainy. On returning he overtook a farmer with a drove of sheep and the two rode on together discussing the value and properties of the land and the current prices of sheep and cattle. 'After satisfactorily answering all His Majesty's enquiries, the farmer asked the gentleman (as he thought) if he had seen the King; and, being answered in the affirmative, the farmer said, "Our neighbours say he's a good sort of man, but dresses very plain"."Aye," said his Majesty, "as *plain* as you see me now", and rode on.'[1]

Among the royal visits was one to Mr. Thomas Baghott de la Bere at Southam, and several to Charlton Park where the King is credited with enjoying some good gossip with Dodington Hunt who had inherited this property from the Prinn family. A favourite ride began with a visit to Mr. Baghott at the Hewletts and continued to Cleeve Hill. The King not only enjoyed the magnificent view from the top of the hill but was greatly interested in 'the vestiges of a Roman Camp', with which, on one of his visits, 'His Majesty indulged himself in contemplation for one full hour'.

There is no record of any exchange of courtesies between the royal visitors and Lord Sherborne, the lord of the manor who lived only twelve miles away at Sherborne. This is all the more strange as expeditions were made to Gloucester, Tewkesbury, Stroud, and Cirencester, where Their Majesties were deeply impressed by the beauty of Earl Bathurst's estate. They also stayed for several days at Worcester to hear the music of Handel performed at the Three Choirs Festival.

On the north side of Cheltenham High Street, in York Passage and almost facing what is now known as Cambray, John Boles Watson had recently built a small theatre to replace the primitive little malt-house where Sarah Siddons had played so successfully. The new theatre was so small that on the occasion of the King's first visit, when his party was increased by the unexpected arrival of the Duke of York and his equerry, there was only standing room for several members of the party in the box which had been hastily prepared for them. The main attraction on that day was the vivacious Dorothy Jordan— Hazlitt's 'child of nature whose voice was a cordial to the heart'. Amid scenes of great enthusiasm she played Hippolyta in *She would and she would not*, and Roxalana in *The Sultan*. Each allusion to the land of liberty, where 'every citizen is a King and the King is a citizen', was wildly cheered—and no one thought of Wilkes and Liberty or the American Declaration of Independence. It was at this performance that Fanny Burney and Miss Planta sat in the box usually reserved for John de la Bere. On this occasion he and his granddaughter— 'sweet little Anne Dewes'—accompanied them.

The King's second visit to the theatre was in the nature of a command performance. Two-thirds of the house was now occupied by boxes; the royal box was canopied in crimson and silver, and the playbills were printed on white satin; tea was to be served to the royal party between the acts, and a loyal address was prepared. Meanwhile Their Majesties, having returned from Worcester at five o'clock, dined at Fauconberg House, went to the Well Walk at six, and, a little later, walked quietly across the Church Meadow and through the churchyard to the theatre, to see Dorothy Jordan and Mrs. Welles in *The Merry Wives of Windsor*.

During the festivities and excursions of his five weeks' holiday, the King did not neglect affairs of state. It is recorded that on one occasion 'the King sat with the parlour window at Fauconberg House open, reading the despatches he had just received by the mail. A great concourse of people from the country took that opportunity of gratifying their curiosity; which His Majesty observing, was pleased very graciously to countenance by showing himself to their full view.'

On the eve of their departure the King and Queen paid their third visit to the theatre. On this occasion, Goding quoting from the *Morning Post* (15 August 1788) mentions the presence of the following 'splendid list of names:—Earls

Bathurst, Oxford, Harrington, Courtown; Lords Rivers, Apsley, Maitland, Falkland, Hamilton, Ducie; and all the fashion that Gloucester, Worcester and the County could send.'

And so, for this short interlude in its history, the Street and the Walks of Cheltenham were crowded with fashionable people of every rank—a pastoral scene of noble lords and ladies who had followed their sovereign to 'this most sweet spot, surrounded with lofty hills', to share with him the benefit of its healing waters. Where they all found lodging remains a mystery, even though Prestbury and Tewkesbury were full to overflowing.

Fanny Burney recalled the last sad scene at the royal departure:

All Cheltenham was drawn out into the High Street, the gentles on one side and the commons on the other, and a band playing 'God save the King'. . . . The journey was quite without accident or adventure . . . And thus ends the Cheltenham adventure.

Alas! the Cheltenham waters did not restore King George's health. One wonders whether, in the long, tormented years which followed, his clouded mind ever recalled the idyllic days when he kept his miniature court in the Well Walk and held levees under the elms and limes.

XII

THE GROWTH OF THE TOWN AFTER
THE ROYAL VISIT

THE royal visit to Cheltenham was followed by the outbreak of the French Revolution, which eventually led to the greatest war in which England had yet been engaged. It was mainly for this reason that there was no immediately large increase in the number of visitors to Cheltenham or in the erection of houses to accommodate them.

The historian Fosbroke[1] described the town as he first saw it ten years after the royal visit when 'the only conspicuous objects were . . . Fauconberg House and a double range of buildings in the High Street above the "Plough"—which buildings, with the exception of one solitary brick house[2] that bore the air of a country mansion and was near the Old Walk, were the only habitations considered fit for the reception of wealth and title'.

He remembered that the two turnpikes, one at Gallows Oak and the other at the lower end of the High Street, were whitewashed and brightly painted and had gay lamps, but that the houses were of all heights, forms, and descriptions—'low, thatched houses with gable ends adjoining slim London fourstoreyed houses, the footway only partially paved and at the lower end intersected by yawning open drains which rendered the path utterly unfit for gossiping or thoughtful promenade, because absence or occupation of mind occasioned a fall into them. Here and there in the fields near the town, new built houses were seen standing alone.'

It is clear, however, that in the last years of the eighteenth century, in spite of the war and the lack of suitable accommodation, the number of visitors to Cheltenham was steadily increasing. According to Goding, 2,000 came in the year 1800. In the census of the following year the number of inhabitants is given as 3,076, and the number of inhabited houses as 710, with 15 being built. Some of this building was at the eastern end of the High Street, and along the narrow paths or lanes which opened from it. Shenton's *Directory* of 1800 explains this: 'As Cheltenham has but one principal street, and many good lodging houses which stand out of the street are situate in places which have no name, the Printer . . . has begun at the top of the street on the north side, and when he came to any turning of that street he has taken in the houses such turning led to, and then turned into the street again, pursuing the same mode coming up the south side of the street.'

On one such opening was built the Colonnade, at the entrance to the future Promenade, which was then a narrow lane across a marshy field. The first stone of these buildings was laid in 1791 by the Earl of Fauconberg. St. George's Place must have been developed much earlier and was for many years the only road to connect the High Street with the Royal Well Spa and with the coach drive to Fauconberg House.

Apart from the effects of the war, development was hampered by four main factors. Firstly, the supply of water at the Royal Well Spa was inadequate for the demands of the visitors, most of whom came to Cheltenham not only for diversion and change but to drink the waters for medicinal purposes. Those who have lived in Cheltenham all their lives without once tasting its saline waters may find some difficulty today in understanding the extraordinary demand for them in the years following the King's visit. King George himself, in the interests of economy, had ordered the closing of the Royal Well on Sundays; and with a view to increasing the supply he had caused another well, known as the King's Well, to be sunk on the Fauconberg estate. Dr. Smith, the Savilian Professor of Geometry at Oxford, who practised medicine during the season at Cheltenham, suggested that 'the inhabitants seeing that they have all the waters to themselves for seven months of the year . . . should be a little more sparing of their draughts during the heighth of the season'. Dr. Jameson, another of the many doctors who were attracted to Cheltenham towards the end of the century, took forty borings on the south side of the present Queen's Hotel; one of these—the first Sherborne Well—was in daily use for two years, during which time three hogsheads of water (approximately 156 gallons) were drunk from it every morning.[3]

Visitors to Cheltenham found not only a shortage of water but a continued shortage of lodgings; as late as 1804 Browne's *Guide* informs us that 'Cheltenham, with all the additions which successful speculations are yearly making to it, will soon be capable of accommodating all the company which resort to it, though at present it is not, in consequence of which, lodgings have been filled up at Charlton Kings, Sandford, Arle, Prestbury . . . which are frequently replenished by the overflow of company which resort to this spot'.

Another difficulty was that of transport—a serious matter for a town as remote from London as Cheltenham. Various Acts of Parliament passed since 1756 had enabled Turnpike Trusts to be set up in a determined effort to improve the roads, but there is considerable evidence to show that they were far from successful. The road from Cheltenham to Gloucester at this time passed from the lower High Street along the Tewkesbury Road, through Boddington to Staverton, and for many years it had been in a notoriously bad condition. The part near Cheltenham was described in 1778 as 'a complete heap of sand, so that it must inevitably become the bed of a river in the rainy season'. Ten years later, Marshall[4] refers to it as 'scarcely fit for Their Majesties' subjects to travel on—and pay for'; and after yet another ten years later, 'All the roads about Cheltenham were execrable, for the native materials, being only of the hardness of loaf sugar, were pulverised by every wheel, and in the winter every track became a gulley' (Fosbroke). The condition of the roads not only made travel to the town unpleasant: it held up the supply of materials that were needed for the building of houses and, even more important, for the repair of the roads themselves. Until the means of transport were improved it was difficult to bring the necessary hard stone from the Bristol area.

Yet another outstanding difficulty was that a great deal of land upon which speculators wished to build was still open fields where separate holdings could not be inclosed because of age-old rights of common pasturage inherent in the system of farming. The land at the back of the High Street—known then as 'the Common called the Marsh'—was likely to become a very valuable building site, but legally it could only be used as common land by the burgage tenants. The common fields of Leckhampton had been inclosed by Act of Parliament in 1778. A similar Act was necessary in Cheltenham before any large-scale building could take place on the north side. In the first few years of the new century, however, all these difficulties which had held back the natural development of the town were dealt with almost simultaneously.

Three Acts of Parliament were passed enabling three new roads to be made. The New Bath Road (1813) passed through Cambray and Bath Street to Leckhampton, with a branch leading through Shurdington and Painswick to Bath. Another road (1810), leaving Cheltenham by the present Portland Street, passed through Evesham and Alcester to Birmingham; the third was the new road to Gloucester which is still the main Cheltenham–Gloucester road. It followed the course of the then recently built railroad for which an Act of Parliament was passed in 1809. Along the tracks of this line horses drew trucks, and a subsidiary line initiated by Charles Brandon Trye ran from the quarries at Leckhampton down the new road as far as the present 'Norwood Arms', and from thence down Norwood Street and across Park Place to join the main line in the lower High Street by the coal wharf.[5] Although parts of these new roads were for many years allowed to remain in an unsatisfactory condition, the development of the town would not have been possible without them. In particular coal could be obtained easily. Griffiths informs us that 'the town and neighbourhood is plentifully supplied with coals from Staffordshire, Shropshire and the Forest of Dean, which are conveyed by the Severn and then by the Railway to the respective wharfs at the extremity of the Town' (1816).

The problem of finding more water was solved only too successfully for the interests of the Old Royal Well Spa. The latter had been an almost accidental discovery; in the early years of the new century, however, determined efforts were made to augment the existing supplies of saline water. In 1801 a chalybeate spring—that is, one with waters impregnated with iron—was located near Barrett's Mill in Cambray.

A second was discovered in the grounds of Wellington House. The main Cambray Chalybeate Spa, however, was developed later (1834) by Mr. Baynham Jones. It was an octagonal building on the corner of the present Rodney Road car-park. A short-lived Spa was built in Alston in 1809. This also had an octagonal pump-room and a small garden. Much more important than these was the Montpellier Spa, where the first pump-room was also built in 1809. In 1801 Henry Thompson, who had gained a fortune in London as a merchant and underwriter, bought a large portion of the de la Bere land. This was a fateful purchase for Cheltenham since it led to the development of the Montpellier Spa and of the building estate of Montpellier and Lansdown.

Thompson began searching for medicinal springs at once; he is said to have made over eighty borings. He built the baths in Bath Road, and nearby a magnificent house for himself which he called Hygeia House. Both these buildings still stand, but at some time after Wellington's great victory in Spain the house was renamed Vittoria House.

In this house the newly discovered saline waters were at first dispensed; in 1809, however, Thompson built the first pump-room at Montpellier on the present site. It was a long unpretentious building with wooden pillars and a veranda, and a small structure over the centre for an orchestra. Following the example of the Royal Well, a tree-lined walk was made as an approach, and opposite the pump-room gardens were laid out. In 1817 this rather primitive structure was pulled down and the present building with the lion couchant was erected. Eight years later the architect John Papworth added the domed circular room which became known as the Rotunda.

In 1818, through the enterprise of Thomas Henney and Samuel Harward, another important Spa was built on the site of the present Queen's Hotel. It was at first called Sherborne because it replaced an earlier well so named in compliment to the lord of the manor. The first Sherborne Well[6] had been located by Dr. Jameson and developed by Samuel Harward at the top of the Old Well Lane. When this well ran dry it was replaced by the second Sherborne Well (1818), which soon afterwards was renamed the Imperial Spa.[7] The great importance of this Spa in the history of Cheltenham is that the approach to it was planted with a double row of trees, after the pattern of the Old Well Walk, and that this avenue, at first known as Sherborne Walk, became in a few years the Promenade.

The extent of the transformation that took place at this time may be judged from the fact that the site of the Promenade was described by a contemporary writer as 'a swampy and scarce passable lane leading from the High Street to the Chelt, over which the passenger could only cross upon the unsteadfast footing of a plank'—and with marshy ground beyond the plank.[8] The purchase of this land for the making of a road and its subsequent resale by the Paving Commissioners is described in Chapter XIX.

In the early years of the nineteenth century, concurrently with the development of the Spas, a great building effort was made. Many houses were completed in St. George's Place; a terrace was planned on the west side of the Church Meadow and was completed as the Royal Crescent before 1810. On the other side of the town John Boles Watson bought a large part of Cambray Meadow (formerly church property) and built there a new theatre which was destined in its short career to be the scene of performances by many famous people, among whom were Sarah Siddons, Charles Kemble, Dorothy Jordan, Grimaldi, Harriot Mellon, Maria Foote, and Colonel Berkeley and his brothers. He also built for himself a small house which he sold later with the land surrounding it to Colonel Riddell— one of the great eccentrics of Cheltenham; and at about the same time James King, the second Master of Ceremonies, built a house known as Cambray Lodge near the present Sandford Gates in the Bath Road.

Colonel Riddell discovered in the grounds which he had bought from Watson a second chalybeate spring. The house itself was at various times enlarged considerably, and from the fact that on several occasions it was let to the Duke of Wellington it became known as Wellington Mansion, but it was known also at some periods of its history as Cambray House. The land adjoining was acquired later by Baynham Jones who built for himself another house, also known both as Cambray House and as Wellington House because the Duke occupied it during one of his visits to the town, and famous later as the first home of Cheltenham Ladies' College. Vernon House, where Charles James Fox stayed in 1803, was a short distance to the east of the theatre. Near the corner of the present Bath Street was another well-known house, Georgiana Cottage, where Byron spent some pleasant hours with his friends. He wrote to Lord Holland in 1812: 'By the waters of Cheltenham I sat down and drank, when I remembered thee, oh Georgiana Cottage.'

Another important building site was developed during the early years of the new century on what was then the extreme south of the town. The Earl of Suffolk bought part of the de la Bere property which included the old Gallipot Farm, and on this site he built Suffolk House for his own residence. His daughter later sold much of the land on which Suffolk Square and St. James's Church now stand.

No Anglican churches were built during the last years of the war, but a large chapel was erected in the High Street for Protestant Dissenters and served by ministers who were prepared to maintain 'the Doctrinal Articles of the Church of England as specified in the Act of Toleration'. The famous Rowland Hill came there from time to time to preach. The building is today in use as Messrs. Dicks furniture repository, and all that survives of its original purpose is indicated by the grave-stones of the adjoining disused graveyard. Behind this chapel a small Roman Catholic church was built in Clarence Street in 1810, mainly for French refugees. Their first priest was the Abbé César, who was succeeded by Father Birdsall. This church survived for fifty years. At the same time the Wesleyans also built their first chapel (which they called Ebenezer) in King Street.

Two other contemporary buildings were erected by the Paving Commissioners—the Market-house (1808) in the High Street, and the prison opposite the chapel on the corner of New Street. A new workhouse was built by the Vestry in the same year near the Knapp, at the back of St. James's Square.

In the meantime the Inclosure Act of 1801 put an end to the

open-field system and made possible the development of the land to the north of the High Street.

The dominant figure in the movement which led to the passing of this Inclosure Act was Joseph Pitt, who was later responsible for the development of the Pittville estate and the erection of the Pump Room. At this time he was forty-two years old and had already made a considerable fortune. Lord Campbell—later Lord Chief Justice—described the beginnings of his career: 'Pitt used to hold gentlemen's horses for a penny when, appearing a sharp lad, an attorney at Cirencester took a fancy to him and bred him to his own business. He soon scraped together a little money by his practice in the law and by degrees entered into speculation.... Everything has thriven with him. He has now [1812] a clear landed estate of £20,000 a year....'9

In the course of his speculations he had bought property in Gloucestershire and Wiltshire. He also bought and sold church benefices and parliamentary seats—in the days of pocket boroughs—and from 1812 onwards he was the Tory Member of Parliament for Cricklade. In Cheltenham he developed large interests in the brewery which belonged to John Gardner and in the banking firm which later became known as the County of Gloucester Bank. At the time when the Inclosure Act was passed he had become (by a recent purchase from the Earl of Essex) the impropriator of the Cheltenham parish church and was therefore entitled to the tithes, and he became the owner of the Cambray Meadow, the Church Meadow, and other church lands. He also bought a considerable amount of burgage and freehold property on both the north and south side of the High Street, and he was later involved in the tontine by means of which some of the Cambray property was developed. His position as chief landowner is made clear at the first meeting of property owners held at the 'Plough' in 1801 to discuss arrangements for implementing the Inclosure Act. 'We whose names are hereunto subscribed, being the Majority in value . . .' runs the minute; Joseph Pitt's name is the first of the three signatures which follow and it is highly probable that the Act was obtained through his influence.

This Act gave permission for the inclosure of the common or

open fields of Cheltenham so that each owner could fence in his land and keep it entirely for his own use or sell it for building purposes. In it Francis Webb of Salisbury was appointed as Commissioner to be in charge of the arrangements. The rights of the lord of the manor were safeguarded, although in the actual operation of the Act he gained singularly little.

By a fortunate chance there survive not only the final Inclosure Award and the plan of the allotments made, but a Minute Book[10] containing records of the early meetings at which the main business of the Inclosure was transacted. These meetings were usually held at the 'Plough', but sometimes further afield, at the 'White Hart' at Upton-on-Severn, or the 'King's Head' at Gloucester; and from the minutes it is possible to reconstruct the actual procedure of the early work of the Commissioner.

His first problem was the distribution of land in the Marsh —technically the property of the lord of the manor—and for centuries regarded as common pasturage for the beasts of the burgage tenants. After this arrangements had to be made for the inclosure of the open fields. Here it was important that no one should be allowed to fence in land until his claim to it had been examined and fully established. There was the further difficulty that some of the very small strips held in separate ownership might be better grouped together, and land redistributed by a series of exchanges, so that each owner had the same amount as before. This would need very careful surveying. The actual fencing-in of the land created a new problem, since it would no longer be possible to cross open fields, and some means of approach to the separate holdings had to be guaranteed. Much attention had therefore to be paid to roads and rights of way. Lastly, much of the land was subject to payment of tithes, and in any redistribution the proportion of amounts due would need careful consideration.

Immediately after the passing of the Act a meeting was held at the 'Plough' where the Commissioner took an oath to carry out his duties 'faithfully, impartially and honestly'; and bankers, solicitors, and surveyors were appointed.

The Commissioner then called for claims to land in the Marsh—a portion of which he ordered to be sold to raise money to defray later expenses. Having called in the assistance of two independent valuers, he proceeded to value the whole of the common lands and some old inclosures. Within four months he had 'made some calculation of the value of the property to be allotted to each proprietor, schemed out some of the allotments and caused the same to be entered on a map in a cursory manner'. Those who thought the valuation unfair were allowed to give evidence, and consideration was given to their objections.

As the expenses increased the Commissioner found it necessary to levy a rate—the first of four—which had to be paid before the work was completed.

A year later the allotments in the Marsh were completed, and half the proceeds of the earlier sale handed over to the twelve claimants who were considered to have lost their property rights by the sale.

In two directions the Inclosure Commissioner experienced difficulty. There was stiff resistance among some of the land-owners to the levy of rates to cover the expenses incurred by the procedure under the Act. As a last resort he ordered distraint of goods when he could not enforce payment by any other means. On the other hand, his order that allotments of land, as soon as marked out, should at once be fenced, was not so much resisted as neglected. Fencing was expensive and many of the owners were in no hurry to carry out this part of the procedure.

The actual process of examining claims, making allotments, arranging compensation for leases and for tithe payments continued for some years. The final award was not signed until 1806, but already in 1802 a significant order had been issued by the Commissioner: 'No person shall stock with Cattle, Horses, Sheep, Pigs, any of their allotments of land so as to suffer or permit the same to run at large nor stock any other of his lands and grounds intended by the said Act to be divided.' With this order there ended a system which had existed in some form at least since the Norman Conquest. The way was now open for modern development and building.

As a result of the award the land at the back of the High Street, including the Marsh and reaching across as far as

Gallows Lane (Hale's Road) and the east side of Bouncer's Lane, was allotted to various owners and the holdings inclosed. At the same time land to the south of the street which was not already built on and was virtually in private possession was also included in the award as far as 'the Moar Stone at the end of the lane near the Cold Bath'[11]—the boundary between the tithings of Cheltenham and Alstone. The latter was not dealt with at this time; the fields of Alstone and Arle remained open and commonable in theory until the Act of 1833 permitted their inclosure; most of the common fields of Leckhampton had been inclosed long before this by an Act of 1778.

In the final award Joseph Pitt, having surrendered (as impropriator of the Rectory) his rights to tithes, received in compensation seven lots of land in the Marsh amounting to 189 acres. On two of these lots was charged the sum of £40 to be paid annually by him to the curate of the parish church—'these two lots', wrote the Commissioner in the award, 'being of yearly value at £100 clear of all deductions and outgoings'. The total of Pitt's lots amounted to 'one-fifth of the arable and tillage lands and one-ninth of all the remainder of lands within the tything or hamlet of Cheltenham (after space has been deducted for roads) liable to pay tithe to Joseph Pitt'. As well as the land allotted to him as compensation for loss of tithe payments Pitt received payments from those in the town whose property was subject to tithe but not affected by the Act itself. A separate schedule of their names and the sums due from each was included in the award; the total sum was £2,325. While it is impossible to make an exact calculation of what Pitt gained by the Act because the amount of his original holdings is not known, there can be no doubt that he was more than adequately compensated for the loss of tithes. As he also held land marked on the award's map on the south side of the street, he emerges as the largest property holder in Cheltenham at this time. On the ground which he received in the Marsh he built the estate of Pittville.

On the other hand, Lord Sherborne as lord of the manor gained very little, except an allotment of land in the Marsh which at some time later was sold to Francis Welles. It should be emphasized, however, that his property rights as lord of the manor, as laid down in the 1625 Act, still held good; he was entitled to heriot or fines on the sale or alienation of lands within the manor and to market tolls. Unlike some of his successors, he did not attempt to revive any ancient claims. The money payments were not considered at the time as burdensome, or as a hindrance to the sale of property. J. K. Griffiths, writing in 1816, says:

> A very considerable part of the real Estates in the Manor and Hundred of Cheltenham is of the tenure of . . . Copyhold of Inheritance which is only transferable by surrender. . . . These estates are in no respect inferior in value to Freeholds of Inheritance. . . . The Fines, Heriots, etc., are merely nominal—the modes of transfer have a most expeditious . . . facility, at a comparatively small extent, and the Records of the Court, which from the 2nd. year of the reign of Queen Mary [1555] to the present time have been carefully preserved, afford all the security and advantage of register counties. . . .

Many of the contemporary Inclosure Acts dealing with other parts of the country caused hardship to the poor, who frequently lost their rights to the use of common land and were induced to sell their small holdings in the common fields so that they became landless labourers. In Cheltenham there is no evidence of such effects. The common land which was inclosed was the Marsh in which from time immemorial rights of free pasture had been restricted to burgage tenants. Rudge, writing in 1803, shows that this right had not lapsed: 'To these burgage tenants . . . the right of common in the Marsh is solely appendent.' On the map of the Inclosure Award[12] a large number of very small holdings remain interspersed among the large blocks owned by Joseph Pitt and others. It appears from the minutes that the Inclosure Commissioner was scrupulously careful to maintain the rights of former holders. This Act is, however, an example of inclosure in a small town, where many interests were concerned and not, as in some country areas, that of a single rapacious lord of the manor intent on enlarging his farm lands in order to experiment with new agricultural methods. From the rise in the Poor Rate and from other evidence it can be deduced that there was a considerable increase in the 'necessitous poor' in Cheltenham at this time. It seems likely, however, that this was due more to the calamitous rise in prices and the other effects of the Napoleonic War than to the Inclosure Act.

As late as 1811 a Supplement of the Award was issued, by which the Commissioner agreed to an exchange of property between one Thomas Smith and the Fellows of Corpus Christi College, Oxford. As a result of this the site of Richard Pate's Almshouse and its chapel, garden, and orchard in the High Street was exchanged for the much smaller site of the present Almshouse (without a chapel) in Albion Street—to the great loss of the inmates. This breach of trust by the Fellows of Corpus Christi is thus glossed over by Griffith in his *Guide*: 'The Almshouses form a neat architectural feature in Albion Street. They were formerly less comfortably situated opposite the Assembly Rooms.' (1816.)

Nearly fifty years later, when the Vestry had won the case against the Fellows of Corpus Christi in regard to the use of funds for the Grammar School, it set up a committee to investigate the facts of this earlier exchange of sites for the Almshouse made under the Inclosure Act, and later chronicled the correspondence with the college agents in the Vestry Records of 1857. From these it appears that one of the Fellows of Corpus Christi College who had been concerned in the original transaction of 1811 was still living, and that he had a clear recollection of the events of that year.

He was well acquainted with the old Almshouses and remembered that general dissatisfaction was expressed to the Trustees at the existence of so mean a building on the principal street of the town. —That interest was made by such inhabitants with Dr. Barton [the Bursar] and another trustee (both Gloucestershire men and having numerous acquaintance in Cheltenham representing the views of the inhabitants) to gain the consent of the Trustees of the Charity to the removal of these incongruous buildings. In this way the Trustees were ultimately induced to entertain the proposal of the parties who were at that time actively promoting the advancement of the interests of the town.

As a result of this proposal an exchange of properties was made between Thomas Smith—banker—and the President of Corpus Christi College. The indenture in which the terms of the exchange were laid down explained clearly what happened. 'The said Hospital or Almshouse had been for a considerable time past and was then considerably dilapidated and out of repair, and the comfort and accommodation which it had afforded to poor men and women was much lessened, and it would take a considerable sum of money to put the same into good repair, and there was no fund or revenue applicable to the purpose of repair.' It was therefore agreed that Thomas Smith should take possession of the original building and its site—covering over five-eighths of an acre—and in return should erect a new Almshouse on a site less than one-eighth of an acre. Because of the difference in area, Thomas Smith was to pay £250 to the college—to be invested in Consols—so that the annual income of £7. 10s. might be used for future repairs of the new building. Immediately after the transfer of the inmates to the new Almshouse the old site was advertised for sale for £2,000, and later it was used to build the Vittoria Hotel, the site of which has been acquired for extension to the premises of Messrs. Woolworth.

Although the legality of this exchange is not in doubt, it would be difficult to justify the transaction on grounds of equity. The old pensioners lost their spacious surroundings and the amenity of their own chapel for a small building on a cramped site in a far less pleasant situation. They were sacrified to the demands of the speculators in lands, bricks, and mortar, who under the guise of promoting the interests of the town were determined to replace all the old buildings, which as new-comers they despised. Nor is it unreasonable to ask why the Almshouse had been allowed to become dilapidated, or why, if it was necessary to rebuild, a direct sale, which would have been more advantageous to the inmates, was not made.

Shortly after this exchange of properties Joseph Pitt also obtained an Act of Parliament (1816) by which he was allowed to exchange the advowson of Bagendon Church (then in his possession) for that of St. Mary's Church, Cheltenham, which had been held by Jesus College, Oxford, since the reign of Charles I. In the same year he sold the advowson of Cheltenham Church—for £3,000—to the evangelical body known as the Simeon Trust.

An indirect result of the Inclosure Act was the production of the first map of Cheltenham in 1806. One of the difficulties of elucidating the terms of the award is that no map of the town, as it was before the Act, is known to exist. This map is therefore of the greatest importance in showing the exact state of development of the town and its surroundings, covering the area from beyond the Gallows Oak at the corner of Old Bath Road on the east side of the town to Alstone and the lower High Street on the west, and showing parts of Charlton Kings and Leckhampton. Unfortunately it does not give the old field names, most of which have been lost. The common fields of Cheltenham—so recurrent a phrase in the medieval records—have now disappeared for ever. In their place will stand the parades and parks of Pittville, the fine church of St. Paul's, and further to the west a large area of working-class houses.

XIII

THE SPA IN TIME OF WAR

THE year when the Cheltenham Inclosure Act was passed saw the end of the first phase of the war with France and the making of the Peace of Amiens. Within two years of this, the second phase—the war against Napoleon—had begun.

It would be easy to over-estimate the effect of the Napoleonic War on a country town like Cheltenham. There was no general compulsory military service. The Vestry was responsible for carrying out a ballot when men were required for the Militia, but those unlucky enough to be drawn could usually pay for substitutes if they wished. In 1811 the Cheltenham Vestry was fined £140 for not arranging a ballot for the three additional men required from the parish within the prescribed time, but they were able to make a successful protest to the Lord-Lieutenant of the County on the ground that they had not been given sufficient notice. It is tempting to assume that the Press Gang would not operate as far inland as Cheltenham. There is, however, at least one case which disproves this. The Bendall family, which has been established in the town for at least 150 years, has a record of one of its members who was captured locally and 'pressed' into service in the Navy.

There are some indications, however, that the war was not merely a background to the gay social life which continued throughout the period. As early as 1793 John Boles Watson devoted the profits of one night's performance at the Theatre Royal in York Passage to the purchase of 'comfortable necessaries for our troops in Flanders'. The financial panic of 1796 hit the town sufficiently to create difficulties for the local banks —each of which at this time issued its own notes. A number of leading residents put a notice in the *Gloucester Journal* to the effect that as 'the present existing alarm is not founded on any real cause' they would be willing to take banknotes for payment. The names include Thomas Baghott de la Bere, Henry Norwood, Thomas Hughes, and James Arkell.

A more definite reaction to the war was shown in the formation of a volunteer force of cavalry in 1795—later under the command of Captain Gray. This was followed three years later by a force of infantry commanded by Sir William Hicks. The terms of association of the latter[1] show the essentially parochial attitude which survived in the midst of a war with battle fronts extending over four continents:

We whose names are herewith subscribed, considering it expedient to form a Corps of Infantry to be trained in the use of Arms for the service of our Country in the Town of Cheltenham and its vicinity do agree to associate under the following Conditions and Regulations:

That we will provide ourselves severally with a uniform (hereafter to be approved by a Committee) and all necessary accoutrements and Arms, unless the same are found by the Government or by the aid of a subscription intended to be entered into towards lessening the expenses of individuals.

That we will at such place and hour as shall be hereafter determined upon meet and will apply ourselves diligently to learn the Exercise under the Instruction of proper officers, during two hours each time of meeting.

That we will be ready to serve on any occasion when the necessities of the Country may render it necessary *at any place within eight miles of Cheltenham.*

It is fair to add that the Cheltenham Cavalry Volunteers were expected 'at all times and in all places to support their King and Country', and that in nearby Winchcombe the Volunteers placed no limit on the area in which they were prepared to serve. A contemporary letter[2] refers to the raising of a subscription at the Theatre for uniforms, 'We had a brilliant house for clothing the Cheltenham Volunteers, when Miss de Camp acted in *Marriage Promise.*' The same correspondent writes in 1803 when Napoleon was collecting his forces across the Channel:

Sometimes I cannot help trembling at the possibility of the success of the invasion, and yet there seem to be many chances of its coming to nothing. . . . I trust Providence will still protect us and our good King. I find that they now have more Volunteers than they want, so I hope they will not take our only man servant who has entered himself in the Cheltenham Volunteers.

From time to time the Cavalry and the Infantry were drawn up together on Cleeve Hill and inspected by Colonel Probyn, after which they were 'liberally regaled at the venerable mansion at Southam' by Thomas Baghott de la Bere. In the later years of the war a few French prisoners were stationed in Cheltenham and were treated with a civilized humanity in marked contrast to some modern practices. Three French officers having given their promise not to move more than three miles away were accepted very much as other visitors in the social life of the town. One of these—General Lefèbre —had been taken prisoner in Spain and sent to England by Sir John Moore. He and his wife became very popular. Their names appear from time to time in the lists of guests at the 'elegant entertainments' described in the *Cheltenham Chronicle*. After a year of such pleasant captivity Lefèbre shocked his hosts by breaking his parole. Disguised as a German count he took his wife (dressed as a boy) to London and so escaped back to France to rejoin Napoleon's Army. After this episode, the remaining prisoners were transferred to Abergavenny.

More exalted French visitors were in Cheltenham at the same time. The exiled daughter of the guillotined King Louis XVI came twice with her husband, the Duc d'Angoulême, staying first at York Hotel in 1811 and later at Cambray Lodge (1813). On this last visit they were joined by two future French kings—Louis XVIII and Charles X—whose dynasty was restored by the Allies after the victory at Waterloo. Another displaced royalty who found his way to Cheltenham at this time was William Prince of Orange—later King of the Netherlands.

The period of social brilliance which developed so rapidly after the end of the war was already beginning. The Prince of Wales—not as yet Regent—came for a short visit in 1807, accompanied by his brother the Duke of Suffolk and his cousin the Duke of Gloucester. He drank the waters at the Royal Well Spa, went to the new theatre in Cambray, and was present at a ball in the Assembly Rooms. This was the first visit of the Duke of Gloucester; it was to be repeated annually for the next twenty years.

The Countess of Jersey—at one time the most influential of all the mistresses of the Prince of Wales—stayed in Cambray for some years; near by the Countess of Oxford stayed at Georgiana Cottage at the Cambray end of Bath Road. Albinia, Countess of Buckinghamshire—one of the most famous gamblers of her time—was at St. Julia's Cottage in Oxford Parade, and Lady Mary Lindsay at Lindsay Cottage which was later enlarged and known as Wolseley House. *Rus in urbe* was the fashion; the new-comers gave enormous parties; a hundred or more guests assembled at a time in these 'cottages' where they were entertained at 'elegant goûters' and 'déjeuners après minuit', with Pandean bands and *fantoccini* performances.

There were frequent balls and card parties at the Assembly Rooms. Mr. King had been appointed Master of Ceremonies on the death of Simon Moreau in 1806, but the fact that he retained the same office during the winter season in Bath, as mentioned by Jane Austen in *Northanger Abbey*, is evidence that Cheltenham was still at this time largely a summer resort. The balls and 'elegant fêtes' undoubtedly finished early. Browne's *Guide* (1804) tells us:

What a contrast does Cheltenham present to Bath, where you seldom meet any fashionable lady, in the streets, earlier than ten or eleven o'clock; but here Aurora no sooner peeps through the East than the fields adjoining the Wells begin to be covered with its fashionable visitants; and soon after six the walks are filled and the company seen thronging to the well with avidity, most of them with glasses in their hands, for the sake of being more speedily served, such is the general anxiety to imbibe the virtues of this celebrated spring.

Among those who came to Cheltenham at this time was Lord Byron. His first visit was in 1801, when as a schoolboy he had greatly enjoyed the view of the Malvern Hills, seen from the top of Bayshill. He came again in 1812 and stayed several months—part of which he spent with a group of intimate friends. He wrote at this time: 'We had a very pleasant set here at first, the Jerseys, Melbournes, Cowpers and Hollands, but all gone and the only persons I know are the Rawdons, Oxfords and some later acquaintances of less brilliant descent.'[3] Among the latter was very probably the Italian opera singer, with whom he found some consolation after the departure of Lady Oxford. In a mood of depression he wrote to Lord

Holland, 'I am disordered by the waters, and diluted to the throat with medicine for the stone by Dr. Boisragon.' His depression was probably increased by the refusal of Miss Milbanke—his future wife—to accept his proposal of marriage at this time. This proposal was almost certainly conveyed by Lady Melbourne (Miss Milbanke's aunt). She was deeply concerned about the affair between Byron and her daughter-in-law Caroline Lamb. Local gossip, however, has assigned the Cheltenham Assembly Rooms as the place of the proposal:

> Was it the Grecian maid or dark gazelle
> That taught the poet how to love so well?
> No, t'was the offspring of a British dame
> Whose pallid beauty fanned the rising flame.
> In Cheltenham's Rooms the accent of her tongue
> Belied the warbling of the fabled song.

On the other hand, Byron wrote that he was not concerned with local entertainment—'As for your rooms and your assemblies they are not dreamed of in our philosophy.'

Before coming to Cheltenham for this visit Byron had stayed for some time at Berkeley Castle with his friend Colonel Berkeley who was already beginning his long dominion over Cheltenham. Two of the main interests of the latter were hunting and the theatre. The Berkeley Hounds were already famous; and the new theatre in Cambray, with John Boles Watson as owner-manager, entered on its most brilliant period under the Berkeley patronage. Colonel Berkeley—and also his brother—took part in both amateur and professional performances at the theatre. He invited several actors, including the great Grimaldi, to stay at Berkeley Castle. Others were entertained in a less orthodox fashion at his residence, German Cottage (at the corner of North Street and the present St. Margaret's Road), which acquired at this time a somewhat unsavoury reputation. He is also credited with maintaining other houses in Cheltenham for his mistresses.

During these years three leading London actresses had close connexions both with the Cambray Theatre and the town. Sarah Siddons, whose performance in Cheltenham had been the occasion of her summons to the London stage by Garrick, returned many times to the town and acted in all three of its early theatres.

Mrs. Neville writes in 1793:

Mrs. Siddons was much admired here not only for her excellent performances for five nights but for the propriety and elegance of her behaviour. At the private houses where she was invited her daughters (unaffected well-behaved girls) accompanied her to the Balls and got genteel partners. She received forty guineas for each night except the last when she acted for the benefit of the performers. . . . Pit and boxes were 5/-d and even the 1/-d gallery was raised to 2/-d.

In 1803, when her health was undermined through grief at the death of her daughter Sally, she came to Cheltenham for a prolonged visit, staying at Birch Farm near the present Clarence Square. In a letter dated 15 May 1803 she wrote:

Our little cottage is some distance from the town, perfectly retired, surrounded by hills and fields and groves. The air of this place is peculiarly salubrious; I live out of doors as much as possible, sometimes reading under the haystack in the farmyard, sometimes rambling in the fields and sometimes musing in the orchard, all of which I do without spectators, no observers near to say I am mad, foolish or melancholy; thus I keep 'the noiseless tenour of my way', and you will be glad to hear this mode of life is so well suited to my taste. Rising at six and going to bed at ten has brought me to my comfortable sleep once more; the bitterness and anguish of selfish grief begin to subside, and the tender recollections of excellence and virtues gone to the blessed place of their eternal regard are now sweet, though sad companions of my lonely walks. . . .[4]

She recovered sufficiently to return to the stage and to play Lady Macbeth with her brother Charles Kemble in the Cambray Theatre in 1807.

Dorothy Jordan, perhaps the greatest comedy actress of her time, had made her first appearance in the Cheltenham theatre during the visit of George III. Since then she had returned several times and on one occasion was principal guest at a large party given for her by the Countess of Buckinghamshire at St. Julia's Cottage. This invitation was no doubt partly due to her charm as an actress and her pleasant personality, but she was also famous at this time as the mistress of the Duke of Clarence.

In the intervals when she was not on the stage she lived with him and with their ten children at Bushey Lodge. It was while she was acting in the Cambray Theatre in 1811—according to a vividly written passage in Oxberry's *Dramatic Diary*—that she received the letter from the Duke which announced his intention of ending their twenty years' union. She did not appear again on the Cheltenham stage.

Harriot Mellon, although never such a great artist as Sarah Siddons or Dorothy Jordan, was for many years a popular actress, both at Drury Lane and in the provinces. She came frequently to Cheltenham to visit her mother and her step-father Thomas Entwhistle, and during her visits she played at the Cambray Theatre. Mr. Entwhistle had settled in Chelten-ham after losing his position with the Drury Lane orchestra. He opened a small music shop at the lower end of the High Street,[5] combining this with the office of postmaster which Harriot had begged for him from Colonel McMahon in 1805. At the same time Mrs. Entwhistle worked hard to raise sub-scriptions for her daughter's 'benefits' at the theatre.

One of the visitors to the town during these years was the elderly banker Thomas Coutts, who found great solace during the illness of his wife in the peaceful shade of the Long Walk. Here one day he met the young Harriot Mellon, and ten years later he married her. After a few years of great happiness he died, leaving her the bank and most of his money. She, in turn, bequeathed most of this great fortune to Thomas Coutts's granddaughter Angela Burdett Coutts, although at the time of her death she had for several years been happily married to the Duke of St. Albans. She returned from time to time to stay in Cheltenham when she was the Duchess of St. Albans.

Although no complete list of visitors exists for these years, much information about the residents is available. Shenton's *Directory* of the town in 1800 names all householders in the order of their houses on both sides of the High Street and the lanes leading from it, beginning with the house of William Hicks, Esq., on or near the site of the present Belle Vue Hotel, after which came the Old Swan Inn and Freeman's Baths, and then the residence of Simon Moreau, Master of Ceremonies. The 'elegant house' of John de la Bere was now occupied by

Dr. Newell; Dr. Minster lived near the Rose and Crown Passage; and the surgeon Mr. Hooper in the Great House (then approached from St. George's Place). At this time a path—the fore-runner of Clarence Street—led from here to the Baptist Meeting-house (now Bethel Chapel), near which lived the solicitor Walter Jessop, while Theodore Gwinnett, who was to play a most active part in the legal affairs of the town, had his practice in North Street, in a house which was the fore-runner of Albion Villa. A third solicitor, Thomas Pruen, lived near by in the High Street; and a fourth, Robert Hughes—between the 'Plough' and the Assembly Rooms which were built by his father. On the other side of these was the farm-house (the old Parsonage) and the Cambray field rented by Thomas Byrch from the Earl of Essex. The last-mentioned house on the south side of the Street is that of William Barrett—the miller of Cambray. The three hundred householders whose names—and in most cases occupations—are listed by Shenton include five bakers and five pastry-cooks; nine shoemakers, nine drapers, six tailors, two hatters, three mantua and dress-makers, two weavers and one stocking weaver; ten gardeners, and two builders. As in all small country communities, some of the inhabitants followed more than one occupation, as Mr. Fricker, hairdresser, perfumer, and dealer in coals, and his neighbour who was a fruiterer and toyman. It is most significant that, according to Shenton, a hundred and fifty of these house holders let lodgings and that there were forty-two laundresses in the town.

Among the residents who were undoubtedly well-known figures in the town were the Reverend H. B. Fowler, the master of the Grammar School (who was most probably more concerned with boarders than with those scholars admitted under the conditions of Richard Pate's endowment), and John Garn, the master of the school held in the little room over the north porch in the parish church. This had been founded soon after 1683 with a bequest from George Townshend 'for teaching poor children to read and write', and re-established in 1713 by public subscription and money from Lady Capel. It bore the unlovely name of the Charity School and its thirty boys wore the clothes provided for them—long coats, yellow stockings, and yellow caps and bands. In an account written by a former pupil there is a lively description of school life at this time.[6]

In my day our playground was the church-yard, which was then minus the iron railings. On its pathways we played marbles, tops, leap-frog, etc., according to season. Hide and Seek and Fox and Hounds were favourite games, for the tomb stones furnished us with splendid hiding places. Many races have I seen run round the Churchyard.

We had a kind of freemasonry between us, and we held the Churchyard as our own, never letting the Grammar School boys invade our territory. If they attempted it they were soon driven out by our fellows or the Beadle. Old Tom, the beadle, is no friend of ours, nor does he recognise us as such, so the feeling is mutual. He is dressed the same as other beadles were: gold lace round his hat, collar and sleeves, with a stoutish cane in his hand. We were only thirty of us, which was all the school would hold, and quite sufficient for our Master to control.

The Master—Mr. John Garn—was a man about 70 years old, of a stoutish frame and middle stature, who suffered at times from rheumatism. . . . He usually wore a dark green cut-away coat with gilt buttons, long waisted vest to match. As to his disposition it was of a mild character, considering the 'rebels' of boys he had to train. This morning he can by no means get up the steps into the school . . . so we had to help him, as we had often done. . . . One boy was in front and one behind: the one in front would walk backwards, and catching hold of the Master's hands, would pull with all his might, their hands locked in each others in a grip of iron. The boy behind, a big strong one, with his head tucked between Master's legs, would with the assistance of another standing behind to steady the operation, lift him step by step up the tortuous staircase.

We reached the schoolroom doorway. Immediately behind this was the wall dividing the school from the church, affixed to which were the stocks, which would hold four boys, two of whom, if they were of the more rebellious type, could have the present of a chain round each ankle. There were likewise three other leg-chains in the School with their staples driven fast into the wall, and once you were padlocked escape was impossible. . . . In one corner of the room was a Moocher's Log . . . a large log of oak, weighing some 14 lb. or 20 lb. which would be impossible for anyone to drag away with him . . . when once he has the chain, which is driven into the cumbrous mass, fastened to his leg. To this tether the culprit remains 'till afternoon school, whence he is removed to the stocks, where he receives strokes with the birch rod, according to his character or according to the number of times he had 'mooched'. For the first offence he would come off lightly; that is he perhaps would only receive one stroke from six boys and six from the Master. During this infliction the Master would stand by and see that justice was properly given, or if not, you would feel the lash of his short whip. This birch rod, the twigs of which were obtained during the time of lopping the lime trees in the Church yard, was much dreaded by all wrongdoers.

One of the most famous residents during these years was Dr. Jenner—famous as the pioneer of vaccination and as a naturalist. Most of his early experiments in vaccination had been carried out at Berkeley and for many years he spent much time in London. His residence in Cheltenham—first at Alpha House in the present St. George's Road, and later at 8 St. George's Place—was usually for part of the year only. It covered almost exactly the period of the war, since he began practising as a doctor in the town in 1795 and returned permanently to Berkeley after the death of his wife in 1815. Like Byron, he was not much interested in balls and assembly rooms. 'Cheltenham is much improved since you last saw it', he wrote to a friend in 1804. 'It is too gay for me. I still like my rustic haunt old Berkeley best.' He preferred the company of a few friends to the great parties. Among these friends was Charles James Fox who came to the town several times in the years immediately before he became Prime Minister. By this time he was no longer a great gambler or an eccentric in dress, but a responsible statesman and a sick man, enjoying the pleasures of rereading the *Odyssey* and making little expeditions with his wife and Dr. Jenner to drink tea in the Grotto at Prestbury.

Dr. Jenner took a considerable interest in the affairs of the town. He was one of the Commissioners appointed under the 1806 Act. In his last years of residence in St. George's Place he was the moving spirit in the foundation of a literary society which was to last for many years after his death. Several other doctors took part in this—among them the fashionable Dr. Boisragon who lived in the Royal Crescent.

Opposition in the town to the principle of vaccination is

reflected in the correspondence published in the contemporary issues of the *Cheltenham Chronicle*. One of Dr. Jenner's own letters,[7] written to a friend in 1812, gives a vivid picture of his work among the poor:

I permitted persons of all descriptions, not only those of the town but from the districts round, to come to me weekly. The small-pox was at their heels, and this drove them to my house in immense numbers. I was literally mobbed, driven into a corner and made a prisoner, necessitated to bow to their will. 'The man shall do me next.' 'No, he shan't—he shall do me' was the language I was often obliged to hear and submit to. For many successive inoculating days the numbers that assembled were on the average about 300. . . . It would be absurd to suppose that out of this vast body all could go through the disease with that correctness which protects them from smallpox infection; in numerous instances, indeed, they did not afford me an opportunity of judging of their security by ever returning to shew me their arms and this teasing occurrence not infrequently happened among the common people of Chelten-ham whom I vaccinated on a reduced scale.

Dr. Jenner's description of the poorer people in Chelten-ham brings us to the question of how they were affected by the war. From a contemporary account (1809) written by Dr. Jameson—the founder of the first Sherborne Well—they appear to have been much better off than their fellows in other parts of the county:

With respect to Cheltenham, it consists chiefly of one open and clear street and the lower classes have separate tenements, so that there is no accumulation of carbonic acid in the air or poor respira-tion, putridity or smoke in consequence of dense population. The people in general are robust through habits of exercise in the open air, for there are no manufactures and few sedentary employments in or about Cheltenham. The inhabitants of the town are chiefly farmers, gardeners, builders, labourers and shopkeepers. The lower classes of the people have little anxious care for the maintenance of their families and exhibit great indifference about employment. They can live a week on four or five days' pay and are therefore slow and leave off outdoor work when it rains. Their diet is wholesome and they are rather temperate. The vegetables, bacon and mutton are uncommonly rich and plentiful. The people eat moderately of animal food and drink freely of home-made ale and cyder but little of spirituous liquor and are seldom intoxicated. They have regular hours of sleep and rise early in the morning. The farmers and most of the cottagers in the vicinity are cleanly in their houses and persons, and the same may be said generally of the inhabitants of the town.

On the other hand, prices rose steeply before the end of the war, and there are indications that the happy state of affairs described by Jameson—if indeed it existed—did not last long. Conditions in the county caused agricultural labourers and underpaid weavers to look for homes and work elsewhere, and despite the settlement orders enforced under the Poor Law system many poor people managed to get into Cheltenham, and being at first without means or work, aggravated a situation already rendered serious by rising prices and unemployment.

In 1811 the Commissioners appointed a committee authorized 'to engage a proper person at a salary not exceeding £20 per annum to make returns of prices of flour and grain twice a month to the Magistrates of Cheltenham for the purpose of fixing the price of bread in the town . . . according to the Statute, and that the same salary be paid out of the Market Tolls'. Unfortunately the magistrates did not immediately consent to this plan, nor to a similar one put forward by the Vestry.

The *Cheltenham Chronicle* reports a meeting held in the autumn of 1813 where 'it was resolved that a plan of supplying a stock of potatoes for the winter to serve out to the inhabitants at reduced prices—to be put into effect immediately, as it appears from the increasing price of provisions that the Parish Poor will be extremely numerous this winter, and there is a disposition in many speculators to monopolise this valuable article of life and sell at an advanced price'.

In the next two years the position grew worse. Public meetings were held in the spring of 1815 to discuss ways of reducing the price of bread, meat, coal, and the carriage of goods. However, apart from the appointment of an Ale Commission, nothing definite was done.

Private charity helped a number of people. The *Cheltenham Chronicle* reports in January 1816 that 'through Mr. Entwhistle upwards of 500 families were, *as is the usual custom*, relieved by the bounty of Mrs. Coutts . . .'.

In addition to private charity, the Overseers of the Poor found it necessary as early as 1809 to rent a new Poor House. Griffiths writes in the first edition of his *Cheltenham Guide*, 'at Easter 1812 it appeared that notwithstanding the Poor Rates had been unusually high, the Poor were murmuring for want of proper relief'.

From the Vestry records we learn that in this year the parish adopted Gilbert's Act of 1782, by which the poor could receive relief without entering the Workhouse, and according to Griffiths the experiment was successful. 'The poor are now judiciously employed and there is a considerable alleviation in the parish rates.'

High prices and shortages must have caused great hardship, but there is little evidence that this was increased in Cheltenham by lack of sympathy or harsh treatment. On the contrary, there were genuine attempts on the part of the Commissioners and the Vestry to mitigate such hardship, and many of the visitors, from the Royal Dukes to the congregation at the parish church, joined with the residents in the dispensation of private charity. In this way Sunday schools had been founded as early as 1787 'through the liberality of visitors seconded by the benevolent spirit of the inhabitants, and about a hundred of the most neglected children of the poor admitted'. The children were then given 'a plentiful dinner' following a sermon in the church, and it was 'a scene for an epicure in philanthropy to behold'. The School of Industry for poor girls was founded under the patronage of Queen Charlotte.

The Dispensary, which developed later into the Hospital, was initiated at a Vestry meeting in 1813, but it was actually organized by a committee of doctors with the financial support of residents and visitors following a resolution 'That from the rapidly increasing population of this town and the consequent increase in the number of the necessitous sick, the establishment of an Institution for administering Advice and Medicine gratis and for promoting vaccination would be attended with extensive advantage' (*Cheltenham Chronicle*).

While it is unlikely that the recipients of such charities felt

quite the same glow of satisfaction as these 'epicures in philanthropy', they at least escaped the harshness of attitude shown
by some contemporary authorities in the county. The end of
the war, however, brought no relief in the matter of food prices
or unemployment. In 1816 the *Cheltenham Chronicle* reports
that the unemployed were set to work on the highways and on
cleansing the pavements and that 'a soup shop was opened
at Mr. Fletcher's premises opposite to the Colonnade'. The
Reverend Charles Jervis and Mr. Newell the surgeon were
appointed to superintend the distribution. They 'served upwards of 500 quarts of soup and as many pieces of bread at
1*d* a time and it was excellent'.

The distresses of the post-war years were, however, far less
acute in Cheltenham than in many parts of the country, partly
because they were to be contemporary with the enormous
increase in the number of wealthy visitors and because of the
subsequent development in building which was to take place
during the greatest period of architectural achievement in the
history of the town.

PLATE I

William Norwood, Lord of the Manor of Cheltenham, 1588–1616

PLATE 2

Henry Skillicorne, founder of Cheltenham Spa

John Dutton of Sherborne, Lord of the Manor of Cheltenham in 1628 [*By courtesy of Lord Sherborne*]

PLATE 3

Thomas Hughes, built the first Assembly Rooms in 1783

PLATE 4

Joseph Pitt

PLATE 5

The Parish Church

PLATE 6

View of Cheltenham in 1748, showing Church, Great House, Long Walk, and Henry
Skillicorne's first Room

High Street, Cheltenham, in 1804, showing Market-house built by the Commissioners
in 1786

PLATE 7

Royal Well, showing Long Rooms built by Henry and William Skillicorne
(by Hulley, 1813)

Richard Pate's Grammar School, taken down 1888

PLATE 8

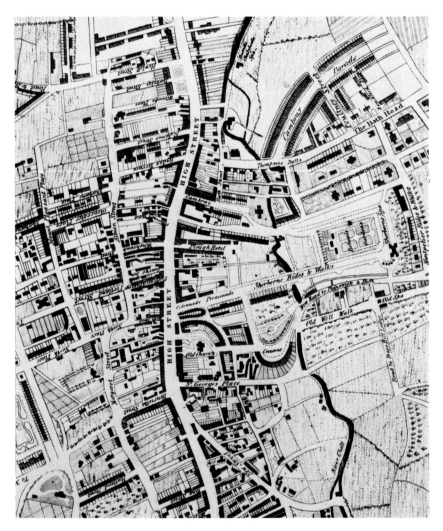

Griffith's Map 1826

PLATE 9

First Assembly Rooms, design usually attributed to Henry Holland

George III and Queen Charlotte driving in the grounds of Bayshill House

PLATE 10

Montpellier Rotunda

First Montpellier Spa built in 1809 by Henry Thompson

PLATE II

Entrance to Montpellier Walk [*Country Life*]

The Promenade, Cheltenham

PLATE 12

Long Walk—early nineteenth century

Old Wells Music Hall, 1848

PLATE 13

The Queen's Hotel [*Trust Houses Ltd.*]

Municipal Offices and statue of Dr. Wilson

PLATE 14

Pittville Pump Room

Pittville Pump Room (interior)

PLATE 15

Porch, North Place

Late Regency House in Pittville Circus,
about 1830

PLATE 16

Cheltenham College—from an early lithograph

Cheltenham Ladies' College in the early 1900's

XIV

THE DEVELOPMENT OF REGENCY
CHELTENHAM
1815–1840

THE twenty-five years after the end of the French wars were from an architectural point of view the most important in the history of Cheltenham, and an examination of Merrett's map of 1834 shows that almost all that is best in the town today was either planned or built during those years. The most distinguished description of this work is given in the 1944 Report on Cheltenham by the Georgian Group, where the town is described as 'unrivalled as a large-scale example of town planning and domestic architecture at its best', and therefore 'a national possession, and its residents the holders of a great responsibility'.

The Report emphasizes that the architectural harmony achieved in these two decades was due to four main factors—a unity of background, of purpose, of style, and of material. Firstly, the builders had a common purpose: they wished to attract wealthy and cultured visitors and residents to the town, and realized that their arrangements must therefore be in the best contemporary taste. This purpose had existed from early days at the Spa, when the Long Walk was planned as an amenity to attract more visitors to drink the waters at the Old Well. With the same object in view, each new spa had its tree-lined walks as an approach and its gardens as a background. In this way Sherborne Walk was laid out as an approach to Sherborne Spa and later developed into the Promenade; around Henry Thompson's Montpellier Spa were the gardens and walks which have become Montpellier Terrace and Parade. The two chief speculative landowners at this time were aiming not merely at building individual houses, but at laying out the new areas of the town in such a way that each would be an attractive whole. Thus the diversity of well-proportioned terraces, graceful crescents, and tree-lined squares in Montpellier and Pittville was combined with a unity of style which is generally known as Regency. This style was uninfluenced by earlier local tendencies. The old houses surviving from the last two centuries usually excited contempt among the new generation, and no necessity was felt to make the new designs fit in with any existing style. Land, though rising in price, was still cheap enough to allow the spacious surroundings of gardens and trees—so beautiful as a green background for the white stucco and graceful ironwork of Regency houses. The use of the same materials emphasized the unity of the style. The new houses were built of brick faced with stone, plaster, or stucco, and this use of materials added to the general harmony. Although Cheltenham is in one sense a Cotswold town, and Cotswold houses and cottages have achieved an unsurpassable beauty in stone buildings, Cheltenham itself has always been mainly a town of brick because so much suitable clay has been available. Only three stone buildings (excluding the church) are known to have been in existence in the town in the eighteenth century: the Grammar School, the Almshouses, and the Market-house. Thus Regency builders continued to use the traditional material.

There is a strong local belief (unfortunately unsupported by any evidence) that Cheltenham brick-fields date back to the reign of King Alfred. There is, however, considerable evidence that it was common practice for the bricks to be made from clay dug on the site of the building for which they were required. We have already seen that the first Bayshill House was built in this way for the Earl of Fauconberg. An advertisement of houses to be built in the Colonnade (1791) runs, 'The proprietors of the land will furnish bricks for the whole of the buildings, made on the spot at 13/- a thousand.' Another advertisement, for the sale of the Plough Inn in 1795, gives a similar indication: '. . . the old Plough Inn Tavern, the frontage of 105 feet, the yard allowed to be the most spacious of any town . . . having stabling for 100 horses; a number of coach houses over which dove houses, straw houses and granaries to hold 5,000 bushels; at one end a Kitchen Garden of half an acre bordering on a piece of rich meadow land . . . where any quantity of bricks can be made.' St. Margaret's Terrace was later built from clay taken from the nearby property of Miss Monson—St. Margaret's Hall.

The new Cheltenham was thus laid out, before the passing of any town-planning Acts, by speculative builders and landowners concerned to make their building a profitable investment. It was fortunate that they built at a time when the level of contemporary taste on which their success depended was high.

Appreciation of the principles of the new plans was not confined to the builders and architects. Contemporary guidebooks and accounts of the town show considerable understanding of what was being done and a great pride in the achievements. Fosbroke wrote in 1826: 'The forms in which Cheltenham is laid out are Streets, detached Villas, Crescents and Parallelograms. The new Walks have all the same character of Malls and Promenades divided by Trees. Streets are capitally ranged and made up . . . like scenes for the Theatre. The general plan is width in the road-ways, decorating houses with verandahs, green lawns and shrubs before and behind. . . .'

S. Y. Griffiths wrote in the same year with even more feeling:

Cheltenham is not now the mere Summer Retreat . . . it has now, with its 20,000 inhabitants, assumed the aspect of a city. . . . The contrast between the former Cheltenham—secured in its lonely loveliness by almost impassable roads—and Cheltenham today—the celebrated, the fashionable, the gay—as its galaxy of white buildings presents itself to the visitor in its everyday array—is miraculous. The bold speculation (which disdaining the usual narrow limits of a town house site at a paltry price per foot) laid out its terraces, its pleasure grounds, its attached enclosures, its plantations, walks and approaches worthy the environs of a palace—has been adopted by the liberal purchaser, and has secured a freedom and magnificence of appearance that an ancient and venerable city can never possess, and that few modern ones will rival.

This first period of architectural achievement was accompanied by a spectacular rise in population. Goding (p. 278), quoting from the census of 1801, gives the figure for the hundred in that year as 3,076, which shows little increase on that given by Sir Robert Atkyns in 1713. Between 1801 and 1826, when Griffiths and Fosbroke wrote their accounts of the town, the figure had reached 20,000. At no time in the nineteenth century was the rate of increase so rapid.

The three landowners mainly responsible for the planning of the new Cheltenham were Samuel Harward, Pearson Thompson, and Joseph Pitt, on whose properties the Promenade and the estates of Lansdown, Montpellier and Pittville were subsequently laid out.

In 1818 the Harward brothers built the Sherborne—later called the Imperial Spa—on the site of which the Queen's Hotel now stands. They laid out the long drive to the Spa, which later became the main Cheltenham Promenade, and developed the gardens which have given their name to Imperial Square. An almost contemporary guide-book[1] described their enterprise:

> The entrance to this new Elysium, which in the course of a few years has been converted from an uncultivated marsh into the present delightful scenery, is from the Colonnade in the High Street, which at once commands an agreeable view of the Spa Room, standing on a gentle eminence at the extremity of the carriage road, nearly half a mile in length, with a spacious gravelled walk on each side . . . bounded by a row of trees and shrubs, mountain ash, beech, larch, pine and sycamore. . . . On the left of the road, near the Pump Room an extensive fruit and flower garden is laid out . . . as a favourite retreat of the subscribers to the Spa, who will enjoy the exclusive privilege of walking in it.

From the surviving prints, the small Pump Room in its woodland setting seems to have been the most charming of all those built in Cheltenham during these years. Its portico was supported by six Ionic columns terminating at each end in 'a light rusticated loggia'. It had a small dome set on a pedestal and supporting the inevitable figure of Hygeia. In the interior, eight Ionic columns on each side 'produced a boldness of architectural beauty rarely witnessed'. The architect, G. A. Underwood, had based the design on that of the temple on the Ilissus, a drawing of which (in Stuart and Revett's *Antiquities of Athens*) must have been well known to most Cheltenham architects. Bernard Blackmantle described it:[2]

And then lower down, in fine Leckhampton stone,
We've the fane of *Ilissus* in miniature shown;
And then crown'd with Hygeia—a bouncer, my lud!
And as plump, ay, as any princess of the blood,
Carved in stone, but a good imitation of wood.

Within a few years building had begun on the Harwards' land on the west side of the future Promenade. In Griffith's map of 1826, the blocks of buildings running from the Colonnade to the present Regal Cinema are shown as completed. They include the group of houses which form the present Municipal Offices and the Imperial Hotel built by a portrait-painter named Millet, which is now the General Post Office. Little credit has been given to the Harwards and to Thomas Henney, by whose enterprise the former swamp became the present Promenade. Even Griffiths does not mention their names although he writes: 'Amongst the many enterprising friends of the town by whom so numerous and beneficial improvements have been designed and carried into effect, to none is Cheltenham more indebted than to the projectors and proprietors of the Sherborne Spa.' The reason for this is probably the fact that (according to a deed of 1818 quoted by the late Mr. C. A. Probert) this scheme required 'great trouble, attention and expense', and therefore John and Thomas Harward 'living at a great distance from Cheltenham and being unacquainted with the management of such matters and relying on the diligence, activity and integrity of the said J. Cossens as well as on his knowledge, experience and supervision' made a contract with the latter to plan and develop the Imperial Spa and its grounds. John Cossens was at one time Postmaster in Cheltenham, and it was while he held this office that he made the well-known and important map of 1820 and dedicated it to the Postmaster-General.

The Lansdown and Montpellier estates were developed by Pearson Thompson on the land bought by his father Henry Thompson, who had himself laid out the Montpellier drives and built the first Montpellier Pump Room (1809). When he replaced this by the Long Room in 1817, he most probably employed Underwood as architect. Pearson Thompson, however, called in the distinguished London architect John Papworth, who had already carried out works in that city, one of which was St. Bride's Avenue on Fleet Street. He was also known for his treatises on a variety of subjects which included architecture and landscape gardening, and later for his work in Württemburg and the Crimea, and his designs for the Shah of Persia and the ruler of Egypt. His best-known work in Cheltenham is the Rotunda, the circular domed hall which was added to Henry Thompson's Long Room at the Montpellier Spa. At the time of its erection in 1825 there were no tall buildings in the rear to blur its outline. Its setting against a background of trees with the hills in the distance must have been very beautiful, though not as magnificent in conception as the long vista of the Pittville design. The interior, with its sixteen Corinthian pilasters, its domed ceiling and original fittings designed by Papworth himself, was used as a ballroom which was graced by the presence of the Duke of Wellington and many of his most distinguished contemporaries.

Amidst his many commitments Papworth could not have spent much time in Cheltenham, but it is generally accepted that he was responsible for the actual layout of the Montpellier and Lansdown area—one of the greater glories of the Cheltenham scene. How many of the houses were built to his design it is impossible to say. It is known that Lansdown Place was begun by Pearson Thompson in 1826 and finished some ten years later by the Jearrad brothers.[3] It is very probable that Lansdown Crescent and Terrace were finished by the same architects, since on the 1834 map all these are shown as incomplete. The present Duke of Wellington wrote in 1926, 'Lansdown Terrace just misses being one of the most interesting and successful designs for a row of houses ever made.'[4]

In the early eighteen-twenties Joseph Pitt began to develop the land on the north of the town which he had received under the Inclosure Act. The architect mainly associated with this development was the resident John Forbes whose best-known works are the Pittville Pump Room and St. Paul's Church. The plan of the new Pittville estate is published in the 1826 edition of Griffith's *Historical Description of Cheltenham*. It shows two central gardens, on each side of which was a road with terraces, varied with individual villas; two squares which were later named after the dukes of Clarence and Wellington;

and a noble crescent. Beyond this was a third garden—with artificial lakes—sloping upwards to the eminence on which the Pump Room was erected as the culmination of the vista in a superb example of landscape gardening. John Forbes's magnificent Pump Room is the largest as well as the most beautiful of all the Spa buildings. Though inspired by the famous Greek temple on the Ilissus, much of its design is original in conception. The dome itself, smaller than that of the Rotunda, is placed on a two-storeyed building which gives it greater height, and the lofty hall from which the Pump Room itself leads is adorned with fluted Ionic pillars. It is generally regarded as the finest surviving Regency building in Cheltenham. On the other hand, it has been severely criticized by the distinguished architect Sir Hugh Casson who calls it a 'stilted high shouldered and rather graceless building'. He also suggests that Forbes was neither skilful nor imaginative enough to have planned the layout of the Pittville estate and that Papworth must have been responsible for this.[5]

The foundation-stone of the Pump Room was laid in 1825, with full Masonic honours, but the national financial crisis of that year affected both Pitt and the prospective purchasers of houses on the estate so that the whole project was held up for some years. It was not until 1830 that the Pump Room was completed, by which time the fashion of drinking English Spa waters was beginning to wane, and the distance from the town was proving a handicap rather than an advantage as Pitt had originally envisaged. On the actual Pump Room he must have lost heavily. He continued with the development of the estate but was unable to complete the original design.

There is considerable evidence that the Pittville proprietors hoped and perhaps expected that an entirely independent area would grow up which would rival Cheltenham, and Griffith, writing in 1826, refers to 'the new town of Pittville'. Henry Davies writes eight years later about the early development of Pittville Spa, 'the first stone of this noble edifice was laid with great parade and ceremony by J. Pitt Esq. the proprietor . . . in 1825. At this time everything promised fair for its becoming, as was indeed intended, *the nucleus of a second town, rivalling its parent Cheltenham both in extent and importance.*' As late as

1839, when the Town Commissioners were trying to obtain an Act of Parliament to extend their powers, Joseph Pitt and the owners of houses on his estate made it plain that they regarded Pittville as outside the town, and so were mainly responsible for the defeat of the Bill.

Two other estates were planned during the period but not completed until later. As early as 1833 the Park—an area of 100 acres—was laid out by its owner Thomas Billings as an oval tree-lined carriage-drive enclosing a central park. Four years later a joint-stock company was formed to establish Zoological Gardens in this park, but the venture was a financial failure. The property was then bought by the Gloucestershire builder and architect S. W. Daukes who converted the gardens into a pleasure park, with flower-beds laid out round the central lake and grounds for cricket and archery. The houses on the estate are shown in outline on Merrett's map of 1834, but not on a contemporary map published by Henry Davies. They appear to have been completed by 1838, according to the map published by Griffith in that year.

The Bayshill estate was developed at a still later date. In 1837 the Skillicorne family sold the land to a company of which H. Norwood Trye, Captain Younghusband, and Captain Newall were directors.[6] The earliest map reference occurs in 1843. Henry Davies, writing in that year, describes it as 'until lately, occupied as pasture and orchard . . . but already two handsome rows of houses, called Royal Well and Bayshill Terrace, have now been erected, as also a number of detached villas . . . several of which are occupied by resident families of affluence and station, and others are in an unfinished state'. The magnificent villas which make Bayshill the finest road in Cheltenham have been attributed to the design of Papworth. According to evidence given by a witness in the Inquiry instituted by the Board of Health in 1848, the Bayshill Company had become bankrupt by that time, and it seems likely that the Trye family lost heavily in this venture.

The development of the older part of the town can very easily be traced from contemporary maps. The Post Office map of 1820 shows considerable building in the area of the Upper High Street—Berkeley Place, Oxford Parade, Priory Buildings; further down there are houses in the newly made North Place and Portland Street. On the south side Cambray has been entirely developed. Suffolk House has replaced the Gallipot Farm; Suffolk Square has been planned but not completed; along the Montpellier Walks houses have already been built.

On the Bath Road the foundations of Thirlestaine House are shown as already laid. The design for the mansion which was to become the most magnificent residence in Cheltenham was taken in part from the same temple on the Ilissus which inspired Underwood and Forbes. It was built by J. D. Scott—a new resident who was nominated a Town Commissioner on the grounds of his great wealth, but he rarely attended meetings. Estimates of the cost of the house vary between £20,000 and £80,000, and it was unfinished at the time of its owner's death in 1831. It was then purchased by Lord Northwick who added a wing on each side of the building for the purpose of housing his pictures—a valuable collection of paintings by Holbein, Titian, Georgione, Poussin, and many other famous artists. It was expected that he would leave them to the town, but unfortunately he died intestate. The next occupant was Sir Thomas Phillipps. He in turn used it to store the manuscripts and books which it was his main passion in life to collect. Finally, in 1949, it was acquired by its immediate neighbour, Cheltenham College.

On the same map appear Lake House—now College House and the residence of the headmaster of the college—and on the main Bath Road most of the villas on the western side. On the north side of the town the Elms, built for Admiral Sir Roger Tristram Ricketts, and Woodbine Cottage (renamed North Lodge when it became the residence of Lord Dunalley) are marked as already completed.

Several books containing good contemporary maps were published in 1826. The best known and most useful, despite its inaccuracies, was by S. Y. Griffith. In his map the houses on the western side of the Promenade, St. Margaret's Terrace, and Oriel Terrace are marked, but Imperial Square has not as yet been developed. It is shown as complete in Merrett's map of 1834, on which the development of Lansdown, the Park, and Pittville can be seen, but not Bayshill.

It was not only in domestic architecture that these twenty years were significant; almost all the finest buildings of nineteenth-century Cheltenham were completed during the same period. The spas have already been mentioned; the new Assembly Rooms were opened in 1816, the new Market and the Masonic Hall in Portland Street in 1823, and four of the numerous churches which were to be built in the first half of the century were completed—Holy Trinity (1823), St. John's (1829), St. James's (1829) and St. Paul's (1831). The Literary and Philosophical Institute—built in the Promenade in 1833—was designed by R. W. Jearrad. Its setting did not show its noble proportions to advantage, and it was pulled down later to make way for shops.

There is a certain ruthlessness in the way in which buildings were demolished at this time. The Lower Assembly Rooms—built in 1784 for Thomas Hughes—appear from existing prints to have been spacious and beautiful. By the end of the war they were pulled down as inadequate and the new Assembly Rooms[7] were built for J. D. Kelley in 1816. The exterior was austere and undistinguished. The famous ballroom, however, was magnificent. It was opened with a ball at which the Duke of Wellington was the guest of honour. These rooms were to remain for many years the centre of social life in the town, until they, in their turn, were taken down and replaced by the present Lloyds Bank.

The size and cost of the new Masonic Hall give some indication of the number of wealthy masons connected with Cheltenham at this time. There is evidence that the moving spirit in this project was Robert Hughes—the son of Thomas Hughes and the builder of Rodney Lodge.[8] The new hall in Portland Street was built by Underwood—himself a mason—and was said to be modelled on a Roman mausoleum.

The faith in the future of the town which is manifest in contemporary local publications led to a demand for a larger Market-house. This—the fourth within 100 years—was built opposite the existing market by Lord Sherborne, to whom as lord of the manor market tolls were due. Griffith describes it:

The building, which is 84 feet in length and 42 feet in breadth, stands in the centre of a spacious square; the principal access to which is *through the Arcade*, containing on the right side of the covered flagway (an uncovered space being on the left for the market people, basket women, porters etc.) a neat and very elegant range of shops. Three portions of the square are appropriated to butchers shops, constructed on a very convenient and airy plan. In the interior, poultry and eggs are sold; and the ground in the rear is occupied by the stalls of greengrocers etc. This arrangement has given the highest satisfaction to all parties, concentrating the sale of all the necessaries of life, and removing from one of the principal promenades of this fashionable town the great inconvenience of a public market. (1826.)

The architectural style of the entrance to this arcade (which is now Bennington Street) was new among Cheltenham designs. Its three arches[9] were Gothic, but the whole effect was oriental. The High Street was still in 1822 the principal promenade for visitors to the town. The Assembly Rooms and the adjoining Williams's Library, Bettison's Library, the Regent Gardens, and the shops made the Street the main centre. The new Market-house may have been built in the design described partly to maintain the attraction of the street; at the same time it should not be forgotten that in the midst of the enormous new industry of catering for visitors the old functions of the market town still continued.

One final aspect of large-scale building remains to be described. In the erection of new churches Cheltenham was following a national trend. For this the Evangelical revival was to a certain extent responsible, while in Lord Liverpool's Cabinet it was probably felt that the revolutionary spirit arising from the appalling depression following the war might be countered if the poor could be led to find consolation in religion. Government grants were therefore available for this purpose after 1825.

It was obvious, too, that the one parish church of St. Mary's was completely inadequate for the great increase in population in Cheltenham. The first of the new places of worship was erected in North Place at the expense of Robert Capper, J.P., of Marle Hill, for the use of the congregation of Lady Huntingdon's Connexion. Its windows foreshadowed the Gothic design which was used, not very happily, by the architect G. A. Underwood for the first new Anglican church of Holy Trinity in the same area. A large part of the cost of the latter was met by Lord Sherborne. On the new Montpellier estate the Gothic church of St. James was designed and built in the perpendicular style by John Papworth and Edward Jenkins. St. John's church, built for the inhabitants of the new houses in and around the upper High Street, was classical in design. Although it was the work of Papworth, it was later pulled down and the present Gothic building erected. The most imposing of all these churches was St. Paul's—designed by John Forbes and also in classical style.

The three former churches had been paid for by the subscriptions of the new congregation in return for guaranteed sittings. At Holy Trinity and St. James's visitors and all those who had not subscribed towards the buildings were expected to pay 1s. for a seat—for which tickets were issued at the door. In contrast St. Paul's—built at the instigation of Francis Close —was known as the Free Church 'where the poor could be certain of finding a welcome'. It was paid for by voluntary subscriptions and a grant of £3,000 from the Government. The situation is well summed up by Henry Davies in 1834.[10]

The three Churches . . . having been altogether erected at the expense of private individuals, or as joint stock speculations, necessarily partook of an exclusiveness scarcely perhaps recognised by the doctrines of the Gospel. While every facility was there afforded to the wealthy and affluent . . . comparatively little care had hitherto been manifested to provide for the spiritual instruction of the poor. . . . The Parish Church, it was quite obvious, was totally inadequate to the accommodation of even a tithe of those persons who, however anxious they might be of worshipping God according to the forms of our national Establishment, were from their situation . . . in life, wholly unable to pay for the use of their sittings. To remedy this evil, the Rev. Francis Close proposed the erection of a Free Church, where the poor might be accommodated as well as the rich; and to the infinite credit of the Town the proposition was so cordially received that . . . the sum of £3,500 was raised by voluntary contributions to carry it into effect.

Joseph Pitt contributed the plot of ground on which St. Paul's was built. It was his last public service to Cheltenham. The period of prosperity for the Pump Rooms was drawing to a close. The first casualty was the Imperial Spa which was pulled down in 1837 and re-erected on the west side of the Promenade, where it remained until it was demolished to make room for the present Regal Cinema. On the original site stands the magnificent neo-Palladian Queen's Hotel (designed by R. W. Jearrad), which looks across the gardens of Imperial Square and down the Promenade created for its predecessor. At Montpellier the decline in the number of visitors was more gradual, but before 1840 the proprietors found it advisable to build a row of shops on the west side of the Grand Walk which had for many years been kept exclusively for the use of privileged subscribers. These shops were built in a style which blended happily with that of the Spa. They were distinguished by the use of statues—the caryatides—instead of pillars. Three of these famous 'armless ladies' (made in terracotta by Rossi) were brought from London by Pearson Thompson as models for the others, which were made in stone by W. G. Brown of Tivoli Street.[11]

Fortunately a new source of livelihood was shortly to be developed for the town. The Regent, who had become George IV, died in 1830. Regency styles continued to be used in Cheltenham for some years, but the main layout of the town had been accomplished within a few years of his death.

XV

'THE MERRIEST SICK RESORT ON EARTH'
1815–1840

SINCE the main purpose of most of the building which has been described in the foregoing pages was to attract people of wealth and rank, it is relevant to ask who were the visitors who came to the town to enjoy the beautiful surroundings created for them by Nature and the lavish expenditure of Joseph Pitt and Pearson Thompson.

A contemporary collection of doggerel verse describes the scene in Cheltenham in the years immediately after the war had ended:[1]

> Men of every class and order,
> All the genera and species,
> Dukes with aides-de-camp in leashes,
> Marquesses in tandem traces,
> Lords in couples, Counts in pairs,
> Coveys of their spendthrift heirs. . . .
>
> Hosts of soldiers, shoals of seamen;
> Droves of squires and herds of farmers,
> Swarms of dandies, flocks of charmers,
> Troops of half-pay light dragoons,
> Stores of cockneys, heaps of spoons;
> Cabinets of politicians,
> Ins and outs of whole divisions;
> Heaps of lawyers, surgeons, proctors,
> Lots of nurses, dentists, doctors,
> Hovering round as ravens do.

The cosmopolitan element is emphasized in the same collection:

> Cheltenham is thus doomed to be
> All mankind's epitome,
> A sort of general congregation
> Culled from every tribe and nation—

> English, Irish, Welsh and Scottish,
> French, Dutch, Flemish, Hottentotish,
> Swiss, Italian, Spanish, German,
> Russ with collar lined with ermine,
> Jolly Danskers, Swedes, Norwegians,
> Esquimaux from Polar Regions,
> Austere Barons with their poodles,
> Tartars, Turks and Yankee Doodles.

Among the numerous visitors the most outstanding was the Duke of Wellington. He had first come to the town in 1806 when he was comparatively unknown. During the post-war years he paid four more visits, of which the first was in 1816. With the memory of Waterloo still so fresh, the town was illuminated in his honour and triumphal arches of welcome were erected across the High Street at the Cambray entrance. He stayed at Wellington Mansion—let to him by Colonel Riddell—in the garden of which he planted an oak tree to commemorate his visit. A fortnight later he and the Duchess attended the ball which opened the new Assembly Rooms, and his presence brought many other distinguished guests.

The *Cheltenham Chronicle* of this time reported faithfully the arrivals and departures of people of rank and fortune. This practice was continued by the *Looker-On*—a weekly journal which was founded in 1834 to report the main events of Cheltenham society. It was the not very edifying custom of some contemporary guide-books to compile from these reports lists of the annual numbers of visitors of rank. One such list is quoted by Goding: 'From the arrival lists of that year (1823) we find that the visitors included 4 Dukes, 3 Duchesses, 6 Marquises, 5 Marchionesses, 4 Bishops, 10 Earls, 8 Countesses, 53 Lords, 70 Ladies—besides a host of Honourables, Baronets and foreigners of title and other persons of distinction.'

Among these distinguished visitors was the Duchess of Clarence—the future Queen Adelaide—for whom the Master of Ceremonies called a meeting of residents and visitors at the 'Plough' to arrange a suitable programme. She was formally welcomed by Lord Sherborne, Sir William Hicks, and Sir William Burdett. The horses were then taken from her carriage and replaced by men who drew it along the new road then under construction (1827) to Liddell's boarding-house, where she was to stay. The proprietor immediately changed its name to the Clarence Hotel—now the Police Station—and the new road was similarly named after the Duchess. Accompanied by Miss Fitzclarence (one of the daughters of her husband and Dorothy Jordan) she was taken to see the principal spas, the Assembly Rooms, and Fauconberg House where King George III had stayed.

It is on record that almost all the members of the royal family who came to Cheltenham during these years showed an interest in the house where the old King had stayed for five weeks. Perhaps this idyllic interlude had remained as a happy memory and had become in the course of the years 'an oft-told tale' in the family circle.

In 1830 the Duchess of Kent, attended by Sir John and Lady Conroy, brought her eleven-year-old daughter Princess Victoria with her governess Baroness Lehzen for a short visit. They arrived at 1 o'clock at 18 Royal Crescent, where the Duke of Gloucester was then staying. Later in the afternoon they were driven to the principal places of interest in the town, drinking the waters at Montpellier. After returning to the Crescent, they proceeded on their journey to Malvern.

The youngest son of George III, Adolphus, Duke of Cambridge, came in 1835. He too spent some hours looking through the rooms of his father's former residence which was at this time in use as a school for boys.

Among foreign visitors, the Duke of Orleans—later King Louis Philippe—came the year after Waterloo; his son the Duke of Nemours arrived with a large suite in 1835. Several members of the Russian royal family also visited the town. The Grand Duke Nicholas stayed at the 'Plough' in 1816; the Grand Duke Michael came the following year; the Grand Duchess Helena in 1831, when she showed great interest in the new infant schools.

Cheltenham's own Duchess—the former Harriot Mellon—twice brought her young husband the Duke of St. Albans on a visit to her former home. They apparently roused more interest than the other visiting dukes and duchesses, since she was the richest woman in England after she inherited the wealth of Coutts the banker, and the Duke, as the King's Grand Falconer, revived the ancient and picturesque sport of hawking in the immediate neighbourhood—to the great delight of visitors and residents. The Duchess might have been a more frequent visitor but in the course of the years she had grown heavy and she objected to the unkind caricature of her figure which was circulated by a local artist.

An earlier and more retiring visitor was Jane Austen, who is always associated more with Bath than with Cheltenham. She did, however, spend three weeks in the town in May 1816, and some months later in the same year her sister Cassandra also came to drink the waters, staying in the High Street in lodgings which at three guineas a week Jane considered very expensive. 'How much is Cheltenham to be preferred in May', she wrote to Cassandra, and in the same letter[2] she remarked that, according to the newspapers, 'the Duchess of Orleans drinks at my Pump'. There is unfortunately no clue by which Jane's own Pump can be identified.

Among the few other outstanding authors who were attracted to Cheltenham at this time was Bulwer Lytton. Both he and his mother stayed in the town several times before the publication of *Pelham* (1830). He seems to have been considerably impressed by the Cheltenham scene:

Accordingly . . . I set off for Cheltenham. I was greatly struck with the entrance to the town; it is to these watering places that a foreigner should be taken, in order to give him an adequate idea of the magnificent opulence and universal luxury of England. Our country has in every province what France has only in Paris—a capital consecrated to gaiety, idleness and enjoyment.

On the other hand, Surtees's cockney grocer Jorrocks could find little to admire. 'It's nothing but a long street with shops . . . with a few streets branching off it, and as to the Prom-men-ard, as they calls it, aside the Spa, with its garden stuff, why I'm sure, to my mind, the gardens by Regent's Park are just as good'. However, he admitted that a short course of the Spa waters had been highly beneficial, and he found himself so much better that he went out with the Berkeley hounds and greatly enjoyed the run through Queen Wood and the slopes of Cleeve Hill.

The Duke of Wellington returned in 1823, staying first at Wellington House and then at Cambray Villa—which because of this visit was also known later as Wellington House. He drank the waters and took a course of baths as systematically as a soldier carrying out orders, but he also enjoyed the social amenities, attending a ball at the Assembly Rooms 'where the brilliant display of fashion and beauty has probably never been surpassed by anything of the kind hitherto noticed in the annals of gaiety and amusement', and a Grand Promenade at Bettison's Library. Eight months later he came back for a further course of the waters. His last visit was in 1828, when he stayed in the Priory in the London Road—the residence of Mr. Marshall who was then Master of Ceremonies. On this occasion he attended a promenade ball at Montpellier with the Princess Esterhazy and her daughter, and was received by Pearson Thompson to the strains of 'See the Conquering Hero comes'.

The High Street remained for some years the main promenade and shopping centre. Social life revolved very much round the Assembly Rooms where, says Griffiths in 1816, 'All the fashion of this mighty empire, from time to time assembled, brings . . . all the youthful loveliness and grace of Britain, and where beauty is—there will be admirers.' Among the earliest surviving rules (1816) which regulated procedure he quotes the following:

> That the public amusements for the Summer Season are as follows:—
>
> Monday: Ball and Cards.
> Wednesday: Ladies' Promenade and Card Assembly.
> Friday: Ball and Cards.
>
> That gentlemen cannot be admitted to the balls in boots or half-boots; officers in their uniforms excepted.
>
> That no hazard, or game of chance, be on any account permitted in these rooms.

Ten years later the rules have become more strict.

The style and well regulated order of society in Cheltenham is not its slightest recommendation . . . and it is the singular good fortune and justly proud boast of our town that among its patrons are included the first personages of the country, in station, affluence and respectability; *whilst no unprivileged footstep is suffered to intrude upon the circle of their pleasures.*[3]

The rule forbidding games of chance has been replaced by the following: 'That no clerk, hired or otherwise, in this town or neighbourhood; no person concerned in retail trade; no theatrical or other performers by profession, be admitted.'

One part of the Rooms was used both as a very extensive auction room and as 'a principal lounge' in the afternoon. Another department of the building was devoted exclusively to the Gloucestershire and Cheltenham Club 'for the gentry and nobility of the County of Gloucestershire'. This was also known as the New Club—a name adopted by its successor in 1875.

On the corner of the High Street and Rodney Road and immediately adjoining the Assembly Rooms was Williams's Library—famous for sixty years far beyond the limits of the town; and further down the High Street, on the same side, was Bettison's Library, which also had a very large collection of books. The town was well provided with what contemporary writers call lounge libraries.

The Royal Well was still holding its own for the drinking of the waters, but the pleasures of the Long Walk were rivalled by those of the gardens at Montpellier. These—laid out by Pearson Thompson and the Jearrad brothers (1830)—covered ten acres and included 'an extensive range of hot and green houses, stocked with choice exotics and rare plants . . . and a light and elegant Chinese pagoda . . . fitted up as an orchestra for the band'.

In the mornings, we are told, 'there are few scenes more animated and inspiring than the Montpellier Promenade . . . between eight and ten, with the presence of the lovely, the titled and the fashionable, as they parade up and down the grand walk to the sound of music . . .'. This promenade is now known as Montpellier Walk, with a row of shops built in Regency style.

By 1834 the Montpellier Evening Musical Promenades, held in the summer on the Grand Walk or in the gardens, have taken precedence over even the attraction of the Assembly Rooms. The band began playing at half-past seven, and as twilight came, the Rotunda and the gardens were brilliantly lighted.

Here again 'no unprivileged footstep' was suffered to intrude. The Promenade was for subscribers only and the rules laid down that 'no servant of any description is allowed to come on the walk during the hours of the Promenade, or into the gardens at any time. . . . Dogs are likewise prohibited.'[4]

The Montpellier balls held in the Rotunda were also popular, partly because the ladies were allowed to wear their promenade dresses and hats or bonnets; the gentlemen, however, had still to wear full dress; and, as in the Assembly Room balls, no clerks or persons in retail trade or theatrical performers were admitted.

Mr. King had died in 1816. The new Master of Ceremonies was Alexander Fotheringham, who devoted his time entirely to Cheltenham. At the time of his election he agreed to pay the rival candidate £200 a year during his own life in return for his withdrawal, so that the office must have been lucrative. On Fotheringham's death in 1820, Mr. Marshall took his place. He was inducted into the office by Colonel Berkeley, and by the terms of his appointment he was expected to confine his activities as Master of Ceremonies to Cheltenham, which by this time had a winter as well as a summer season.

The summer balls were usually held at the Rotunda and the winter balls in the Assembly Rooms. At the Ball for the Master of Ceremonies held at the Rotunda in 1836 the *Looker-On* informs us that 'the Band was enforced from London', and that there were 'delightful sets of quadrilles and waltzes, among which were . . . the famous Princess Victoria Waltz . . . and the Vocal gallope which still continues a great favourite'. In the same year a grand Pittville fête was reported as 'a dream of enchantment; the illuminations were brilliant and dazzling; the lake girdled with a zone of light'.

The public balls and musical promenades were to a certain extent controlled by the proprietors of the rooms where they were held, but there were also committees of residents—one for the winter balls and one for the summer balls—and a General Committee for Public Entertainments.

It was from the Committee of Summer Balls (presided over by Lord Sherborne) that Mr. Marshall, after serving for fifteen years as Master of Ceremonies, requested permission to give up some of his duties to enable him to accept an offer from London to preside over the Hanover Square Balls. As a result of this request he became so unpopular that he was forced to resign his office (1836). The committee then made arrangements for a new election, and decided that the right of voting should be limited 'to Heads of families, whether Ladies or Gentlemen who had been residents in the town as owners, occupiers or tenants of houses for not less than twelve months'. At the election, which was conducted in the Assembly Rooms by the General Committee for Public Entertainments, Captain Andrew Hyacinth Kirwan was chosen and soon established himself as a popular figure in the town. He was later described by a well-known resident as '*the* character of the place . . . the Beau Brummel of the town who presided at all the public Balls in silk stockings, blue tights, blue tailed coat, a cocked hat under his arm and a blue sash over his shoulder'.[5] He was kept busy with the many public functions at which he was expected to look after the guests.

The Races were established in 1819 as an annual three-day event under the patronage of the Duke of Gloucester. Colonel Berkeley, a good all-round sportsman though not primarily a racing man, supported them with a subscription of £1,000 a year. Dr. John Fosbroke tells us that they were held on the picturesque elevation of Cleeve Hill.

'A Town Cup of costly workmanship is annually run for. The chief subscribers are Lord Sherborne, Lord Ducie . . . and the Berkeleys. . . . Well crammed hotels, profusion of gambling, balls and plays are the natural consequences.' Alongside the course were Punch and Judy Shows, candy sellers, booths for 'shyers of sticks for snuff boxes', and travelling minstrels. Contemporary estimates of the numbers present at these early race meetings varied from fifteen to twenty thousand. They proved a major attraction until the new curate-in-charge of the parish church—the Reverend Francis Close—made them a target for his attacks from the pulpit.

It may be judged therefore that there was no lack of entertainment during these years at

> The fount of health and mirth
> The merriest sick resort on Earth.

The local eulogies on this brilliant social scene were by no means universally approved. The bitterest critic of post-war Cheltenham was William Cobbett. It should be remembered that this period of Cheltenham's post-war gaiety was probably that of the greatest poverty and hardship for rural and industrial workers that England had yet experienced—and a time when they probably came nearer to revolution than ever before or since. For this suffering Cobbett blamed—among other causes, such as Inclosure—the heavy taxation levied by a Parliament in which none of the poor and very few of the middle classes were represented; and he hated those whom he thought benefited most from these taxes: pension-holders, stock-jobbers, and fund-holders—in his own words 'tax-eaters'. In 1821 he set out on his 'Rural Rides', in the course of which he reached Cheltenham, where he described the visitors and new residents as idle parasites on the body politic:

Cheltenham is a nasty, ill-looking place, half clown and half cockney. The town is one street about a mile long; but then, at some distance from this street, there are rows of white tenements, with green balconies, like those inhabited by the tax-eaters round London.

Indeed, this place appears to be the residence of an assemblage of tax-eaters. These vermin shift about between London, Chelten-ham, Bath, Bognor, Brighton, Tunbridge, Ramsgate, Margate, Worthing and other spots in England, while some of them get over to France and Italy. . . .

Cheltenham is at the foot of a part of that chain of hills which form the sides of that dish which I described as resembling the vale of Gloucester. Soon after quitting this resort of the lame and lazy, the gourmandising and guzzling, the bilious and the nervous, we proceeded on, between stone walls, over a country little better than that from Cirencester to Burlip-hill.

This attack made Cobbett so unpopular in Cheltenham that when nine years later he attempted to deliver a political speech near the Market, he had to retreat hurriedly. His enemies, unable to seize his person, burnt his effigy in the Street.

Cobbett was by no means the only critic of the idleness and frivolity associated with the life of the town at this time. Catherine Sinclair gives a less provocative but more succinct description of the visitors: 'I never saw such resolute idlers with such a lounging indolent do nothing air. It is one of the places where card playing continues as a constant business, and where old people can be seen going to the grave with a pack of cards in their hands.'[6] Bernard Blackmantle, in *The English Spy* (1826), describes a similar scene: 'Cards, cards, cards, nothing but cards from "rosy morn to dewy eve" at the town of Cheltenham. *Whist*, with the *sun* shining upon their sovereigns, one would think a *sovereign* remedy for their waste of the blessed day—*écarté*, whilst the blue sky is mocking the blue countenances of your thirty pounds losers in as many seconds.'

The *Gentleman's Magazine* complains that there is not a literary institution in the whole place and that 'as to intellectual matters its stock is only that of a book milliner's shop or a tabernacle tract office. . . . Cheltenham is Attica in architecture and Boeotia in understanding. It is an elegant constructed case of fashionable butterflies and evangelical beetles . . . where it is deemed that man was only made to flutter or crawl.' The reference to evangelical beetles and tabernacle tracts shows an unflattering recognition of the already strong influence of Francis Close. It seems strange that Cheltenham, which had so much to offer in the healing of the sick, the provision of civilized entertainment, sport of all kinds, and the combination of rural beauty with noble architecture, should be expected to develop into an intellectual centre as well. Fosbroke met the critics admirably: 'If Cheltenham were London it would no longer be Cheltenham.' He thought its pre-eminence over all other watering-places lay in 'the indiscriminate mixture of many things mightily well contrived for the diversity of human dispositions, affording the most sovereign remedy on earth for all the shades of blue devilry . . .'. In fact the small Literary Society formed by Dr. Jenner was revived in 1834 and shortly afterwards the members erected in the Promenade the fine building known as the Literary and Philosophical Institution.

Among the new residents at this time were many who were neither wealthy nor distinguished. Cheltenham was attracting large numbers of very poor people, anxious to escape the hardships of life in other parts of the county and to find settlement in the town. Farm labourers and domestic servants from the surrounding countryside came to the annual Cheltenham Mop which acted as a sort of employment exchange; here the work-people renewed their employment or found new masters. Their wages varied from £3. 10s. a year to a very occasional £10. From the Quarter Session Records we see how frequently they tried to move away from their villages into the towns. Some of them took to the roads and became trampers—confirmed vagabonds. Hundreds of these visited Cheltenham, attracted by the reputation of its comparatively mild Poor Law régime, and lodged in the overcrowded lodging-houses at the lower end of the High Street. Many others, who were utterly destitute, tried to get the right to settle here and were sent away by the Overseers of the Poor. In 1832, when the cholera epidemic was raging in many parts of the county, nine men were stationed at the main entrances to the town to prevent the entry of vagabonds, two thousand of whom were conveyed around the outskirts, given food, and sent on their way.

Fosbroke, writing in 1826, had thought it extraordinary that the town escaped epidemics of smallpox and pestilence 'considering the general system of subdivision of houses into lodgings and the density of the population of the inferior streets', but he was aware that, in comparison with other over-crowded towns like Gloucester, even the lower end of Cheltenham's High Street was comparatively healthy. He also knew that a great deal was done, which was neglected in other places, to maintain cleanliness in order to avoid epidemics. Behind the scenes of gaiety and the façade of the entertainment industry, the old vigorous life of the town went on. There was much agricultural land a short distance from the centre of the town and local produce was sold in the market, which still played a large part in the economy of the town until the increase in the number of shops in the thirties and forties lessened its importance. The malting industry flourished and there was considerable employment for blacksmiths and saddlers in a town where the Berkeley Hunt was such a popular feature of social life. The old fairs and cattle markets were still held; pigs were sold in Henrietta Street, horses in Albion Street, while the High Street was the scene of the fairs for the first half of the century. 'It forms a curious and amusing sight', wrote Griffith in 1816, 'to behold the mixture of London elegance with Gloucestershire fashion; to view the street with its booths... decorated with ribands and trinkets, and the crowding together of rustic lads and Bond Street beaux [*sic*]—of rural lasses and Westminster belles. Many a lass on her return to the dairy has learnt a new method of decorating her bonnet.'

It would therefore be entirely wrong to believe that the whole life of the town during these years was given up to providing entertainment for visitors. In addition to the balls and promenades, the card parties and the plays, the races and the hunting, there was a strong current of healthy activity concerned with local government and a lively interest in party politics, although Cheltenham was not entitled to its own Member of Parliament until 1832.

In local government, as will be shown later, there was far more continuity of policy and purpose than might have been expected from the large numbers of new residents. Many of these were from the Army and the Navy and the East India Company. Doctors came in numbers to look after the health of the new-comers; solicitors came to deal with the legal side of the enormous development of new property; business men of all types came to serve the needs of the growing population, and the letting of lodgings remained a major industry. Some of the new-comers took an active part in the affairs of the town, serving on the Vestry or as Town Commissioners with members of older families who survived to carry on the earlier traditions.

Among the many doctors who played an important part in the life of the town two were outstanding. Thomas Newell, who was Surgeon Extraordinary to George IV, was a Town Commissioner, an active member of the Vestry, a founder member of the Conservative True Blue Club, and for some time Chairman of the Committee for Public Entertainments. Dr. Boisragon—Physician Extraordinary to the King—had been Lord Byron's friend and physician. His interests were equally wide. As a young man he was a popular figure at private and public balls; he enjoyed attending the Races; he shared the musical interests of his son Conrad, who was a talented professional singer. His private journal and accounts book survives for the years 1830-2 and re-creates the background of his hard work, by which, in a widespread as well as fashionable practice, he earned £3,000 a year. One of his recorded fees is that of £2. 2s. from Sir Richard Greeley— 'for endeavouring to meet his Maker'. Unlike Dr. Newell he was a strong Liberal and acted as vice-chairman at the great Reform dinner held in 1832 when Lord Segrave (Colonel Berkeley) was in the chair. With other doctors he was instrumental in the revival in 1834 of Dr. Jenner's Literary Society.

The chief solicitors who had established themselves in the town and whose firms survive to this day were the Pruens, the Jessops, the Winterbothams, and the family of Thomas Griffiths. John Brend Winterbotham was the son of the famous Nonconformist William Winterbotham. Theodore Gwinnett—Clerk to the Commissioners—has already been mentioned. His residence —Albion Villa—is now the headquarters of the Liberal Club.

One of the most active men in public affairs during these years was a hard-headed business man John Gardner—owner of the principal brewery in the town and a partner with Joseph Pitt in the County of Gloucester Bank, then situated in the Cheltenham High Street. During the financial panic of 1825, when a run on the bank was expected, he made the journey to London and back again in record time to bring back enough money to meet the demands of the shareholders and so save the bank. His wife was the sister of Major Agg of the Hewletts; Major Agg's youngest son James took the name of Agg-Gardner and purchased the Manor of Cheltenham in 1843, paying Lord Sherborne £39,000. John Gardner's partner Joseph Pitt, despite his many activities in Cheltenham, was never a permanent resident.

Pearson Thompson, who played such a major part in the development of Regency Cheltenham, acted for a time as Town Commissioner and was also concerned in the founding of St. James's Church and Christ Church. At his residence in Hatherley Court he found time for the dinner parties which were reported from time to time in the *Looker-On*. With all these activities it was impossible for him to practise as a barrister, although earlier in life he had been called to the Bar. Unfortunately his building speculations were not confined to Cheltenham, and he lost so heavily on transactions in London properties that in 1850 he had to sell out his interests in Cheltenham and emigrate to Australia, where he died twenty-three years later.[7] Some years before his departure the Jearrad brothers had taken over his interests in the Montpellier Spa.

Major Agg of the Hewletts was one of the first of a long stream of arrivals who, having made ample fortunes in India, were prepared to settle permanently in Cheltenham. In Hickey's *Memoirs* he is described as a man 'who had acquired a handsome independence in the Bengal Corps of Engineers and returned home (1802) to become deputy Lord Lieutenant of the County and Justice of the Peace for Cheltenham'. Shortly afterwards three doctors who had also acquired wealth in the service of the East India Company came to Cheltenham and built for themselves three magnificent houses in Suffolk Lawn. Two of these, Robert Sherwood and William Ingledew, took an active part in the affairs of the town, serving for many years as Commissioners. They were the fore-runners of many who retired from service in India and brought their money to the town. It was indeed very largely on the foundation of the wealth acquired in the East that the new Cheltenham was developed, and throughout the nineteenth century Anglo-Indian society was a marked feature of Cheltenham life.

Among these outstanding personalities the two dominant men in Cheltenham during this period were undoubtedly Colonel Berkeley and his antagonist the Reverend Francis Close, who was for thirty years incumbent of the parish church to which he had been appointed by the Simeon Trustees in 1826. As an undergraduate he had studied under Simeon and was deeply imbued with his ideas. He was therefore both the product and the exponent of the Evangelicalism which was changing the whole temper of English society and nowhere more than in Cheltenham. Under his influence it developed into an ecclesiastical stronghold and an educational centre—nicknamed by his opponents the 'Close Borough'.

He was described by a contemporary writer as 'the Cheltenham Gamaliel—and emphatically the great man of the place, Monarch of all he surveys in that resort of fashion, and never did Beau Nash rule with more absolute supremacy. The authorities of the town sink into insignificance when their influence is placed beside that of the potent Vicar.'[8]

William Fitzhardinge Berkeley was the eldest son of the fifth Earl of Berkeley and Mary Cole. He sat in the House of Commons for a few months in 1810 as one of the members for the county of Gloucester, resigning his seat on the death of his father, when he expected to enter the House of Lords as the new Earl of Berkeley. His claim to the earldom, however, was not sustained before a Committee of the House of Lords, on the ground that the marriage of his parents had not taken place until after the birth of their first three sons. Since Morton Berkeley, the rightful heir as the first son born in wedlock, believed (under the influence of his mother) that this decision was wrong, he refused to accept the title or the property. William therefore remained as head of the family and owner of Berkeley Castle and the family estates. He continued to be known as Colonel Berkeley for many years because of the commission he held in the Gloucestershire Yeomanry, although he received the title of Lord Segrave in 1831 and ten years later became Earl Fitzhardinge.

In the first half of the nineteenth century the powerful family of Berkeley had a predominant influence in the parliamentary representation of Gloucestershire. One of William's brothers was member for the city of Gloucester, one for Bristol, and yet another for West Gloucestershire; while after the Reform Bill Cheltenham was held for an almost unbroken period of sixty years by two of his brothers and a nephew. As the Berkeleys were Liberals and Francis Close a Conservative, their opposing views added zeal to the contest over moral values which enlivened the town for many years. Francis Close was backed by the new *Cheltenham Journal* (founded in 1824 to support the Conservative Party) and later by the *Cheltenham Chronicle* which became openly Conservative after the publication of the new Liberal paper—the *Cheltenham Examiner* (1839).

It is therefore unsafe to accept in entirety the figure of Colonel Berkeley presented in the opposition Press as a mere hard-riding libertine and rake. His letters reveal an educated man who could express his point of view with force and clarity. He was an able public speaker, deeply interested in politics, and sincerely concerned for parliamentary reform; he received his first peerage for his active support of the Reform Bill against the Duke of Wellington and his Tory followers. He was an enlightened patron of the theatre and a gifted amateur performer. He was also a most capable master of hounds, with his own high code of ethics for hunting, and even in this capacity he claimed that his efforts in building up his first pack were inspired by his literary interests. Undoubtedly his services in the hunting field and his generous patronage of the theatre and of the Races contributed considerably to the amenities of Cheltenham and attracted many visitors.

Each year at the opening of the hunting season the church bells rang out to welcome the arrival of the Colonel and his friends, and they were escorted by the Cheltenham contingent into the town. Each year, according to Dr. John Fosbroke, the season ended 'with the cavalcade of the hunt, which drives into Cheltenham four-in-hand upon stage coaches in the appropriate costume—the Berkeley scarlet mounted with a black velvet collar and a fox thereon worked in silver, the lining yellow; and a subsequent Ball is given with great magnificence at the Theatre' (1826).

Of the theatre, Dr. Fosbroke speaks in a similar manner: 'With the visits of the stars it ought to do well, but were it not for the crowded houses on the amateur nights . . . with Colonel Berkeley and his brother Captain Berkeley playing as amateurs . . . there would be more labour than profit.'

Colonel Berkeley was concerned not only in the sporting and social side of life in Cheltenham; he took an active part in promoting other aspects of its progress. Thus he was in the chair at the meeting held at the 'Plough' (1820) to discuss the erection of the bridge over the Severn at Haw Passage. Among those present were Joseph Pitt, John Gardner, Baynham Jones, Thomas Henney, Thomas Smith, William Gyde, Theodore Gwinnett, and Captain Matthews. It was then decided to raise subscriptions of £50 each, 'to be secured on the Toll', for the erection of the bridge.

It should be remembered that Colonel Berkeley grew up in the last years of the eighteenth century and that if in some aspects of his life he resembled the sons of George III, he was a child of his times. The fact that his patronage of the theatre extended sometimes to the actresses themselves, and that his relations with women gave him an unsavoury reputation enabled the *Cheltenham Journal* to pursue him with innuendo and with very direct references to his private life. In one case, following a blatant attack on his parentage and on his relations with the actress Maria Foote, who was his mistress for some years and for whose benefit he had arranged performances in the Cheltenham Theatre, he took the law into his own hands. With two friends he overpowered the defenceless editor in his own home in Northfield Place and horsewhipped him. It is fair to add that certain letters of Colonel Berkeley have survived, from which it is clear that he tried to get legal redress from the editor on grounds of libel, before he took this extreme step. In the subsequent lawsuit he was ordered to pay £500 damages to the editor; he himself, however, was awarded £100 in damages in an action against the *Cheltenham Chronicle* some years later.

The most consistently outspoken criticism came from the *Cheltenham Looker-On*. Its attack in 1847 is typical. 'The ogre of the Castle, himself held in thraldom by his lady loves, in turn holds all in thrall for twenty miles around. The dread and terror of his name seem to exert such a baneful paralytic influence that all who breathe the same air are at once deprived of political freedom and cease alike to act or think for themselves.'

In the meantime Francis Close was thundering from his pulpit against the activities of the Berkeleys and their friends. The first object of his attack was the Races. In the second year of his incumbency he preached the first of his many sermons in this connexion. He noted the gambling and profligacy which he thought were essential concomitants of all horse-racing. Within four days of its delivery this sermon had been printed and 3,500 copies sold. Almost immediately the opposition retaliated and a war of pamphlets developed, indicating that the unregenerate section of Cheltenham intended to enjoy its pleasures despite attacks from the evangelical pulpit. This conflict continued for many years, and though it might be said that Francis Close finally won the battle, a number of devoted sportsmen, including many Irishmen, detested his views. Among the well-known sporting patrons of the Races were the colourful Berkeley Craven—cousin of Colonel Berkeley; the eccentric Fulwar Craven of Brockhampton; and the great gambler and victor of steeplechases, the Irish Colonel Charretie.

From the comparatively early days of the Spa, Cheltenham seems to have had an attraction for the Irish, which continued through the nineteenth century:

> The Churchyard's so small, and the Irish so many,
> They ought to be pickled and sent to Kilkenny.

This was obviously written before the provision of the new cemetery at the lower end of the High Street in 1831. Some of the Irish, as, for example, Colonel Charretie, were drawn by the opportunities for racing and hunting and perhaps by the general gaiety of the town. Others—passionate amateurs—were interested in the Cheltenham Theatre which had provided scope for many Irish since the early management of the Irishman John Boles Watson. Others who were Roman Catholics were happy to be in a town where there was a large and flourishing Catholic church, which had begun with the arrival of French refugees in the course of the French Revolution. The early services were conducted by the Abbé César in a room in the York Hotel and later in the first church built (on the present site) as a result of the exertions and wealth of Father Birdsall, a few months before the death of the Abbé.

Among other more eminent Irish residing in Cheltenham were Lady Clonbrock, Lord Clancarty, and Lord Dunalley, who served as one of the Town Commissioners and was a great supporter of Colonel Berkeley; James Corrie of the Kilkenny Theatre; Charles Bushe—the retired Chief Justice of the King's Bench in Ireland—and his son-in-law Admiral Sir Josiah Coghill; Thomas Fortescue (brother-in-law of James

Agg-Gardner) who lived in a colony of retired East India Company officials in Suffolk Lawn. The Irish song-writer Tom Moore visited Cheltenham several times to collect information for his life of Byron, and always received a warm welcome from his compatriots. Among the many references in his diary there is one to a dinner at the Imperial Hotel with a party of twenty, 'almost all of whom were Irish'.[9]

From the reminiscences of Colonel Kendall Coghill the social scene in Cheltenham at this period emerges sharply, showing an almost self-sufficient group of men who shared the common background of service in the French wars and enjoyed their retirement in Cheltenham to the full, whether on the hunting field or at the exclusive New Club. Colonel Coghill writes of his father, the Admiral, as 'a big jovial man whose laugh could be heard from Lansdown to Pittville, who was always entertaining old naval and military warriors of Nelson's and Wellington's day, and whose whole conversation seemed to refer to "old Boney". Daily these old warriors used to haunt the Club which was then in the Assembly Rooms, and there they fought their old battles over again, and new ones, over long whist and billiards.'[10]

A similar picture, but from the point of view of the wives and daughters of these heroes, is presented in the papers[11] of the Whinyates family, which consisted of Admiral Thomas Whinyates, General Sir Edward Whinyates, Captain George Whinyates, and their five sisters. Sarah Whinyates married Captain Younghusband—later one of the most active of the Town Commissioners. She accompanied her husband on the ship carrying Napoleon to St. Helena. Her letters describe dinners with the ex-Emperor and his apparent enjoyment of the songs which she and her eight-year-old daughter sang to him. In the same year her sister Amy Whinyates writes, 'I never recollect Cheltenham one quarter so gay and pleasant . . . as it is at present. . . . We were at a Ball every night, Saturdays and Sundays excluded.' A similar impression of an unending round of balls and entertainments is given by a third sister Rachel. In this there is a charming picture of the wedding of her sister Octavia at St. Mary's Church in 1828. 'At nine o'clock we were all ready. . . . Octavia, wearing sprigged muslin and white

satin with orange flowers and a veil . . . went to the Church in
a sedan chair . . . and the rest of the party in carriages separately.' Some time later, when the married couple arrived at
the Clarence Hotel after their honeymoon the church bells
rang merrily to welcome their return. There followed a continuous round of parties with music and dancing, family
dinners, and a grand ball.

Rachel Whinyates also describes the magnificent scene at
the opening of the new Pittville Pump Room in 1830, and the
public breakfast attended by all the leading families in the
county.[12] The next year the Whinyates family attended
the Assembly Rooms to hear the unforgettable performance of
Paganini—'the wonder violinist of the day'.

These private parties, so much in evidence in Rachel Whinyates's diary, increased to such an extent that it was found
necessary in the late eighteen-thirties to limit the number of
public winter balls at the Assembly Rooms to one a fortnight
instead of one a week. The *Looker-On*, commenting in 1837
on the fact that Cheltenham had never before been so full of
winter residents, referred to the private parties which 'held
ceaseless round'. Again, in 1842, 'Private parties, frequently
more numerously attended than the public Assemblies, follow
each other in nightly succession, each emulating its immediate
predecessor in costliness, elegance and splendour. They serve
to keep society in a constant state of pleasurable excitement
and provide occupation and employment for the industrious
[*sic*] and trading portion of our population.'

Sometimes, however, in this paradise of parties and violin
performances the outside world obtruded unpleasantly.
Towards the end of 1832 Rachel Whinyates recorded two such
intrusions—the fact that the cholera epidemic had reached
England from the Continent; and that riots had broken out in
Bristol culminating in the burning of the Mansion House and
the Bishop's Palace, following the rejection of the Reform Bill
by the House of Lords. Rachel's own attitude to this Bill had
been shown earlier: 'This place is in a bustle owing to the
Reform Bill being brought into Parliament, as Cheltenham

will be among those towns returning a new Member of Parliament. But I trust it will never pass and that they will all be disappointed' (1830).

In the wave of revolutions which swept Europe in 1830, England did not entirely escape. So strong was the demand for a reformed and more representative Parliament that in many parts of the country there was a genuine revolutionary feeling, directed not against the Monarchy itself but against the privileges of the old land-owning aristocracy which dominated Parliament through the pocket boroughs. Even in remote Gloucestershire, extreme poverty among agricultural and industrial workers was causing great misery and there were riots and acts of incendiarism in support of the Reform Bill, and even in Cheltenham the echoes of these were felt.

A public meeting was held in the Assembly Rooms as a result of the Home Secretary's circular calling on magistrates and all in authority to deal firmly with riots and incendiarism. The meeting was presided over by Sir William Hicks as one of the leading magistrates, and ended with a resolution put by Francis Close: 'This meeting has the satisfaction to be enabled to declare, that the general conduct of the inhabitants of this town and district, so far as their experience goes, has been loyal and peaceable.'

A further reference to the riots is to be found in a contemporary letter of Lord Ellenborough[13] who had recently purchased the estate of Southam following the death of Thomas Baghott de la Bere (the last surviving member of his family): 'I find the villagers in a happy state of ignorance, and have neither school nor beer shop. They are said to have behaved well in the late disturbance with the exception of two, one of whom was thrashed into a more correct mode of action. The farmers were excellent. . . .'

While Cheltenham was thus happily free from rioting, it was very much involved in what had been a nation-wide struggle for the Reform Bill. Early in 1830 the Tory opponents of the Bill organzied a True Blue Club in Cheltenham on the lines of the one established in Gloucester in 1788. Two years later, at a meeting held at Yearsley's Hotel, the first Cheltenham Conservative Club was formed—'upon principles of the

Conserving of Property'. Among the main supporters were Sir William Hicks of Witcombe, Admiral Mordaunt Ricketts of the Elms, Colonel Limond, and Colonel Munroe—all of whom were Town Commissioners, William Ridler of the Cheltenham and Gloucestershire Bank, Dr. Newell, Robert Bransby Cooper (chairman of the new Board of Health set up in Cheltenham to take precautions against cholera), John Gregory Welch of Old Arle Court and later of Arle House, and the newly arrived Earl of Ellenborough who was in the chair. The latter might have been expected to take a most forceful part in the political fortunes of Cheltenham, since his wealth, influence, and ability were sufficient to counteract even the strength of the Berkeleys. He was credited with enjoying a sinecure of £7,000 a year obtained for him by his father the former Lord Chief Justice, although the actual amount seems to have been £3,800. He had served in the Duke of Wellington's Ministry as Lord Privy Seal and was most bitterly opposed to the Reform Bill which, in its abolition of pocket boroughs without compensation, he and his fellow Tories regarded as an unwarrantable interference with the ownership of private property.

The Cheltenham Liberals replied by forming a society known as 'the Cheltenham Loyal and Patriotic Association for the purpose of obtaining a full, fair and free representation of the People in the Commons' House of Parliament'. Colonel Berkeley—now Lord Segrave—was its president. The two secretaries were Captain Gray and Colonel Olney. Committee meetings were held in the office of the solicitor J. B. Winterbotham, while another solicitor, Thomas Griffiths, took a hand in the correspondence, much of which has been preserved.[14] It includes letters from some of those who joined the Association—the Berkeleys, Lord Sherborne, Lord Dunalley, Sir Berkeley Guise, and Charles Hanbury Tracy of Toddington Park. Other supporters were Robert Capper of Marle Hill, Dr. John Fosbroke, Dr. McCabe, Dr. Boisragon, Francis Jerrard, the solicitor Edward Pruen, R. E. Marshall, Thomas Henney, and William Gyde.

The Association began at once to exert pressure on the Government. The blind but indefatigable Captain Gray organized a petition to be sent to the House of Commons pressing for Parliamentary Reform; an address to the King thanking him for dissolving Parliament on the rejection of the Bill; and later a petition with 5,000 signatures to the House of Lords, begging them not to reject the Bill a second time. Lord Segrave (Colonel Berkeley), although suffering from gout and rheumatism, was called upon to arrange for the presentation of the latter, and Sir Berkeley Guise was expected to do the same for the petition to the Commons. The letters which have survived reveal the close co-operation between these two and the Association.

As a result of similar pressure from all over the country, King William agreed to create enough Liberal peers to swamp Tory opposition if the House of Lords should insist on a further rejection of the Bill. In view of this promise, the Duke of Wellington and the Tory followers abstained from voting when the Bill was sent to the Lords, and as a result it became law in 1832.

From contemporary accounts[15] it appears that never before or since has Cheltenham been so illuminated and so decorated as when it celebrated the passing of the Act which gave it the right to elect a Member of Parliament. Transparencies representing busts of King William appeared in many parts of the town, with mottoes appropriate to what was considered his patriotic action. The 'Plough' was illuminated with two crowns and a star; the Assembly Rooms and the 'Fleece' also had stars; the Royal Hotel and Yearsley's had crowns; the 'Old Swan' the motto—'a patriotic King and a Parliament reformed'. Harper's printing works had a transparency of Hercules destroying the serpent. Dr. Boisragon's house in the Royal Crescent displayed in large letters the inscription:

> Magna Carta   1215
> Maxima Carta   1832   esto perpetua.

Captain Gray was presented with a massive service of plate at a dinner attended by Lord Segrave and Sir Berkeley Guise. One hundred tradesmen marked the occasion with a dinner at the 'Sussex Arms' when 'hilarity, good humour and excellent singing continued to a late hour'; and a hundred members of the Poor House were given a dinner of roast beef and plum-pudding 'with a liberal allowance of strong ale' by John Hatton, the builder, so that they too might share in the celebrations.

The next grand celebration was held in 1838 to commemorate the centenary of the Old Well and the planting of the Long Walk. A public breakfast was followed by music and dancing and a procession to plant a young oak tree.[16] When the fête began in the evening 'the whole scene was enchanting'; the avenue of trees in the Long Walk was illuminated with thousands of 'lights forming innumerable arches of gold and green, in the manner of a cathedral nave . . . the commingling of all ages of rank, position, beauty and fortune, in dense masses, revived the remembrance of Grecian festivals . . . the entertainment ended with a clever pyrotechnical representation of the eruption of Mount Vesuvius'. Rachel Whinyate found it 'a scene of enchantment which no one could forget'.

At this distance of time it is easy to see that this celebration marked not only a centenary but a farewell salute. The vogue for drinking English medicinal waters was declining before the competition of continental Spas, and the hey-day of the Cheltenham waters was over. The Imperial Spa had been demolished a year before this celebration took place and the Royal Well Spa buildings were pulled down ten years later. The Pittville Pump Room, within a few years of its completion, failed to attract enough regular visitors and subscribers to make it a profitable concern, although the beauty of its garden and lake made it a fairy-land setting for occasional fêtes and balls. Montpellier retained its popularity for some years after its rival the Royal Old Well Spa had been rebuilt as a music hall; it was, however, used less for the drinking of waters than for the balls and concerts at the Rotunda.

One phase of life in Cheltenham was drawing to a close. Apart from the decline of the Spa, the forces of the evangelical movement were altering the character of the town. If we except the Queen's Hotel, the Hospital, and the villas on the newly developing Bayshill and Park estates, the most important buildings of the next phase were churches and schools—in the development of both of which the influence of Francis Close was dominant. The power of the Berkeleys was by no means ended, but the general mood of the town was to become more in accord with the aims of Francis Close than with those whose presence had made Cheltenham 'the merriest sick resort on earth'.

XVI

THE STRONGHOLD OF THE
EVANGELICALS
1840–1875

THE most succinct description of Cheltenham at the beginning of this period was written by Tennyson and founded on his own observation of the social scene while he lived in the tall house in St. James's Square: 'Cheltenham—a polka, parson-worshipping place of which Francis Close is Pope, besides pumps and pump-rooms, chalybeates, quadrilles, and one of the prettiest counties in England.'

For many years the parties and the polkas continued at a furious pace among the wealthy residents, but amidst the gaieties the evangelical spirit was making strong headway. Even the circulating libraries could claim in their advertisements in 1844: 'Theology has now become a necessary part of polite education.'[1] Much of the change in Cheltenham was due to the influence of Francis Close whom the Simeon Trust had appointed, first as curate to the new Holy Trinity Church in 1824, and then in 1826 as incumbent of St. Mary's, because he so exactly represented the evangelical views of the Trust. He desired to spread the gospel according to Low Church principles by the building of churches and the founding of schools; to succour the poor by well-organized charity societies; to extol sobriety and to uphold strict sabbatarian observance.

The most fruitful work which he accomplished outside his church was concerned with education. Early in 1826 he founded a Sunday school in the tithing of Alstone, which he was soon persuaded to convert into a day-school for infants—the first of its kind in Gloucestershire. Samuel Wilderspin, one of the pioneers in such schools, came down to initiate the experiment and later settled in the town in Dr. Jenner's old house in St. George's Road. Shortly afterwards Francis Close opened a school of the same kind in a new building in St. James's Square. By 1844 there were six such infant schools in the town. Francis Close did not entirely agree with Wilderspin's principles of letting the children learn through 'playing and doing'. A great deal of the curriculum was concerned with the teaching of the scriptures as interpreted by current evangelical views. Thus[2] the children sang:

> Children just as young as you, as gay
> As playful and as strong,
> Are dying, dying every day,
> And so may you.

The money for these schools came mainly from public subscriptions, raised partly through appeals from the pulpit and partly from visitors who were encouraged to visit the schools. Money was also required for the maintenance of the National Schools, the first of which, in Cheltenham, was founded in 1816 with financial help from the Church of England National Society for Education. Since the first Government grant of money towards schools was not made until 1833 and might then only be used for the provision of actual buildings, considerable sums had to be raised, even though Dr. Bell's Monitorial System (whereby much of the teaching was done by the older pupils) was in use. After the first flush of enthusiasm waned, it became increasingly difficult to raise adequate funds, although there was probably not the same objection in Cheltenham to the provision of schools which existed in the county, where landowners and farmers feared that education of the poor would lead to the rise of 'an effeminate class of persons, averse to rough work, conceited and insubordinate'.[3]

'It is a grief to me that we can never raise a numerous meeting on education in Cheltenham', Francis Close once told a meagrely attended meeting of the Cheltenham National and Sunday Schools Society. It was only as a result of herculean efforts and with the help of other clergy of the town that he brought into existence four National Schools and converted Lady Capel's Charity School, then held in the room over the north porch in the church, into a similar institution in Devonshire Street.[4]

While Francis Close was occupied with the development of

the church schools he was also fighting the advance of the High Church influence. The growth of this movement within the Church of England National Society for Education caused a split which ended in three hundred evangelical supporters—clergy and laity—walking out of a meeting of the Society held in London, and in the formation of the Church of England Education Society, of which a branch was established in Cheltenham. Francis Close was henceforth determined that no Tractarian or High Church views should take root in any Cheltenham school. He therefore threw the whole weight of his influence into the founding of what became known later as St. Paul's Training College, and its sister foundation St. Mary's. He presided at a meeting held in London to discuss this project at which it was agreed that Cheltenham was peculiarly well situated for the location of such a college and that it already had efficient National Schools from which 'more than 200 masters and mistresses had already gone forth to different parts of the Kingdom'. The final resolution declared 'That an Institution for the training of masters and mistresses upon scriptural and evangelical principles in connection with the Church of England is urgently called for and that an effort should be made to establish such a Training College in Cheltenham'. The Government scheme of allowing grants to approved colleges had come into force in 1846 and in the following year two houses were rented in which seven students formed a nucleus of the new training college. Francis Close spent his energies in addressing meetings in many parts of the country in an appeal for funds. The new building, designed by the architect Daukes in Gothic style of the 'decorated' period, was finally erected on a piece of land given by Miss Jane Cook. On the foundation-stone, laid by Lord Ashley (Shaftesbury) in 1849, the object for which the building was erected was clearly inscribed: 'For the purpose of instructing masters and mistresses . . . upon scriptural, evangelical and Protestant principles in accord with the Liturgy and Articles of the Established Church.'[5]

St. Paul's Training College is often regarded as the greatest achievement of Francis Close, but Cheltenham was making history during these years in another type of education, and in this too he played a leading part. With the increase in the number of well-to-do residents, the problem of educating their children became urgent. From its earliest days as a Spa the town had attracted men who had served abroad, particularly in India—in the Army and the East India Company. Not all the new-comers were wealthy. Many of them had retired on Army or Navy pensions and felt the need of a good but not too expensive day-school for their sons. Cheltenham College was founded in 1841 by the efforts of a few of these residents— among whom were George Harcourt, Major-General Swiney, Captain Iredell of the Bombay Native Infantry, and Captain Richard Litchfield (Royal Artillery). It was financed with money raised privately from the proprietors—a company of small shareholders—and therefore called the Proprietary College. It was the first new English public school to be founded in the nineteenth century and was the model for many successors.

The idea had been mooted at a meeting in General Swiney's drawing-room on 9 November 1840 when a provisional committee was elected 'to devise the best means' of founding a school. The committee met the next day and invited 'local parochial clergy shareholders' to attend its meetings—three of which were held during the next fortnight. At the first meeting of proprietors held on 26 November, Francis Close took the chair and was appointed one of the four vice-presidents and thus joined the Directors. He proved to be a most active vice-president and in this capacity frequently signed the minutes of the meetings of the Directors and nearly always prepared the annual reports. Lord Sherborne was President of the Council for the first twenty years, and one of the early secretaries was Captain Robertson, R.A.—the father of the Reverend Frederick Robertson.

The school opened in the central houses of Bayshill Terrace, but very soon outgrew this habitation. In addition to the sons of residents, boarders from other parts of the country were accepted. With a growing population there was a shortage of schools all over the country and the soundness of the education offered at Cheltenham was a considerable attraction. At the same time the opening in 1840 of the railway line between

Cheltenham and Gloucester as part of the main Birmingham line to Bristol, together with the work being carried on by the Great Western Railway Company in extending the London line from Swindon to Cirencester, made the town more easily accessible. Thus the time and the place were wisely chosen, as the subsequent history of the college has shown. The first block of the present building—designed in Perpendicular style by the Bath architect J. D. Wilson—was opened in 1843; ten years later additions were made from the designs of D. J. Humphris, including the first chapel, which was replaced as a chapel by the present building in 1891. The recent acquisition of Thirlestaine House added an impressive dignity to what had already become such a pleasant feature of the Cheltenham landscape and a happy setting for the work of the college.

There is some doubt as to whether this important new school would have come into existence if Richard Pate's Grammar School had been restored earlier. Francis Close thought it would not. He said publicly, 'Had the Grammar School taken its start only a few years sooner, we should not have had in Cheltenham any Proprietary College, because it was the necessity of the case, and the absence of any public school of a high educational character which had led to the foundation of the noble structure of which we were now so justly proud'.[6]

Francis Close clearly believed that the college was founded on evangelical principles, but no religious controversy ever hindered its purely educational objects, despite the very strong influence exerted by him in its early years. There was indeed no pronounced evangelical prejudice shown by the Reverend William Dobson, Principal of the college from 1844 to 1859. His interests were not bounded by the college walls. He was much drawn to Frederick Robertson and was one of the small group which enjoyed the friendship of Tennyson during his short residence in St. James's Square. In the public controversy over the provision of a free library for the town he vigorously supported his friends, the Reverend C. H. Bromby of St. Paul's and the Reverend H. W. Bellairs—Her Majesty's Inspector of Schools for Gloucestershire. It was at the residence of the latter that these three, with a few friends, decided to found a Proprietary College for girls similar to that established for boys, and financed by shareholders who were members of the Church of England. They formed the resolution 'That an Institution for the daughters and young children of Noblemen and Gentlemen be established in Cheltenham, and be entitled the Cheltenham College for the Education of Young Ladies and Children'. With the small capital raised by the first shareholders, a lease was taken of Cambray House[7]—formerly the property of Baynham Jones—and the first prospectus was issued for the 'Cheltenham College for Young Ladies', with Mrs. Proctor and her daughter in charge.

The new school faced great difficulties. Education for girls consisted mainly at this time of giving them such accomplishments as were considered useful in the acquisition of husbands, and there were strong prejudices against extending to girls the advantages of subjects taught in boys' schools.

Francis Close accepted the office of President, but played no part in the early struggle. Shortage of money and differences of opinion between the first Principal and the Council nearly wrecked the new foundation. The appointment of Miss Beale in 1858 was immediately challenged by evangelical critics; she was, however, able to convince the Council that she was not a Tractarian. In other hands than hers the school might have developed—as many of her critics wished it to do—into a small day-school for the daughters of gentlemen. Instead she made it one of the instruments which during the next half-century changed the position of women in modern society. Entirely dedicated, she spent the rest of her life in developing a college which provided a comprehensive scheme of education at all stages, from kindergarten to preparation for university degrees, and included a teachers' training department. Any great school inevitably has an influence far beyond its immediate place and the generations educated there; and in this sense the children of Dorothea Beale, whether as wives or women working in the professions newly opened to them, carried her ideals across the world. Her influence, however, was more direct than this; she was recognized far and wide in her own lifetime as a pioneer and a leader. She is the one great figure whose work in Cheltenham at this time achieved a more than national importance.

Not the least of her difficulties was concerned with the need to find larger premises as the college grew. Fauconberg House in St. George's Road (which was built by Samuel Onley for Doctor Fowler) was early acquired as a boarding-house, but it was not until 1871 that the Council purchased part of the grounds attached to the Old Well Spa, and on this site erected the first section of the new buildings which ultimately covered the whole of the former site of the Spa. The Music Hall, with which Samuel Onley had in 1848 replaced the original Long Room, was not finally pulled down until 1896, when the Princess Hall was built. Only a few sad elms then remained—for a short time—to remind the passer-by of that famous walk.

One aspect of these great educational achievements in Cheltenham was that they were largely inspired by religious purpose. It should not be forgotten that the Noncomformists also developed their own schools. A boys' school—known as the Cheltenham Protestant Union School—was maintained in a room under the Portland Chapel by Robert Capper of Marle Hill House, and by the Countess of Huntingdon's Connexion. A great part of their work, however, was concerned with Sunday schools.

Francis Close appears in retrospect to be the dominant figure in the religious life of Cheltenham, but there were other outstanding clergy interested in education, such as the minister of Highbury Congregational Chapel, Doctor Morton Brown, to whom Colonel Berkeley in his old age turned, and not in vain, for help; Archibald Boyd of Christ Church—later Dean of Exeter—and Frederick Robertson his curate from 1842 to 1845. It must be admitted, however, that the great driving force by which the Evangelicals achieved so much was often accomplished by a narrowness of viewpoint and an intolerance which helped to create conflict and bitterness. During these years the controversy between the Tractarians and the Evangelicals was at its height all over the country. Francis Close entered the conflict by attacking any church organization in which he thought Tractarian influence was powerful, such as the Society for the Propagation of the Gospel and the Cambridge Camden Society which was concerned with the restoration of the medieval aspects of church buildings. The conflict was also fought out in the town itself with the vicar of St. John's—a follower of Pusey.

In the widening rift Cheltenham has been described as a hotbed of religious excitement. In this atmosphere Frederick Robertson, who was curate of Christ Church, seems to have been so unhappy that after four years he resigned. It was only after his appointment to a church in Brighton that his great powers matured and that he became accepted as one of the great preachers of his day. His published sermons had a nation-wide circulation at a time when theological works seem to have been a popular form of escapist reading. Although he began his duties in Cheltenham with a great admiration for Francis Close and for his vicar—Boyd—he was never spiritually at home in the atmosphere of the town. Thus he wrote: 'The state of the Evangelical Clergy [in Cheltenham] is, I think lamentable. I see sentiment instead of principle, and a miserable mawkish religion superseding a state which once was healthy —I stand nearly alone. The Tractarians despise me and the Evangelicals loudly express their doubts of me.'[8] He appears to have disliked not only the narrow evangelical outlook of his congregations in Cheltenham, but their ability to combine with this a never-ending round of exclusive social engagements: 'My work is less satisfactory here than at Winchester—partly from the superficial nature of the place, in which I would not remain another day but for my coadjutor and leader [Boyd]; partly from the effects of the temptations and frittering away of time almost inseparable from a residence here.'

Undoubtedly as a result of the hammering from the pulpits libertinism disappeared from the external social scene, but the congregations of the fashionable churches and particularly of Christ Church consisted very largely of well-to-do, leisured people living in extreme comfort in spacious houses, maintained by staffs of well-drilled servants. To Robertson, who was deeply conscious of contemporary social injustices and of the poverty during the 'hungry forties', their piety was super-ficial. His political views, although never paraded, were Liberal, and he read widely at a time when by no stretch of the imagina-tion could the Cheltenham of the leisured Evangelicals be called cultured. Against these barriers of religious intolerance and narrow social exclusiveness Robertson felt he could make no headway. He resigned in 1845 and shortly afterwards began his most successful ministry in Brighton.

Very great emphasis was laid by the Evangelicals on the keeping of the Sabbath, and there is ample evidence that it was most strictly kept in Cheltenham. According to a Presbyterian Scot, 'The Sabbath was better kept in Cheltenham than any-where else in Britain—outside Scotland.' A Presbyterian gathering in Edinburgh told Francis Close that he was 'the only Church of England clergyman who had succeeded to a great degree in obtaining Sabbath observance'. When the Midland Railway Company opened their line in 1840 from Birmingham to Cheltenham, local efforts were at once made to prevent the running of Sunday trains. For six years these were successful. Francis Close himself made an appeal to the Directors and later to the 'Railway King', Hudson. He had many fervent supporters among his parishioners who had the double motive of maintaining the Sabbath and keeping the people of industrial Birmingham from polluting the atmosphere of Cheltenham.

The passing of a Railway Act (1846) enforcing the running of certain passenger trains on Sundays on all lines called forth from Close the comment: 'Another page of Godless legislation is recorded in the annals of our beloved country and another national sin invokes the displeasure of the Almighty.'[9]

Evangelical censure fell less successfully on the theatre, although Watson's Cambray Theatre where so many famous players had appeared had gradually lost its appeal. After its destruction by fire in 1839 it was not rebuilt. Occasional per-formances were given in the Assembly Rooms and in the Royal Wells Music Hall which was built by Samuel Onley on the site of the Old Well Long Room. Some of these performances were by amateurs, and were equally frowned on by the clergy. When, however, Fanny Kemble gave a series of readings from Shakespeare in 1850, most of fashionable Cheltenham turned out to hear her, despite the counter-attraction of a public lecture by Francis Close on 'The Tendencies of the Stage, Religious and Moral'. The performances of oratorios, whether by the choir of St. James or the Three Choirs Festival at Gloucester, were equally condemned.

The spirit of religious controversy continued for many years. The underlying cause of the bitter attacks by Francis Close against the Tractarians was his fear that their views would ultimately lead to large conversions to Roman Catholicism—a fear which was strengthened when Newman acknowledged his conversion to that Church in 1845. For many years Francis Close had used the 5th of November to preach a sermon against Popery. The appointment in 1850 of Roman Catholic bishops with territorial titles in England was the occasion of an outbreak of anti-Roman feeling in the town. At a large public meeting a loyal address of protest was sent to the Queen. It was an unusually representative meeting at which not only the leading clergy but the Member of Parliament, the lord of the manor, Captain Robertson and many other distinguished residents were present. This was followed at a lower social level by an attempt to burn the Pope in effigy. The effigy concerned was exposed in a tailor's shop and all preparations had been made when the action was stopped by order of the magistrates. A disappointed crowd advanced on the Roman Catholic church of St. Gregory, tore down railings, and tried to set fire to the building; later some shops belonging to Roman Catholics were broken into. The next month an anti-papal address carrying 4,000 signatures was sent from Cheltenham to the Queen. The outcome of this and similar protests was the passing of the Ecclesiastical Titles Bill, which was, however soon repealed because of the impossibility of its enforcement.

In view of their increasing antagonism towards the Roman Church, the Evangelicals and the Dissenters were prepared to sink some of their differences and—as will be explained in the account of the Vestry—Francis Close himself proposed a solution to the problem raised by the refusal of the Dissenters to pay Church Rates.

The most vindictive spirit, however, was directed, as was perhaps natural at the time, against current secularist views, some of which developed in reaction against the alliance of the Church with the forces of Conservatism, and against its general lack of concern with poverty among the working classes. Not until the Christian Socialist movement of Charles Kingsley and Frederick Maurice was there any attempt within the Church to support political action as a means of improving economic conditions. On the other hand, the followers of Robert Owen were actively disseminating his views, some of which had more in common with atheistic Marxist communism than with the religious background of the greater part of later British Socialism. It was as a missionary of Owen's plans for the development of Socialist colonies as a remedy against increasing poverty that a young man—George Jacob Holyoake—came to Cheltenham in 1842. He delivered his lecture in the Albion Street Mechanics' Institute—Cheltenham's contribution to the great movement initiated by Birkbeck. Following the general policy of Owen, he made no direct reference to religion, but after the lecture he was closely questioned by two men who were locally credited with being agents of Francis Close. 'The Lecturer has told us much about our duty to Man; what about our duty to God?' Holyoake replied with a protest against the amount of money devoted to the upkeep of the Church at a time when large numbers of the people were starving. 'I appeal to your heads and your pockets, if we are not too poor to have a God?'

The meeting ended in an orderly fashion, but was reported at length in the *Cheltenham Chronicle* which by this time strongly supported Conservative policy and the views of Francis Close. It called for legal action against the blasphemous views expressed by 'a person called Holyoake who had delivered a lecture on Socialism (more appropriately called Devilism)'.

A fortnight later Holyoake returned to give another lecture on 'Civil and Religious Liberty'. When he had finished speaking he was immediately arrested without warrant by the superintendent of police and was charged the next day before the local magistrates with having at a previous meeting uttered statements deemed to be blasphemous. The magistrates were Robert Capper of Marle Mill House, who had built Portland Chapel a few years earlier, and the Reverend T. Newell; with the police surgeon they expressed their horror by heaping angry

abuse on the prisoner. The following day he was conveyed—
his hands in irons—to Gloucester Gaol, but his friends saved
him from the ignominy of being marched in this condition
nine miles through the streets by paying his fare and that of the
escorting police on the new railway. In his own words he was
on arrival 'thrust into a dirty cell, with hands bolted together
until the skin was pinched off, kept parched with thirst for sixteen hours without any water to drink, and then fed on convict
gruel for fourteen days'[10] while awaiting the granting of bail.

By this time the case had aroused considerable controversy.
At a public meeting a resolution was passed condemning the
conduct of the Cheltenham magistrates as cruel and tyran-
nical; later a memorial was sent to the House of Commons in
protest. The Home Secretary admitted in the Commons that
certain irregularities had taken place, but despite this admission
Holyoake was later sentenced at the Gloucester Assizes to six
months' imprisonment which he served under conditions of
extreme hardship in the common gaol. In the same decade a
boy entered Cheltenham College who was later to hold similar
views. This did not, however, prevent him from receiving the
Order of Merit in 1902 or from entering the House of Lords in
1908 as Lord Morley of Blackburn. Holyoake lived to be the
Grand Old Man of Secularism, the doyen of the Co-operative
movement, and a highly respected figure in public life.

Immediately after serving his sentence Holyoake returned
to Cheltenham and there repeated his original statements, but
on this occasion no further legal action was taken. The publicity
given in the Press had already proved damaging to the in-
stigators of the trial. The Liberal *Examiner*, however, had
joined the *Cheltenham Journal* and the *Cheltenham Chronicle* in
expressing satisfaction at the prison sentence. It was left to the
radical *Cheltenham Free Press* to point out 'the unchristian
spirit of using a prison sentence to teach Christian truths; the
need for men to be drawn and not driven to Christ; and the
fact that religious feelings cannot long prevail where misery
and destitution exist'.

Even in Cheltenham there were in the 'hungry forties' many
direct indications of such misery and destitution. In a letter

sent in 1841 to the *Cheltenham Journal* Christopher Cole—the Secretary of the National Schools—refers to 'the thousands of neglected and ignorant children with whom the streets and courts of this town abound'. Two years later the *Examiner* proposed that the distressed poor should be set to work laying stone pathways in the town. An influential committee was elected, £700 contributed, and with the co-operation of the Town Commissioners the scheme was put into operation.

In 1850, 240 people left Cheltenham as emigrants to Quebec, dispatched by the Board of Guardians and assisted with money from local subscriptions. Hadley's *Guide Book* of 1856 tells us that 'poverty seems to follow in the train of wealth and it has been remarked of Cheltenham that notwithstanding its numerous public and private charities, there is an unaccountable over-proportion of paupers to the population'.

The attitude of the Evangelicals towards contemporary poverty was reflected in Lee's *Guide Book* (1843):

> Since we learn from the Scriptures that wealth is the gift of Him who putteth down one and setteth up another, and that the poor shall never cease out of the land, it is the duty of the rich to relieve their necessities. . . . As wealth and influence increase, charity should extend the circle of its sympathy, and we are happy to state that the charities of Cheltenham have multiplied, and that her zeal and activity in relief of the necessities and distresses of the poor have kept pace with her increasing reputation and growing splendour.

The *Guide Book* then lists a number of the forty local charities and the names of the ladies and gentlemen by whom they were organized and administered. It had been estimated that over £3,000 was annually subscribed to these societies (in addition to another £2,000 for foreign missions), but this was probably a very conservative estimate. There had been apparently some lack of discrimination in the earlier distribution of these alms, and this, combined with the administration of Poor Relief by the Vestry which was perhaps not as harsh as that of some other towns, had attracted vagrants. Francis Close seems to have welcomed the change in administration enforced by the Poor Law Amendment Act (1834).

Despite all the generosity and expressions of sympathy the division between Rich and Poor—the 'Two Nations' of Disraeli's contemporary novel—was most clearly marked. In the same *Guide Book* the site chosen for the infants' school in St. James's Square was praised as being 'near to the Poor and not far from the Rich'. Queen Charlotte's original foundation in Winchcombe Street for orphan girls had been renamed the Female Orphan Asylum, and the *Guide Book* described it as intended 'to instil into the orphans the principles of religion and morality . . . to make them good household servants . . . and to teach them that the lowest stations in life may be rendered respectable by good principles and honesty'. In the newly built hospital (1848) the first house surgeon and Secretary of the Institution was David Hartley, who had formerly been in the service of the East India Company. When he entered a ward all the patients, whether men or women, stood in military fashion at the foot of their respective beds.[11] The 'Free Church' of St. Paul's had been built expressly to serve the needs of the poor, who could not afford the pew rents or the payments at the door which were required from worshippers in other churches.

Of the horrors of the factory system there were few or none in Cheltenham, but at a time when the Factory Acts were beginning to enforce a limitation on working hours, there was no legislation to protect either domestic servants or shop assistants. Shops in Cheltenham remained open until 10 p.m. A movement was set on foot in 1842 to make shopkeepers close at eight, but for many years it made little headway in spite of support from the churches and the Nonconformist ministers.

The main sources of employment available at this time in Cheltenham were the building industry, the many forms of domestic service, and of work for tradesmen and shopkeepers who in their turn served the needs of the wealthy residents. In fact the whole economy of the town was geared to serving these needs, at a time when the Cheltenham waters were attracting fewer visitors and residents. Indeed the population, which had reached 36,000 in 1841, had increased only to 39,500 in 1861—a marked decline in the rate of increase.

It was frankly recognized that the schools had replaced the waters as a source of income. Hadley's *Guide* (1856) tells us:

Cheltenham can no longer depend upon the annual influx of visitors for support. Its present large population requires some more settled means of livelihood and it cannot rely on a safer source of revenue than that derived from our educational institutions. . . . To the welfare and prospects of the town the College is of the greatest importance, because, directly or indirectly, it causes to be expended in the town little short of £150,000 per annum. This estimate is made after due regard of the number of families it causes to reside here for the education of their sons. . . . When it is considered also that the Grammar School has brought numerous families to reside here, whose style of living approaches the aristocratic, we can safely say that this Institution, next to the College, will prove hereafter of eminent use in promoting the prosperity of the town. If it causes to be spent here £20,000 or £30,000 annually, it must be considered a great public adventure.

While allowing for probable exaggeration in these figures, it is clear that the value of the schools in the economy of the town was fully realized.

At the same time the presence of the schools and the influence of the Evangelicals had produced other less tangible effects. There is an unpleasant smugness reflected in the guide-books of the 1860's.

The town is now no longer a type of fashionable watering-place. . . . The frivolities once so prevalent here are now more honoured in the breach than in the observance. . . . Education has also powerfully done its work for good in Cheltenham. The gross and vicious habits of a past generation have fled or died out before the spread of education and intelligence, and a comparatively healthy moral tone now permeates all classes. Occasionally a character of the old stamp may appear on the fashionable horizon . . . but he is carefully avoided and excluded from family circles.

The exclusive nature of upper-class society in the town increased as time went on. Earlier in the century many distinguished Army and Navy men had served as Town Commissioners, but after the passing of the 1852 Act this situation was reversed (Chapter XXIII). It was observed during the conflict which arose over the incorporation of the borough in

1876 that for many years previously only solicitors and trades-men could be induced to serve. The Master of Ceremonies and the Committee of Resident Noblemen and Gentlemen still regulated balls. Another exclusive club, known as the Imperial because it occupied the former Imperial Hotel which is now the General Post Office, was founded in 1856. There were two musical societies and according to the *Guide Book* of 1863 one 'was recruited from the best families, and the greatest vigilance was exercised' in the admission of both members and audience; the other 'drawing its support mainly from the middle classes'.

This exclusiveness was no doubt inevitable where there was such a close-knit society sharing the same background of service to the Crown in various parts of the world. To many of its members life in Cheltenham was merely an extension of the former social round to which they had been accustomed before retiring, and the circle was so large that it was self-sufficing. Not all the members were wealthy. The old gibe against the town as being 'poor, proud, and pretty' was a reflection on the number of retired Service people living on small pensions, but rich or poor they tended to share the same outlook and to form a somewhat exclusive group.

There were indeed many distinguished residents in this group. In the fifties and sixties the obituary columns were filled with the names of generals and admirals who had fought Napoleon, by land and sea; and at the same time their sons and grandsons—often educated at the College—were on active service in many parts of the rapidly expanding Empire. The close connexion between India and Cheltenham was main-tained during these years. Lord Ellenborough—a familiar figure in the town during his residence at Southam—was appointed Viceroy in 1842. During his term of office, in spite of the policy of the East India Company, war broke out in the Punjab and Sind. Among the heavy casualties in the battles with the Sikhs were many whose homes were in Cheltenham. Sir Charles Napier, who (by what has been called a 'very useful and humane piece of rascality') had annexed Sind, came to stay in Imperial Square in 1848. He drank the waters and rode around the town on his little Arab horse and was very much at home in the society of the many soldiers who had served with him in various parts of the globe—from the United States to India. When in the same year war flared up again in the Punjab it was to Sir Charles Napier that the Commander-in-Chief—the old Duke of Wellington—turned with the words, 'If you don't go, I must'. A representative Cheltenham gathering bade farewell to Sir Charles at the Great Western Railway station as he set off on his expedition.

The outbreak of the Indian Mutiny caused acute suffering in the town. The *Examiner* wrote of 'the hundreds of our families who have friends and relatives in India—the hundreds more whose connections are on the way thither to avenge the outrages—who are all at this moment moved with deep feelings of sorrow and anxiety'. The same mood is expressed by a local versifier.

> What English town
> More 'whelmed with anguish? Where the happy hearth
> More robbed than ours?

The Crimean War, which immediately preceded the Mutiny, had a similar local effect because of the large number of families directly affected. Goding, who was an actual eyewitness, refers to the large crowd of relatives in Imperial Circus waiting daily for the bulletins which were issued from the office of the *Examiner* in the days following the battles of Alma and Inkerman. At a time when heavy black was worn by all relatives of the dead the fashionable part of the town seemed to be in general mourning. There can indeed be no doubt that military and naval circles in Cheltenham rendered great service in the expansion and defence of the Empire, and that they did this with the blessing and goodwill of the evangelical clergy of the town, to whose congregations they mainly belonged.

Not all these, however, had fitted themselves into the straitjacket of Evangelicalism. The sporting circle continued its activities untroubled by the pulpit fulminations of Francis Close or the ideals of respectability extolled by the guidebooks. The popularity of flat racing waned, but steeplechasing took its place, organized very largely by Colonel Berkeley, and from 1844 it became an annual event. The race of 1847 was won by Holman over a gruelling course mapped out by

Colonel Berkeley himself—through Noverton Lane in Prestbury 'over a stone wall into an orchard, over a stanked brook
with gorse bushes on the taking-off side, across the meadows
towards the Hewletts'. It came to be regarded as 'the steeple
chase of history, the "Country rider's Classic"', because it was the
theme of Adam Lindsay Gordon's poem, 'How we beat the
Favourite'.[12] In this poem the winner was the poet himself, on
the mythical 'Bay Iseult', and the favourite he imagined he had
beaten was George Stevens, one of a small group of Cheltenham immortals, who later rode five Grand National winners
but was unfortunately killed when his horse bolted down
Cleeve Hill. He was trained by Tom Oliver whose stables were
at Prestbury, and who had himself won the same race three
times. Another rider whom he taught was Thomas Pickernell
—friend and contemporary of Adam Lindsay Gordon at Cheltenham College. Pickernell too won the Grand National three
times—a feat which was also achieved later by Jack Anthony
(Dean Close School). Not far from Tom Oliver's stables in
Prestbury, at the 'King's Arms', Fred Archer spent his child-
hood. He grew up to be one of the greatest of all jockeys and
had won the Derby five times before his tragic suicide at the
age of twenty-nine.

Adam Lindsay Gordon[13] was for two short periods—as a
child of nine and later as a young man of eighteen—a pupil at
Cheltenham College, where his father was a master. It was
during this last period that he became friendly with Tom
Oliver, George Stevens, and Tom Pickernell. Horse-racing
was not the only sport for which Cheltenham was known at
this time. The middle-weight champion of England—Jim
Edwards—had a boxing saloon at (or near) the 'Roebuck'—
a public-house situated in a turning from the lower High
Street. In this saloon Pickernell and Gordon used to receive
instruction, and on one famous occasion Gordon by some
lucky chance knocked out the champion. The two boys seem
to have spent much of their time in this saloon and on Tom
Oliver's horses. Eventually Captain Gordon decided that his
son was wasting his talents and dispatched him to South
Australia. In that country his genius developed and he was
later recognized as the national poet. His memories of the

great days of hunting and steeplechasing in Cheltenham never left him. 'How we beat the Favourite' was published only a year before his suicide in 1870. In his 'Legend of Cotteswold' he recalls an earlier hunting scene:

> I remember the lowering wintry morn,
> And the mist on the Cotswold hills,
> Where I once heard the blast of the huntsman's horn,
> Not far from the Seven rills.
>
> Jack Esdaile was there, and Hugh St. Clair,
> Bob Chapman and Andrew Kerr,
> And big George Griffiths on Devil May Care
> And black Tom Oliver.
>
> And one who rode on a dark brown steed,
> Clean-jointed, sinewy, spare,
> With a lean game head of the Blacklock breed,
> And the resolute eye that loves the lead,
> And the quarters massive and spare,
> A tower of strength with a promise of speed
> (There was Celtic blood in the pair).

Among the names mentioned George Griffiths belonged to the family who had succeeded Robert Capper at Marle Hill House. Jack Esdaile, also a very fine rider, had married Ianthe Shelley,[14] the daughter of the poet by his first wife Harriet Westbrook. Unlike her famous father she held strong evangelical views. The 'one who rode on a dark brown steed' was Edward Nolan who in the Crimean War carried the order for the Charge of the Light Brigade and was killed instantaneously. Sixty-three years after Gordon's death a plaque in the Poets' Corner of Westminster Abbey was erected to his memory by the Australian Government.

Another small group continued its way unconcerned with the main stream of Cheltenham social life. In a house in St. James's Square Alfred Tennyson lived with his mother and sisters, who had come to the town in 1844. For six years the house seems to have been the poet's headquarters, and in a room overlooking the Great Western Railway station he spent long evenings with the few friends whose society was congenial to him. Parts of *In Memoriam* must have been written in this house. In poetic vision he saw the age-old Cheltenham Street:

> There where the long street roars hath been
> The silence of the central sea.

In the year of the publication of *In Memoriam* he succeeded Wordsworth as Poet Laureate. The impact of this event upon contemporary Cheltenham may be judged from Miss Beale's experience shortly after her appointment to the Ladies' College (1858). 'I tried to get Tennyson's last poem in one of the principal shops of the Promenade. I was told, "We have never had any poetic effusions in our Library, and I do not think we shall begin now".'[15]

Among the small circle of his Cheltenham friends Dobson and Robertson have already been mentioned.[16] Others were Dr. Ker and Sydney Dobell who was writing poetry which in his own time had a considerable reputation and brought him a wide circle of friends among contemporary writers. As a Liberal—in his early days a Radical—he felt strong sympathy with the Italian revolution which he expressed in the long poem *The Roman*. He was also deeply moved by the beauty of the Gloucestershire scene; but to the modern reader much of his poetry seems largely derivative, with echoes from Keats and Shakespeare.

Another distinguished resident was Sir Thomas Phillipps, tenant and later owner of Thirlestaine House, for the eight years preceding his death there in 1872. Neither he nor his wife, who was an invalid, took an active part in the social life of the town, but he continued to amass manuscripts and books on a scale which made him one of the most famous collectors of all time.[17] It is significant that both Ranke and Mommsen thought it worth while to examine the Thirlestaine House collection.

In the year of Sir Thomas Phillipps's death occurred that of Lord Ellenborough. In his later years he was credited with a dislike of Cheltenham, although he had a residence there in addition to his house at Southam. He was the last of the great eighteenth-century figures in Cheltenham, whose standard of morals was so markedly different from that of the mid-Victorian era in which he died. Earl Fitzhardinge had died in 1857 following a fall from his horse while hunting. It seemed a fitting end for the Colonel Berkeley who had dominated the sporting scene for so long. At the time of his death, however, he was regarded with respect and affection not only for his sporting qualities, but for those described in his obituary in the *Examiner*. 'He was a true aristocrat, a consistent politician, an honest man, a good landlord, a constant friend, a charitable nobleman, and a first-rate Lord Lieutenant of the County.' None the less in the struggle against evangelical forces he had been very largely defeated and at the end of his life was himself much influenced by the Congregational minister, Dr. Morton Brown. The reign of Francis Close came to an end in 1856, in which year he was appointed Dean of Carlisle. Shortly afterwards Boyd moved from Christ Church to a London vicarage and later became Dean of Exeter, so that these leading personalities in the struggle left the Cheltenham scene at the same time.

This composite picture of Cheltenham life with its many-sided activities was probably not the image which was presented to the rest of the country. Large churches and eloquent preachers were undoubtedly a considerable contemporary attraction for visitors, and it was on these grounds as well as for its beauty of setting that its reputation mainly rested during these years. This point of view is well presented by George Eliot in *Middlemarch*: ' "We will make a journey to Cheltenham in the course of a month or two", Bulstrode said to his wife. "There are great spiritual advantages to be had in that town, along with the air and the waters, and six weeks there will be very refreshing for us." '

XVII

THE CHANGING SCENE

In the early days of the Spa, as we have seen, difficulties of
transport had held back developments. The old Gloucester
Flying Machine had taken three days to travel from Gloucester to London in the year 1738. By 1773, according to
William Winterbotham, the time for the journey from Cheltenham to London was reduced to 26½ hours, and by 1783,
when the second Cheltenham *Guide Book* was published, a
coach from Gloucester could reach London in 18 hours. The
major improvement on the roads approaching Cheltenham
took place just before and just after the beginning of the nineteenth century, with a corresponding increase in the facilities
for travel. An advertisement in 1826 shows that a fast coach
ran from the Plough Hotel every morning, reaching London
in ten and a half hours. There were also at the same date two
daily services to London from the Plough, three daily services
to Birmingham, two to Bath, and one to Liverpool; while
from the Royal Hotel there were three other coaches running
daily to London, three to Birmingham, two to Bath, one to
Exeter, Coventry, Wolverhampton, Manchester, Sheffield, and
Chester. In 1831 Gurney's Steam Coach was tried out by
Sir Charles Dance between Cheltenham and Gloucester but
its use was abandoned following complaints of the damage
done to the road. It has been estimated that in the years
immediately preceding the construction of railways from thirty
to forty four-horse coaches passed along the High Street each
day. 'Many of the best whips of the time were then on the
road between Cheltenham and London, Cheltenham and Bath.
The Plough Hotel was the very heart of the town and was the
scene of healthful vigorous life from morning till night', writes
the anonymous author of *The Golden Decade of a Golden Town*.
In a few years the old inns were to be superseded as starting-
points by the new railway stations.

It was perhaps natural that a town through which such a volume of traffic passed should show an early interest in the development of railways, although no action was taken until the Great Western Railway Company obtained an Act of Parliament in 1835 sanctioning the building of a line from London to Bristol.[1] A group of Cheltenham residents then considered plans for the construction of a line from Cheltenham through Gloucester and Stroud to join this line. Brunel was called in to make a survey. At a public meeting held shortly afterwards it was proposed that an application should be made to Parliament for a Bill to sanction the making of a line from Cheltenham via Gloucester to join the G.W.R. at or near Swindon. The local company which was then formed (the Great Western Union under the chairmanship of W. H. Hyett and later of Henry Norwood Trye) proceeded to apply for the required Bill. The opposition in Cheltenham was led by Thomas Henney and in the House of Commons by the spokesmen of a company recently formed for the construction of a line to London via Northleach, Witney, Aylesbury, and Tring. The Bill, however, was passed, largely owing to the initiative of Pearson Thompson and his partner Roy, and the company proceeded with the project of a line to Gloucester and on through Stonehouse, Stroud, and Kemble to a junction near Swindon, with a branch line to Cirencester. In the meantime the Birmingham and Gloucester Company (later the Midland) had also applied for a Bill to permit the construction of a line from Cheltenham to Gloucester as part of their main project of a Birmingham to Gloucester Railway. The two companies then made an agreement to share the Cheltenham to Gloucester line, and at the same time purchased jointly the old tramway between the two towns, although they did not immediately close it to the horse-drawn trucks which carried coal and other heavy goods along the line.

Soon afterwards the local company ran short of money and the Birmingham and Gloucester Company took over the almost completed line to Gloucester on which Brunel had been working. This was then opened in 1840 with a station at Lansdown as part of the new line from Birmingham, but it was known locally as the Roy Thompson[2] line.

In the meantime the local company had managed to find the money to construct the line from Swindon to Cirencester, but was then obliged, because of financial difficulties, to sell even this to the Great Western Railway Company and with it the right to buy back their original share in the Cheltenham to Gloucester line. Finally, after heavy losses, the local company was absorbed into the Great Western Railway in 1844. In the same year, by a working agreement between the Birmingham and Gloucester Company and the Great Western, an Act was obtained by which a short line ($1\frac{1}{4}$ miles) was made to connect the line near Lansdown Station with the new Great Western Station to be built in St. James's Square. When this was opened in 1847 Cheltenham was connected directly by railway with Birmingham, Bristol, and London. For two years it had been necessary for Cheltenham and Gloucester passengers to travel by coach from Gloucester to Cirencester, whence they took the train to Paddington. In 1845, however, the Swindon to Gloucester route was completed by the Great Western Company and at last the journey could be made directly to London.

The new mode of travelling made an immediate appeal. Rachel Whinyates wrote in her diary (October 1840): 'Got up early to see Laetitia off. We went to the train station at a little after 7 o'clock and at 8 the strange and wonderful steam conveyance set off, moving slowly at first. The carriages are very comfortable, like armchairs, for six persons in each. At Birmingham (50 miles in 3 hours) they enter a fresh train for Liverpool. One cannot but feel nervous. God grant a safe arrival.'

Within a few years the scene had changed. The coaches had disappeared and the inn yards were quiet. One of the oldest of the coaching inns—the 'George'—went out of business completely and was used as an auction room by Messrs. Engall & Sanders. The old tramway lasted until 1859 when the two railway companies closed the main track.

The project for making a shorter line to London via Tring, which had been defeated in 1837, was revived in 1845. It was backed by many influential people in the town, but there was strong opposition because in Cheltenham itself the line would have passed unpleasantly near to various churches and chapels and would have meant the raising of the level of five roads. A public meeting was organized in protest, presided over by Francis Close, and a fund of £1,000 was raised to oppose the scheme. The Bill was thrown out in the committee stage, perhaps unfortunately for the town, since the proposed route would undoubtedly have been shorter. Two years later another company made a similar attempt and succeeded against all opposition in getting a Bill through Parliament. Certain properties in the lower High Street were then actually purchased for the site of the new line, but the scheme had then to be dropped for financial reasons.

One of the properties concerned was the present Idminston House which had been used as a general hospital since 1839. With the growing population a larger hospital was in any case becoming necessary and a site in Sandford Road had already been provided some years before the sale. The architect chosen was D. J. Humphris, later Borough Surveyor and known at the time for his designs for Keynsham Terrace in Hales Road. The new hospital—completed in 1849—is the last important building in classical style to be erected in the town. It is entirely Greek in design, having for its entrance a central portico with four Ionic columns, and as it was built very shortly after Lord Northwick had completed his additions to the nearby Thirlestaine House, Humphris may well have been influenced by the design of this earlier Greek building.

A less happy design—by the architect John Middleton—was chosen for the isolation hospital in Charlton Lane. This somewhat grim and forbidding building was not completed until 1877. It was founded very largely with money bequeathed for the purpose by Miss Delancey,[3] but was delayed partly because of complications arising from her will and partly because of a rise in labour costs. The remainder of the money required came from public subscriptions which were doubtless raised more easily because of the memory of the earlier scarlet fever epidemics. In recent years it has been converted into a hospital and a home for old people, and a similar conversion, for other types of patients, has been made of the workhouse erected in 1841 in Swindon Road for the Cheltenham Union of

Parishes set up under the Poor Law Amendment Act (1834). This building was sarcastically described by a contemporary guide-book as being 'of the plainest character;... it will readily be admitted that no public money has been wasted upon ornament or external decoration.'

Most of the other important buildings erected after 1840 were schools, which have already been described, and the churches and chapels which were considered essential to serve the needs of the newer areas of the town. Between the Park estate and Leckhampton the Gothic church of St. Philip's was erected in 1844. Its first minister was the scholarly J. E. Riddle who lived at the nearby Tudor Lodge, and it was for many years the church where Miss Beale worshipped. Its mural tablets show that the congregation included many fashionable people, but it also provided for the poorer residents in the area. The first building was pulled down in 1882 when the present church of St. Philip and St. James was erected in its place.

St. Peter's Church, designed by S. W. Daukes in neo-Norman style, was consecrated in 1849, in an area where crime and ignorance were at this time most prevalent. A draft[4] which has survived of a petition from the parishioners to the magistrates is undated, but it was probably drawn up between 1850 and 1860. It makes a strong case for a separate police station: 'People of respect are afraid to live here, because life and property are not safe.... Persons are stoned or pelted with mud . . . one or two have lost their lives. . . . The country people are robbed of their baskets. . . . The church has two clergymen, and is nearly empty of a Sunday morning. No town in England can equal this parish. The rich can protect themselves, but where ignorance and superstition dwell, there is slavery.'

St. Luke's was the third church which was considered necessary because of the growing population. In 1845 the Church of England school in Bath Road had been licensed for public worship and it was widely felt that a new church must be built in the area. The money required was raised by subscription. It did not, however, come mainly from wealthy shareholders as with earlier churches, but from small amounts given by large numbers of poorer people; £600 alone was raised in one shilling subscriptions. It was during the sermon at the consecration of this church in 1854 that Francis Close publicly admitted his regret for the earlier method of building churches by the raising of share capital.

> More than half the seats in the best parts of this Church are dedicated to the poor for ever, only sufficient being reserved to support the Minister and maintain the decent performance of divine worship. I deeply regret that through ignorance I ever assisted in building churches on any other principle. But we knew no better, knew not of the depth of Christian piety and sympathy on which we could draw. We therefore had recourse to the cupidity of individuals by creating property in churches. I wish that every church could be redeemed from private property entirely, but it is better to have these churches than none at all.[5]

He did not stop at vain regrets but took steps to effect a change in connexion with the management of St. James's Church shortly before he left to be Dean of Carlisle.

Three other Anglican churches were built before the borough received its Charter of Incorporation. St. Mark's (designed by John Middleton) was consecrated in 1862 to serve the religious needs of the area around Gloucester Road and the Midland Railway station. All Saints' Church (1868) was erected for a parochial district taken partly from Holy Trinity and partly from St. John's. The third—the church of St. Matthew —was not completed until 1879. Its erection was due mainly to the efforts of Canon Bell, at that time Rector of St. Mary's. He wished it to become the parish church in place of St. Mary's which he proposed should be a chapel of ease. There was, however, such strong opposition that he was unable to proceed with this change. St. Matthew's replaced the temporary church which had been built in 1859. In that year the discovery was made that the vaults under the pews in the south aisle of the Parish Church were in a most insanitary condition, that the galleries erected in the last century were unsafe, and that the buttresses of the tower were cracked. As these galleries and pews had been erected as a result of faculties, and the owners were entitled to refuse permission for their removal, the incumbent (the Reverend Edward Walker—the first Rector) decided to close the Parish Church, and a large temporary church of corrugated iron, complete with porch and a small spire, was erected where St. Matthew's now stands. To make way for the new building the old Great House was at last pulled down. The adjacent Clarence Hotel, built in the original grounds of the Great House by Lord Sherborne, had been purchased in 1859 and altered to make the present Police Station. In the meantime the repair of St. Mary's had been made possible after an application to the Home Office. A sanitary officer was sent from the Burial Board and after the report which followed his inspection an Order in Council was issued by which the pews and galleries could be moved, the vaults sealed, the floor covered with concrete nine inches thick, and all the other necessary repairs completed. In the course of these operations three ancient stone coffins were discovered, the origin of which is unknown, but unfortunately the sites of the burial places of many earlier inhabitants were covered over and their identity lost. The ancient font had been removed some years before to the Sun Inn—where it was used as a watering trough. St. Mary's church was reopened for public worship in 1861.

Three important Nonconformist chapels were built in the Gothic style during these years. Salem Chapel in Clarence Street was opened by the Baptists in 1844; another branch of the Baptists built the Cambray Chapel in 1855 from the designs of Dangerfield—also at one time Borough Surveyor; the Congregational Church in Winchcombe Street (built in 1852) was designed by Samuel Onley for the congregation of Dr. Morton Brown, which was too large for the Highbury Chapel in Grosvenor Street. This large building was acquired in 1932 to make way for the Gaumont Cinema then built on its site, and a new Congregational Church was erected in Priory Terrace. The St. George's Street Wesleyan Chapel was built in classical idiom, as was the later United Methodist Free Church (Royal Well Chapel, 1867). Bethesda in Great Norwood Street was built in 1846, by Wesleyan Methodists. In 1844 the Unitarians built their church at the foot of Bayshill. Goding described it as 'an elegant structure in the Anglo-Norman style', but as a member of its congregation he was no doubt prejudiced in its favour.

In 1836, the Society of Friends built a new meeting-house in Manchester Place, adjacent to the one in which they had worshipped since 1702. The Jewish congregation apparently considered purchasing this old meeting-house, since in 1836 they paid for a survey of the building to be made. The subsequent report was presumably not to their liking and the next year the Unitarians took over the building and used it until they moved to their new church in 1844. In the meantime the Jews had bought land near St. James's Square and built a synagogue which was consecrated in 1839. Five years later they acquired land in Elm Street for a burial ground.

It is uncertain when the first Jews settled in Cheltenham. Ephraim Alex, the founder of the Jewish Board of Guardians in London and a well-known social worker, was born in Cheltenham in 1800, but the earliest existing record of a congregation is dated 1826. From receipts dating from 1830, it appears that their place of worship was in Manchester Place, probably near the Friends' meeting-house. The land for the synagogue was purchased in the names of Isaiah Alex (surgeon dentist), Andrew Isaacs of Stroud (pawn-broker), Abraham Levi (watch-maker), Ephraim Moseley (boot- and shoe-maker), Levi Isaacs (gentleman) and Israel Moses (pawn-broker). During the next fifty years the Jewish congregation included many well-known residents, among whom were the Da Silva family and Miss Lousada, M. R. Henriques (bookseller), E. Samuel (furrier), W. Isaachar and H. Karo (jewellers) and, later, M. Hart—the owner of the Fleece Hotel. The congregation received some support from Sir Francis Goldsmit—the first Jewish baronet in England—who at one time lived near Cirencester, and was for many years the leader of the movement to enable Jews to sit in Parliament. It appears from the records, however, that from 1874 financial difficulties had arisen, and in 1897 the synagogue was closed. It was not in general use again until 1939.

The best of the Gothic buildings of this period was the Roman Catholic church of St. Gregory with its fine spire and tower. It was designed by the well-known architect Charles Hansom and completed in 1857, to replace the earlier church built in 1810 after the arrival of French refugees from the Revolution.

One of the greatest external changes was caused by the demolition of the Market-house, with its pleasing front, which Lord Sherborne had built in the High Street in 1822. This had been sold by the lord of the manor to the solicitor R. C. Chesshyre, who in 1867 removed it to make way for shops and converted the Arcade into a public thoroughfare which is now known as Bennington Street. The following year pens were set up in the street for a cattle market. The Commissioners greatly disliked this arrangement, especially as the old fairs were still held in the High Street, although they had long outlived their original purpose and constituted a nuisance to traffic and pedestrians. It was not, however, until the Commissioners purchased the Albion Brewery ground and caused the transfer of all markets and fairs to this new site that the town was cleared of cattle-pens and fairs (1876).

Some of the other changes have already been mentioned. In 1856 the sign of the Imperial Hotel was removed from the old building on the west of the Promenade and for many years the building itself was the home of the newly formed Imperial Club under the chairmanship of William Nash Skillicorne. Finally, on the decline of the club, the premises were purchased for use as the General Post Office of the town (1874).

The Imperial Club was succeeded by its rival the New Club which in 1874 built for itself the spacious premises it still occupies next to the Town Hall. According to a guide-book of 1883 it was 'open to Visitors of approved rank in society'. It seems to have taken over much of the prestige of the original New Club (1816) which was, however, still housed in its much smaller quarters above the Assembly Rooms. For many years it represented the ultra-Conservative section of Cheltenham society, preferring the maintenance of old ties with the county to the development of municipal independence and the incorporation of the borough.

It was significant of the changing times that the house on Bayshill[6]—once famous as the residence of King George III— was pulled down to make way for a more modern building. The new Bayshill House, on the same site, became the residence of the Baron de Ferrières who came to the town in 1860. It is now known as Sidney Lodge and is the property of the Cheltenham Ladies' College.

The demolition of the Old Well Spa in 1848 has already been mentioned. In its place Samuel Onley built the much larger and more imposing structure which was known at first as the Royal Wells Music Hall and later as the Theatre Royal. The portico was supported by four Corinthian columns, on either side of which were two larger plate-glass windows (Goding, p. 393). In the interior eight Corinthian columns supported the roof, although two of these were removed later because they blocked the view of the stage. The dispensing of the Spa waters was relegated to a small conservatory at one end of the Long Room, while at the opposite end there was a stage suitable for concerts and dramatic performances— an arrangement which indicated the great decline in the use of the waters. At the same time the surrounding gardens were relaid and a very pleasant scene set for what was virtually a small theatre. Unfortunately, however, it was not large enough for mid-nineteenth-century audiences, and though it served a useful purpose for a few years it was already becoming obsolete when it was bought by the Governors of the Ladies' College in 1889. They had already acquired a strip of land on the east side of the Old Well Walk on which they erected the new building in 1872. The old Music Hall was then repaired and was used by the College until 1897, when it was replaced by the present Princess Hall. 'The elm trees of the Old Walk were still standing beside the Theatre Royal—and stood for many years after the Hall was built. The College buildings had advanced step by step to the Old Well; and by a freak of history, the Princess Hall built in the last phase of its Gothic revival, links the College with Regency Romance.'[7]

This purchase had thus brought to an end the last attempt to maintain the Old Well Spa as a centre for social gatherings and the dispensation of the waters. The character of the town had completely changed, and it is significant that the purchase was made by one of the new educational institutions which were to replace the Spa as a source of revenue by attracting to the town (for entirely different reasons) people from many parts of the world.

XVIII

PARTY POLITICS AND GENERAL
ELECTIONS

B Y the Reform Act of 1832, as we have seen, Cheltenham became a parliamentary borough entitled to send one member to the House of Commons. From the surviving poll books of the eighteenth century it appears that the majority of Cheltenham freeholders entitled to vote for county members were Whigs, and it is therefore not surprising that, in the first election after the passing of the Act, the Liberal Craven Fitzhardinge Berkeley (younger brother of Colonel Berkeley) was returned unopposed. The next day he was 'chaired' in a procession beginning from the 'Plough' 'in a superb car drawn by six beautiful horses all tastefully decorated with laurel and orange drapery'. Rachel Whinyates in her diary describes the scene from the Conservative point of view:

A member for Cheltenham is chosen today. The Whigs have prevailed; Lord Segrave's heavy purse has attracted the Tradespeople. . . . This day was the chairing. The Honourable Craven Berkeley sat embowered in laurel. The voters—tradespeople— walked four abreast in front; two flags of England went before, with those of 'Reform' and 'Berkeley and Independence'; it was a pretty sight, though it was said to be a shabby procession, as no gentlemen were in it on horseback. Lord Segrave glories in having his brother returned by the middle and lower classes and not by the gentry.

Although there had been unparalleled rejoicing at the passing of the Act, it was soon realized that large numbers of people would not benefit under the new voting qualification. In the boroughs only those with a house worth £10 a year were entitled to vote. The population of Cheltenham in the census taken in 1831 was 22,942, and yet Craven Berkeley, when describing the results of his pre-election canvass, referred to the 900 potential voters in the town.

Grave discontent followed the realization of the inadequacy of the Reform Act. The working classes had three main grievances. Primarily, food was still dear, and for this they blamed the Corn Laws. They felt cheated because they were still unrepresented in the House of Commons, and they objected to the existing restrictions on trades unions. Many Radicals at this time found it difficult to distinguish between Liberals and Conservatives, especially as the latter had in general accepted the Reform Act as a *fait accompli*, and the former were responsible for the hated Poor Law Amendment Act and the persecution of those attempting to form trades unions. The Radicals in Cheltenham had in 1834 founded the *Free Press*, a weekly journal which had a wide circulation, and they were already using the Mechanics Institute in Albion Street for political meetings and discussions. At the general election in 1835 Craven Berkeley was therefore opposed not by a Conservative candidate, but by the Radical, William Penn Gaskell, who demanded in his election address the repeal of the Corn Laws, the extension of the right to vote, and the repeal of the Poor Law Amendment Act. The hustings were put up in Barnett's Riding School,[1] and on a show of hands Craven Berkeley was elected by 412 votes to 25. The system of voting in Cheltenham has been well described by Sir James Tynte Agg-Gardner, who was later Member of Parliament for the town for forty-three years:

When the system of 'Open voting' was in vogue, the nomination of the candidates (now a mere formality) was a conspicuous and important ceremony. On the appointed day the rival candidates with their respective proposers, seconders and hosts of supporters, accompanied by bands and banners, marched in procession to the hustings. On arriving there the Returning Officers, who presided, invited the proposers and seconders to describe the claims and merits of their respective nominees. After these duties had been discharged, the candidates themselves were called upon to speak, which they did as well as they could, to the accompaniment of rival bands, cheers, jeers, hisses, and volleys of eggs, dead cats and other missiles. At the conclusion of this entertainment, the Returning Officer called for a show of hands, and gave his decision on the result. If his decision passed unchallenged, the candidate in whose favour he had decided was declared *ipso facto* duly elected; but it generally happened that the proposer of the candidate who had lost on the show of hands demanded a Poll. This was granted, and the polling took place on the following day. The Poll opened at eight o'clock and closed at four. Hourly statements of the number of votes recorded were issued. As soon as the Poll was over, the Presiding Officer revisited the hustings, formally announced the result, and the election was over.

Without attempting to discuss the advantages and disadvantages of the two systems of open voting and voting under ballot, I will merely remark that the general cost of the election under the old system was about six times as much as that which rules at the present day, because certain expenses then permitted are now prohibited. For instance, a candidate was expected to defray the railway fares of voters from whatever distance they might select to come; also provide them with banners and colours, and to engage what was called a 'bodyguard' for the protection of the candidate and canvassers.[2]

The first Conservative opposition came in the election rendered necessary by the accession of Queen Victoria in 1837, but their candidate Jonathan Peel was defeated by 632 votes to 298. By the time of the next election in 1841, Liberal ministries had held office for eleven years and there was a strong reaction in the country against them. The Cheltenham Conservatives put up James Agg-Gardner whose family had recently purchased the manor from Lord Sherborne. The Radicals also had a distinguished candidate in Colonel Peyronet Thompson, a graduate of Queens' College, Cambridge, who had seen active service in the West Indies and the Peninsular War, and in recent years had been campaigning against the Corn Laws. The election was held in a field in Bayshill. James Agg-Gardner was proposed on the grounds that 'he holds such an extent of property, including the Lordship of the Manor, that his interest is identified with the prosperity of the town, and that his heart and soul are devoted to its welfare'. Pearson Thompson rose to second the nomination but was howled down as a renegade and turncoat—since he had formerly supported the Liberal demand for the Reform Bill and had recently changed sides. The nomination of the Radical candidate came as a surprise to both parties. He was proposed by Samuel Harper, the editor of *Cheltenham Free Press*, in a speech attacking the inaction of the last Liberal ministry. John Goding rose to second the nomination but was temporarily silenced when one of his opponents drenched him with a bucket of water. Further interruption came from Craven Berkeley, who called Samuel Harper 'a damned blackguard', John Goding 'a wolf in sheep's clothing', and accused both of them of being in the pay of the Tories. The Returning Officer then asked for a show of hands for each candidate and it appeared that the Radical had won. A poll was demanded, and when this took place the next day the figures showed how few of the Radical supporters at the hustings had the necessary property qualification to vote. Craven Berkeley received 764 votes, J. Agg-Gardner 655, and Peyronet Thompson only 4 (*Cheltenham Free Press*, 10 July 1841). After this failure the Radicals did not put up any more candidates.

The size of the Conservative vote was not only due to the general reaction against the Liberals. It marked the begininng of the change brought about as the result of the purchase of the manor by a popular Conservative family which was resident in the town. There were other more general causes. The antagonism between Berkeley Castle and Francis Close was carried into the political field and the whole weight of the influence of the latter was thrown on the Conservative side. It was in the year of this election that Francis Close told the Working Men's Association:[3]

I cannot for the life of me separate politics from religious preaching. . . . There is no distinction between politics and religion. I cannot teach a man his duty without in some degree talking politics. In my humble opinion the Bible is Conservative, the Prayer Book Conservative, the Liturgy Conservative, the Church Conservative, and it is impossible for a Minister to open his mouth without being a Conservative.

With few exceptions the other Anglican clergy, while less outspoken, belonged to the same party.

The Nonconformists, on the other hand, were traditionally Liberal and they were engaged during these years in resisting the demands enforced on them for church rates. When four Quakers refused on principle to pay this rate in 1841 a distraint order was levied on their property. Six years later the minister of the Baptist Chapel (Bethel) had certain of his goods seized for a similar refusal. The Vestry itself instituted a series of polls on the question of church rates, and each year an increasing number of the parish voted against their imposition on the unwilling Dissenters. It was much to the credit of Francis Close that in 1851 he proposed a compromise by which all expenses concerned with the Anglican services in the church should be raised by voluntary subscriptions from the congregation, and not included in the general church rate, which would in future be used for the maintenance of the church fabric, the churchyard, and objects of public welfare. In this he anticipated the Act of Parliament which finally lifted the burden of rates for church expenses from those who had their own chapels to support. Until this happened, however, the question of rates was one of the causes for the adherence of Nonconformists to the Liberal party. At the time of the general election of 1847 six of the leading Nonconformist ministers, including Dr. Morton Brown of Highbury Chapel, issued the following invitation: 'To the Protestants and Dissenters of Cheltenham. We the undersigned Ministers of Protestant Dissenting Chapels and Congregations in this town, feeling it to be our duty to state the grounds on which we give our support to the Honourable Craven Berkeley in this election, request you to meet us at the Town Hall, when we will severally address you on this subject.' In a long speech Rayner Winterbotham referred to the Tory persecutions of Dissenters (of which his own father was a victim) and to the fact that the Whigs (Liberals) had always stood for civil as well as religious liberty. He reminded them that in that very hall (then a riding school) the announcement of the passing of the Reform Act—a great Liberal achievement—had been made. Dr. Morton Brown also emphasized the traditional policy of the Liberals in upholding religious freedom and civil liberty, and it is clear from the speeches of other ministers that they were concerned not only with the removal of the disabilities of the Dissenters but with the extension of the franchise and with vote by ballot.

Politics at this time entered into almost every activity of the town. The Guardians of the Poor were elected very largely on a party political basis, and even the appointment of the medical officer for the Workhouse was the occasion of the triumph of the party to which he belonged.[4] The election of the Liberal Septimus Pruen as Coroner by somewhat dubious means (1850) led to a Conservative meeting of protest presided over by Lord Redesdale. A new election was called for, and later the candidate supported by Lord Redesdale was successful. Even the election of manorial officers, which had hitherto been uninfluenced by party politics, was affected. In 1848 at the traditional November meeting of the Court Leet the jury were told to make nominations for the High Constable from which the steward of the lord of the manor would choose the High Constable. Objections were raised on the ground that the jury had always directly elected the officials. 'For the first time anything like a political feeling has been allowed to creep into the Court—almost the only neutral spot in Cheltenham. It should be urged that when Lord Sherborne held the Manor, nothing like party feeling marked the appointments.'[5] Happily at the dinner given at the 'Plough', which followed the meeting of the Court Leet, politics were excluded and agents of the Liberal and Conservative parties might be seen hobnobbing over Churchill's Port, and toasts were given to 'Lord Fitzhardinge and his Fox-hounds' and 'Mr. James Agg-Gardner, Lord of the Manor, with loud and unanimous honours'.

A less happy example of party political bitterness was the attack by the solicitor R. S. Lingwood on the local magistrates. As will be shown later, there was considerable ill feeling (which was to some extent connected with party politics) between the Cheltenham Town Commissioners and the local bench of magistrates. In 1848 R. S. Lingwood was reported in the Conservative *Cheltenham Journal* as having accused the magistrates of 'prostituting their office for political purposes' by excusing the payment of Poor rates to Liberals and making Conservatives pay the full rate. Lingwood denied that he had made the statement, but the magistrates brought a suit against Hadley, the editor of the *Journal*. The case was tried at the Assizes and the editor was required to publish a full apology and to pay all costs, although he maintained that the report was accurate.[5] The *Examiner* in its comments on the case of

Hadley *v.* the Queen pointed out that, in season and out, the Conservatives never ceased to attack the magistrates. The *Journal* commented: 'After all, the real evil consists in the exclusive character of the Cheltenham Bench. Had the majority of the acting magistrates not been active parties on the Liberal side... the charges of Mr. Lingwood would have fallen harmless. It is a great misfortune ... that gentlemen of Conservative opinions should be practically excluded from the Commission of the Peace.' To this assertion the *Free Press* replied that 'Tory Magistrates were in the Commission, but failed to attend'.

A few months before this the local Press had been divided in its comments on the case of the Reverend W. F. Wilkinson, who was Theological Tutor at Cheltenham College and according to the *Examiner* 'was known to be a gentleman of Liberal principles'. A lecture on 'Some Tendencies and Characteristics of the Age' had been given at the Literary and Philosophical Institute by the Radical Nonconformist George Dawson, minister of the Church of the Saviour in Birmingham, after which Wilkinson had proposed a vote of thanks on behalf of the meeting. He was immediately afterwards censured by the Board of Directors of the College, who took the view that Dawson was 'a person whose theological and religious principles were inconsistent with those on which the College was founded', and as a result of this censure he felt obliged to resign. The Directors of the Literary and Philosophical Institute then issued a memorial in which they condemned the action of the College authorities and expressed their sympathy with Mr. Wilkinson.[6] The matter was taken up by the newspapers of all three parties and finally reached the London Press. The *Looker-On* supported the right of 'the Directors of an entirely privately owned institution to dismiss any of the people they employed'. The *Examiner* referred to 'Mr. Close, the reverend instigator of the persecution of Mr. Wilkinson' and regarded the censure as a violation of the rights of the individual. Shortly afterwards George Dawson visited the town again to speak at a public meeting called in protest. He was supported by many of the leading Liberals including Dr. Wright, the solicitor G. E. Williams, and Dr. Morton Brown. A resolution was passed that a memorial should be sent to Lord John Russell (then Prime Minister) 'praying him to confer on the Reverend W. F. Wilkinson the first vacant Church preferment that might be placed at the disposal of the Crown'. Apparently the memorial was successful since, according to Goding, 'a valuable living in the City of Derby was presented to Mr. Wilkinson by the Lord Chancellor'.

The general election of 1847 was fought with more than the usual bitterness. The Conservative candidate Sir Willoughby Jones was accused of holding Tractarian views—which was even more damaging in an evangelical town than the rumours of vicious living which were circulated about his opponent Craven Berkeley. In neither case was there any truth in the accusation. On the other hand, the Conservatives made good use of Craven Berkeley's reported statement in the House of Commons that 'more deaths from miasma occurred in Cheltenham than in any other town of the same size in England'. The statement was made in a speech supporting the Government's policy (later embodied in the Public Health Act of 1848) of creating new sanitary authorities to carry out preventive measures following the cholera and fever epidemics of previous years. The impact of this speech on a town which was still striving to attract visitors to the Spa was serious.

Craven Berkeley explained that he had spoken entirely in the interest of improving the sanitary conditions of the town which the Commissioners had failed to alter, but the incident undoubtedly lost him support in the election. The Conservatives won by eight votes. They celebrated their first victory with a procession half a mile long through the town and with a magnificent dinner party at the Assembly Rooms attended by 400 of their supporters, among whom were some of the leading Conservatives of the borough and the county. The dining tables on this occasion were decorated with flowers and fruit in silver baskets lent by the jewellers Messrs. Martin & Co., and the venison and pineapples were presented by Lord Northwick of Thirlestaine House.

The *Looker-On*, 7 August 1847, emphasized the importance of the victory as the end of the Berkeley supremacy:

The emancipation from a bondage the more degrading, because more dishonourable, than that of a rotten borough of the oldest times.

For nearly fifteen years the town has submitted to every kind of indignity offensive to a free and moral people; and yet, as if obedient to some enchantment which held our volition in thraldom, we continued still to return the Castle nominees, albeit other constituencies taunted us with wearing the Berkeley collar and bartering the franchise for a few days' hunting.

Unfortunately for the Conservatives the rejoicing was premature. The Liberals immediately presented a petition accusing their opponents of bribery and corrupt practices, including the payment of money to 300 voters. After the earlier hearings Sir Willoughby found himself unable to defend his case; the petition was successful and he was therefore unseated. In the new election (1848) Craven Berkeley defeated James Agg-Gardner by 169 votes. The Conservatives then presented a similar petition, complaining that the Liberals had won by means of bribery and 'treating' voters to 'beer and breakfasts'. This petition too was successful and another election became necessary. It is unlikely that either of the unseated candidates were concerned in the bribery. It must indeed have been difficult for them to control their agents and supporters in dealing with some of the voters who by local custom expected at least a supply of food and drink from the candidates.

In the new election of 1848 Grenville Berkeley (a cousin of Craven Berkeley) was elected by 151 votes, so that the Liberal hold on Cheltenham remained unbroken. The petitions had at least one good effect in that the state of affairs revealed by the evidence convinced not only Liberals but some Conservatives of the need for a system of voting by ballot.

There was at this time a concerted attack on the house of Berkeley by Conservatives in various parts of the county. At the end of 1847 two petitions were sent to the Queen asking for the removal of Earl Fitzhardinge from the Lord-Lieutenancy of the county. One was from some of the electors of the Western Division accusing him of illegal interference in the recent elections, and one from 'the Mothers and Daughters' of the same division calling for his dismissal from office.[7] Neither petition was successful and for at least twenty years the family retained its ascendancy. Earl Fitzhardinge's brother Francis was M.P. for Bristol; his brother George Charles Grantly sat for West Gloucestershire (1832–67); his brother Admiral Sir Maurice sat for Gloucester City for many years until he was created Lord Fitzhardinge, when his place was taken by his younger son Charles (1861).

In Cheltenham the Berkeley family was in general supported by the Radicals who did not in this area align themselves with the militant section of the Chartist movement. A body of Chartists indeed marched to the Parish Church but listened peacefully to the sermon by Francis Close admonishing them to be grateful for their many blessings. The effect of the Radical support, however, was to keep the more progressive aims of the Liberals—the extension of the franchise and the vote by ballot —in the fore front of their political promises. So the triumphant Cheltenham Liberals sang the song of the Berkeleys:

> When Tory foes and Tory gold
> Would bid our Liberty succumb
> The name of Berkeley will uphold
> The freedom of our island home.

At the same time Craven Berkeley was partly vindicated in his statement about the health of the town. The Commissioners received a sharp reprimand from the Registrar-General for manipulating the statistics to their own advantage. In a letter addressed to their clerk he wrote: 'I will thank you to state to the Commissioners of the Town of Cheltenham that in their Memorial to the General Board of Health I consider that an improper and unwarrantable use has been made of the information furnished to them by Mr. Ticehurst [the local Registrar], from the public records confided to him of Births, Deaths, and Marriages.'[8]

In the election of 1852 the two former candidates, Sir Willoughby Jones and Craven Berkeley, returned to the contest. Craven Berkeley won by a majority of 130, but his death in 1855 caused another election in which the Conservative candidate William Ridler—a local bank manager—was defeated by over five hundred votes by the former member Grenville Berkeley. Shortly afterwards the appointment of the latter to an office of profit under the Crown led to his resignation and to yet another election in 1856. The new Liberal candidate was his nephew Captain Francis Berkeley, son of Sir Maurice, the member for the City of Gloucester. The Liberal majority was reduced in this election to 186, but in the next election of 1857 Captain Berkeley was returned unopposed. This election had been caused by Lord Palmerston's defeat in the Commons following his justification of the British bombardment and the capture of Canton in the dispute with China. In Cheltenham Liberals and many Conservatives supported Palmerston's Chinese policy, and as a result the Conservatives did not put forward a candidate. For the Liberals, however, the year marks the zenith of their power in Cheltenham.

In the election which followed two years later the Conservatives had a very strong candidate in Charles Schreiber, a former pupil of Cheltenham College, a Fellow of Trinity College, Cambridge, and nephew of Captain Schreiber of Pittville. He had recently married the widowed Lady Charlotte Guest—daughter of the Earl of Lindsey—and although she was by conviction Liberal, she accompanied him in his campaigns in which he showed himself a hard worker and a very good organizer. After a close fight he was defeated by only twelve votes, and the Conservatives treated the result as a virtual victory. His wife describes in her diary the triumphal reception she and her husband received on their return to Cheltenham a week later. The Great Western Railway station was decked with flags, a band played, and a large crowd greeted them. House fronts and windows were filled with supporters and shops were shut. Charles Schreiber made a speech from the balcony of Roden House in Pittville and introduced his wife to his supporters but—as she wrote—'taking care not to mention my radical politics'.[9] Thirteen hundred supporters attended the dinner arranged for him at the Pittville Pump Rooms. A petition to unseat his opponent was prepared but subsequently withdrawn for want of evidence.

In the meantime he carefully nursed the constituency, and in the election of 1865 he won the first real victory for the Conservatives by twenty-eight votes, and so brought to an end the unbroken Liberal ascendancy of over thirty years. The two candidates and some thousands of their supporters had met at the hustings in St. Anne's field in Hewlett Street. The proceedings were described by an eyewitness,[10] who related that when he called out 'Blue for ever' he was belaboured with an umbrella by an old woman wearing the orange favour of Captain—now Colonel—Francis Berkeley. Charles Schreiber was wearing a silk waistcoat which was soon stained with rotten eggs. Other missiles followed, including dead cats. The ladies of both parties wore ribbons and carried parasols of the colour of the parties they supported.

In the indescribable confusion the Returning Officer read the writ and the Bribery Act, after which the candidates were duly proposed. Colonel Berkeley's speech followed. His watchwords were 'Civil and Religious Liberty', by which he meant the extension of the right to vote and the abolition of church rates levied on Nonconformists, and he promised to work for Free Trade and cheaper tea and bread. At this stage his supporters waved aloft two loaves of bread—one labelled Berkeley's 4d. and the other Schreiber's 10d. loaf—which immediately became targets for brick-bats.

Charles Schreiber's speech made shrewd hits at the fox-hunting activities of his opponents, and offered a counter-blast to the Liberal claims that the Berkeley family's patronage and their annual expenditure of money were important factors in the economy of the town. He also explained his objections to the extension of the franchise and the removal of the disabilities of the Nonconformists.

What is to be the political future of our Country? [he asked]. Is it to be constitutional or democratic? (Cheers). Democracy has been well said to resemble the grave in this, that it devours itself, but it gives nothing back... Of all the existing forms of government democracy is the lowest and worst. Shall England abandon her Protestant Faith, her Established Church, the blessing she enjoys, for the evils offered to her clothed in the specious garb of Progressive Reform and Civil and Religious Liberty?

Turning to the interests of the town he continued:

There has been a time when that sacred animal the fox had a large share in the return of your member of Parliament. That day is past and we come to that which is of vital interest to the town, and what do we find it to be?—the College. Remove your College, and your property (land and houses) will depreciate by about 50 per cent, and Cheltenham will be a residence surrendered to owls and bats. If you had accompanied me in my canvass through the town, you would have seen how the labour of Cheltenham finds its occupation. It is in ministering to the comforts, necessities and luxuries of the rich; and, if I may raise the question, which side of the hustings gives most employment to the Labour of the Poor?'[11]

It was clearly impossible in the crowded scene for this election to be decided by a show of hands. The Returning Officer therefore 'as a matter of courtesy' awarded the victory to Colonel Berkeley. Charles Schreiber then demanded a poll, which took place the next day at the booths arranged in the five wards. By the evening feelings had risen dangerously high. William Lynes—one of the Berkeley runners—was walking up the High Street with a friend and singing, 'Hurrah for the bonnets so yellow', when an excited young Conservative supporter named John Glasse called out to him, 'I'll give you yellow, you ——', and at point-blank range shot him dead. After the declaration of the poll in his favour (by a majority of 28), Schreiber was unable to make a speech because of the crowds, and he left the field in deference to a request from the Chief Constable. The Liberals were deeply shocked at the result of the poll. 'You will hardly believe me when I tell you we are beaten', said Samuel Onley when making the first announcements, and Colonel Berkeley left it to Frederick Munroe to speak on behalf of the defeated Liberals. 'We are unaccustomed to defeat,' he said, 'and if we do not behave well under it, it is because we are not used to it. . . . Retribution will come. We unseated Sir Willoughby Jones and we shall unseat Schreiber.'

In the meantime a coroner's jury brought in a verdict of wilful murder against Glasse and he was committed for trial at the Assizes where he was later sentenced to fifteen years' imprisonment for manslaughter. The Conservative *Looker-On*, which had stated in his defence that he was rudely accosted and insulted, referred to the trial of 'the unfortunate Glasse'. It seems that the latter was drunk not so much with alcohol as with excitement, as were many others of both parties on the same day.

One reason for the Conservative victory was that Colonel

Berkeley had attended the Grand Prix in Paris *on Sunday*—a deed which shocked both Evangelicals and Dissenters; but the Liberals assigned their defeat partly to the effect of Schreiber's arguments as to the source of the prosperity of the tradesmen, and partly to the influence of the clergy. 'It is bad to see clergymen of the Church of England, with the Reverend Principals of our College and Grammar School, together with a host of other clerical partisans stepping out of their way to diminish their legitimate influence by placarding their names on the list of canvassers for the Tory Candidate.' They failed to record one strong reason—that since the death of Earl Fitzhardinge in 1857 the influence of the Berkeleys had waned. The point was well made by the counsel for defence during the hearing of the petition presented by the Liberals in an attempt to unseat Schreiber for corrupt practices during the election. 'The influence of the Berkeleys has long been in a state of decadence and now was in a state of absolute death. In the time of Earl Fitzhardinge the noble Earl kept a large establishment and the influence of the family was then large. But those times were now gone.'[12] The petition failed. Schreiber himself and his agents were exonerated from all responsibility for the action of two of his supporters in 'inducing several voters by corrupt means to vote against the Honourable Francis Berkeley'.

From the surviving correspondence concerned with this petition[13] a sorry picture emerges of the state of affairs in the Cheltenham Liberal party at the time. Colonel Francis Berkeley and his father Lord Fitzhardinge felt strongly that William Boodle and R. C. Chesshyre—the solicitors who handled the local side of the petition—were making capital out of party loyalty by charging outrageously for their services, and by their failure to pay the expenses concerned. Colonel Francis Berkeley wrote to his solicitor in Berkeley: 'The people at Cheltenham are always very greedy in election affairs. They keep writing to me for money on account and declare that neither Chesshyre nor Boodle will settle their claims.'

One of the few disinterested men in the party headquarters was the barrister James Fallon, who was closely related to the Skillicorne family. In his letters[14] he tells of his great concern that 'the Borough, which ought to belong to the Castle after the generous way Lord Fitzhardinge has behaved, should slip from us from want of tact and management, and at half the money it costs us. . . . I will cheerfully give all the help I can to make the best of our indifferent position.' At the same time, while he blames the Tory Press—'There is no limit to their lies and misrepresentations'—for the loss of the petition, he admits the real hard work put in by his opponents: 'The Blue Party aided by Schreiber in person are indefatigable in improving and securing their position. . . .'

Shortly afterwards, however, he was cheered by the result of the local elections for the Commissioners. 'The Liberal party carried away everything at the Commissioners' Election. It cost a lot of money; we have a capital subscription; if well managed we should have a good majority at the Board and keep it.'

Colonel Francis Berkeley was by no means pleased with the situation. He wrote to his father: 'The place is very dear and more money is spent on political matters than it is worth. I wish I had never seen the town of Cheltenham.' It is significant that neither he nor any of his relatives fought an election in Cheltenham again, and in this abrupt way the long political connexion between the Berkeley family and the town came to an end.

Charles Schreiber also withdrew from the Cheltenham scene, and in the next election in 1868 the Liberals regained the seat with the comfortable majority of 171 in a large poll. Their candidate was an Oxford undergraduate, H. B. Samuelson, who defeated a Cambridge undergraduate, James Tynte Agg-Gardner, the young lord of the manor. When the same candidates stood in the next election (1874), however, the situation was reversed. James Tynte Agg-Gardner attributed his victory to the general swing of opinion in the country against Gladstone and to the introduction of the ballot. Almost at the same time, however, in the first local government elections held after the incorporation of the borough, the Liberals held a majority of seats with the result that the first two mayors—William Nash Skillicorne and the Baron de Ferrières—were Liberal, although they had originally opposed incorporation.

When opinion in the country swung back in 1880 and Gladstone was returned to power, Cheltenham also returned a Liberal—the popular Baron de Ferrières. Unfortunately for his party he was unwilling to continue his parliamentary career, and for the next twenty years the Conservatives were returned. They were not defeated in Cheltenham until the great national landslide of 1905 when the Liberals swept the country.

There were various interacting causes for the failure of the Liberals to maintain their long hold on the town. The influence of the Church was for many years thrown on the side of the Conservatives. The Proprietary College attracted as residents many families who were traditionally Conservative. The sale of the manor to a resident Conservative family was followed shortly afterwards by the withdrawal of the Berkeleys from the political scene. After the retirement of de Ferrières, the Liberals had difficulty in finding a local candidate who was socially eminent in a town where this factor was considered important. In later years the local party was considered too radical by some of the potential candidates such as Alfred Milner and Sir Henry Hoare. In actual fact their old rallying cry, 'Civil and Religious Liberty', which had sounded so long from the hustings and the Nonconformist pulpits, was no longer valid. Political and religious freedom had been largely won before the retirement of de Ferrières, and the Liberal programme of economic and social reforms had to await the arrival of Asquith and Lloyd George. On the other hand, the Conservatives were fortunate in having a popular and wealthy resident, involved in local interests, as the lord of the manor. He was prepared to devote his life to a political career and thus he provided an element of permanence which was lacking among the Liberals. When Sir James Agg-Gardner died in 1928 he had represented the borough in parliament—though not consecutively—for forty-three of his eighty-four years.

XIX

THE ADMINISTRATION OF THE VESTRY
AND THE COMMISSIONERS
1786–1821

UNDER the already mentioned Act of Parliament of 1786, a body of Commissioners was appointed and given power to make the changes considered essential for the development of the town. Since the greater part of the manorial jurisdiction had disappeared beyond recall and the authority of the bailiff of the borough had not developed to take its place, the only contemporary local government authorities were the Vestry and the justices of the peace. The administrative functions of the latter have already been described; those of the Vestry, inadequate as they were to deal with major changes, were of great importance in the day-to-day administration of the affairs of the town.

The Vestry and its elected officers were responsible not only for the maintenance of the church fabric and the churchyard but for the administration of the Poor Law, the repair of the roads in the parish, the maintenance of the fire-engine, the destruction of vermin, and many other matters such as carrying out the ballot for the militia.

The Cheltenham Vestry Books[1] have been preserved only from 1755, although Goding had access to earlier books, rating lists, and Overseers' Accounts which have since disappeared. From these records a picture emerges of a small community managing its affairs at somewhat informal and infrequent meetings of ratepayers summoned to deal with problems when they arose—sometimes only once, sometimes three or four times a year. At the Easter annual meeting the churchwardens were appointed, and the overseers of the poor and the surveyors of the highway were nominated for their later appointment by the justices of the peace.

Since in general only ratepayers could attend, the very poor were excluded from Vestry meetings, but from the signatures in the first surviving Vestry Book it appears that a fair cross-section of the community attended. The numbers present varied from six to over thirty, and included some who were unable to write and therefore made their mark instead of signing, as well as the more literate tradesmen, farmers, land-owners, and professional men—the curate, the schoolmaster, and, in later years, the doctor. Among the signatures are those of Thomas Hughes and his enemy William Miller; Thomas Humphreys of Cambray Mill and James Arkell of Sandford Mill; William Barrett, flour merchant and baker and later miller; William Pope, baker, whose family at one time owned the 'Plough'; Thomas Gregory from Alston and William Gregory from Arle, both farmers; Thomas Gardner, malster; Thomas Meekyns, draper; William and Giles Ash-mead; John Clutterbuck and Thomas Nettleship, gentlemen; Edward Timbrell, who is described at one time as schoolmaster and again as gentleman, and his son who was probably steward to the Earl of Essex; John de la Bere, steward to the lord of the manor; and Thomas Baghott de la Bere of Southam and Thomas Higgs, names well known in Cheltenham at least as far back as the reign of Elizabeth I.

One of the main functions of the Vestry was the administration of the Poor Laws and the closely related Settlement Acts which were intended to prevent vagrants from moving from parish to parish. The churchwardens and the Overseers of the Poor—the latter unpaid but obliged to serve when appointed—were responsible for the relieving of the poor, using the Poor Rate levied on the parish. The details of the administration of the Poor Law will be dealt with more conveniently in the next chapter on the Vestry, but it should be noted that the Poor Rate was used for a multiplicity of purposes.

A resolution recorded in 1764 orders that 'the Church-wardens and Overseers of the Poor, at the expense of the Parish, provide volunteers for the Parish of Cheltenham to serve in the militia and that they produce such volunteers at the next meeting of the Deputy Lieutenant of the County to be held at the Swan at Bibury . . .'. During the last years of the American War of Independence it was agreed 'that the Overseers of the

Poor shall pay to Edward Townshend and John Squires the sum of £1. 11. 6d over and above the money allowed by Parliament in consideration of these having procured by our desire two single men as deputies for them'.

The maintenance of the fire-engine was another charge on the Poor Rate. 'Agreed to pay £1. 5. 0d a year of the Poor Rate to put and keep the Fire Engine in proper repair' (1788). Expenses of litigation were also paid from the same source. When the Vestry ordered proceedings to be taken in Quarter Sessions against the 'Occupiers of a house or houses where, by all report, bad and fatal consequences must follow the iniquitous proceedings', the cost and charges were to be defrayed out of the Poor Rate.

This case illustrates the responsibility of the Vestry for handing over to Quarter Sessions matters concerned with criminal law. It should be remembered that there was at the time no police force in the modern sense. The constable, who like other parish officials was compelled to serve when appointed, was responsible primarily to the justices of the peace whose orders for arrest he carried out. He could also make arrests without their orders when necessary. The Vestry seems to have maintained—until the appointment of the first Commissioners—the little two-roomed prison which was situated in the High Street in front of the 'Eight Bells' and near the church. It was used mainly for housing prisoners awaiting trial. There were stocks and at least one whipping-post,[2] which could be used only on the orders of a justice of the peace, but as there are no records of the work of the justices acting singly or in Petty Sessions, little is known of how frequent these orders were at the end of the eighteenth century.

Another function of the Vestry and churchwardens was the maintenance of the fabric of the church and the burial ground, for which they were entitled to raise a church rate. Thus in 1776 'the Churchwardens desire the Inhabitants to meet at the Vestry on Friday, 11th of April at 2 o'clock in the afternoon—to consult them about repairing the Church and Steeple and also the Burial Ground, and the Church Rates and other things relating thereto'. At this meeting an order was given for the payment of the annual rent of 30s. for the churchyard to the steward of the Earl of Essex (impropriator of the benefice) although the churchwardens 'shall keep the Churchyard Walks and Trees in good repair'. In 1787, with the permission of the Earl of Essex, it was decided to block up the door in the chancel to make room for more pews 'for the accommodation of the Nobility and Gentry that frequent the Cheltenham Spa'.

The churchwardens were also responsible for the care of the church property within the building. When Henry Skillicorne and William Barrett became churchwardens in 1755 the list of goods they took over is given as: '1 gilt dish, 1 silver flagon, 1 green bag, 2 books of accounts, 2 keys belonging to the Church coffer.' An earlier list had included 'five fourms and a table in ye chancel'. Whether these forms were placed round the Communion table as at Deerhurst and Winchcombe is not known, but in view of the later statement in the Vestry Records (1807) that 'it is resolved that an Altar piece shall be erected in the Chancel' this seems likely.

Undoubtedly the work which was carried out least efficiently by the Vestry was the repair and upkeep of the roads of the parish. Each year the Vestry nominated two probably unwilling surveyors of the highways. After their appointment had been confirmed by the justices of the peace[3] they became directly responsible for the maintenance of all such roads in the parish as were not in the charge of the Turnpike Trusts.[4] All persons in the parish were bound, by various Highway Acts, either to give six days' labour service a year, or lend a cart and team of horses, or provide a sum of money in lieu of these services. If the available labour and money was not adequate for the necessary repairs, a highway rate could be raised on the order of the justices of the peace. At the end of their year of office the two surveyors handed back any money they had in hand. Thus it is recorded in 1756: 'Mr. Sarsons and Mr. Edward Timbrell gave up their accounts as Surveyors of the Highways and upon balance left due to ye Town twelve shillings.' A record quoted by Goding tells a different story of two surveyors who ended their year of office in debt to the parish since 'they had not collected so much money as they had disbursed by £2 by reason of taking too little money of the substantial inhabitants of the town. We, therefore, elect them to serve for the said office for the next year [1721] and by the consent of the Vestry they are not to exceed the expenses of 20 shillings for Ale.'

As the surveyors were unpaid as well as untrained, and acted more or less under compulsion, the roads were for the main part kept in poor condition. In addition to their ignorance of principles of road-making and their unwillingness to impose financial and other burdens on the parish, their work was hindered by the limitations of their obligation, which in fact entailed nothing more than keeping open and safe 'a passage for the King and his lieges'. Neither they nor any other authority in the parish were legally entitled to raise rates to light or cleanse the existing roads, to make new roads, or to draw up rules for the position of new buildings, or in fact to carry out any of the changes which were necessary whenever there was a rapid growth of population.

The situation in Cheltenham was by no means unique. Already other towns such as Worcester, Bath, Birmingham, and Plymouth had found it necessary to apply for private Acts of Parliament under which Commissioners with special powers were appointed. The enterprising new-comers to Cheltenham must have known of this procedure. The first guide-book had forecast the removal of 'certain old coarse buildings'. According to Goding there had been an attempt in 1784 to obtain powers to divert the stream from the centre of the street. In the next year an application was made with the permission of the lord of the manor for leave to bring in a Bill 'for the Paving, Repairing, Cleansing and Lighting of the Street of Cheltenham and for removing the present and preventing future encroachments, nuisances and annoyances therein'.

The subsequent Act of 1786 appointed fifty-eight Commissioners—sometimes known as Paving and sometimes as Town Commissioners—and gave them the powers applied for. Among their names are many we have already met in the Vestry Records. The old families are represented by William Gregory, Robert Cox, and Thomas Higgs. The millers are there—James Arkell of Sandford and Thomas Humphreys of Cambray Mill, with Thomas Pope, one-time owner of the 'Plough', Edward Timbrell, former churchwarden and Surveyor of Highways, and the Reverend Hugh Hughes, the incumbent of the parish church. The three enterprising businessmen Thomas Hughes, William Miller, and William Skillicorne are included, together with Samuel Harward, whose family later developed the Imperial Spa. The aristocracy of Cheltenham was represented by John de la Bere, his son the Reverend John de la Bere, and the Honourable John Dutton, the son of the lord of the manor. Of the bailiff of the borough, formerly such an important official, there is no mention.

These Commissioners were chosen on a fairly wide basis, representing many interests, old and new. The only qualification insisted on was the ownership of real estate of £400 or the enjoyment of not less than £40 in annual rents; and each Commissioner was forbidden to act in matters where he had a personal interest. Their proceedings were to be entered in a book and they were to appoint a Treasurer, Clerk, Collector, Surveyor, Scavenger, and other officials. They were empowered to raise a rate, not exceeding for the first year 2s. 6d. in the pound on yearly rents and property value, and 1s. 6d. in the pound for succeeding years.

They were also empowered to force owners and occupiers of property 'adjoining the streets, lanes or passages' to pave the full width from the house to the road, under the direction of the Surveyor appointed, and using the materials ordered. Failure to comply with any part of the order carried a heavy penalty. On the newly paved street there was to be no 'cock throwing, bull-baiting, bonfires or squibs, serpents, rockets or fireworks whatsoever . . . or playing of the game called football'.

Apparently parking problems were recognized, since the Act expressly states that 'no one is to leave any waggon or cart to stand or remain in the said street or any public passage for a time longer than is necessary for unloading'.

The Market-house and the Butter Cross were to be pulled down—the materials sold and the sites thereof 'laid into and made part of the said principal street' and new ones erected, 'belonging as before to the Lord of the Manor but taken for public use'. The streets were to be lighted with lamps set on posts, and a penalty was provided in anticipation for anyone who should damage such unusual objects.

Lastly the Act provided that the householders should clean that part of the street or lane immediately in front of their houses, and they were not to leave in the Street any dunghills or other obstruction. A scavenger was to be appointed to go round each week and collect such material and deposit it on 'a piece of land near the town bought for the purpose'.

This Act marks the beginning of a new and most interesting experiment in the government of the town. Cheltenham is extremely fortunate in having preserved most of the Minute Books of the Commissioners from their first meeting until their office came to an end nearly a century later.

These early Minute Books are short and laconic records of the stages by which what might be called the modern municipality came into being. Thus the first Town Clerk and the first Treasurer (with annual salaries of eight guineas and six guineas respectively) were appointed at the opening meeting, and the first loan of £600 for public works agreed upon. After this the Commissioners acted with great speed. Within three months they had put the old Market-house and Butter Cross up to auction, sold the materials for a combined sum of £64. 10s., and made an order 'that a Market-house shall forthwith be built on the scite [sic] where the old Blindhouse and where the present Prison stand. That the Prison shall be removed to where the Pound is, and that a new Pound shall be made within the Common called the Marsh and near the gate there'. Following this order they accepted an estimate by which John Everis and Thomas Keyte were to build the new Market-house 'according to the plan and at the prices described in certain papers signed by them and delivered to our Clerk'. This new Market-house—a small stone building with pillars —was erected in the High Street almost opposite to North Street and in front of the 'Eight Bells'. It is shown clearly in a water-colour of the High Street, made in 1804,[5] by which time it was already considered obsolete. It was left standing, however, and used as an additional market when the new Market-house was erected next to it in 1808. The new stone prison was built a little later in Henrietta Street and consisted of 'two apartments of the same size as the Prison lately pulled down'.

Having thus cleared the 'coarse old buildings' from the Street, the Commissioners proceeded to pave it, light it, and arrange for keeping it clean. There is no reference to the diversion of the water from the Street. The contract for paving the street was signed after a majority vote of the Commissioners early in 1787, so that presumably the diversion had taken place by then. One result was that for the next fifty years succeeding owners of Cambray Mill raised objections to the town's claim to access to water from the river at the point where the mill-pond was constructed. Goding states that when the sewer was laid down the High Street in 1834, the old stepping-stones were found.

In the meantime the occupants of the houses on each side of the street had been ordered to make a footpath outside their houses, 'of flat Hannam stone $4\frac{1}{2}$ feet wide and $2\frac{1}{2}$ to 3 inches thick, with a stone border 3 inches wide'. Where the order was neglected, the Commissioners had the work done by contract and recovered 'from the several inhabitants the Paving and Pitching money according to the respective accounts to be signed by our Surveyor and agree to pay him £10 for his trouble'.

This is the first mention of the Town Surveyor—an official who was to play a most important part in the development of the town in the next half-century. Two other important officials —the Scavengers—had been appointed at a salary of £10 a year each, with the duty of keeping the streets clean, and at the same meeting 120 lamps had been ordered for lighting them. By a later order these lamps were to burn from daylight to 12 o'clock, excepting that 'when the moon rises at 10 o'clock or before they were to burn bright one hour only after the moon rises'.

The money for these improvements came from a loan raised at 5 per cent. and from a rate of 2s. 6d. in the pound, which was soon afterwards reduced to 1s. since the inhabitants, already paying Poor Rates, Church Rates, and Highway Rates, regarded it as 'inconvenient'. The difficulty of raising money was to handicap the Commissioners throughout the period of their power. Another difficulty was inherent in a system under which the Commissioners—appointed and not elected—did not feel bound by a sense of responsibility to the electorate to maintain regular attendances at what were intended to be monthly meetings. Even at the first meeting, held at the 'Plough' immediately after the passing of the Act, only thirteen of the fifty-eight Commissioners were present. At the November meeting only two were present and no business could be done. The speed with which the early work was carried out is therefore all the more surprising. A third difficulty resulted from the fact that the Act had not defined the town boundaries within which the powers of the Commissioners held good. A laconic record was made at the March meeting in 1787: 'Upon a question arising where the town of Cheltenham did begin—it was upon being put to the vote unanimously agreed by the Commissioners "that the Town or Street of Cheltenham begins at the stile leading into the field at the top of the said town. We do adjourn. . . ." '

The boundary question was to cause considerable trouble in the future, but for some time to come the Commissioners seemed to be content with the improvements carried out before the visit of King George III. Their initial outburst of energy was not maintained; indeed until the end of the century meetings were poorly attended and there were long intervals between meetings, in one case of six months and in another of one year. Their work was mainly concerned with lighting, paving, and cleansing the streets, and even within this limited scope, the results were so far from satisfactory that a demand arose for a new Act of Parliament which would confer greater powers. The Commissioners themselves recorded in 1803 'that it is absolutely necessary for the comfort of the inhabitants and gentry resorting to the town that the public streets should be watered in a different manner than it is [sic] at present'.

A new Act was obtained in 1806. In the preamble it was stated that 'the streets both old and new are still incommodious, unsafe for passengers and not sufficiently lighted'. During the three years before the passing of the Act there was a larger attendance at meetings and new names appear among the signatures. Among these were Thomas Hughes's son Robert, who was at this time building Rodney Lodge for his residence; Francis Welles of Marle Hill—the new steward of the manor; the Reverend Richard Nash Skillicorne—the heir of the Skillicorne property; Thomas Smith (Bank), so designated to distinguish him from Thomas Smith (Grocer) who was also postmaster; Captain Thomas Gray—in command of the Cheltenham Volunteers; and Theodore Gwinnett who became clerk to the Commissioners and was concerned in the legal side of most of the public work in the town.

All these names were given in the list of seventy-two Commissioners appointed under the new Act of 1806, which list also included the Earl of Suffolk, Charles Hanbury Tracy of Toddington, Thomas Baghott de la Bere, William Humphris Barrett—the owner of Cambray Mill, John Boles Watson who by this time had built the theatre in Cambray, Henry Thompson, the founder of Montpellier Spa, Joseph Pitt of the future Pittville, the famous Colonel John Riddell of Wellington Mansion, Charles Brandon Trye of Leckhampton—sometime senior surgeon to Gloucester Infirmary, his friend Doctor Jenner, and the solicitor Thomas Pruen. They were joined shortly afterwards by another solicitor, Walter Hylton Jessop; by the well-known Dr. Jameson who took a great interest in developing the medicinal waters of Cheltenham; Baynham Jones, already mentioned as having built Cambray House and as the owner of the main Chalybeate Spa at Cambray; and William Gyde—a forceful personality who built Gyde's Terrace and played a most active part in the affairs of the town. The Reverend Hugh Hughes Williams, the Baptist minister of Bethel Chapel, also became a Commissioner at this time and gave loyal and constant service for the next thirty years. Cheltenham was indeed fortunate in that it was already attracting many professional men, able and willing to give voluntary service in the administration of the town's affairs.

The Act of 1806 gave the Commissioners increased powers to deal with paving and repairing the existing streets, with certain rights of compulsory purchase of property if necessary. They had the duty of keeping the streets clean and free from nuisance and annoyance, and were empowered to maintain a police force and to issue regulations for the control of all hackney carriages and sedan chairs. Since the new activities would involve heavier expenditure, the Act allowed greater latitude in raising money by loans and annuities, but it enjoined stricter attention to the keeping of accounts.

A new sense of responsibility seems to be indicated by a declaration at an early meeting 'that it is the duty of all Commissioners who take part in a debate on any question to attend meetings until the conclusion of the same and give their vote thereon'. Apparently meetings were becoming more formal. 'On any subject debated, Gentlemen shall address the Chair standing and no gentleman shall speak twice unless in explanation.' At the same time the clerk was ordered to obtain a box[6] in which important papers were to be placed for safe keeping. A year later, however, at a meeting when only eight Commissioners were present, a circular letter was ordered to be sent to the others, stating 'the expense incurred to the public and the serious consequences arising from their non-attendance, and requesting their regular attendance in future'.

In the meantime there began the first town-planning that Cheltenham had as yet known. The Commissioners felt it necessary to open communication between the High Street and the New Well near Suffolk House (Gallipot Farm) which was attracting many visitors. This well must be distinguished from the Old Well where King George had drunk the waters and from the new Montpellier Well over which Pearson Thompson later built the Rotunda. As already explained, the 'New' well stood at the end of what was then known as Well Lane, where the present Montpellier Street now runs at the back of the Rotunda, and parallel with the Old Well Walk, on which the Ladies' College now stands. At this time there was no means of reaching Well Lane from the High Street except by footpaths and by crossing the plank bridge across the Chelt. The Commissioners' first plan was to develop and continue the road in front of the Royal Crescent, then being built. They finally decided, however, to continue the road already begun at the opening from the High Street called the Colonnade, and they accepted Samuel Harward's offer to sell the right of way for £450, 'which land was duly taken over by our Surveyor'

(1806), and in this way the future Promenade was planned. The next year they purchased from Harward for a further 100 guineas a right of way from this road already planned 'across the Brook, and so in a straight direction . . . then turning short to the right and communicating in a straight line leading to Gallipot'. The brook is of course the Chelt which then ran its course in the open. Two years later they planned to extend this road from the Colonnade to connect with Henry Thompson's Montpellier Spa and Rides, and in this way the road leading up to and past the Queen's Hotel was developed. They also contributed £200 to help the tithing of Alston repair the Well Lane, and accepted Henry Thompson's offer of a loan at 5 per cent. towards the making of the road. It was not until 1813 that an order was given to the Surveyor: 'to cause the road down the Colonnade to be staked out'. How far this had advanced when the Commissioners in 1817 resold the right of way back to the Harward family at the original price is not clear. This enabled the Harward brothers to develop the Promenade as a tree-lined avenue to the new well—shortly to be known as the Sherborne and then the Imperial Spa (1818), and this development gave the Promenade the character it has since maintained.

These and other projects required money, which the Commissioners were raising at this time by means of a series of annuities at the rate of 9½ per cent. for life on the capital advanced. In the years to come these annuities were to prove a heavy burden, as most of the annuitants had singularly long lives.

In the meantime it should not be forgotten that although rapidly developing as a spa, Cheltenham was still a market town and that the Commissioners were constantly being pressed to build a new Market-house. The old one, although built only seventeen years before, was the subject of a strong complaint in Browne's *Guide* (1803): 'The Market House is at present far too small to contain one half of the marketable produce that is constantly brought to the Town. . . . We wonder that the very great inconvenience has not been remedied. . . . We should earnestly recommend, not its enlargement, but its removal.'

The Commissioners finally bought, for £702, a piece of ground almost adjoining this building, and by compulsory purchase acquired two nearby houses to be pulled down for extra space. On this, by agreement with the lord of the manor who leased them the tolls for twenty-one years, they built the new Market-house with a council room for themselves on the second floor, and a shambles adjoining. The old building was left to be used for the sale of earthenware and glass. It seems to have survived in a dilapidated state until 1811[7] despite various proposals to remove it. The Commissioners at the same time planned to widen the street at this point by the compulsory purchase and demolition of two houses belonging to William Humphris Barrett and his mother, but as with matters concerning the right of water from his mill Mr. Barrett proved obdurate and it was not until 1817 that the sale was achieved and then at his own price. At first a Clerk of the Market was appointed to collect tolls; shortly afterwards, however, the Commissioners found it easier to let the tolls by yearly auction from which they received in 1815 as much as £490.

With the completion of the Market-house it was decided that a new prison was necessary 'to replace the dangerous hole in Fleece Street', although this had only been erected in 1786. The project, however, was held up because of a financial crisis in the affairs of the Commissioners. This coincided with a similar crisis in the affairs of the Vestry which—as we shall see later—was finding difficulty in the collection of the rates necessary to pay for its increased expenditure. In 1810 the Vestry decided that a survey of the parish should be made with a view to the making of a fairer assessment. In their records of the same year the Commissioners made a significant entry:

> We consider it our duty to provide for payment of Interest on sums due to the Mortgagees and Annuitants under this Act, and of the Salaries of Officers serving, and of the balances now due to the Treasurer in execution of these payments, before any sums on any other accounts whatever be paid:
>> Resolved that from the first monies collected by the Rates sufficient sums be in future set apart for such purposes. . . .
>> Revolved that to prevent a recurrence of the circumstances

which have rendered the foregoing Resolution advisable, the Accounts of the Treasurer be audited every three months and produced to the Commissioners at the subsequent meeting (1810).

These resolutions were shortly followed by the levying of a savage rate:

Resolved that the present valuation of the property in the Town be increased in the proportion of adding £13 to every £20 now rated and that a rate of 5/-d in the pound be raised on such compound valuation (1811).

Eventually the Commissioners decided that their rates should be raised on the same basis of assessment as the new Poor Rate 'by doubling the amount of the charge upon each respective property in the said Poor Rates and charging them thereon after the rate of 2/6 in the £'.

During the last years of the Napoleonic War the Commissioners were largely occupied with problems of lighting, paving, and cleansing the streets. It would be possible, even without maps, to trace the growth of the town by the orders for lamps recorded at their meetings. The expenses of paving and cleansing were sometimes shared with Turnpike Commissioners who had some responsibility for the High Street as part of a turnpike road. These expenses were heavy. For example, £150 a year was now being paid to whoever undertook to act as scavenger. A long struggle developed over the right of the town to use the water which passed from the Chelt to the Cambray mill-pond owned by William Humphris Barrett. In 1807 the latter agreed 'to permit the water to run down the Street as heretofore, on his being indemnified by the Commissioners against claim for damages by the owners of Mills on the stream below'. Despite this agreement notice had to be served on Barrett in 1813 to induce him to open the sluices, and the Commissioners ordered the Court Rolls to be searched to vindicate their claim. The matter dragged on and twice Counsel's opinion was sought; as late as 1822 it is recorded that a demand was made for the use of the water, but with the founding of the Water Company shortly afterwards, the claim seems for the time being to have been dropped.

During these years the Commissioners were also much concerned with the issue of orders and prohibitions which came under their general heading of nuisances. A typical entry is in 1807: 'The Surveyor to enquire into the state of pig-sties in and about the town and public roads and footpaths to see if offensive to persons passing ... these and any other nuisances, privies, wells ... also to be removed if offensive.' But pig-sties and privies were not the only subjects of orders. Owners of blacksmiths' shops and brew-houses and slaughter-houses were frequently warned to abate the nuisance caused, under penalty of an order for removal. Chimneys had to be raised to prevent smoke from annoying visitors. The firing of bricks— a frequent operation in Cheltenham—was forbidden if complaints were made. One man was ordered to remove his cocks and asses from a yard near the Street; another was forbidden to have his carriage washed on the pavement in Cambray. The constables were directed 'to prevent all boys playing with hoops, tops, etc., in the streets, the same having been represented as a nuisance to the Company'.

The main difficulties, however, arose through the lack of a water system and modern sanitation. The only sewer in existence before the war ended seems to have been in St. George's Place. Dr. Jenner's only recorded utterances at the Commissioners' meetings were, first, a request in 1806 to be permitted to open a drain from his house in St. George's Place into this public sewer, at his own expense, and two years later a proposal that a common sewer should be made to serve the whole town. A committee, which included Dr. Jenner, Colonel Agg, Thomas Pruen, and the Reverend Hugh Williams, was appointed to make further inquiries and empowered to call on professional advice, but like so many other inquiries it failed to achieve any immediate result. Innumerable proposals of the same nature were made in the coming years until, in 1834, a private company was formed.

Despite all the efforts of the Commissioners, however, there was considerable dissatisfaction in the town, one reason being that they had not brought into being a satisfactory police force. The two High Constables and the petty Constable— manorial officials—seem to have been the only men actively engaged. The Vestry put it on record in 1811 that the establishment of a more permanent police force was necessary. The correspondence of the recently established *Cheltenham Chronicle* (1809) gives the same impression of dissatisfaction. There were complaints that the street was not clean, and that the pavements were not reserved for the use of foot-passengers but were often invaded by animals and carts. It was difficult to enforce orders dealing with these on a farming community unused for centuries to the niceties of pavements.

The powers of the Commissioners had been increased by the Act of 1806. Their number had also been increased and the property qualification necessary for their appointment raised, but many of them were new-comers to the town or residents only in the sense that they owned property there. It is clear that the number was far too large to be an efficient, administrative body.

A correspondent of the *Cheltenham Chronicle* writes in 1809: 'The Commissioners appear to me to be too numerous ... select from the whole a certain number and let these lay down plans for improving roads and walks about the Town.'

The Commissioners were encountering the same difficulties which the Manorial Courts had faced for so many centuries. They could make orders but they could not permanently enforce them on a highly individualistic community. As late as 1813 they issued 200 notices with orders to prevent horses being exercised in the High Street—and fifteen years later they were still trying to enforce the same order.

There is a prophetic note in the next letter (published in the *Cheltenham Chronicle* in 1809):

It is equally to be feared and lamented that Cheltenham which is clearly increasing in public importance will . . . in its future character of a beautiful town, be sacrificed at the shrine of private individual interests, unless some gentleman of fortune rescue it from the present miserable and disgraceful system that is falsely called improvement of the place. It is submitted that as a preliminary step some men of fortune shall purchase the whole of the land in the most favourable situation and then employ an Architect to give a plan for the creation of a new Town.

Fortunately, such men—Pearson Thompson and Joseph

Pitt, with the architects Papworth, Forbes, the Jearrads, and others—were able in the near future to carry out this same design and build the planned new town. The greater part of the development, however, did not take place until after the Napoleonic War had ended in 1815 and until, by the Inclosure Act of 1801, the land was freed from medieval restrictions and made available for building purposes.

XX

THE WORK OF THE VESTRY (1806–1852) AND THE REORGANIZATION OF PATE'S GRAMMAR SCHOOL

THE appointment of the Town Commissioners under the Act of 1786 did not have an immediate effect in lessening the Vestry's functions, most of which remained in force for the next fifty years.

As both authorities were empowered to raise rates, the control of local government finance was to a certain extent shared between them, although in the case of the Vestry the justices of the peace maintained definite powers of control. The distinction between the functions of the two authorities was not always sharply drawn and, as in the matter of the repair of the roads, there was overlapping and friction.

The most important work of the Vestry remained the administration of the various Poor Laws under which the Workhouse was maintained and the poor relieved with money provided by the Poor Rate. The early sources on which Goding drew for his description of this administration have since disappeared, but it appears to have been extremely informal. In the last half of the eighteenth century, however, the Vestry Books record the various experiments made in methods of dealing with the poor of the parish.[1] In 1755 a Workhouse Master had been appointed at a salary of £8 a year, with two guineas extra for wood, an allowance of 1s. 4d. per week per head for the maintenance of the poor in the house provided and the value of their work, and '1/- for every vagrant he takes before a Justice of the Peace, and if convicted 1/6 more; 1/- for every person who has not obtained a settlement in this Parish when he shall have obliged him to bring his settlement'.

This system must have caused great hardship to the poor, while extra payments show the anxiety of the Vestry to keep out all persons who came from other parishes without money or without the certificate which under the Act of 1697 gave permission to move to those likely to be able to support themselves. The next year it was agreed that the overseers of the poor should take a lease of the Workhouse then in occupation, at a rent of £10 a year for twenty-one years, and shortly afterwards 'it was agreed that no pauper shall be relieved out of the workhouse except in extraordinary cases'. There are, however, cases of allowances made which show that the rule was not very strictly kept. The determination to keep down the rates is shown again when in 1778 a decision made to purchase property for a Workhouse was reversed shortly afterwards at a heavily attended meeting, on grounds of hardship to the ratepayers. The system of renting a house therefore continued for some years.

In 1793 it was recorded that Ichabod Painter and his wife were to be Master and Mistress of the Workhouse for one year at a salary of twenty guineas 'allowing them meat and drink, washing, lodging and eight bushells of malt (tea, sugar, butter only excepted)'. In the same year Thomas Minster was appointed by the Vestry as doctor for those poor for whom the Vestry was responsible at a salary of eighteen guineas a year, but 'broken bones, small pox and lying-in women were to be exempt from the said sum'. A few years later Doctor Minster was being paid 5s. a head for vaccinating certain poor children. In 1796 it was recorded that 'Henry Smith, one of the Overseers of the Poor, shall agree with Messrs Haines and Company of the City of Gloucester to establish the Pin trade in the Workhouse belonging to this parish'. The making of pins and of mop-heads seems to have been the main occupation of the inmates of the Workhouse. In 1800, however, the poor were 'let to farm to John Dobbins for £850 a year'—an arrangement which was apparently unsatisfactory since it was soon terminated. At last, in 1809, a new Workhouse was built to the specifications of the Vestry. It was rented for £246 annually for seven years and then purchased for £2,578—an expense which was one of the causes of later financial difficulties.

The churchwardens and overseers also enforced with some vigour what became known as the Bastardy Laws, taking sworn evidence from the mothers concerned as to the fathers of their illegitimate children and exacting payment from them on the orders or with the concurrence of the justices of the peace. They were also concerned with finding premiums and arranging apprenticeships for the children of the poor, undoubtedly with the intention of preventing them from being a burden on the rates when they grew up. Nowhere, however, in these or other contemporary Cheltenham records is there any direct evidence of individual cases of inhumanity which characterized the administration of the Poor Laws in various other places, although there is, of course, no actual proof that cases of this kind did not occur.

During the years of the war with Napoleon food prices in Gloucestershire, as in the rest of the country, rose in a manner out of proportion to the rise in agricultural and industrial wages. The distress in Cheltenham itself was very serious and there were many efforts, as, for example, those made by the Entwhistles and the Reverend Charles Jervis, to provide food for the poor during these years; and not only food but houses for the poor were difficult to obtain. In 1800 the Vestry agreed to pay the rent of a Cheltenham man then living in Withington because 'from the great and increasing want of houses to accommodate the Poor . . . there would be no house in Cheltenham to receive him. It is further agreed that the Cheltenham Overseers undertake to pay the rent for the ensuing year to induce the Withington Overseers to let the said man continue in the said house in Withington.' In the next year's records there is a reference to the necessity of building immediately 'some cottages for the residence of the poor', but there is no account of this being done. The problem was accentuated by the attempts of labourers from the surrounding countryside, where agricultural wages varied from ten to four guineas a year, to settle in the town. By 1811 the rise in food prices was so serious that the Town Commissioners, at the instigation of one of their members—Eyles Irwin—were considering enforcing the Assize of Bread by which maximum prices could be fixed, but the justices of the peace would not agree. However, as the situation grew worse, Eyles Irwin, acting as a member of the Vestry, put forward the same proposal which then received the required sanction from the justices. Measures were taken to ascertain the market price of corn in Gloucester and Tewkesbury and to fix the prices in Cheltenham accordingly. It is of course impossible to be certain how far this measure alleviated the distress, which was certainly very serious.

At the same time both the Vestry and the Town Commissioners were faced with a financial crisis. The Commissioners had built a prison and the Vestry a workhouse and neither authority had enough available money to pay other legitimate expenses. The Vestry appointed a committee to carry out an Inquiry which revealed not only considerable discrepancy in the accounts, but 'that the amount of uncollected dues under the assessments made from time to time in years past, for the relief of the poor, requires immediate attention, lest from small beginnings evils of considerable magnitude arise from certain years' accounts not having been available'. Apparently every effort was made to put an end to peculation of this sort. For some months the members of the committee, which included Theodore Gwinnett, Dr. Jameson, Edward Pruen, Thomas Tucker, James Agg, and Captain Gray, met twice a week to work on a new rating assessment which was to be made after a survey of property had been carried out by a Cirencester surveyor. This survey, however, cost £500, which added to the existing financial liabilities. According to Griffiths's *Cheltenham Guide* (1816):

At Easter 1812, it appeared that notwithstanding the Poor Rates had been unusually high, the Poor were murmuring for want of proper relief; and the Overseers, after expending all the money they had collected, incurred debts, on the Parish account, to the amount of £1,580—£500 of which was for surveying the land in the Parish, £242 for rent of the Poor-House, and £820 owing to sundry tradesmen, for provisions and clothing, attornies, the law expenses, etc. etc. This alarming state of things induced the Parish to adopt the provisions of the Act of Parliament made in the 22nd year of George 3rd's reign 'For the better relief and employment of the Poor', which has produced a salutary effect, the above debt being now entirely discharged, all the provisions, clothing etc., carefully purchased with ready money, the employment and comfort of the Poor in the House particularly attended to, those who need assistance out of the House properly relieved, and the Poor Rates not increased.

Under this Act, usually known as Gilbert's Act (1782), a salaried Guardian of the Poor and a salaried Governor of the Workhouse, nominated by the Vestry, were appointed by the magistrates. Both these officials were subject to the authority of an unsalaried Visitor of the Poor, appointed in the same way under this Act. The Overseers retained their original powers, but at the same time a yearly statement of their accounts was to be submitted annually to the Vestry. After the passing of the second Sturges Bourne Act (1820) a salaried Overseer was appointed to assist the others. Under this system the Cheltenham Vestry administered the Poor Law until the passing of the Amendment Act of 1834, which transferred many of their powers to a newly constituted Board of Guardians, elected for a Union of Parishes. Each year until then the Vestry nominated a list of men from whom the justices appointed three new officials. The annual salary of the doctor appointed to look after the poor had now reached £40 a year and was to be advanced to £50 in succeeding years.

During these years the Vestry, as in other towns, waged a constant war against the numerous poor who came into the town from other places and tried to acquire a settlement and so qualify for Poor Law benefits from the Cheltenham rates.

In Hulley's drawing of the Royal Well (1813) a notice is shown posted on the exterior of one of the buildings: 'All vagrants coming to this town under pretence of protection shall be committed to goal [*sic*].' Wherever these new-comers were found to be indigent an order from the magistrates was obtained by the Overseers of the Poor for their removal to the parish of their birth. It seems likely, however, that a number of such strangers slipped in and found work in the growing building industry and in domestic service.

Friction between the Vestry and the Town Commissioners is revealed early in the nineteenth century. One of the great problems that arose from the rapid growth of the town must have been that of the maintenance of law and order with the primitive police methods still in force. The petty Constable was nominated by the Court Leet and was responsible to the High Constables and finally to the magistrates. In 1810 the Vestry discussed the necessity of the establishment of a permanent police force which they recorded 'could only be obtained by the powers of a royal Charter of Incorporation for the town'. Although nothing further is heard of their proposal to apply to the Prince Regent for such a charter, the incident marks the beginning of the long-drawn-out agitation against the powers of the unelected Town Commissioners.

Some of the other duties of the Vestry which were not directly concerned with the church have already been mentioned: the arrangement of the ballot for the militia, the administration of the parish charities, the repair of the parish roads, the provision of stocks or pillory, and the destruction of vermin. Apparently sparrows were the only 'vermin' for which the Cheltenham Vestry was prepared to pay the customary price of 3d. a dozen; in other parts of the county foxes, hedgehogs, badgers, kites, jays, woodpeckers, and tom-tits were included in this category. For a fox as much as a shilling was paid and fourpence each for hedgehogs and kites.[2]

In 1811 the Vestry was ordered to pay a fine of £140 for not carrying out a ballot within the time prescribed 'for three men opportioned upon the parish to supply the deficiences of the Militia'. In great perturbation the Vestry sent a letter— drafted by Captain Gray—to the Lord Lieutenant of the County, asking him to appeal on their behalf to the Court of Exchequer, since the omission was not due to their neglect but to a mistake over the date made in the original order for the ballot. Since the thanks of the meeting were given to Captain Gray for the able way he had conducted the investigation and for his general exertions on behalf of the parish, presumably the fines were not enforced. The record of the incident is signed by Dr. Jameson, William Binckes—wine merchant, Moses Yearsley of the 'Eight Bells', Edward Hatch—a carpet maker(?), and the solicitors Robert Hughes and Benjamin Newbery.

A far more serious problem was the lack of burial space, and although the difficulties were not comparable with the outrageous conditions[3] in the London area during these years, the

Vestry was deeply concerned. It is recorded in 1812 that 'It is the opinion of this meeting that the imperious wants of the Parish loudly call for additional burial ground', and this is followed by a resolution to buy land adjacent to the existing churchyard. As this land had already been acquired by Joseph Pitt, who also owned the churchyard itself as a result of his purchase of the Impropriation, it was then decided to buy both from him. Theodore Gwinnett was asked to interview Pitt but was instructed not to pay more than 100 guineas for the churchyard itself. Eventually this was bought for £100 with the 'poor houses' lying near and £500 was offered for the additional ground. The Vestry then approached Pitt with a request 'that he will indulge the Parish by taking the purchase money—being £600 and the interest thereof—by instalments of £100 per annum with the interest'. Apparently this arrangement was accepted since a resolution was passed at the next meeting 'conveying thanks to Mr. Pitt for the handsome and liberal way in which he had met the wishes of the Parish'.

Nineteen years elapsed before the same problem had to be faced again. In 1829 the Vestry received a notice from His Majesty's Commissioners for the building of new churchyards, pointing out the need for a new burial ground and asking them to submit plans for this. As a result the Vestry acquired land for the purpose on the south side of the lower end of the High Street, where the Georgian entrance and the small chapel of this now long-disused burial ground may still be seen.

In the meantime, as accommodation in the church itself was inadequate for the increasing number of visitors and residents, more galleries had to be erected. Again the indefatigable Theodore Gwinnett played his part. 'Mr. Gwinnett considered and digested a scheme for alterations and improvements and offered to produce the same at the next meeting, with a plan for removing the belfry and completing one above it and for repairing the galleries.' By this time a new altar piece had been provided in 1807 and an organ had replaced the bassoon which had accompanied the choir at the time of the royal visit.

The repair of the roads which were not under the jurisdiction of the Town Commissioners or the Turnpike Commissioners constituted a heavy burden on the Vestry's resources. Some-times these repairs were undertaken willingly as an obvious duty; sometimes, however, difficulties arose as to which auth-orities were liable for the necessary repairs. Thus in 1819 a Vestry meeting of the inhabitants of Westhall, Naunton, and Sandford was called by the Surveyor of Highways for those areas in order to determine whether they should repair the road 'through Sandford Field from New Bath Road to the Old Bath Road, and also the Well Lane', and it was decided that 'the said Surveyor shall not repair the road through Sand-ford Fields, it appearing that the same hath not been put in good repair by the parties who have enclosed the fields on each side'.

On the other hand, as new roads were developed from the old footways, their owners sought to 'dedicate' them to the public use so that repairs would be carried out by the parish. Thus Engine House Lane—now Rodney Road—was taken over in 1827 and 'the Surveyors of the Highway of the Tything of Cheltenham shall henceforth keep the said road in repair as a public highway'. As late as 1831 the inhabitants of Westhall were indited by Pearson Thompson for not repairing Hatherley Lane. They lost their case at the Gloucester Assizes, although they had pleaded that this road had never been repaired within the memory of man, that as it lay between Naunton and Westhall only part of the obligation lay with Westhall, and that part of it ran through a former field which had been enclosed without the lane being first repaired.

The Vestry was in general as much aware as the Commis-sioners that the repair of the streets was an important factor in the prosperity and health of the town. A Vestry Committee was appointed in 1821, consisting of Dr. Briggs, Baynham Jones, Thomas Henney, and John Gardner—all of whom were also Town Commissioners—with the duty of reporting on the state of roads not under the jurisdiction of the Commissioners. Among the various streets included in the report, Rutland Street (with its accumulation of dust and filth) was described as reflecting disgrace on the inhabitants, and 'in the event of epidemic diseases as being a means of promoting and extending the influence of such a calamity.' Devonshire Street and Milsom

Street required cleansing, but the chief owners of property there were the Fellows of Corpus Christi College, Oxford, who refused to allow any interference. At the same time the committee also condemned a number of privately owned roads which were in a disgraceful and neglected condition and which they considered should be put in order so that they could be taken over by the parish. Finally, they made the appeal (already quoted) for 'co-operation among the various authorities in the interest of the comfort and advantage of the Residents and the convenience of those who visit the town for health or pleasure'. The difficulties arising from the overlapping of authorities continued until the Act of 1852 transferred the obligation of the repair of the roads to the Commissioners.

The Vestry report of 1821 was signed by its chairman, Dr. Briggs, and is an indication of the services rendered to the town by the doctors who settled there during these years and who were more aware of the dangers of disease in congested areas than the authorities in many other towns. During the unhappy period in 1832, when many parts of England were attacked by cholera, the Government took strong measures to prevent the epidemic from spreading. Among these were the setting up of local Boards of Health (under the Act of 1802) with authority to impose sanitary measures and to demand the money necessary for these. Some members of the Vestry took great exception to the attitude of the board set up in Cheltenham, which they complained had been privately formed without any consultation with them, and they pointed out that two of its members (including the President—Bransby Cooper) were not even inhabitants of the town from which they proposed to raise the rates for the measures they imposed. Undoubtedly this Board of Health did useful work and, as Henry Davies says in his almost contemporary book *Cheltenham Past and Present*, may have been partly responsible for Cheltenham's escape from the cholera. 'All the low and unhealthy places in the town were under their superintendence thoroughly cleansed and purified and the utmost care taken to prevent the spread of those fevers prevalent . . . among the dwellings of the wretched and the poor. . . . Nearly 2,000 vagrants were prevented from entering the town, being escorted by its officers around the outskirts, relieved and passed on their journey.' From another source we learn that 'In the poorer streets houses were lime-washed, the privies, cesspools and dry wells emptied and purified with lime, while upwards of 100 vagabonds were sent out of the town. . . . Nine men were constantly employed from morning to night at different entrances to the town turning back vagrants.'

At the same time the Town Commissioners were engaged in negotiations with the Vestry for the making of a new sewer, and were themselves more than usually active at this time in their enduring campaign against insanitary privies and pig-sties. They supported the Board of Health in every way. Its secretary, Dr. Newell, was also a Town Commissioner and acted as liaison officer between the two bodies. On the other hand, the Board of Health took a high hand with the Vestry, demanded money without being prepared to submit detailed accounts of spending, and refused to divulge any information concerning the reports which it sent to the Privy Council. The Vestry protested that much of the work done was a duplication of that already carried out in a town heavily rated for cleansing purposes by the Commissioners, and that '£50 had been paid for a Cholera hospital but neither the Hospital nor the accounts were forthcoming, and now the Board was asking for another £150 from the Parish'. They were further incensed when in reply to their inquiries, Bransby Cooper abused them as 'A radical lot' and they recorded a resolution 'that this meeting regards with regret the intemperate use of the words "radical lot" as applied by Mr. Bransby Cooper', and another that 'it is the duty of the Ratepayers never to relax in their endeavours to accomplish by constitutional means the dissolution of the present Board of Health'. In the same mood they put it on record that 'it was highly unconstitutional that any community should be taxed for the expenditure of money by individuals over whom they have no control and in whose appointment they have no voice', and in the next year they were considering a petition to Parliament pointing out this anomaly.

It is thus clear that the Vestry regarded itself as the guardian of the liberties of the parish. These events, however, occurred during the passing of the Reform Bill, when political emotions ran high, and it is easy to detect that undercurrent of party feeling which ran through every aspect of public affairs in Cheltenham at this time. Bransby Cooper and Dr. Newell were founder members of the Conservative True Blue Club formed to protest against the passing of the Reform Bill. From this time the balance of power among the active Town Commissioners was Conservative because of the increasing number of Army and Navy officers recently appointed; but when the latter served on the Vestry, as they were entitled to do if they were ratepayers, their influence was diluted by a number of Radicals and Liberals. Among these were Edward Hatch—for many years churchwarden—Samuel Harper, a schoolmaster who later became proprietor of the *Cheltenham Free Press*, and Captain Gray who was the prime mover of the campaign in Cheltenham for the Reform Bill. Under the Sturges Bourne Act (1819) it had been enacted that when voting took place in the Vestry Meeting, a system of plural voting should be adopted by which a person rated at £50 and under should have one vote and that an additional vote should be allowed for every additional £25 concerned. It appears from the records, however that such votes were not very frequently taken in the Cheltenham Vestry.

One incident reveals that the Radical element was not always in the majority in Vestry meetings and that what the Webbs refer to as 'government by public meeting' did not always go unchecked.[4] James Fisher, who was partly responsible for the development of Suffolk Square, came to a Vestry meeting with a proposal to hand over the road round the Square to the parish so that any repairs could in future be paid for by the Vestry. A resolution to this effect was passed and the register was signed by James Fisher, Sir Richard Wolseley, John Wolseley, and Captain James Matthews. Edward Hatch, the churchwarden, seems to have been the only member of the opposition present. He wrote across the page concerned: 'I protest against making the road round Suffolk Square out of the rates—as being only for the benefit of the few and not to the advantage of the many. Signed Edward Hatch.'

On many occasions, however, there was unanimous agreement in the Vestry—as in the investigation into the administration of the funds of Richard Pate's endowment, and in the following protest to the magistrates in 1834:

The application of the Magistrates relative to the parish stocks was taken into consideration, and it was resolved that Mr. Griffiths do convey to them the following message, viz: 'That while this Meeting are [*sic*] prepared to obey the law by the erection of stocks if the Magistrates require the Parish so to do—they beg to express to the Bench their strong feeling against such a mode of punishment in Cheltenham; and that they indulge a hope that on further consideration the Worshipful Bench may discover some means of avoiding such punishment.'

There is no record that the Vestry bought the stocks, although stocks were in actual use in nearby Winchcombe until 1860.

At the time of this protest the Government were passing through Parliament the Poor Law Amendment Act. Despite the application of Gilbert's Act, many parishes throughout the country had for some years been forced to raise unbearably heavy Poor Rates, not only because of the very great distress and poverty which had caused the earlier riots and disturbances of 1830–1, but because, owing to the procedure which developed after the decision taken by the magistrates of Speenhamland (1795), labourers' wages were supplemented out of the Poor Rates, with the natural consequence that wages decreased and Poor Rates increased to an alarming extent. Cheltenham itself does not appear to have been seriously affected by the Speenhamland decision, but the Poor Law Amendment Act (largely the work of Chadwick) was put into effect in the area from 1835. By this Act poor relief could only be given within the Workhouse, except in a few specified cases. Unions of parishes were created and each Union provided a Workhouse which was managed by Boards of Guardians elected from the parishes concerned. An Assistant Poor Law Commissioner visited Cheltenham and as a result of his Inquiry the Cheltenham Union came into being, comprising the parishes of Cheltenham, Charlton Kings, Leckhampton, Swindon, Prestbury, Uckington, Badgeworth, Shurdington, and Great Witcomb. Only ten guardians were to be elected from Cheltenham itself. The Overseers of the Poor retained their functions with regard to the raising of the Poor Rate, but the Cheltenham Vestry lost its powers of direct control over its own Workhouse and its own poor. Thus the Act marks a definite stage in the decline of the importance of the Vestry.

The new Board of Guardians held weekly meetings in the old Cheltenham Workhouse. Among those elected for the Cheltenham Division were Thomas Henney, G. A. Williams (the Librarian), George Russell, R. E. Marshall, and S. C. Harper; among the local justices of the peace, who were all *ex officio* Guardians, were Robert Capper, R. Bransby Cooper, Henry Norwood Trye, and the Reverend C. B. Trye. For some years the Cheltenham Workhouse was used for the able-bodied poor in the Union; the old Charlton Kings Workhouse for the children; and the Prestbury building for the aged and infirm.

The Cheltenham members of the Board may well have felt their loss of independence since the Poor Law Commissioners —more especially Edwin Chadwick himself—kept a tight control over the Boards of Guardians. When proposals were made for a new Workhouse at an estimated cost of £10,000, Sir Edmund Head was sent from London by these Commissioners to discuss the means of lessening the cost—and the amenities—of the proposed building which was erected in 1841.[5] The Commissioners also issued suggested dietaries from which the Boards of Guardians could decide on the most suitable food for the inmates of the Workhouse. While these dietaries were certainly not on the starvation level which seems to have existed in the fictional workhouse of Oliver Twist or indeed in the actual building at Andover where the starving paupers tore the rotting gristle from the bones in the grindmill, they do indeed seem grimly unsatisfactory to modern feeling. It is noteworthy that the Cheltenham Board in choosing the dietary considered suitable for the elderly allowed meat on three days a week instead of two and added an allowance of half a pint of table beer with the meat, for each individual concerned. Indeed the annual consumption of beer and spirits was so much higher than in some other Union workhouses that the Medical Officer was questioned as to the necessity for such an amount, but he firmly resisted the attempt to lessen it.

The powers of the Vestry were again lessened by the passing of the private Act of 1852, under which thirty Commissioners were to be elected as the sole local government authority for Cheltenham. The responsibility for the maintenance of the roads was then transferred to the new Commissioners so that from this time the functions of the Vestry were mainly limited to activities directly concerned with the church.

Valuable work had also been carried out during this half-century in connexion with the administration of the charities for which the Vestry was responsible. The Cheltenham Hospital originated at a Vestry meeting held in 1813, at which it was resolved to convene a general meeting for the purpose of founding a Dispensary from which the General Hospital developed. Perhaps the most important achievement in this connexion was concerned with the Inquiry into the affairs of Richard Pate's endowment of the Almshouse and the Grammar School.

The outcome of this Inquiry was a long-drawn-out but successful suit in Chancery, to compel the Trustees—the President and Fellows of Corpus Christi College, Oxford—to administer the property according to the original purpose of the founder.

Unfortunately, no records of the early history of the Grammar School have so far been found, although it is known that the first headmaster was Christopher Ocland who published poems on Queen Elizabeth I, and whose *Anglorum Proelia* was ordered to be used in every Grammar School in the country. The documents relating to Pate's endowment, which are preserved in the archives of Corpus Christi College, Oxford, deal mainly with leases and with the suit in Chancery and have no reference to the early administration of the school or the Almshouse, although the Trustees were bound by the conditions laid down by Richard Pate in the indenture of 1586 to keep a register of all the masters and ushers appointed. The school seems to have been in a satisfactory condition during the reign of Charles I and the Commonwealth, since Christopher Bayley, who died in 1654 after thirty-four years as master, left £80 in his will for the erection of a Market-house 'out of his prime desire to

advance the good of the town of Cheltenham, where he gained
the greater part of his estate'.[6] Half a century later Prinn, in
the description of the town which he wrote on a page of the
court books, referred to another Master, '—— Rogers, a
Master of Arts in the said University [Oxford], a good man and
an excellent scholar'. Prinn also wrote that both the school and
the Almshouse were 'well endowed', and yet by the beginning
of the nineteenth century the Almshouse had been replaced by
a smaller and inferior building, and the Grammar School, like
many others with similar endowments, was in an unhappy
state of decline.

The original annual salary allotted to the master of the
School by Richard Pate was £16, an amount which was not
sufficient at the beginning of the nineteenth century to allow
a headmaster (who must be a Master of Arts) to devote all his
energies to the school. The Reverend H. B. Fowler had combined his position with the holding of two church livings. In
1815 the Trustees appointed as his successor the Reverend
Thomas Gray and (probably under local pressure) raised the
annual salary to £30. They also promised to appoint an usher,
according to the terms of the endowment, but apparently did
not carry out their promise. Unfortunately Gray died almost
immediately and the Reverend William Hawkins was appointed
in his place. He too held two church livings. Under these circumstances it is not surprising that a contemporary guide-book
states that 'latterly the School has been deficient in Scholars'
(Griffiths, 1816).

It was a keenly felt grievance that although under the terms
of the original endowment the school was to be a free Grammar School, Hawkins interpreted his duties to the foundation
as referring only to the free teaching of Latin and Greek, and
charged fees for instruction in other subjects. His action may
have been in accordance with Lord Eldon's recent definition
(1806) in a case concerning Leeds Grammar School, but it was
unmistakably contrary to the purposes indicated in the actual
wording of the original endowment: 'to maintain the Free
Grammar School . . . aforesaid and the exercise of Grammar
and other Liberal Arts thereat'. Undoubtedly the Vestry
records reflect the general belief in the town that the funds were

mismanaged, the property neglected, and the school of little value to the neighbourhood. With the rise in land values in the preceding two centuries the income from the property of the endowment should with careful management have increased proportionately, enabling the amounts received for the Grammar School and Almshouse to be more in keeping with the contemporary value of money.

The Vestry also complained that all the leases of property negotiated on behalf of the Trustees were drawn in Oxford in the most expensive manner by lawyers who knew little of local conditions and were not concerned with increasing the income of the endowment; they were therefore determined to find out the exact value of the endowment and to insist that it should be administered for the good of the town. In 1816 Theodore Gwinnett was instructed to continue the inquiry into the administration of the Grammar School and Almshouse 'which charities appear of late years to have wholly failed of their original intentions'. He reported to the Vestry that he had consulted an eminent Chancery Counsel who had given his opinion that 'by an application to the Lord Chancellor the funds of these charities might be very considerably increased and the Charities themselves rendered much more agreeable to the intentions of the Founder'. He was then instructed to make such application. Captain James Matthews (one of the churchwardens) agreed that action should be taken in his name on behalf of the parish and in this way there began the suit of James Matthews[7] and others *v.* the President and Scholars of Corpus Christi College, which was not finally closed until 1857. A committee was appointed to act on behalf of the Vestry, and although this committee was of necessity reconstituted from time to time, the new members showed the same dogged resolution to force the Trustees to agree to their demands. The first committee, consisting of Dr. Minster, Dr. Newman, Robert Hughes, Thomas Henney, and E. L. Newman, was concerned with three main points: they wished the parish to have some share in the negotiations of future leases; they were concerned that a full valuation of the estates should be made; and they were determined that the salary of the headmaster and the usher should be raised in accordance with the increased value of the estates, so that the Grammar School might be reorganized and restored to its original purpose.

In the copy of the original application, which is included in the Corpus Christi College collection, the main charge was that of 'the mismanagement and misappropriation of certain Trust Property—although the said property was daily increasing in value', and this was supported by examples concerning the neglect of the Grammar School and the granting of leases 'at nominal or small rents wherein the said College hath taken large fines from the Tenants for the granting or renewal of such rents and applied same to their own use'. Some idea of the attitude of the Trustees can be gathered from other documents in the same collection—in particular from the brief drawn for the defence in 1822 and from a contemporary letter of an unnamed correspondent who appears to have had a close connexion with the college. This letter states that the earlier delay complained of by the Cheltenham Vestry was inevitable, since at that time the President of the College was 'aged 87, weak and feeble, and in the habit of late years of not communicating to the Bursar or the Fellows' any information he received from the Master of the Grammar School; that the Bursar was appointed (although sometimes reappointed) annually and it 'cannot be expected of him who has so little interest in the matter . . . that he will enter into all the intricacies of the case'. The same correspondent claimed that 'Hawkins from his own showing received at least 400 guineas per annum for the last four years independent of what he gained from boarders', and he quoted Dr. Williams—a Fellow of the college and nephew of the President—as saying that there were thirty-four boys in the Grammar School in 1818, all of whom were private pupils, and that there were none being taught according to the terms laid down in the indentures. Under these circumstances, he wrote, both he and Dr. Williams thought there was a strong case against raising the salary of the headmaster since 'if he had a large permanent salary he would no more attend to his duties at the School . . . but join in the festivities of Cheltenham like any other independent person'. Dr. Williams therefore suggested (according to the correspondent) that instead of such an increase a capitation fee of £4 or £5 should be paid to the headmaster for every boy received under the foundation, and that in order to raise the status of the school, the School House itself should be enlarged and that exhibitions to Corpus Christi College should be offered to the pupils. The correspondent's own attitude is summed up in his statement: 'I am sorry to say that such a Charity is considered odious . . . the opinions and feelings of mankind are considerably altered since the school was endowed . . . only the children of inferior tradesmen could be sent to the school in its present state, and what benefit in the world would Latin and Greek be to them?'

From the actual brief it appears that the main line of defence with regard to the Grammar School was that the Trustees thought the Vestry's claim to be untimely, since so much consideration had already been devoted to the problem! They were also opposed to 'the proportional participation in the increased revenue of the Charity by the inmates of the Almshouse since such an increase of benefits would make these 'not Almsmen' but 'Gentlemen'!

The pressure of the Vestry was so far successful that in 1821 the Trustees had requested the consent of the parish to the renewal of certain leases, and a professional survey of Pate's property was made. Thomas Henney twice published the terrier of these estates at his own expense.[8] Five years later, however, the committee could not 'conscientiously say that the Charity Estates had been properly let'. A new committee (appointed in 1828) met a deputation from the Trustees with a view to bringing the proceedings in Chancery to a close. It recommended in 1833 that the headmaster of the Grammar School should be allowed £35 a year for the previous sixteen years of his service and £116 a year for the future; that additional almshouses should be built and the allowance to the inmates increased; that no leases of Pate's property should be granted without the consent of the incumbent and the church-wardens; that the expenses arising out of the suit in Chancery should be paid by the Trustees from their own quarter of the income from the endowment. At the end of the report the members recorded their satisfaction

at the termination of the proceedings in the suit which will have disclosed the real situation of the Charity Estates and the rights of the Inhabitants of Cheltenham to the advantages to be derived from them, the more in particular *as it will be seen in the recollection of many present at the meeting that the College always treated these estates and probably actually believed them to be their own absolute property, subject to the trifling allowances heretofore made to the Master of the School and the poor persons in the Almshouses.*

Among the signatures to the report were those of Francis Close, Edward Hatch, James Humphries, Thomas Henney, and Thomas Griffiths.

Unfortunately, whatever agreements were made were not entirely kept and in the following year the committee made an unsuccessful application to the Court of Chancery to compel the college to carry into effect the arrangements proposed. Lengthy negotiations ended in a compromise; the Trustees finally agreed to an arrangement by which the headmaster of the Grammar School should be paid the increased salary proposed by the Vestry Committee, with £2 per head for every scholar over the number of fifty. The salary of the second master was to be raised to £60 and the allowance of the inmates of the Almshouse was to be increased to 8s. a week with a quarterly allowance of 5s. 4d. Also, for the future no leases were to be granted without the consent of the incumbent and churchwardens of the parish church. On the other hand, the Trustees refused to render an annual detailed financial statement of the administration of the estates; they refused payment of any legal expenses in the Chancery suit out of their own quarter of the income; they were most firmly opposed to the free teaching of English subjects in the Grammar School; and they refused to increase the number of beneficiaries in the Almshouse. The report of the committee in which this agreement was recorded again recommended that an appeal should be made to Parliament as this would be less expensive than the Chancery proceedings on which 'so much of the funds had been wasted in the past twenty-five years', but at the same time the committee advised that the suit in Chancery should be kept open because it was 'the only present means of making the inhabitants aware of the way in which the income was being expended by the Trustees'.

As happened so frequently in Cheltenham after such resolutions, no immediate action was taken. The next recorded report of the Vestry Committee was written in 1843, by which time Samuel Harper and John Goding were among its members. It made the same recommendation of a petition to Parliament. In a long and indignant attack on the policy of the Trustees it pointed out that although some of the lands were let at a very low rental and although leases were still being drawn by agents of the Trustees in a most expensive manner, the income on the estates had increased more than tenfold, and the increase was not being directed to the original objects of the Charity. Despite this increase, however, the School 'had fallen into inutility and perfect uselessness . . . and the Headmaster by his negligent manner is bringing the school into discredit and has very few scholars to teach'. The number of these given for the current year was twenty-two. Deep regret was also expressed that the portion of the Charity concerned with the Almshouse 'had not increased in usefulness with the large increase in the annual value of the estates'.

This report seems to mark the worst phase in the relations between the Vestry and the Trustees. Shortly afterwards an improvement began. This was made possible partly by the growing change in opinion in the country towards the fate of its old grammar schools. The facts revealed in the Report of the Brougham Committee (1837) had made many people uneasy. This report was followed in 1841 by an Act of Parliament 'for improving the condition and extending the benefits of Grammar Schools'. It seems clear that the Fellows of Corpus Christi were not only aware of this change of opinion but were themselves beginning to adopt a new attitude towards Richard Pate's foundation.

In Cheltenham the death in 1848 of the reactionary headmaster Hawkins, who had opposed all changes except the increase in his salary, lessened the difficulties of reorganization. The school was then actually closed for a short time. A Vestry Committee of resolute men, among whom were Francis Close, R. S. Lingwood, D. J. Humphris, John Goding and Samuel Harper, were determined that it should be restored to its original purpose. In the same year the Master in Chancery

approved the scheme for a new and extended system of education. This was finally carried out 'with the cordial co-operation
of all parties—particularly the President and Fellows of Corpus
Christi', and in 1852 the newly organized school was reopened
under the able and scholarly headmaster Dr. E. R. Humphrey.
Within a few months there were 150 scholars and a large
number of applicants whom the original building could not
accommodate. A new schoolroom was erected in the rear of the
old building and the neighbouring Yearsley's Boarding House
was purchased to provide further accommodation. In 1857
the long and expensive proceedings in Chancery were finally
brought to a close with an order from Vice-Chancellor Kinders-
ley who complimented the Vestry Committee on their resolute
action. In this, the interests of the town had been well served
by all parties in the Vestry, but particularly in the last years by
R. S. Lingwood and G. A. Williams—political opponents but
alike in giving their professional services freely to the town;
and even more particularly by Francis Close who had acted
on every committee appointed to negotiate with the Trustees
since he had been appointed as incumbent of the parish. It may
well be left to him in this connexion to summarize the events
of the last forty years. At the ceremony of the reopening of the
school it fell to him to convey to the President of Corpus
Christi in person the vote of thanks to the college passed at the
Easter Vestry meeting.

Allow me to say, let this be a great day of amnesty and entire
forgetfulness of whatever may have taken place in bygone years.
Let us look at Corpus Christi College as they are presented to us
this day, and we may then, without fear, say that they have done
all that men could do to further the interests of this important
institution. . . . There may be many causes, as suggested by the
President, why the school has fallen into comparative desuetude
and obscurity; but it should be remembered that it is in common
with a great many schools throughout the Kingdom, and much of
this must be attributed . . . to the indifference of the great bulk of
the population to the advantage of a liberal and enlightened education. Its revival now is mainly to be attributed to that conviction
which, I thank God, is now so extensively felt . . . that no earthly
thing, no riches . . . no advantages of birth, no position in society

can bear comparison in value with an intelligent, moral, enlightened and Christian education.⁹

Despite this new-found harmony, the Vestry continued with an almost terrier-like persistence to demand information from the Trustees concerning the conditions of the former exchange of the Almshouse site in 1811. They finally elicited a detailed account of what happened at that time (Chapter XII), but met with an absolute refusal to discuss the fate of the £250 paid to the college as part of the exchange.

The future of the school itself seemed bright. In many ways, however, it appeared to have been dogged with ill luck. Its able and much respected headmaster, Dr. Humphrey, disappeared from the town in the company of the wife of a local resident.¹⁰ From this cloud of scandal it was rescued by the Reverend Henry Hayman, later headmaster of Bradfield. Further reorganization became possible when the income of the endowment increased with the rise in land values. After the passing of the Endowed Schools Act of 1881, a new scheme was put into force by which Corpus Christi College gave up its complete control over the school. Under this scheme a governing body was set up which included four nominees of Corpus Christi College, four appointed by the Borough Council, four by the magistrates, and two by parents of the scholars. The college continued to maintain the estates and to collect the revenues, but after keeping the share allotted in the original deed of gift, transferred the remaining three-quarters to the new governing body under which the affairs of the school and the Almshouse were to be administered.

It had long been realized that a new building was essential for the school. A difference of opinion arose as to whether this should be erected on the existing site or whether new land should be purchased which would allow room for future expansion. Although the latter scheme was strongly opposed by W. H. Gwinnett, it was accepted by the majority of the Governors. A piece of land was purchased near Christ Church on which, subject to the consent of the Charity Commissioners, the new school was to be built. Unfortunately this consent was not given. While a small but vociferous group was opposed on grounds of sentiment to removing the school from its original position, the majority of the inhabitants were not sufficiently concerned to insist on the retention of the new site, which was ultimately acquired by the Ladies' College for a playing field. As a result the new school, completed in 1889, was erected on the old site. No grounds of sentiment, however, caused the Governors to retain any part of the original building which had survived through the centuries to this date, and by an act of vandalism, similar if differently motivated from that of the pulling down of the Almshouse, the last stones of Richard Pate's building were removed. Time has vindicated those who opposed the plan of keeping the school in the centre of the town, where the limited space prevented future expansion. Within thirty years there was a demand for a larger building. The school was again unfortunate in that plans for this were delayed by the outbreak of war, and perhaps by the building of the Girls' Grammar School. A decision was finally reached to build the new school in Hester's Way, where on 19 July 1963 the foundation-stone was laid by the President of Corpus Christi College. With a strangely apathetic attitude to historical background the name of the founder has in recent years been dropped from the title of his school, which is officially known as the Cheltenham Grammar School. On the other hand, the girls' school which was founded as recently as 1905, has now the title of Pate's Grammar School for Girls.

XXI

THE WORK OF THE COMMISSIONERS
1821–1839

IN the period that followed the end of the Napoleonic War, the two administrative bodies—the Paving Commissioners and the Vestry—were occupied with work that was unspectacular, but of the greatest importance. Cheltenham undoubtedly owes much to its architects and speculative builders, but it is also indebted to the two authorities whose concern for the planning and cleansing of streets, regulations for the building of houses, provision of wells and drains, saved it from the fate of so many towns with a similarly rapid development of population, where congeries of slums grew up and epidemics of smallpox and cholera created a national problem.

The powers of the Commissioners were strengthened by a new Act passed in 1821. This third Act, like its predecessors, was precipitated by affairs connected with the Market, thus showing once again that the Market was still a most important factor in the economy of the town.

The Market-house erected by the Commissioners in 1808—the upper room of which they had designated the Town Hall and used for their monthly meetings—was after twelve years considered too small for the volume of trade concerned. Attempts were made to extend it by transferring the vegetable market to a building to be erected in the Rose and Crown Passage, but it was found that, short of undertaking the expensive work of pulling down and rebuilding most of the passage, this situation was not suitable.

At the same time the Commissioners ran into unexpected difficulties with Lord Sherborne, from whom they had a twenty-one years' lease of the market tolls. The annual amount for which these were let had risen in 1819 to £650, and it was therefore unlikely that, if they built a new Market-house on a new site, Lord Sherborne would renew the lease on the same terms. The Commissioners therefore took Counsel's opinion as to their rights and were told that they could not proceed any further in the matter without a new Act of Parliament which would give them additional powers. This they obtained in 1821.

The Act empowered them to sell their interest in the old Market-house and take a lease of the tolls for a new one. They decided, however, to relinquish their interest in the tolls and in the project of the new building, if Lord Sherborne would compensate them for the expenses in which they had been involved. After long negotiations he finally agreed to take over the old building and to pay as compensation £500 a year for nine years. He allowed the Commissioners to continue to hold their monthly meetings in the upper room until the building was required for other purposes, and he afterwards paid for a suitable meeting-place for the remainder of the nine years. From 1823 they adjourned to a room provided for them at the 'Fleece', which remained their permanent meeting-place for some years.

The old Market-house was then altered and refronted (Goding, p. 105). It was for some time used as the offices of Messrs. Pruen & Griffiths, and for the Public Office where the magistrates held their Sessions three times a week. After the Act of 1852 the Town Commissioners and later the Borough Council held their meetings in this building. It was purchased by Messrs. F. W. Woolworth & Co. in 1915, and resold by them to Tesco in 1960. In 1827 Messrs. Pruen & Griffiths had offered to allow a clock to be placed there if maintained by the Commissioners, and from that date until 1958 the Town Clock projected from the upper storey. It was for many years kept in repair by the clock-maker William Howlett.

The new Market-house built by Lord Sherborne was situated almost opposite the former one, and the oriental front of the arcade stretched across what is now Bennington Street. As Lord Sherborne leased the tolls and the management of the Market to Baynham Jones, the Commissioners had no further connexion with it.

The 1821 Act ratified many of the powers which the Commissioners had been exercising for some years, such as their insistence that the plans of all new buildings and all additions and alterations to old buildings should be submitted to their surveyor, who enforced regulations concerning the thickness of party walls and stopped the use of thatch for roofs. It also enabled them to widen streets where necessary, and in 1824 they accepted Joseph Pitt's proposal that he should undertake the widening of Portland Passage provided that the Commissioners paid him £3,000 towards expenses. The account of the transaction as given in the Commissioners' Records has the same obscurity which exists in every record of Pitt's financial dealings with the town—as in the Inclosure Award and in the Vestry Records of purchase of land for the churchyard. However, when the Commissioners were attacked some years later on general grounds of inefficiency, one of the accusations was that they had paid as much as £3,000 to Pitt for widening Portland Passage (now Pittville Street).

It must be emphasized that the maintenance of the carriageway of existing roads still remained with the Vestry or with the Turnpike authorities, while the Town Commissioners were responsible for repairing but not actually for laying the footpavements. From the time of the 1786 Act the occupants of houses in the Street had been required either to lay the pavement or pay the Commissioners for laying it; as late as 1835 the Commissioners refused a demand from the Vestry to lay pavements from the Belle Vue Inn to the Old Bath Road on the ground that 'the laying of new pavements is unprecedented'.

Rapid building development necessitated the making of new roads. Under the Act of 1821, when in any such road three parts of the buildings to be erected were finished, each proprietor was required 'to pave the footway and stone the road to the centre', in a manner satisfactory to the Commissioners' surveyor. When this was done the proprietors could apply to the Commissioners to declare the same a public road, after which the Commissioners took over the responsibility of lighting, cleansing, and repairing the road and pavements. Thus in 1828 when three-quarters of the new houses to be built were completed, the occupiers of Hewlett Street, were ordered 'to pave and pitch the footpath adjoining and in front of their respective houses . . . the work to be done under supervision of the Surveyor', and to stone the road to the centre.

It was inevitable that there would be a certain amount of confusion and overlapping between the separate authorities—the Town Commissioners, the Vestry, the Turnpike Commissioners, and the Justices of the Peace, who still retained their administrative powers. In practice the separation was modified by two factors. First, the Town Commissioners and the Vestry shared the same viewpoint—that the present and future prosperity of Cheltenham depended on the number of visitors who could be attracted by such amenities as clean, well-paved, well-maintained roads. Thus a committee of the Vestry set up in 1821 issued a report which was identical in sentiment with a report made by a committee of the Town Commissioners a few years later. This emphasized the necessity of 'maintaining the Roads and Walks . . . in good repair all over the Town, as it is unquestionably of the first importance to the interest of Cheltenham, materially supported as it is by a temporary and fluctuating population, that every encouragement and facility should be given to the enjoyment of the Visitors . . .'.

The second factor was that while the two main bodies were independent of each other, the more active of the Commissioners frequently attended Vestry meetings and helped to direct Vestry policy, especially after the Sturges Bourne Act (1819).

Despite this liaison, however, various complaints passed from one administrative body to another. Thus in 1819 the Commissioners gave notice to the Surveyors of the Highways (acting for the Vestry) 'to cause the[1] Fleece Lane to be put in complete repair', and a little later their committee waited on the same surveyors 'respecting the state of New Street, Sherborne Street, Rutland Street and others—and to induce them to put these into a proper state of repair and attend more carefully to their condition in future'. In 1825 the Commissioners appointed a special committee to work in conjunction with the By-road Surveyors—'to improve the state of the Town generally and particularly narrow streets and to remove filth therefrom which may affect the health of the inhabitants'.

There was some liaison too between the Town Commissioners and the Commissioners of the Turnpike roads—
who were responsible for repairing their own roads. Three
groups of Turnpike Commissioners held monthly meetings
in Cheltenham: the Commissioners for the road from Cheltenham to Bath through Birdlip, who met at the 'Fleece', with
their clerk Theodore Gwinnett; the Commissioners for the
Cheltenham to Gloucester Road, and those for the road from
Cheltenham to Evesham—both of whom met at the Masonic
Hall and had as clerk J. C. Straford, himself one of the Town
Commissioners. Baynham Jones of Cambray House, one of
the most active of the Town Commissioners, was also one
of the Turnpike Commissioners. On at least two occasions
the Town Commissioners sent a committee to attend the meetings of the Turnpike Commissioners to complain about 'the
state of the High Street and to make arrangements for keeping
the Turnpike roads of the town in proper order'.

More generally these conferences were concerned with
cleansing the streets—one of the major problems at the time.
During the ten years after Waterloo there were attempts to
share the work and the expenses with the other two authorities,
but by 1826 the Commissioners finally decided to buy carts
and employ their own workmen for cleansing the streets.

The Commissioners made many efforts during these years
to maintain or regain the right to the water from the Chelt,
which formerly flowed down the street for at least two days
a week from the mill-pond at Cambray. It has already been
stated that William Humphris Barrett had to be reminded in
1813 of his earlier agreement 'to permit the water to run down
the Street as heretofore'. In the next twenty years the Commissioners made twelve attempts to regain this right, but
apparently they failed.

Apart from the necessity of watering and cleansing the
streets there was the problem of obtaining a domestic water-
supply for a rapidly growing population dependent so far on
private wells. As the Commissioners failed to supply the need,
a private Water Company was formed in 1824 which constructed a reservoir near the Hewletts to conserve water from
nearby springs and piped a supply to those willing to pay. In

the meantime the Commissioners sank their own wells in different parts of the town—near York Hotel, at Sandford, and Westhall. They were then threatened with legal action by the owners of the mills at Cambray, Alstone, and Twyning, on the ground that the wells drew water from the source of the water-power used for the mills. Finally the Commissioners cut off their wells entirely from supplies from the Chelt, but they still used water from other wells wherever possible, as it was less expensive than paying the Water Company for supplies.

The lighting problem had been solved much earlier by the formation of a private Gas Company (1818). This was regarded at first with great suspicion by the Commissioners, who insisted on certain rights being safeguarded by clauses inserted in the Act of Parliament concerned. Among these they reserved the right to decide the placing of new lamps, and with monotonous regularity for many years the monthly meetings deal with demands for lamps as newly built streets are completed. By the Act of 1821 the Commissioners were empowered to erect a gasometer and supply gas directly to the town, but they showed great hesitation and indeed timidity in embarking on public enterprise, and so the private company was formed.

This timidity is most marked in their greatest problem—the provision of sewers. Nothing had been done, apart from setting up a Commission to implement Dr. Jenner's proposal (1808) to make a Town Sewer. Not until 1822 was any actual work begun and this was concerned with the enlarging of the old sewer in St. George's Place. In the following years a number of special meetings of the Commissioners were held to consider the practicability of making a common sewer under the High Street. They even employed Papworth—presumably the architect—to take the levels and prepare estimates, and paid him £52 for his services. This energetic action held up temporarily the proposal to form a private Sewerage Company. The meetings continued, but whenever a decision was taken to build this sewer, it was revoked at the next meeting as inexpedient. The only outcome of all these deliberations was the construction of a sewer running from the Montpellier area down Old Well Lane into the Chelt, and of this achievement they were inordinately proud. 'An important common sewer upwards of half a mile in length has been constructed entirely free of expense to the public.' Finally, however, under a private Act, a Sewers Company (1834) was formed and a somewhat inadequate sewerage system developed. The reluctance of the Commissioners was in part due to fear of the cost, and in part to the belief that there was no strong demand for new sewers from the greater part of the inhabitants; neither of these reasons excuse what appears to a later generation as a neglect of their duty to provide a necessary public service. It is, however, quite certain that many of their number were shareholders in the private companies which were formed to give the three main services to the town, and were therefore not anxious to develop public enterprise.

The Commissioners did not show the same timidity in two other spheres of action, in both of which their attitude caused a conflict between them and the magistrates. In the age of the sedan-chair they laid down detailed regulations, later changed to by-laws, which fixed charges and parking-places for vehicles and imposed a code of restrictions on their owners. From 1807 all chairmen had to be licensed, and when other types of chairs —wheel-chairs and fly-chairs—were introduced, and in 1828 hackney coaches, the by-laws were revised. Each chairman was ordered to wear a long, loose, blue coat and on the sleeve of this a scarlet badge three inches in size with the licence number of his vehicle in blue on it. The conditions laid down in 1827 caused the equivalent of a strike and no chairmen presented themselves at the special meetings held for the purpose of granting licences. The Commissioners advertised in the local newspapers and as far afield as Bath and Bristol for applicants. Neither their records nor the contemporary newspapers reveal how the matter was settled, but undoubtedly there was considerable ill feeling against the Commissioners. Ten years later the number of horse carriages and hackney coaches had increased considerably in proportion to the number of chairs. Complaints of cruelty to the horses caused new by-laws as to the size of horses to be used and the weight to be carried. These by-laws also ordered the driver of every carriage 'to provide himself with and at all times wear a neat and clean

frock-coat of blue cloth reaching below the knees and also
. . . to wear a number corresponding with the number of the
licence of his carriage conspicuously attached to the front of his
hat . . . every such coat and number to be approved of by the
said Commissioners'. At the same time all drivers were required
to remain seated in or on their vehicles while waiting for fares.

The last two orders were so unpopular that the horse fly-men
paraded the streets with placards in protest, and they also
published a statement in the *Cheltenham Free Press* complaining of the high-handed action of the Commissioners and asking
for the support of the public. The Commissioners retaliated
by refusing to renew any licences to the drivers concerned
unless the latter signed a written apology. From the records
of the succeeding months it appears that a few of the drivers
found themselves obliged to sign the apology.

In the meantime the local magistrates protested. The Chairman of the Bench, Captain St. Clair of Staverton Court,
informed the Commissioners' Surveyor, in the presence of the
other magistrates and of many of the horse fly-men assembled
at the Public Office, that some of the proposed by-laws were
absurd, particularly those relating to the fly-men sitting constantly on their boxes and wearing numbers in their hats. He
protested also against other proposed orders, by which no
butchers' trays or bakers' baskets might be carried on the footpath, and no traders might sell goods from baskets or barrows
in the streets after ten in the morning. He stated that neither
he nor his fellow magistrates would convict persons breaking
such by-laws, and complained of a want of courtesy on the part
of the Commissioners towards the magistrates in not having
submitted their proposed by-laws to them.

The Commissioners replied by passing a resolution 'That it
is the opinion of this meeting that the communication from the
Magistrates was uncalled for and unwarranted', and that the
threat to refuse to convict 'was improper and calculated to
hold up the Body of Commissioners to contempt, and obstruct
them in the exercise of their legal functions'. They pointed out
that there had been no discourtesy, since 'the powers of making
by-laws are by law clearly separated, upon sound principles,
from the jurisdiction which the magistrates alone in their legal

capacity possessed of putting such by-laws into execution'. They also took Counsel's opinion on the matter and when this was given in their favour, a committee which included R. E. Marshall and Thomas Henney met the magistrates. The only final concession the Commissioners made was an offer to delay for three months the proposed by-law which enforced the carrying of butchers' and bakers' trays in the road instead of on the footpath.

This was not the only occasion of argument between the Paving Commissioners and the magistrates. There had been earlier differences of opinion in connexion with the police.

For the first twenty years of their appointment (1786) the Commissioners had accepted the situation in which the only police were two High Constables and the petty constable, all of whom were originally manorial officials, and now were responsible to the magistrates. Shortly after the Napoleonic War ended, the Surveyor was authorized to appoint from one to four watchmen as a nightly patrol, and an order was issued for a pair of stocks to be set up. There is some evidence that there was trouble with lamp-breaking and 'nightly depredations'. For four years police duties were carried out by these watchmen and the two High Constables, to whom the Commissioners paid a small salary. It was then decided that a permanent Watch Committee should be set up, which divided the town into eight districts, each with its own night-watchman, under a superintendent who was a former gaoler of Northleach prison. For these watchmen the Commissioners bought ten great-coats, twelve cutlasses and belts, twelve police rattles, twelve dark lanterns and long staves with crooks, and eight watch boxes. Despite these formidable weapons, the system does not seem to have worked very well. Within a year another committee was appointed 'to find a better way for watching the town'. Under the new arrangements, two beadles and street keepers were appointed with the full authority of Constables; it was, however, soon found necessary to revive the system of having night-watchmen.

For a time this was organized on a voluntary basis—some of the residents acting as watchmen themselves or paying substitutes. In 1823 the Commissioners decided to employ the beadles—now increased to four—exclusively within the town as opposed to the tithings. The magistrates took strong objection to this, but a compromise was arranged by Theodore Gwinnett by which the magistrates were requested to regulate the special duties of the constables. Two years later, however, the Commissioners sent a committee to consult the magistrates 'as to the best mode of effecting a more efficient Police'. Robert Capper (of Marle Hill), who was both a magistrate and a Commissioner, suggested placing the police under an experienced superintendent who would report directly to the magistrates. At the recommendation of Capper's friend—Sir John Birnie, the Chief Magistrate at Bow Street—a former Conductor of a Night Party in that area was brought in from London to take charge of the Cheltenham Police Force, at an annual salary of £150. Again the arrangement worked well for a short time; unfortunately later investigations held by the police led to the resignation of the superintendent. At the same time Billings—the Surveyor of Buildings—resigned, but offered to retain the work of Surveyor of New Buildings while the new surveyor, George Russell, was given the additional duty of taking charge of the police, at a composite salary of £200 a year on the understanding that he provided a room with a coal fire for the meetings of the Police Committee! The town was divided into twelve districts, with four constables to each. Among other duties the constables were expected to make a daily visit to each lodging-house which received vagrants and report on the numbers and on those who stayed there more than one night. They were also enjoined to enforce injunctions against 'furious driving' and exercising horses in the street. Shortly afterwards Sir Robert Peel instituted the Metropolitan Police Force, and in 1831 the Commissioners adopted a similar system, and made no further experiments.

The year 1832 was outstanding because of a cholera epidemic which affected many parts of the country. Among the attempts to prevent this from spreading, the central Government ordered the setting up of local Boards of Health.[2] The Cheltenham Vestry, as we have seen, resented the high-handed action of this Board of Health, but the Commissioners did all in their power to co-operate, particularly by enforcing literally the law ordering the summary arrest of all vagrants whom they believed might be carriers of the disease. The magistrates insisted, however, that no vagrant should be arrested unless he had been first cautioned by the police, and they fined a constable £1 for having made such an arrest. As a result serious trouble developed between the magistrates and the Commissioners (1834). George Russell (the Surveyor), acting on behalf of the latter, pointed out that their police were under orders to arrest vagrants at sight, and liable to a fine by the Commissioners if they disobeyed orders, and also that the police were paid by the Commissioners. Captain St. Clair replied for the magistrates that the Commissioners had no legal right to fine their constables; he stated firmly that on grounds 'both of humanity and regard for the County Purse' the magistrates would only convict a vagrant if he had previously received a personal caution from a constable. A joint meeting was then arranged which, on the insistence of the magistrates, was held in public. The Commissioners offered to replace the boards which had formerly been erected at all entrances to the town cautioning vagrants not to enter. The magistrates at first refused to compromise and insisted on their right 'to the implicit obedience of the police constables to every legal order given by the Magistrates'. Eventually, however, some of the latter seemed to realize that the police might have experience enough to distinguish between cases of genuine hardship and confirmed trampers. Finally, there seems to have been an unwritten understanding. 'We collected it to be the opinion of the Magistrates', wrote the committee representing the Commissioners, 'that discretion would be allowed to the Constables, but no formal order was given.' There the matter rested.

The end of the struggle as to who should control the police came when the Act of 1839 allowed the county magistrates to form a paid police force for the county. The Cheltenham Commissioners resisted vociferously on the grounds that Cheltenham as a residential centre needed a specially large force of its own. The magistrates won their case, and judging from the comments of contemporary guide-books the new system seems to have been satisfactory.

The Commissioners, having lost the initiative during these years by failing to provide the town with a gas service, a water-supply, and adequate sewers, were facing unpopularity for other reasons. The Municipal Corporation Act passed by the Liberals in 1835 had enabled[3] ratepayers in corporate boroughs —irrespective of property qualifications—to elect Town Councils with full responsibility. There was at this time in Cheltenham a strong body of Liberal and Radical opinion which was opposed to the system by which unelected Commissioners were in charge of the affairs of the town, more particularly after the passing of the Act. Provocation had been added to this feeling by the refusal of the Commissioners to allow the general public access to their meetings, and by their rescinding an earlier order by which the names of those voting for and against resolutions in their meetings were recorded.

This unpopularity was clearly revealed when the Commissioners decided in 1839 to apply for a new Act of Parliament to increase their powers so that they could assess for rates property on the newly developed estates—particularly Pittville. Pearson Thompson, who had inherited the Montpellier Spa and the land around it from his father, and the Jearrad brothers who by 1834 had become proprietors of Montpellier Spa, the Imperial Spa, and much of the Lansdown estate, were themselves active Commissioners and on the whole co-operative with their general policy. On the other hand, Joseph Pitt (who rarely attended Commissioners' meetings), his son William, and the owners of houses on the Pittville estate regarded their property as outside the town and not subject to the Commissioners' jurisdiction; in fact, there is considerable evidence that the Pittville proprietors hoped and expected that an entirely independent area would grow up which would rival Cheltenham. Pitt was therefore strongly opposed to any increase in the powers of the Commissioners, and was supported in this attitude by Thomas Billings who was at this time beginning the development of the Park estate.

For three years before they finally decided to apply for a new Act, the Commissioners had been occupied with making a new assessment for rating purposes and in trying to enforce rates on the very considerable amount of new property which up to now had not been assessed. This assessment had been carried out in co-operation with the Vestry, which still levied the Poor Rate. For the first time there was genuine co-ordination between the two rating authorities. At the same time the Commissioners were faced with the absolute necessity of overhauling the fire services and building a new fire-engine house following a disastrous fire at the premises of R. E. Marshall in Clarence Street in 1838. Defective hose-pipes, scarcity of buckets, inadequacy of water-supply, and delay in bringing the engine, revealed the complete inefficiency of the services provided by the Insurance Company to which the Commissioners paid an annual premium for maintaining fire services. The expenses of building the Fire Station and providing efficient engines amounted to £993, and quite naturally the Commissioners wished to collect the amount of rates they considered due to them. They argued that the proprietors of Pittville benefited considerably from the general services provided by them, but were unwilling to pay towards the expenses. The proprietors continued to lodge appeals against the rates. The solicitor J. B. Winterbotham suggested that a test case should be taken to law in order to get a judgement in Queen's Bench on the matter. At this critical stage the Commissioners' Clerk, Edmund Newman—a man of much legal experience—resigned because he did not agree with the proposed Bill, his place being taken by J. L. Packwood. The Gas Company, acting on the Commissioners' orders, had begun to lay pipes in Pittville with a view to the lighting of the streets and had been served with a notice from the Pittville proprietors claiming damages. The Commissioners, uncertain how far their powers extended, asked for Counsel's opinion. They received the following statement: 'None of the sections of the existing Act define to any legal certainty the limits of Cheltenham. . . . I think it would be proper for the Commissioners to apply for an Act of Parliament to explain and amend the Act and I think that without such an Act the Commissioners cannot carry into effect the purposes of the Act now existing.'

They therefore decided in 1839 to proceed with an application for a new Act and to borrow £1,800 at 4½ per cent. interest for the expenses likely to be incurred. In the first draft of the Bill they asked for a definition of boundaries which would enable them to extend their powers of lighting, paving, cleansing and rating to the newly developed areas. In deference to popular demand, they proposed that future Commissioners should be elected by ratepayers but insisted that the method laid down for Vestry elections by the Sturges Bourne Act (1819), which established a system of plural voting, should be adopted. They also insisted that rates on houses valued annually at £12 or less should be paid by the landlord, thus disfranchising the poorer tenants.

Early in the year they had asked the churchwardens to call a parish meeting to discuss the proposed Bill and had published a summary and asked for suggestions and objections from the public. A storm broke at the parish meeting, held actually in the church. After what the *Cheltenham Free Press* called 'scenes of indescribable confusion and tumultuous altercation', a resolution was passed—largely the work of James Boodle acting as Secretary of the Liberal Association—'That it was not expedient to apply for any Bill in the present session and that the Borough member should be instructed to oppose any that should be applied for'. Boodle was supported by other Liberals —William Gyde and his son the solicitor W. H. Gyde. Samuel Harper—more Radical than Liberal—emphasized 'that the unpopular manner in which the Commissioners had administered their existing powers was no inducement to anyone to support the increase of their powers'.

Shortly afterwards a petition against the Bill was organized, which received 2,368 signatures. It was soon followed, however, by a petition with 543 signatures in its favour. The Commissioners claimed that of the 2,368 signatures only 351 were ratepayers, and that their contribution only constituted an amount of £788 in rates, whereas the petitioners for the Bill contributed £3,583. They saw no reason why the non-propertied classes should express any opinion as to the government of the town.

The first petition against the Bill was presented to the House of Commons by Henry Berkeley, the brother of Craven Berkeley, who as member for Cheltenham had been persuaded earlier to introduce the Bill itself into the House, but without any pledge of his future support. The Berkeley family were in difficulties. They realized the need to clarify the powers of the Commissioners, but as Liberals were strongly opposed to the proposed methods of plural voting. Eventually they decided to oppose the Bill. At a second public meeting held in the York Hotel, Craven Berkeley's letter conveying this decision was read. There was also opposition from the Gas and Water Companies, and particularly from Pitt and Billings. A letter to the Commissioners' Clerk from Pitt's London solicitors runs: 'Mr. Winterbotham is now with me in Town, but we leave this evening for Cheltenham . . . having fully instructed our Parliamentary Agents. We wish to offer no factious opposition to the Bill, but to that Bill in its present shape and extent Mr. Pitt and the purchasers under him have the most insuperable objection and will oppose it by every method in their power. It interferes with vested rights to an extent which we are quite sure the legislature will not tolerate. . . .'

As Joseph Pitt commanded Conservative support in the House—he had long been a silent but reliable party member—there seemed little chance for the Bill.

At this juncture Pearson Thompson did his best to mediate by arranging a meeting between the conflicting parties. Lord Segrave (Colonel Berkeley) took the chair at this meeting, but the negotiations failed. The Liberals demanded that each rate-payer should be restricted to one vote, and that the poorer tenants should be allowed to vote. They objected also to a clause which Lord Shaftesbury had insisted on inserting at the Committee stage, by which the main control of the town's roads should pass from the Highway Surveyors to the Commissioners, but they were ahead of their times in asking for a clause empowering the Commissioners to purchase five acres of land for public amusement and recreation. The Commissioners, while prepared to make some concession to the poorer tenants, were adamant on the matter of plural voting.

They were prepared to concede far more to the demands of Joseph Pitt and the proprietors of the Pittville estate. They agreed that it should be written into the Bill that 'their powers of watering, watching, cleansing and widening the streets shall

not extend to the estate of Joseph Pitt', and they were prepared to light the Pittville Streets on a special rate if asked to
do so. They were also willing to allow the occupiers of Montpellier, the Old Well, and Bayshill 'to erect fences and shut
gates to exclude the public from private roads on the occasion
of public fêtes as fully and amply as they have been accustomed to'.

Despite these concessions the Bill was defeated by nine
votes, the Berkeleys having used the influence of the Reform
Club and Pitt that of his Conservative friends to oppose it.
The report signed by the Committee of the Commissioners
—J. S. Cox, James Fisher, R. E. Marshall, G. A. Williams,
Robert Younghusband—laid the blame for this mainly on Pitt.
'Notwithstanding all their exertions [the Berkeleys] we should
have been successful but for the opposition of Pitt and his
Agents who used their utmost endeavours to prevail on mem-
bers who otherwise would have been favourable, to vote against
the Bill.'

As a result Cheltenham was condemned to a further fourteen years under Commissioners not directly responsible to an
electorate and with powers ill defined and inadequate to meet
the changing situation.

XXII

THE COMMISSIONERS—AN UNPOPULAR OLIGARCHY
1839–1852

T HE unfortunate defeat of the 1839 Bill left the Commissioners in an unenviable position. They were bound by the 1821 Act to maintain certain services in the town, but the area over which their powers ran, hitherto ill-defined, was now narrowed by the generally accepted view that the Pittville and Bayshill estates could not be included for rating purposes. With the problems created by an ever-increasing population the Commissioners needed more rather than fewer powers. Their position, moreover, was rendered less tenable by their refusal to make any real concession to the demand for a freely elected body to take control of the government of the town—a demand accelerated by the recent passing of the Municipal Corporations Act, which had virtually brought about a revolution in municipal affairs. They wished to remain a self-appointed oligarchy at a time when the prevailing political opinion in the town was Liberal and was strongly supported, in this matter at least, by a small group of somewhat vociferous Radicals who were in the happy position of being able to express their views in the *Cheltenham Free Press*—a Radical newspaper published weekly.

The Liberals also had their paper, the *Cheltenham Examiner*, founded in 1839 with the backing of the house of Berkeley and, according to Goding, with that of most of the magistrates of the Cheltenham Bench.[1] If this statement is true, it would explain some of the animosity shown by the local magistrates towards the Commissioners during these years. There was, however, no clearcut political issue in which the Commissioners represented one party and their opponents another.

If the general attitude of the Commissioners during these years was Conservative, several leading Liberals were themselves Commissioners, and the principal opposition to the recent policy of the Commissioners had come from the life-long Tory Joseph Pitt. It is safe to emphasize that the main body of the Commissioners was at this time opposed to the Liberal demand that they should be elected by the ratepayers without plural voting, and that they were certainly over-zealous in maintaining the secrecy of their proceedings and in refusing access to their meetings to the Press or the public. It should also be remembered that many of the fifty Commissioners were either non-resident or did not care to attend, and although in theory—and sometimes in fact—non-attendance disqualified a Commissioner, some of those appointed under the 1821 Act remained in the position only nominally and took little part except in occasional opposition to popular demands.

An incident in 1840 seems to indicate a growing disrespect for the powers of the Commissioners. On this occasion, while they were dealing with rating appeals in their monthly meeting held at the 'Fleece', a noisy mob collected outside, shouting 'Down with the Commissioners' and 'Hang them on the nearest lamp-post', and 'Rogues, thieves and Tories'. Nine men forced their way into the room and the meeting broke up in confusion. The men concerned were later tried in Glou-cester at the Assizes on the charge of creating a riot.[2] Two of them were sentenced to a month's imprisonment, in one case with an additional fine of £10. The fact that after they had served their term of imprisonment they were brought back by their friends in a carriage drawn by four greys, and enter-tained at a public dinner at the 'Lamb', gives some measure of the unpopularity of the Commissioners among one section of the people. The *Cheltenham Free Press*, however, showed little sympathy with this demonstration, which it considered was fomented by certain Liberals for personal reasons.

A more serious threat to their power occurred in the same year when a man named Strickland questioned the legal right of the Commissioners to force him to pay their rate. The case was taken to Quarter Sessions where the magistrates, in direct opposition to the opinion of the Chairman of the Bench, quashed the rate. The Commissioners put in an appeal to the Court of Queen's Bench, but until the case was settled they felt that they could not legally enforce the collection of rates of any kind. They therefore sent out notices to explain 'that a rate which they were advised was valid having been set aside on grounds which, if good in law, would be fatal to any other rate, they could no longer continue to employ the men working for them on the credit of the rates until a higher Court had decided on their powers'. Their clerk informed the Chairman of Quarter Sessions that 'in all probability the Town Police will not act after this weekend', and requested him to instruct the Chief Constable of the County to direct the rural police to act in Cheltenham. George Russell, the Commissioners' surveyor who also acted as Superintendent of the Police, reported that he had informed the police under him that the Commissioners had no money to pay them if they continued their services, and that 'such Police had discontinued to watch the Town, and he had so informed the Chief Constable'.

In the course of the next six months the Gas Company sent in demands for payment for two quarters' gas, with interest on the amount concerned, and threatened to discontinue lighting the town if the amount was not paid quickly. The Commissioners replied firmly that they had no funds, and would make no attempt to obtain them by raising rates until the case had been legally settled. Pearson Thompson and other rate-payers then gave notice of their intention to apply for a mandamus to force the Commissioners to raise a rate to pay for the essential services in the town. The Commissioners replied with an expression of regret for the position in which they were placed, and refused to take any further action.

Pearson Thompson lost his case for obtaining a mandamus, but in the course of the proceedings in the Court of Queen's Bench, Lord Chief Justice Denman threw out the opinion 'that the application pending in the Court ought not to interfere with the measures which may be necessary to sustain the local interests of the Town'. On the strength of this statement the Commissioners who, as they explained, were only too anxious to conform to any suggestion which would help them in the dilemma, decided at last to order that a new rate should be imposed. The matter was indeed urgent. The police had been disbanded for lack of funds to pay them. The Commissioners were faced with a writ for payment of £1,756 from the Gas Company, with demands for payment of interest on various loans and annuities, and also with a demand for repayment of the principal and interest of money borrowed by them from the County of Gloucester Bank to pay for the expenses of the 1839 Bill. Five months afterwards their appeal came before the Court of Queen's Bench. The verdict reversed the decision of the Gloucester magistrates and established their legal right to raise rates. Thus after an interval of more than a year, during which they seem to have acted with dignity and restraint, the Commissioners resumed their normal responsibilities.

The resignation of the police force was less serious than it might have been because the episode coincided with the putting into force of an Act of 1839 by which, with the concurrence of the magistrates of Quarter Sessions, a force of County Police might be established and maintained by a county rate. The Commissioners fought hard to prevent Cheltenham from being included in this arrangement. They had recently increased the numbers of their own force and they were most reluctant that this should be superseded. Early in 1840 they addressed a petition to the Home Secretary asking that the town might be excluded altogether from the Bill, or that a clause should be inserted by which Cheltenham would be allowed the same number of the County Police as those formerly employed by the Commissioners. 'The Town of Cheltenham is the resort of a great number of invalids . . . it is essentially necessary for their welfare to give them a feeling of perfect security and freedom from annoyance, and for such purpose a large Police Force is necessary.' The Commissioners believed, almost fanatically, that this security and freedom from annoyance depended primarily on the maintenance of their by-laws. Their own police force brought an average number of thirty cases each month before the magistrates for the infraction of by-laws—'the greater part of which was for obstructing streets in the delivery of Merchandise, Bread, Vegetables, etc., from Waggons, Trucks and Barrows, and also from the misconduct of Flymen and Fly Carriage Drivers'. The Commissioners had good reason to doubt whether a police force under the county authorities would act as effectively. They also sent a memorial to the magistrates in Quarter Sessions asking for their support for the petition.

The value of property in Cheltenham is constantly fluctuating and the town has no staple trade to support it; it is entirely maintained by its being a place resorted to for health and recreation. . . . It has been brought to its present state of prosperity by an immense outlay of Capital and can only be maintained in this state by its being managed strictly in accordance with the regulations . . . for the prevention of Nuisances and the provisions of sufficient police to enforce these.

Despite the fervour of their pleading, the petition was rejected; the magistrates preferred to enforce the Act. The Town Police Force was thus superseded by the County Police. There is a sad record in May 1841: 'Ordered the sale of Police Clothing and other articles getting damp in the Station House.'

The Commissioners, however, were determined that their by-laws should be enforced, and for this purpose within a few weeks after the sale of the old uniforms they appointed two beadles, and shortly afterwards two others. Each of the four was expected to patrol a specified area; he was paid £50 a year and had to find his own clothes—a blue cloth frock-coat with a red collar was recommended. He was also expected to carry a copy of the Act of 1821 and of the by-laws with him so that when he had to deal with a case of infringement, he could show the person concerned the exact terms of the by-law. He was expected 'to pay constant attention to conduct of drivers of carriages and wheel chairmen and to give notice to the police of any beggars importuning passers-by'. The position appears to have required delicacy and tact. 'The Beadles are at all times to conduct themselves with good temper and urbanity towards all parties . . . they are to avoid entering into disputes and discussions . . . and not to go beyond simple warning that they will duly report such parties to the constituted authority.'

There was such a strong feeling among the Commissioners that the magistrates were not enforcing their by-laws that in 1843 they sent a complaint to the Home Office. An acrimonious correspondence followed between their clerk and the chairman of the Bench, who said that after perusing the 1821 Act and the by-laws, he calculated that 349 types of offences existed under the Act and 326 under the by-laws! He therefore submitted that the County Police could not be expected to deal with all these offences. However, Sir James Graham, on behalf of the Home Office, wrote requesting the magistrates and the Gloucester County Constabulary 'to carry into execution the provisions of the local Act and the by-laws, recommending the subject to the attention at the earliest meeting of the Magistrates'. Whatever their reply to Sir James Graham, the deputy clerk of the magistrates was ordered to write to the clerk of the Commissioners that 'the County Constabulary have *not* been specially directed to carry into operation the provisions and by-laws of the Cheltenham Commissioners'.[3]

The major part of the Commissioners' work was still concerned with maintaining the safety and cleanliness of the roads. The records of the confusion which existed between the various authorities because of their ill-defined powers make tedious reading. In 1836[4] a Board of Highways had been elected for the township of Cheltenham. Some years later the legality of the Cheltenham board was disputed, and there was a strong belief in the town that if the board was not the legal authority for the repair of roads within the township, the Commissioners ought to be held responsible for such work. It was therefore decided that Counsel's opinion should be taken on both points.

With regard to the Board of Highways, the opinion given was that a board of the kind could only be legally elected for a whole parish, and as the township of Cheltenham was only part of the parish, it therefore could not legally elect a Highway Board. The same barrister also gave his opinion that the Commissioners were only responsible for the repair of those roads 'within $1\frac{1}{2}$ miles of the parish church which were in existence at the time of the 1821 Act and not under the care of the Trustees of Turnpike roads', and for the roads which they had actually 'taken to' since that date.

In this extremely confused state of affairs the magistrates were with some difficulty induced to agree to the appointment of a Surveyor of Roads who carried on the work of the former board, and the Commissioners took steps to find out the actual roads for which they were responsible. The account of these, as prepared by John Surman Cox—their able clerk—is a most interesting document because of the light it throws on the early development of the town.

From this time the Commissioners dealt faithfully with the upkeep of the streets for which they were liable and for which they could levy rates. They were fully aware, at a time when legislation was under consideration to raise the general standard of public hygiene in towns, that the health of the town might be affected by unclean streets and bad drainage. When in 1846 the Board of Guardians[5] applied to them for information concerning the state of sewerage and drainage in the town, they immediately set up a committee to collect the information required. The conditions described in the report of this committee seem incredible in a town which took pride in its beauty and amenities:

Coltham Lane,[6] the boundary of the Parish of Cheltenham, is a deep road several feet below the land in Cheltenham Parish. The muck and filth in it arise from the Parish of Charlton Kings, as the road in question, being lower than the adjoining land, is made use of as a common drain. It is much feared that the Commissioners have no jurisdiction over this lane. . . .

After a long list of roads which, as a result of being left unrepaired, had filthy ditches, defective drainage, and pools of stagnant water, and of others rendered unsavoury by nearby pig-sties and privies, they proceeded to describe the state of the Chelt into which sewage was discharged at this time:

A great nuisance arises from the river Chelt between St. George's Place and Alston Mill, and the Commissioners have agreed to pay one-third of the expense of arching over the river between St. George's Place and the Cold Baths, but greater nuisance arises between these and Alston Mill, where the Commissioners have no jurisdiction—as it runs between private property and they must ask for power under the Sewers Act to order the nuisance to be put down.

In a further statement issued a few months later, the committee reported '240 cases of defective drainage and neglect of common cleanliness, 220 of which have been temporarily or permanently dealt with', probably with a supply of lime which the Commissioners were prepared to supply free to house-holders too poor to buy it.

The Commissioners' surveyor was ordered to deal with all public nuisances reported; private individuals were given notice in cases where the nuisance was their responsibility. Undoubtedly the Commissioners were genuinely determined to maintain an efficient system of sanitary inspection; at the same time they were probably only too accurate in their estimation of the general situation in the country: 'The Committee believe that in most Towns of the same size a much greater number of nuisances of all kinds may be found, and with the general healthiness of Cheltenham, they have every reason to be satisfied.'

Other difficulties arose from the fact that the three main services were in the hands of private companies over which the Commissioners had no control, and that none of these services was satisfactory. The recent investigation had shown how far the Sewers Company had failed in providing an adequate service. At the same time, J. S. Cox (in his capacity as Clerk) reported what he considered to be the unsatisfactory attitude of the Water Company, which by turning off the main in Hewlett Street could withhold supplies of water from other mains and so create a most dangerous situation in case of fire. He had also inquired into the cost of water supplied to other towns by private companies and reported that in most cases prices were lower than in Cheltenham and that profits were restricted by clauses in local Acts. A few months after this warning a fire which broke out at Alder's cabinet works in Albion Street caused extensive damage because of insufficient water, broken-down stand-pipes, and the refusal of at least one of the company's servants to co-operate with the firemen.

In the meantime the Gas Company, on the expiration of their contract with the Commissioners, demanded an increased price and a guarantee of a seven years' contract. Lord John Russell's Ministry during these years was continuing Lord Melbourne's policy of reforming municipal government. Chadwick's Report and the successive epidemic of typhus and cholera had taught many people outside the Ministry the danger of leaving sanitary and drainage systems in the rapidly growing towns under the control of authorities with inadequate powers. The Commissioners, therefore, felt their position to be insecure and they refused to be bound by a seven years' contract with the Gas Company.

They were at this time harassed by the pressure of Government policy, hindered by cross-currents of conflicting interests among themselves, and constantly attacked on their status as an unrepresentative and secretive oligarchy. In deference to this last point of attack, they at last decided, at the time when the Health of Towns Bill was passing through its final stages in the Commons, to publish the minutes of their monthly meetings, but they still refused to allow either the public or reporters to be present.

The purpose of the Health of Towns Bill may be seen from the preamble: 'Whereas more effectual provision ought to be made for improving the sanitary condition of Towns . . . and it is expedient that the supply of water to such towns for the sewerage, drainage, cleansing and paving thereof should, so far as is practical, be placed under local management and control, subject to such general supervision as is hereinafter provided. . . '.

In the fifty-two clauses which follow an attempt was made to give the existing central authority in towns—under the supervision of a central Board of Health—control of water, sewerage, drainage, and road repairs; and where the central authority was not adequate for this purpose, to set up a local Board of Health with similar powers. In towns such as Cheltenham, where the Commissioners were appointed under a local Act (1821), the consent of a majority of these would be necessary before their powers could be transferred to another body such as an elected Board of Health; and in all towns the consent of one-tenth of the ratepayers was necessary before an application for the adoption of the Act could be made.

The Commissioners decided to support the Bill (which became the Public Health Act of 1848) on the ground that their existing powers were not adequate for the making of the changes necessary for a rapidly growing population. At their request a Vestry committee convened a meeting of ratepayers, which after a lively discussion passed a resolution calling for the adoption of the Act.[7] The supporters of this resolution considered that the Commissioners had outgrown their usefulness as an institution and that 'it was monstrous for a town of 40,000 to be taxed at 1s. 4d. in the pound without any say in the matter'. The main opponent—W. H. Gwinnett—thought that the adoption of the new Act would increase the rates. As the result of a further resolution calling for a Government inquiry into the state of the town, Edward Cresy was sent from London to examine the position. His visit is an example of how the central Government attempted during these years to guide local authorities in implementing the legislation which was passed to deal with problems of a rapidly growing population.

The Inquiry[8] itself shows the town trying to solve the very difficult problem of how to reconcile private interests with the general good, so succinctly expressed by R. S. Lingwood when protesting against the principles of the 1851 Bill: '... the great difficulty would be to make the interests of private Estate owners and private Companies coincide with those of the Town.' It also reveals the personalities of the leading figures in the town in a way that is not achieved by the records of meetings of either the Commissioners or the Vestry. All the main interests of the town were represented at the Inquiry, including the Commissioners (who offered full co-operation), the ratepayers, the three private companies, and the proprietors of the estates of Lansdown, Pittville, and Bayshill. There was also present a number of other residents: James Agg-Gardner, the solicitors John Bubb and Samuel Pruen, James Fallon, William Hollis—gunsmith, and John Goding.

Cresy was extremely critical of the general layout of the company's sewers, although old Thomas Henney, who avowed himself the father of the Sewers Company, pointed out how much the company had achieved since its initiation, 'when even the High Street was in a disgraceful condition'. On the other hand, William Tartt, himself one of the Commissioners, admitted that 'unfortunately the houses which most required drainage were in streets where there was no main sewer'. Dr. Wright roundly accused the Sewers Company of seeking dividends rather than the health of the town. Charles Hale, the Town Surveyor, added that though the company had power to sewer any streets where required, 'they only did so where the amount of remuneration would recompense them for the outlay'.

On the question of the water-supply, Cresy found the company out of date, both in regard to its charges, which made it impossible for most of the inhabitants to afford the amount recognized as necessary—'100 gallons of pure water for each household per day'—and in its failure to use gathering grounds to collect their water-supply.

G. E. Williams, acting as solicitor for both these companies, insisted that their rights must not be interfered with, but when the Inquiry turned to the position of the Commissioners, he joined whole-heartedly with Boodle in the attack: 'Whatever the diversity of opinion as to the necessity for the Act, there was one point on which there was no difference of opinion— that if the Enquiry enabled the Town to get rid of the present Commissioners, the majority of the rate-payers would rejoice in its adoption.' On the other hand, W. H. Gwinnett said with equal conviction that a large number of residents doubted the wisdom of applying for the Act, not only because of the expense and the obvious increase in rates, but because the good health of Cheltenham made it unnecessary. Dr. Wright, however, emphasized that the last statement did not apply to the poorer classes.

Cresy next turned his attention to conditions in the poorer areas of the town. Here he found streets not well cleansed; dirty, unventilated lodging-houses letting accommodation at threepence a night for a bed, and sometimes allowing four or five persons in one bed; tenement houses with insanitary yards and the inevitable pig-sties; and a very unhealthy system by which about 100 people with donkey carts sifted rubbish from the scavengers' collection and scattered dust as they did so. The large Union Workhouse, however, was found to be satisfactory.

Some months later the Inspector's final report[9] was published. In addition to the points already made, the report laid considerable emphasis on the high rate of infant mortality and on the heavy incidence of epidemic disease in the preceding year, when in three months 107 deaths occurred from scarlet fever, mostly in the poorer parts of the town. 'We may trace the source of sickness and premature deaths in a great measure to the condition of the crowded and ill-ventilated habitations of the humbler classes.' A list of twenty streets with additional courts and alleys was given where conditions were insanitary, the water-supply inadequate or non-existent, and where in general 'the scavenger, the water cart and the sewer were unknown'. Some of the lodging-houses in the poorer areas were in a pestilential condition and disease could also be spread in them by the pauper tramps who combined 'the greatest aversion to labour with an abhorrence of cleanliness'; evidence supplied by a member of the Board of Guardians revealed that 8,891 of these tramps had received poor relief in passing through the town in 1848. The sewerage system was severely criticized and condemned. The Chelt was polluted with sewage from the town; Wyman's Brook (the Swilgate) from the Prestbury (Pittville) estate; and the Hatherley Brook from the Park estate.

The report recommended that in accordance with the Public Health Act, a local Board of Health consisting of twenty-five rate-payers should be elected; that a more satisfactory system of sewerage and a better water-supply should be brought into operation. It concluded with a statement of opinion that 'A very large amount of sickness and premature mortality might be prevented by the application of the provisions of the Public Health Act, and that ... a very great saving in existing charges for lighting, repair of roads, sewerage and water might also be effected'.

The report angered the opponents of the Act, and alarmed many others, who feared that it might deter visitors from coming to the town. The Conservative *Looker-On* stated: 'This document is likely to lead to much angry discussion, and if its suggestions are acted upon, it will assuredly inflict a very serious injury upon the property of the Town, seeing that a variety of most expensive works are recommended to be done, which would load the inhabitants with a burthen of local taxation.'

The Commissioners took the opportunity to send a memorial to the General Board of Health, using information supplied to them by the local Registrar of Births, Deaths, and Marriages, in order to contrast their own and Cresy's estimates of the comparatively low death-rate in the town from infectious disease. They were then sharply rebuked by the Registrar-General, who accused them of using for comparison a different statistical system, and different dates for the period of calculation, from those adopted by the Inspector.

After acrimonious party spirit had lessened, there was a general feeling, except among the more extreme Conservatives, that change must come. It was realised that the Public Health Act alone was not adequate to make these changes. The private estates would still remain unrateable. The Turnpike roads would be beyond the jurisdiction of the governing body, and the old Board of Commissioners would continue in existence despite the election of a local Board of Health. Early the next year a public meeting was held and a committee was appointed under the chairmanship of Agg-Gardner, to arrange for an application for a Bill to deal with Cheltenham's special problems.

This Bill passed quickly through the early stages in the Commons, but to the general surprise it was thrown out in the Committee stage. A clause in the Bill gave the town the right to buy out the Sewers Company. Lord Abinger pointed out that the price named in the clause was £5,000 more than the sewers were worth, and that in any case a money clause could not be allowed in the Bill, and the Committee then threw out the whole Bill.

There was naturally great disappointment. Within two months, however, a decision was reached to apply for a new Bill (without the offending clause) to be introduced in the next session of Parliament. The vexed question whether the Commissioners should be nominated in the Bill or elected was settled by a compromise by which the first Commissioners were to be nominated in the Act and were to hold office for one year only; after this they were to be elected by the ratepayers, but on a system of plural voting.

With the passing of the Improvement Act in 1852, Cheltenham received its first measure of self-government. The new governing body was given full authority to provide the services necessary for health—especially a new sewerage system and an adequate supply of water—and if necessary the right to 'buy out' the private companies. It was also empowered to raise rates in all parts of the borough and given complete control of the roads. The progressive forces had won their battle and the conflicting jurisdictions of the last century were at last transferred to a central authority.

XXIII

THE DECAY OF THE MANOR

DURING the last phases of the jurisdiction of the Town
Commissioners, another authority which was much
older than theirs—that of the lord of the manor—was
also drawing to a close.

We have already seen that by the end of the eighteenth
century the manorial courts had lost most of their judicial
power. The court leet, however, maintained some of its
functions far into the nineteenth century. It was in this court
that the copyholders elected the manorial officials, the most
important of whom was the High Bailiff, who was regarded
as the ceremonial head of the town in the years before there
was a mayor.

In the court leet, too, all copyhold property had to be
'surrendered' to the lord of the manor before it could change
hands, and the transaction was then recorded in the Court
Rolls. The fees which were collected by the steward, together
with the ancient fines, rents, and heriots, formed the major
portion of the manorial income. Copyhold property was still
subject to the restrictions defined by the Act of 1625. It differed
from freehold principally in that its owners, being still legally
tenants of the lord of the manor, paid him an annual rent; and
in that whenever the property was transferred by inheritance,
sale, or lease, a heriot or fine—the amount of which was fixed
by the Act—had to be paid to the lord of the manor. In the
course of years many of the original copyhold properties had
been broken up into smaller holdings. The Act provided that
with each division of property the payments should also be
divided. This fact, together with the change in the value of
money, meant that many of the fixed payments amounted only
to a few pennies, but the actual fees charged by the stewards
had been steadily raised after the manor changed hands in 1843.

By the middle of the nineteenth century copyholders in

Cheltenham shared a feeling which had developed in many parts of the country that the existence of copyhold property was a medieval survival which had now become anomalous. A movement had been set on foot for 'enfranchisement', by which all restrictions would be removed and copyhold property would be converted into freehold. This feeling received recognition in the passing of the Copyhold Acts of 1852 and 1858 which appointed Commissioners with power to settle disputes that might arise in matters of enfranchising copyhold property, and made provision for the terms under which this might be carried out.

As long as the Manor of Cheltenham remained in the possession of the Sherborne family there seems to have been little friction. The second Lord Sherborne was not slow to assert his rights with regard to the Market and such minor matters as fallen trees on the highway, but as he never extended his claims beyond those which were generally accepted, and as he was personally much respected, relations with his tenants remained happy. 'He was as good a gentleman as ever lived' said Thomas Teal when giving evidence against the claims of a later lord of the manor. In 1843 Lord Sherborne sold the manor to James Agg-Gardner for £39,000 and for the first time since the days of William Norwood, Cheltenham had a resident lord of the manor. Whereas Lord Sherborne was a landowner of ancient family, the new lord derived his income very largely from brewing and banking interests inherited from his uncle's family. There was another important difference. The Sherborne family were in general Whigs, and Lord Sherborne had contested the county in 1810 as a Whig, whereas James Agg-Gardner was Conservative—a fact which was to have a considerable effect on the future political representation of Cheltenham.

Ten years after this change of ownership the copyholders in Cheltenham held a public meeting with a view to forming an association to protest against the recent rise in the fees demanded by the steward of the manor. The chairman of the meeting was Sir William Russell of Charlton Park, lord of the Manor of Ashley (part of Charlton Kings), and the owner of considerable copyhold property in Cheltenham. He was supported by the barrister Samuel Gael who had also inherited much copyhold property in Charlton Kings, by the solicitor John Bubb, and by many other well-to-do copyholders.[1] At this meeting they expressed resentment not only against the actual rise in fees, but against the addition that such an increase would make to the income of the lord of the manor, on which the price to be paid for enfranchising the property would be calculated. A particular grievance was that 'whereas by the ancient custom of the Manor, where a party was possessed of several lots of copyhold property, the whole might be sold, devised or mortgaged in one document for the payment of one fee . . . a separate fee was now demanded for each lot. . . . The whole of the Delabere Estate—including copyhold land from Charlton Kings to Uckington—had passed from owner to owner between 1760 and 1807 and was repeatedly treated as one entire property.' Gael complained that because he resisted such fees he had been proclaimed an outlaw in the lord's court.

The steward of the manor had protested strongly against the holding of this meeting, but despite this protest, the copyholders showed great determination to resist the increase of fees. Shortly afterwards a test case of Treherne—a copyholder who refused to pay the additional amount—was tried at Gloucester Assizes. The case was finally transferred to the Court of King's Bench and taken before Lord Chief Justice Campbell. Judgement was given for Treherne, and the increase in fees beyond those of ancient practice was declared illegal. In the course of this case Lord Campbell forcibly expressed his views on the need to reform the law of copyhold tenure and 'to change this tenure into free and common socage. . . . We are not by any means to be supposed as sanctioning the practices which have prevailed in this Manor of Cheltenham, which appears to be an instance of a Manor kept up for the sake of obtaining fees which are very oppressive to the copyholders.'[2]

James Agg-Gardner died in 1858. He had taken an active part in the affairs of the town, particularly in the struggle to obtain the 1852 Act and later as the efficient chairman of the first Board of Commissioners elected under this Act. He appears to have been a keen business man, getting as much as he could from his copyhold tenants and unwilling to sell the market tolls at what the Commissioners regarded as a reasonable price. On the whole, however, he was popular. His heir was the twelve-year-old James Tynte Agg-Gardner who was made a ward in Chancery. Shortly afterwards, the manor was put up for sale by auction. Particulars of the property were issued to the auctioneers by Messrs. Gwinnett & Ticehurst, the stewards of the manor:[3]

> The principal part of the revenue of the Manor arises from the court fees payable to the stewards on admittances and surrenders which have for many years been, and now are, accounted for by the steward to the Lord of the Manor. The net income arising, after deducting the fixed yearly sum paid for the performance of the duties, has amounted to nearly £1,000 per annum, in each of the two years ending 1860 and 1861. . . . The above is exclusive of all sums received from enfranchisements. . . . This lot is especially worthy the attention of any solicitor who may be willing to give the necessary attention to the subject of the Manor and encourage enfranchisements.

In 1862 the manor was purchased for £33,000 by the solicitor Robert Sole Lingwood. He was already known in the town as an uncompromising Tory who had opposed the 1852 Act because it introduced the principle of election into local government. He had also opposed the institution of a public library, and his attack on the county magistrates on the ground that they showed favour to Liberals had led to a lawsuit. It seems likely that he bought the manor as a business speculation, hoping to derive a profit from the payments made for the enfranchisement of copyhold property. If the copyholders refused his terms, he intended to revive certain claims of medieval lords of the manor against them.

Within three months of the purchase he had instructed the stewards to send a notice to the copyholders pressing them to enfranchise their property. The same notice also warned them that he intended to claim copyhold property in absolute forfeiture in cases where:

1. It had been leased without the transaction having been carried out in the manorial court.
2. Where timber had been cut down on such property without permission from the lord of the manor; and

3. Where clay had been dug for brick-making without similar permission.

The notice, instead of causing the copyholders to hasten the process of enfranchising their property—as was intended—caused an outburst of rage. The angry copyholders held another public meeting at which they formed the Cheltenham Copyholders' Protection Association. A committee was appointed which included Sir William Russell, William Nash Skillicorne, Samuel Gael, and John Brend Winterbotham. Copyholders were advised in general to refrain from any attempt to enfranchise 'until some general rule can be laid down'. It was finally decided that a case must be taken under the compulsory clauses of the Act of 1852 to test the claims of the lord of the manor. The two lots of copyhold property which were selected for enfranchisement belonged to William Gyde who, although he was now an old man, was very well able to defend his rights. Described in the forthcoming case as a grocer, he had built Gyde's Terrace (now Grosvenor Street) at the beginning of the century; he had been appointed a Town Commissioner as early as 1806, and for many years he had been active in party politics as a Liberal.

In due course valuers were appointed for both sides and a meeting arranged between them before an umpire chosen by the Copyhold Commissioners. William Gyde then exercised his right[4] of putting forward a number of questions dealing with the claims of the lord of the manor which he asked to have referred to the decision of the Copyhold Commissioners. The result was as the copyholders wished it to be. An Assistant Commissioner was appointed to hold a full inquiry into the manorial claims in Cheltenham.

This dramatic inquiry opened at the end of 1863 in the Old Well Music Hall and lasted for four days. It ranged far back over the centuries, illustrating from Domesday Book and the court rolls of the manor the long continuity of the history of Cheltenham, and it was attended by most of the leading citizens.

The case for the copyholders was put by George Edmund Williams acting as honorary solicitor to the Copyholders' Protection Association, and for the lord of the manor by the barrister Mr. Sheldon, instructed by Messrs. Gwinnett & Ticehurst. Williams was now in his sixtieth year and was suffering severely from gout, but he still retained some of the fervour and persistence with which he had fought for the 1852 Act of Parliament. His main case rested on the 1625 Act which was passed, as he pointed out, to put an end to the disputes between the lord of the manor and his tenants by having the position of the latter exactly defined. For this Act the tenants had paid the Crown £1,200 and received in return a clear statement of the amount of their obligations to the lord. Since in this statement there was no mention of any restrictions on the cutting of timber or the digging of clay for bricks or of any forfeiture of actual property, he declared that the claims of the present lord could not be substantiated. He went centuries further back into history and produced in evidence the relevant extract from Domesday Book in which the Manor of Cheltenham was described as Terra Regis, and he therefore claimed it as ancient demesne in which the copyholders had certain freehold interests in the land which would entitle them to timber and clay.

He supported his case by calling a number of witnesses who gave evidence that the claims made by the present lord of the manor had not been put forward within living memory.

William Gyde was called first. He deposed:

I am the owner of considerable copyhold property in the Manor . . . and have had a good deal to do with the purchase and sale of such property, to the extent of many thousands of pounds. . . . I am now in my 85th year and have lived in Cheltenham nearly seventy years. I have had a great deal to do with the business of the town and I believe I am the oldest magistrate of the county. . . . Formerly I frequently attended Copyhold Courts, but I never heard of any forfeiture or claim of the Lord on account of clay, brick, earth or timber in respect of copyhold property. The copyholders have always exercised full power over the soil both above and below, without question or payment or any acknowledgment to the Lord of the Manor of any sort. The number of bricks made in Cheltenham would be immense, the houses being principally built of them. . . . Copyholds have always been considered equal to freeholds. . . . I have never heard of any forfeiture for any lease being granted out of Court, or of any forfeiture on any ground whatever . . . . I have made leases for 7, 14 and 21 years . . . and I have constantly been a party to leases without going to Court.

Gyde's evidence was followed by that of William Nash Skillicorne:

> I am a magistrate of the County of Gloucester and Chairman of the County Bench here. My family is one of the oldest in Cheltenham, dating back 158 years . . . and has owned a good deal of copyhold property. The whole of the Bayshill Estate belonged to my great-grandfather, Henry Skillicorne. . . . I sold the Bayshill Estate for £50,000. . . . Just before I sold it I cut down £200 of timber on it. . . . I have other copyhold property, on which I have also cut down timber. . . . I purchased seven acres of this property from Miss Monson's trustees . . . from which a large quantity of bricks were made which were used to build a property here, known as St. Margaret's Terrace. I never heard that the Lord of the Manor had any claim or account of brick, earth or timber—or any claim at all beyond the rents, fine and heriot, as set forth in the surrender. . . .

Charles Cook Higgs, descended from an old Charlton Kings family, was called next. He, too, owned considerable copyhold property. 'There is a good deal of brick earth on it', he said. '. . . I have let portions for brick-making for the last twenty years and I never heard of any claim of the Lord of the Manor in respect to brick earth. . . .'

Samuel Gael, the owner of copyhold property known as Ryeworth and Battledown Knoll, gave evidence that he had cut down much timber but could remember no protests from Lord Sherborne's agent except when a roadside tree was lopped and when a copyholder took stone from Charlton Common.

Further support came from the evidence of Samuel Onley, who had bought much of the Bayshill property, including the Royal Old Wells, from the Bayshill Company.

> I have dug, during the last fifteen years, enough brick earth to make a million bricks. . . . I never thought of any claim from the Lord of the Manor. As a Surveyor and a Builder, I have known every Brickyard for the last 25 years; I never heard that the Lord of the Manor made any claim against them for violation of his rights. The late Lord resided here and must have seen me constantly doing it. I have cut down 150 timber trees. . . . I never heard of any claim in respect of timber. . . . I have made fifty leases of my property,

but I never went to Court about it. I have never had any property claimed as a forfeiture. . . .

With almost monotonous repetition, evidence as to recent custom was given, enlivened from time to time by phrases peculiar to the Gloucestershire countryside. 'I remember a smart bit of timber being cut down . . . twelve large oaks and as many elms . . . I never heard anything about forfeiture', said the brickmaker Joseph Collier.

There was considerable evidence that leases were by general custom drawn up without reference to the manorial court. The most important witness to this effect was Edmund Newman. He had been steward of the manor for the fifteen years preceding the death of James Agg-Gardner, and a practising solicitor in partnership with Messrs. Gwinnett & Ticehurst, who then acted occasionally as deputy stewards. He went on to identify particulars of property of which sales and leases negotiated by this firm were arranged without being registered in court and in which the purchaser was required to pay for timber. In several instances the former lord of the manor had himself purchased timber from copyholders under these conditions, and the present lord had bought a house which was under a similar and unexpired lease. He emphasized that the descriptions of these properties were issued from the office of Messrs. Newman, Gwinnett & Ticehurst as 'copyhold equal to freehold . . . with heriots and fines normal and of fixed amount'.

Since Messrs. Gwinnett & Ticehurst refused to produce the actual contracts in evidence, Newman affirmed that he had himself attended certain of these sales and could say of his own knowledge that the particulars had in truth been issued from his office.

John Brend Winterbotham, now in the thirty-seventh year of his practice as solicitor in Cheltenham, produced nine forms of advertisement from his own office with the same description of copyhold property as being equal to freehold, where the timber concerned was to be taken by the purchaser at valuation. He too was the owner of considerable copyhold property and admitted that he had openly cut down timber and dug and burnt brick earth to form ballast for roads.

The case for William Gyde occupied a day and a half. On the afternoon of the second day, the case for the lord of the manor was opened by Mr. Sheldon. He appears to have been an old man, very learned in the general laws affecting copyhold and content to draw his arguments from these laws. He was therefore contemptuous of those whom he called 'mushroom lawyers' who had no knowledge of the main books available on the origin of copyhold. He wished to remind 'the unfortunate copyholders of Cheltenham that they were descendants of villeins and serfs and held their properties under the strict and literal terms of base tenure'. He thought that as the new lord had probably paid too much when he purchased the manor he was certainly entitled to the profits which derived from his legal rights. 'Nobody could blame him for seeking to obtain compensation.'

Both Mr. Sheldon and the stewards of the manor relied entirely on documentary evidence and called no witnesses. R. J. Ticehurst brought into the Inquiry the large box containing the court rolls and from these he produced twenty-five cases of leases (grants) recorded immediately before and after the 1625 Act, in order to prove that it was customary for the leases to be transacted in the manorial court. Mr. Sheldon then occupied the next two days with an address consisting largely of extracts which he read from the fifty-four law books in front of him. From time to time he apologized, with a passing gleam of humour, for the dullness of his theme. 'Really, Sir, I am afraid I shall send you to sleep.' The Commissioner protested that the cases quoted were irrelevant, and the reporters were relieved to give up the attempt to follow the theme.

His main argument appears to have been that the Cheltenham copyholders were not exempted by the 1625 Act from the general law of copyhold excepting in those matters specifically defined in the Act, and that this left a wide field where the lord of the manor had rightful claims. He cast no imputations on the character of the witnesses, but pointed out that they spoke under strong bias, and that although they all gave evidence that the claims under discussion had not been made within living memory, this did not prejudice the lord's right to revive them.

In contrast to this long-drawn-out 'somnolent wandering through the trackless ocean of Case Law', Williams in reply dealt specifically with the documentary evidence put in from the court rolls, claiming that, in contrast to these twenty-five leases, there were many thousands of leases which had not been registered in the court. Mr. Ticehurst interrupted to say that these twenty-five were put in merely as examples. Williams challenged him to produce any others and suggested an adjournment so that this could be done—a challenge which was not accepted. He drew a graphic picture of the stewards poring over the court rolls 'spelling over every one of them dating back for four hundred years', in the unsuccessful effort to find additional cases and even one case of forfeiture of property.

He was unable, however, to deny that by the Act of 1625 a fine had legally to be paid on every lease, but he claimed that as this was usually merely a matter of pennies the actual collection would cost five hundred per cent. more than the fine was worth, and that it was notorious that it was included in the lump sum demanded by the steward when the property came into court for surrender.

This latter argument apparently did not entirely convince Commissioner Wetherell. In his final decision he included the following main points:

I do determine and decide

1. That in this Manor [of Cheltenham] the Lord is not entitled to claim any consideration in respect of timber.
2. That in this Manor the Lord is not entitled to claim any consideration in respect of facilities for improvement.
3. That in this Manor the Lord is not entitled to enter for a forfeiture for any other kind of waste committed by a Tenant.
4. That in this Manor the Lord is entitled to enter for a forfeiture in respect of Leases of Tenements held of the Manor by copy of Court Roll, which may have been made and granted contrary to the provision of the Act of Parliament passed in the first year of the reign of His Majesty Charles the First [1625]. . . .

This decision was jubilantly communicated to the copyholders by Messrs. Williams & Brydges:

It is all fours in your favour, excepting the Lease point, for which we care but little—because the object of the lease can be effectually attained by another form of document . . . altogether the fact is that the Lord is entitled to nothing beyond the Rent, Heriot and Fine, as set forth in the surrender.

After this adverse decision, the manor was sold back to the Agg-Gardner family, in whose possession it still remains. The next blow to the ancient manorial claims was to be the compulsory sale to the Commissioners of the market tolls; and the election of a mayor following the incorporation of the borough was to render unnecessary many of the duties of the manorial High Bailiff who had formerly been regarded as the ceremonial head of the town.

Almost all that remained of the great powers of the medieval owners of the manor was the right to the collection of the somewhat valueless heriots and fines. Even these disappeared with the Act of 1925 by which the last restrictions on copyhold property were removed.

THE LAST PHASE OF THE
COMMISSIONERS' POWER, AND THE
BATTLE FOR INCORPORATION

THE thirty Commissioners appointed under the Act of 1852 were chosen almost entirely on party political lines so that one-half were Conservative and the other Liberal. The Conservatives included the lord of the manor—James Agg-Gardner, R. S. Lingwood, Henry Davies, editor of the *Chronicle*, Baynham Jones, William Ridler of the Cheltenham and Gloucester Bank, and among the Liberals were John Brend Winterbotham, James Fallon, and William Nash Skillicorne. Their work was necessarily concerned with 'homely matters like sewers and gutters, water and gas', but they were none the less initiating a new form of local government in Cheltenham. As a newly constituted body they had to work out methods of procedure, make their own standing orders, and decide on the number of officials required to carry out the necessary work, as well as on matters of policy.

As was to be expected, party political differences were apparent in the appointment of these officials. By a narrow majority James Agg-Gardner was elected chairman of the Board, largely because, as lord of the manor, he had been chairman of the committee which promoted the Act; the vice-chairman was the Liberal barrister James Fallon. The election of G. E. Williams was not so much a party decision, since he had been responsible for much of the legal work connected with the two recent Bills. A majority which included members of both parties chose him as clerk in preference to the strong Tory W. H. Gwinnett.[1]

The matter of most immediate urgency was the provision of an adequate sewerage system. This was made clear in a supplementary report drawn up in London on behalf of the

Central Board of Health by its own surveyor, following an application from the Cheltenham Commissioners to borrow the sum of £11,000 for additional sewers.

Although the town of Cheltenham is exceedingly well situated for drainage, and a considerable amount of work for this purpose has been executed . . . much of it appears to be defective. . . . The river Chelt running through the centre of the town from East to West, and receiving a large share of its drainage, is in an exceedingly bad state, and has long been a fruitful source of disease and injury. Along its course are three water mills, the dams of which, penning back the foul matters discharged, constitute so many huge open cesspools which in warm weather are intolerable and from which in times of flood the water and filth flow back into the houses, an evil which has occurred three times in six weeks (1853).[2]

The Commissioners had to decide whether to buy out the Sewers Company and add to their existing and inadequate system or to set to work on an entirely new plan. The Sewers Company at first refused to sell at the original and generous offer of £12,000 suggested in 1848, but finally in 1857 they were bought out for £9,000. In the meantime an additional sewerage system was successfully added, using Wyman's Brook and Hatherley Brook in the extended service. The demand for excessive compensation for the land taken by compulsory purchase from the lord of the manor illustrates the persistent conflict of private interest with public necessity. The proceedings were also obstructed by an attempted refusal of the Fellows of Jesus College, Oxford, to allow the Commissioners' surveyors to proceed with their work on the main Cheltenham sewer[3] 'without a previous payment by the Commissioners of the amount of compensation to be paid to the College for so doing . . .'.

The other important contemporary problem was the water-supply, upon which the success of the new sewerage system largely depended. In this case the Commissioners failed to realize the urgency of the situation, and the policy of dallying was later to prove an expensive matter for the town.

The shortage of water was immediately evident. The newly appointed Scavenger had contracted to water the High Street three times a day, and the other streets twice a day excepting on Sundays, but a number of streets in the poorer areas were to be omitted, including Sherborne Street and Grove Street which were 'in the very midst of the fever area', as John Bubb reminded the Board. 'The Cholera might again visit this county and Cheltenham might not again escape. . . . It was indispensable that the poorer portion of the town should be looked after even more than the richer.' Because of the many protests made by the general public, the number of streets to be watered daily was increased, but there were then complaints that none were satisfactorily cleansed owing to a shortage of water. For some years to come there were constant complaints of the dusty streets and fears that visitors would be prejudiced against the town. The wells constructed by the former Commissioners for cleansing the streets were running dry, and the Water Company, high as were its charges, was unable to supply the deficiency if it maintained a full supply for household purposes. There was also the danger of inadequate supplies in case of fire. A correspondent writes in the *Examiner*:

The Town Scavenger was 'had up' a few days ago and mulcted in a fine of 10/- for 'lâches' committed in his department, but who, Sir, who is to 'have up' the Water Monopolists for their shortcomings? At the fire which broke out at the Full Moon there was no water to be obtained at any of the fire plugs for upwards of half an hour. The engines were there, the firemen were there, the neighbours were there, but the water was not there. . . . (1 June 1853.)

The next year the Commissioners gave notice to the Water Company that for the purpose of maintaining the conditions laid down by the Public Health Act they required an additional supply of 400,000 gallons of water a day, and asked whether the company could supply it.

Following an unsatisfactory reply from the Water Company, the Commissioners called in an engineer and instructed him to draw up plans for obtaining an adequate water-supply from local sources, so that a Bill might be introduced to give parliamentary sanction to the scheme. The engineer produced the necessary plan, but twenty-three years were to elapse before the Commissioners acquired their own water-works, and then it was by purchase and not construction.

During this interval the Commissioners followed a policy of almost incredible inefficiency and delay. The Water Company, shaken by the possibility of the Commissioners providing an alternative supply, offered to sell their works at a price to be fixed by arbitration. Unfortunately, the Commissioners then decided that it would be cheaper to provide their own supply, but they also agreed that it was expedient to defer application to Parliament until the following year. The Water Company made a final offer (1863) to sell at £100,000, and as this was not accepted the directors applied to Parliament for their own Bill by which they might develop further supplies near Boxwell Springs (South Cerney); and though the Commissioners were now willing to buy them out, it was too late. This Bill, however, was thrown out before it reached the Committee stage, largely because of the opposition of certain London water companies which drew their water from the Thames, and feared that their supplies would be affected if the Cheltenham Water Company took water from its head springs.

A newly constructed Cheltenham and Gloucester Water Company then introduced another Bill to enable them to draw water from the Severn. There followed an outbreak of rage in the town at the idea of Cheltenham being forced to drink from 'the filthy Severn', polluted, as it was believed, by sewage and industrial waste from the city of Worcester. At a public meeting a resolution to petition Parliament against the passing of the Bill was passed with acclamation. The Commissioners spent over £3,000 in opposing the Bill, but the Water Company triumphed and proceeded with their scheme.

Unfortunately, although the new sources then available were adequate for all purposes, the prices charged by the company were too high for the poorer people to pay. By the end of 1868 the Water Committee reported back to the Board of Commissioners that 'they considered, in the present state of the Law, it was hopeless to get the Company to supply water for the poorer areas'. They next dallied with a scheme worked out by their own surveyor 'for watering the streets and getting a supply to the poor parts of the town', but decided against it in favour, once more, of asking for a parliamentary Bill 'to enable them to provide their own complete supply'. They were influenced in this by a statement in the recently issued report of a Royal Commission (1868) 'that the placing of the water-supply under public control affords the best and only feasible means of ensuring a proper and compulsory supply to the Poor'. Despite the statement, nothing was done. The Commissioners continued to pay a high price for the water required for the sewers, and the poorer inhabitants remained without the water which they could not afford.

It was not until 1877, when Cheltenham had received its Charter of Incorporation, that the Water Company was bought out at a price of £220,000; in addition the town also paid the expenses of the Act of Parliament required to enforce compulsory purchase. The Water Company during these years had acted with energy and determination in its own interests; the Commissioners, on the other hand, were dilatory and indecisive. It is not possible, however, to assess how far their attitude was affected behind the scenes by the fact that some of their members had interests in the companies concerned.

A similar position had arisen with regard to the supply of gas. In 1866, following complaints about its quality and cost, the Gas Committee recommended 'that the Commissioners should consider taking the supply of gas for the public lamps under their own management'. They then obtained an estimate of the cost of the erection of their own gas-works and decided that 'it appears that a great saving would accrue to the rate-payers by the enjoyment of the public works . . . forthwith'. After months of bickering over prices and inefficient lamps, they obtained the services of an engineer and paid him £40 for his plans for new gas-works, but decided (1867) that a final attempt should be made to reach an agreement with the Gas Company. The contract was renewed for one year, 'after which they [the Commissioners] will proceed immediately to erect gas-works of their own and make gas'. During this year there were continued complaints of the service provided. The Commissioners' inspector reported that in one month 116 lamps were extinguished by deposits in the gas and that in 93 other lamps the power had fallen. The contract was, however, renewed for a further year, although the Committee concerned had reported that 'it was absolutely necessary that the Board should take some active measures to improve the supply of gas to the town, either by encouraging the formation of a new Gas Company, or by implementing their resolution to proceed *immediately* to erect their own gas-works'.

The position remained unsatisfactory. The inspector reported in 1871 that 273 lamps had been notified as being without light in the preceding month, and that the quality and price compared unfavourably with that in other towns like Brighton and Canterbury. In 1872 the Gas Company obtained an Act to raise more capital to extend the area of its operations and refused to consider any qualifications suggested by the Board of Commissioners or the newly founded group of Gas Consumers. The company then raised prices, claiming that the town had been paying an inadequate amount during recent years for its gas. The only advantage to the public was that the company agreed to maintain its lamps at a candle-power more in accordance with general usage in the more progressive towns. Even this did not entirely ease the situation since the Commissioners felt it necessary to cut down the amount of time during which the lamps were to be lighted, in order to keep down costs. In the year before the Incorporation of the Borough there were constant complaints of the darkness of the streets and the Commissioners were still discussing the possibility of providing a separate gas-supply for public lighting although they were debarred by the Gas Company's monopoly from selling it to private consumers.

Apart from these three main services, the Board of Commissioners were enabled under the Public Libraries Act of 1855 to provide the additional service of a free library and a museum if two-thirds of the ratepayers wished for it. They therefore called a public meeting (1855) with Frederick Munroe, their own chairman, presiding.[4] The subsequent speeches illustrate the widespread prejudice against spending public money, particularly for furthering the education of the poorer classes for whose benefit most people thought that the Act would provide. This, however, was not the view of the Reverend C. H. Bromby, the Principal of the Training College, who was surprisingly outspoken on the deficiencies of education and of the unhappy state of many working men. 'Why', he asked, 'has primary and elementary education failed in this town . . .? Because the Labour Market comes in and interferes with their work just when the children are beginning to leave, although in other countries, even those under despotic governments, the children remain at school until they are 14.' He thought that if England was to retain her commercial supremacy she must educate her operative classes, and that this Act —passed as it was for the further education of working men —ought to be implemented in Cheltenham.

He was supported by William Dobson, the Principal of Cheltenham College, who attacked those who were afraid of educating the working classes, and by Canon Boyd of Christ Church. The latter, as one who worked with his brains and his pen, counted himself one of these classes and was ashamed to admit to visitors that Cheltenham did not possess a public library. He was not supported, however, by his churchwarden, R. S. Lingwood, who held strongly that it was dangerous to educate the public unless there was sufficient control over the books provided. If a free library were to be provided he prophesied: 'There is not a man in this town who will not be sorry he has done it.'

Another member of the Christ Church congregation, H. Davies—proprietor of the *Looker-On*—feared that a library might be opened on Sunday, and could see no reason why public money should be spent on providing books for the poor. 'The Almighty (in his earliest laws) expressed the need for providing bodily sustenance for the poor—but there was no positive Commandment for supplying their mental wants.'

The primary argument expressed against the proposal was that it would cause an increase in the rates, and this at a time when taxation was likely to rise because of the Crimean War. The feeling against what was considered waste of public money was so strong that the meeting broke up in confusion and uproar. The chairman was unable to count votes, or even to decide which among the audience were ratepayers; but it was clear to him that the required two-thirds of the latter were not in favour. Another meeting was held in the following year with a similar result. The matter was then dropped and it was

not until 1888 that Cheltenham fell into line with more enlightened boroughs and built the Public Library.

In 1860 the Commissioners were also unsuccessful in their
attempt to provide a building which could be used as a Town
Hall and as a centre for transacting their own business. At this
time they could have bought for £2,500 the Institute, originally built for the Literary and Philosophical Society on the
eastern side of the Promenade, but there was an outcry against
'the reckless squandering of public money'.⁵ William Ward
reminded his fellow Commissioners that 'time was when the
business of the Commissioners was held in the back room of
a public house [the "Fleece"], and he saw no reason for any
change'. There was a counter-proposal to build a new Town
Hall and finally the whole project was dropped. As a result
the Institute, a noble Regency building in the Promenade, was
pulled down and shops put in its place.

Among their achievements during these years the Commissioners could claim the opening of the Bath Road directly
into the High Street; the provision of the large new cemetery
at Oakley; and the acquisition of the tolls from the markets
with the transfer of the market itself to a new site away from
the centre of the town.

In this last matter the Commissioners acted with firmness.
Although they had been looking for a suitable site for a new
market as early as 1852, they had hesitated, as their clerk
explained, to purchase land for this when the tolls concerned
were claimed by a lord of the manor who was unwilling to
negotiate for their sale. However, after the death of James
Agg-Gardner in 1858, parts of the manor were sold to Robert
Sole Lingwood—of the firm of Messrs. Bubb & Lingwood,
solicitors. He offered to resell the Market-house and the tolls,
and on the failure of the Commissioners to purchase at the
required price, he sold them to another solicitor, R. C. Chesshyre. The latter pulled down the Market Arcade and opened a
cattle market in the thoroughfare known as Bennington Street,
with cattle pens and an open part for the trotting of horses.

By 1873, however, the Commissioners were determined to
buy out Chesshyre and put an end to 'the objectionable position
in Bennington Street'. After a public meeting on the matter

had been held they asked for a Government Inquiry which would be necessary if they applied for permission to borrow money for the purchase.[6] An Inspector was sent from London to inquire into the conditions and the purpose of the purchase, and as his report was favourable, the Commissioners proceeded to buy the tolls for the town and to lay out a new market in the lower end of the High Street near the site of the old Albion Brewery. On this site, and this site alone, all future fairs, markets and hirings were to be held. In this way a picturesque element was removed from the town in the interests of public health and convenience, and at the same time another stage in the decline of manorial jurisdiction was reached.

The purchase of the market tolls was to be the last important achievement of the Board of Commissioners. They were under the constant fire of criticism, as summed up in a leader in the *Examiner*:

The way in which the very moderate Agenda placed before our Governing Body on Monday last was dealt with was not such as to increase our respect for the capacity of the Board or to rekindle any very ardent desire for their reign over us. A lighter programme could not have been desired, and yet for five dreary hours twenty business men were content to discuss only a part of it and to leave the only matter of public interest for a future meeting. A revision of street lighting ought not to have been delayed a day. The present arrangement, which leaves the High Street in a state of darkness for nearly two hours each night is a scandal to the Town and produces a state of inconvenience which the Commissioners appear to be the last to realise. (*Examiner*, 7 July 1875.)

Criticism of this kind was used as an argument for the abolition of the Board of Commissioners and its replacement by a Mayor and Corporation with full powers, but before this could take place a fierce battle had to be fought.

During the middle decades of the nineteenth century many towns with rapidly increasing populations were beginning to outgrow the restricted forms of local government permitted to them by private Acts of Parliament and were seeking the greater independence conferred by incorporation. In Cheltenham the demand for the change was put forward by men of widely different opinions. There were three main reasons for this: discontent arising from the inefficiency of recent administration; a feeling of growing civic pride which demanded a greater dignity and style than the Board of Commissioners could give to the town; and an urgent need to put an end to the corruption which prevailed during elections of members of the Board.

It should be remembered that under the 1852 Act, a system of plural voting was in force, allowing a maximum of twelve votes to any individual voter according to the amount of rates paid. Owners as well as occupiers, even if the former were not resident, were allowed to vote. As many of these did not live in the town and as no conclusive register of voters was kept, impersonation was comparatively easy. In each ward there was only one returning officer and one polling booth, which was usually surrounded by a noisy crowd often inflamed with beer supplied by candidates; and since no provision for the application of the Corrupt Practices Act had been made in the 1852 Act there was little hope of removing electoral bribery and corruption unless the Act was superseded.

The demand was by no means a matter of party politics. It was first publicly suggested at a Liberal party meeting (1872) when H. B. Samuelson, who then represented the town in Parliament, stated that 'Incorporation would do away with much of the corruption which appears to run through the whole municipality'. He was supported by William Nash Skillicorne, who asked, 'Why not Cheltenham, when Tewkesbury, Gloucester and Worcester—all smaller towns—have the dignity of a Mayor and Corporation?'[7]

In the general election which followed two years later, Samuelson was defeated by the Conservative James Tynte Agg-Gardner. The new member, anticipating, as he said, a lull in party politics, took the opportunity to send a letter to the chairman of the Board of Commissioners in the hope of initiating public discussion. 'One change I should like to see effected,' he wrote, 'the substitution of a Mayor and Corporation for the Board of Commissioners. I am inclined to think this change would be beneficial to Cheltenham (1) by giving it a civic head, (2) by bringing it into close relation with other corporate towns, and (3) by the superior system of electing the Municipal Parliament which would then be introduced.'[8]

At a Board meeting held to discuss Agg-Gardner's proposal, twenty Commissioners were in favour and five abstained from voting. The usual procedure then followed. A public meeting was held early in 1875 at which a resolution was passed that a petition for a Charter should be presented to the Queen, and an amendment calling for delay put forward by W. H. Gwinnett and James Winterbotham was defeated.

These two opponents of the scheme were strongly supported by the Baron de Ferrières, a wealthy resident living in the house built on the site of the recently pulled-down property once occupied by King George III. He was destined to be one of Cheltenham's most public-spirited mayors and to represent the newly incorporated borough as its Liberal Member of Parliament. In this opposition he was joined by William Nash Skillicorne, who had changed his point of view as a result of his fear that additional expenditure of public money would be involved and the rates would have to be substantially raised.

After the petition (signed by 4,530 householders) had been forwarded by the promoters of the scheme, the opponents collected 1,020 signatures for a counter-petition against incorporation claiming 'That the town having prospered under the present system, no change is required—That owners of property have a vested interest in the maintenance of the present system of voting—That by the change proposed local rates and expenditure will be increased'.

As a result of this counter-petition, a Government Inquiry became necessary.[9] This was held in the Commissioners' Board Room, in which for four days the promoters and opponents of the scheme faced each other and gave their evidence before the Commissioner appointed by the Privy Council.

The evidence showed the marked change which had taken place in the composition of the governing body. The earlier Commissioners had been criticized because so many of them had been retired high-ranking military and naval officers, whereas now the foremost criticism was directed against the numerical superiority of tradesmen, who were almost the only men prepared to face the existing conditions of rowdy and corrupt elections. The evidence also revealed the special problems of Cheltenham, still largely a residential town for retired well-to-do people who feared that their exclusive society might be invaded by the dignitaries of the new municipal body.

The clerk of the Board of Commissioners, E. T. Brydges, opened the Inquiry with an account of the long history of the town and its progress until the time had come, as he thought, for its incorporation. He was followed by George Parsonage, speaking as chairman of the Board of Commissioners and as High Bailiff of the manor. 'I consider the want of a Head to take the lead in matters connected with the town as most serious. . . . As High Bailiff I call meetings and preside over them, but I am elected not by the inhabitants of the town, but by the Lord of the Manor and the Court Leet which represents only copyholders, who are a limited section of the inhabitants and getting smaller every year.' He emphasized that Cheltenham could not be invited to take part at national functions such as the recent Thanksgiving Service in Westminster Abbey for the recovery of the Prince of Wales, because it had no Mayor to represent it. He claimed that many important societies would hold their conferences in Cheltenham if there was a civic head to receive them. He was also concerned that the present Board was in no way representative. 'I do not consider that the gentry have taken much interest in the local government. . . . There are a great many people of ability in the town, whom it is desirable to have on the governing body, but I do not think we shall get them on the present Board. If we had a Corporation I think we should get them. At Bath there are nine gentlemen on the Council and an Admiral is the Mayor. . . .'

Most of the opponents of the scheme, including J. B. Winter-botham and Gwinnett, denied that electoral corruption existed on any large scale. Others, as the Baron de Ferrières, refused to believe that it could be lessened by having a Mayor and Cor-poration. James Winterbotham took a very strong exception to the injury which would be done to property owners who, under the electoral system in force for incorporated boroughs, would be able to claim only one vote instead of a possible twelve under the existing system. Gwinnett objected to the abolition of an ancient and picturesque office of High Bailiff which he considered carried sufficient authority to sustain the dignity of the town. He also envisaged, in agreement with William Nash Skillicorne, that a Bench of Magistrates for the borough would be a necessary consequence of the incorporation and as some of these magistrates were likely to be the tradesmen elected for the new corporation, he did not think the new Bench would be suited to the character of the town. He was satisfied that the old Board, which consisted of twenty-five tradesmen and five professional men, had been successful in carrying out the duties assigned to it, but he did not wish the same type of candidates to be elected to the greater dignity and powers of a borough council.

The Baron de Ferrières, cross-examined by Winterbotham, replied to the latter's question, 'What is the feeling of the Upper Classes in Cheltenham with regard to Incorporation and what do you think its effects will be on the Town?'—

I consider that Cheltenham Society is peculiar. . . . We have no 'great guns' amongst us. We meet very much on equality and I think that to introduce into it a certain number of people who could claim official precedence, including their wives and daughters, would be to throw an apple of discord into it and would be injurious to the town. It must be borne in mind that we have no Merchants, no Manufacture, only Trade. It might be said that the Mayor and Aldermen would not wish to intrude into the Balls, but I think they would stand up for their rights.

You think the ladies would look upon it with apprehension? I think they would.

Apparently the recently formed New Club took the same view. The chairman, Colonel Stevenson, said that its members represented the greater part of fashionable residents in the town and that they were decidedly opposed to the idea of incorporation. He thought, too, that many ladies were against it. 'There are a great many unprotected ladies who come here to reside, and can walk about and enjoy themselves with the greatest freedom without coming into contact with anything disagreeable under the existing system.'

'Will these unprotected ladies be prevented from walking in the streets if there is a Mayor and Corporation?' he was asked. 'I cannot say', he replied. 'But at present Cheltenham is one of the most peaceful places and I should be sorry to see the present arrangement disturbed. . . . If the whole of the gentry were polled there would be a strong majority against it.'

This point of view is reflected strongly in the *Looker-On*, a paper which still chronicled Arrivals and Departures, Balls, and other events of the social scene.

The final decision of the Government Commissioners, after the four days' hearing of evidence, was to recommend that the petition for the charter should be granted. Instead of accepting this decision, however, the opponents took a somewhat unusual step in a matter of this kind by appealing to the Privy Council. Their case[10] was heard in London six months later when Sir Henry James, instructed by E. T. Brydges, acted as counsel for the promoters, and Henry Thesiger, instructed by James Winterbotham, for the opponents. George Parsonage, James Fallon, W. H. Gwinnett, and the Baron de Ferrières were present during the proceedings.

Most of the evidence and comment had already been given before the earlier inquiry. Thesiger made a strong point of the injustice which he thought would arise from the loss of votes by property owners, and pointed out that plural voting was still permitted in many local government bodies. He showed that although the proportion of petitioners for incorporation was numerically $4\frac{1}{2}$ to 1, with regard to property holders it was only $1\frac{1}{2}$ to 1. 'No doubt the feelings of the majority are entitled to have some weight, but where you find the majority is attempting to take away a considerable number of rights possessed by the minority, there ought to be some stronger argument than the mere wish of the majority.' He also emphasized where the real opposition lay.

Among the gentry there is an absolute majority against it. The town is socially and in other respects closely connected with the neighbouring County, possessing on the one hand a position and reputation of a peculiar and distinctive kind; it stands in no need of the status which it is supposed will be conferred upon it by the grant of a municipal Charter, but which would in fact be inconsistent with and in derogation of its existing status. . . . To impose this Municipal Corporation would materially, and to the great injury of the town, interfere with existing social arrangements and would tend to introduce disputes from which the town is at present free. It would in no respect increase its status and would give opportunities for increased expense without any corresponding advantages.

Counsel for the promoters stated that of the 231 existing corporate boroughs in the country, only 29 had a population greater than Cheltenham's 43,000. He denied any injustice to property owners, pointing out that the system of plural voting, which they wished to retain, had been abolished in all the recently incorporated boroughs. He thought the opposition from the gentry 'came with a very bad grace from those who confessedly and avowedly held aloof hitherto from the management of the town, and now came here somewhat selfishly to protect the vested rights of their property by voting against persons who do take a material interest in the town'. Finally he considered that there was conclusive evidence of scandalous and disorderly elections and of the evils of bribery, treating, and personation.

By a decision of the Privy Council this appeal was lost, with the result that in April 1876 Cheltenham became an incorporated borough by virtue of the charter granted by Queen Victoria: 'We do . . . hereby grant and declare that the Inhabitants of the said town of Cheltenham . . . and their successors, shall be for ever hereafter one body politic and corporate in deed, fact and name, and that the said body corporate shall be called the Mayor, Aldermen and Burgesses of the Borough of Cheltenham.' The coat of arms was granted in 1887.

In this coat of arms the long history of the borough is only partly illustrated. The cross is that of Edward the Confessor—the first known owner of the manor; the fountain symbolizes the healing waters of the Spa, and the tree and branches commemorate the tree-lined avenues which were features of the Regency town; the books stand for its famous schools and colleges. The market—for centuries a main source of livelihood—received no recognition.

After the grant of the Royal Charter the last traces of the medieval jurisdiction of the manor vanished with the extinction of the office of High Bailiff, and the 'ancient Burrough abounding in Sundry Priviledges' was merged in the newly incorporated municipality. With its increasing population and the recognition of its importance as an educational centre, incorporation was inevitable. The inevitability was finally accepted by most of those who had strongly opposed the change, and it is significant that two of these—William Nash Skillicorne and the Baron de Ferrières—became the first Mayors of the new Borough of Cheltenham.

Description of the Arms of the Borough of Cheltenham

The Arms following, that is to say a Chevron engrailed Gules between two Pigeons in Chief and an Oak Tree eradicated in Base proper, on a Chief Azure a Cross flory Argent between two open Books also proper, binding and clasps of the first, and for the Crest on a Wreath of the Colours upon a Mount between two branches of Oak a Fountain thereon a Pigeon all proper.[11]

POSTSCRIPT

HAVING traced the history of the ancient borough of Cheltenham as far as its incorporation in 1876, it only remains to indicate the more important developments of the following years.

Excitement ran high over the election of the first Mayor. Crowds assembled on the streets and angry scenes developed between the supporters of the two political parties. According to a contemporary writer,[1] special services were held in some of the churches and chapels in an attempt to counteract the prevailing mood of unrest.

The Liberals had won the first municipal election by a large majority and had celebrated their victory with a torchlight procession headed by their own yellow band playing 'Old Dan Tucker'. Their candidate for Mayor was William Nash Skillicorne, although he had earlier opposed the scheme for incorporation and had been defeated as a candidate in the recent election. The Conservatives wanted George Parsonage, the former High Bailiff who had taken a leading part in obtaining the Charter of Incorporation. A public meeting held in support of Skillicorne was nearly broken up by a gang of hooligans, and the Conservative agent had to be ejected by the police.[2] The excitement in the town died down, however, after the Council with its Liberal majority appointed the first six aldermen, and chose Skillicorne as one of them to be the first Mayor. As the great-grandson of the founder of the first Spa and of the eighteenth-century prosperity of the town, he was a fitting choice.

He was succeeded the next year by de Ferrières and in the following year by Alderman Wilmot. He then served as Mayor for three consecutive years. It was not until 1882 that George Parsonage came to office, when he retained the mayoralty for the succeeding five years.

During this period every effort was made to enhance the dignity of the new municipality and particularly by the second Mayor, Alderman the Baron de Ferrières.

Charles Conrad Adolphus de Ferrières was the grandson of the Napoleonic General du Bois who commanded the French brigade in Holland. He was naturalized as an Englishman by special Act of Parliament and in 1860 came to Cheltenham, where he spent the remaining forty-eight years of his life in the new Bayshill House built on the site of King George III's former residence. During these years he devoted much of his wealth and his time to the service of the town of his adoption. He was elected as Liberal Member of Parliament in 1880, but refused to stand for a second election. By no means a strong party man, he was genuinely concerned with the need for social reform. The fact that he included support for the repeal of the Contagious Diseases Act in his election programme of 1880, and that in the same year he took the chair for Miss Becker at the first meeting in support of the Women's Suffrage movement held in the town, shows that in his sympathies he was somewhat in advance of his time. It was his pleasure to uphold the dignity of the new borough and to strengthen it with munificent gifts—the massive silver gilt cup still used for municipal functions, and the valuable collection of Dutch pictures for an Art Gallery for the town. His banquets caused even the *Looker-On*, soured as it was by the Liberal victory, to become almost lyrical. At the inaugural banquet 'the Rotunda was specially carpeted and decorated with exotic plants and pennants of the nations, and the tables were laid with a profusion of flowers and glittering épergnes of fruits for a banquet fit for an epicure'. The guests included the Mayors of Gloucester, Bath, Worcester, and Tewkesbury, and a number of friends of de Ferrières from the county, together with the Parliamentary member (James Tynte Agg-Gardner), the Principal of the College, and not only the Bishop of Gloucester and Canon Fenn of Christ Church, but Dr. Morton Brown of the Congregational Church. The latter was the leading Nonconformist minister in the town and a very strong Liberal; the toast to 'the Bishop of Gloucester and the Clergy' also included 'and all the Denominations'.

Another of the banquets of de Ferrières'—this time held at the 'Plough'—marked the opening of the first of the festivals which in recent years have become part of the Cheltenham scene. It was given in honour of W. G. Grace and his Eleven during the first Cricket Week to be held in the town (1877). This was followed shortly afterwards by the Social Science Conference which was the first of the many important conferences for which Cheltenham was to be a congenial meeting-place. With de Ferrières as Mayor, it became a brilliant social occasion as well as a conference, and in this way he inaugurated what became almost a new industry for Cheltenham.

During the four decades after the granting of the Charter a programme of municipal enterprise was carried out which has never since been equalled. The first measure was the purchase of the private Water Company which, while paying dividends of 8½ per cent., was supplying water at a price which the poorer inhabitants could not afford. The Commissioners had most foolishly refused the earlier offer of the Water Company and it was left to the new Borough Council—following the customary procedure of a public meeting giving its sanction to the promotion of a parliamentary Bill for compulsory purchase—to take the necessary steps. The Water Company, seeking permission to increase its sources of supply, had its own Bill before Parliament at this time. This Bill was, however, defeated and the Cheltenham Borough Council was able to take over the Water Company and its undertakings at a price of £220,000 —nearly twice the amount for which the Commissioners could have made the same purchase—in addition to the costs of the Act concerned. At the same time permission was given for the making of a new reservoir near Dowdeswell which could safeguard the supply for some years to come.

Shortly afterwards the Council purchased the old mills at Cambray and Alston with a view to lowering the level of the Chelt and preventing the floods which were then of frequent occurrence. At the same time it also obtained permission for the widening and improving of certain streets, among which were North Street, Manchester Place, Regent Street, and the Colonnade.

The next object of attention was the provision of a public library which had been bitterly opposed on two occasions since the Libraries Act was passed. In 1878 the Council arranged for a meeting at which public opinion could again be tested. The majority shown at the meeting in favour of the library was so small that a poll was held in the town (1878) and the decision was reversed. A small group of people, led by Canon Fenn of Christ Church and encouraged by de Ferrières, continued their campaign until they won their case for the library by a narrow majority in 1883. The Council then imposed a ½d. rate and used it to provide in 1884 small premises in Liverpool Place in the High Street. As part of the Jubilee celebrations they were determined to provide the town with a larger and more distinguished building. The rate was raised to 1d. and voluntary subscriptions were called for. The new library in Clarence Street was at last built at a cost of £16,000 and was used also for the temporary accommodation of the School of Art and Science. The foundation-stone was laid to the singing of a most appropriate hymn, 'Now thank we all our God', and the occasion of its opening by Sir Michael Hicks Beach was felt to be of great importance. The Mayor and Corporation led a carriage procession from the Queen's Hotel and were accompanied by the Cyclist Corps of the Volunteers, the Engineer Volunteers, and the Rifle Volunteers. The bells of the parish church rang merrily and the town was gay with flags in answer to the mayor's request 'that the townsmen will kindly decorate their houses on the day of opening'. It was indeed a famous victory.

The Art Gallery was ceremoniously opened in 1899 with a banquet given within its walls by de Ferrières, through whose initiative it was largely built. He contributed £1,000 towards the cost of the two galleries and presented forty pictures by early Dutch artists from his private collection to form a nucleus.[3] The Museum was not opened until 1907, although the Corporation had adopted the Museums Act eight years earlier.

Another progressive measure which followed the Jubilee Year was the lighting of the streets by electricity. Perhaps because the relations between the Commissioners and the privately owned Gas Company had for many years been far from happy, the new undertaking was entirely a municipal enterprise. At the same time an Improvement Act was obtained which gave the Borough Council increased power with regard to sanitary matters, hospitals, and the provision of public parks.

The surviving spas were at this time fighting a losing struggle for existence since few residents or visitors were willing to pay for admission. Pittville, heavily mortgaged, was administered by the Court of Chancery, and the proprietors of Montpellier failed even to keep in repair the ugly wooden railings which screened the gardens from public view. In 1888 Sir James Agg-Gardner, who was generous both in his private and his public charities, presented the town with a recreation ground in the Pittville area. Three years later the Borough Council proceeded to purchase the Pittville Spa and Gardens for £5,400, and shortly afterwards to enlarge the latter by adding a further 3½ acres of the grounds of Marle Hill House which included Robert Capper's Pond. The next purchase was the Montpellier Spa and its gardens, for which £7,400 was paid. By this enlightened policy the Council preserved the Spa buildings and saved their grounds from the speculative builder, thus maintaining a large part of the Regency heritage as a priceless and permanent possession of the town. They continued this policy with the purchase in 1895 of the Winter Gardens— a glass building erected some sixteen years earlier by a private company on the land facing Queen's Hotel. Since its demolition the site has recently been laid out as the Imperial Gardens which greatly enhance the beauty of the centre of the town. The Promenade fountain (supplied with water from the Chelt) had been erected in 1893 and the nearby long garden laid out with care, while the earlier widening of the Colonnade had already improved the vista from the High Street. The most important Regency buildings which the Borough Council failed to preserve were the Assembly Rooms on the corner of Rodney Road. Externally they were the least distinguished of the surviving buildings, but with their purchase and subsequent demolition by Lloyds Bank in 1900, the scene of many great occasions in the life of the Regency town vanished for ever. Shortly afterwards the Town Hall was built, and by a happy inspiration the central block of five large Regency houses in the Promenade was purchased for use as Municipal Offices in 1915.

Thus Cheltenham, which received its Charter of Incorporation so late in its long history, showed during these years a remarkably rapid development of municipal enterprise. In this a great part was played not only by Sir James Agg-Gardner and de Ferrières—who were the first to receive the freedom of the Borough—but by many other less wealthy though equally public-spirited citizens. Among these were James Alexander Hay, who built the Cottage Homes which adjoin Naunton Park, and W. H. Gwinnett (an old pupil of Pate's Grammar School), who gave money for scholarships for his old school and for many other causes.

The old families—the Marshalls, the Winterbothams, the Gwinnetts—members of which had served as Town Commissioners under the earlier Acts, continued to be represented in the new Borough Council. It was therefore fitting that the first woman to be chosen as Mayor (1921) should be Miss Clara Winterbotham—the great-granddaughter of William Winterbotham who left the town in 1775 and the daughter and granddaughter of earlier Commissioners. No other woman held this office until Alderman Miss F. L. Carter was appointed in 1961.

In the meantime the town was still largely residential in character, partly because of the attraction of its natural beauty, but even more because of its educational facilities.

The Cheltenham Ladies' College under Miss Beale was developing during these years into one of the foremost schools for girls in the country. The reputation of Cheltenham College may be gauged from a speech made there in 1883 by the Duke of Cambridge—then Commander-in-Chief. 'I have come a considerable distance to be present today because I know of no College or institution of this kind that has done so much for the general utility in the various professions of Her Majesty's services as Cheltenham College. . . . Nothing in my mind can be better than the manner in which the education of the College is at present conducted.'

A new public school was founded in 1886—four years after the death of Francis Close. At a small meeting presided over by Canon Bell it was 'resolved that the most fitting memorial would be a middle class school for the West of England which would provide a thoroughly useful education based on the scriptural and evangelical principles of the Church of England'. With the assistance of the Dean of Canterbury £10,000 was raised in subscriptions and used to endow the Dean Close Memorial School.

The Grammar School, as we have seen, moved into the new buildings in 1889. It was in the least happy position among the schools and its numbers fell drastically after the setting up of a separate school for Technology and Science (with funds provided by the 'Whisky money'). This was finally, however, incorporated in the old foundation. In 1904 the Governors responded to a long-expressed demand and took over Livorno Lodge for a girls' school, which in the following year became known as the Girl's Grammar School under Pate's Foundation.

Three men of very great distinction were almost contemporary as pupils at these three schools. From Cheltenham College came Dr. Edward Adrian Wilson, who owed much of his scientific knowledge to his boyhood observation of birds and animals near his home at the Crippetts. His father was medical secretary at the Delancey Hospital and he himself was for a short time Junior House Surgeon at Cheltenham General Hospital. In 1910 he accompanied Robert Falconer Scott on his expedition to the South Pole and died there with him two years later. Captain Scott's last, most moving letter to Wilson's wife is well known.[4]

Gustav Holst was a pupil of Pate's Grammar School where his father was music master. His earliest known composition —an operetta called *Lansdown Castle* in reference to the old toll-gate on the Gloucester Road—was performed at the Corn Exchange in the High Street and was followed by the *Cotswold Symphony* (1900). His major work—the *Planets*—was written much later and did not become famous until the end of the 1914–18 war.

James Elroy Flecker came to Cheltenham as a child when his father was appointed headmaster of Dean Close School. His poems recall his memories of the daisied lawns and the rose garden of the School House, the nearby elms, and the Leckhampton lanes. Although he was deeply attracted by the exotic imagery of the East, as shown in *Hassan*, he never lost his love for the quieter colours of his Gloucestershire home.

Cheltenham was at this time a town of sharp contrasts as were so many of its contemporaries. While the public schools flourished and the Corporation developed its programme of municipal enterprises, a large section of the community was by no means prosperous. There was little industry or manufacture in the town. This latter fact is confirmed in the verse spoken by Lily Langtry at the opening of the new Theatre in Regent Street in 1891:

Hail sylvan city, for thy vanished stage
With us returns at last—a golden age.
'Tis strange that Thespis hence so long should roam.
Where could he find a more congenial home
Than this fair valley sheltered from all ills
In the broad bosom of the eternal hills,
Where shrines of Faith and Learning greet the eye
Nor fog nor factory smoke pollute the eye?

The majority of the working classes still depended for their livelihood on the well-to-do residents, either directly through some form of domestic service or indirectly through employment connected with trade, shopkeeping, or building. Conditions for shop-workers were still hard. Evidence collected by the Commission on the Employment of Children (1865) had revealed many cases in Cheltenham of young girls working in the drapery and millinery trades for twelve hours a day over long periods of the year. In 1870 there had been a determined effort in which the Rector—the Reverend Edward Walker—Dr. Jex-Blake, then Principal of the College, and de Ferrières were actively concerned to shorten the hours of shop-workers. Progress was slow, but by 1890 it appears to have been generally accepted that the better shops closed at 5 p.m. on Wednesdays and at 7 p.m. on other days.

There was poverty and unemployment in many areas of the town. In 1878 the *Looker-On* published an appeal from the Vicar of St. Peter's who 'having 4,000 poor in his charge and but few to help him, seeks aid from all who can spare something . . . to support his winter relief work . . .'. Ten years later a General Committee formed for the relief of the town's unemployed distributed 18,000 quarts of soup in ten weeks and continued the work in the succeeding winters.

During these years most important and unselfish work was carried out by the Reverend James Owen—the senior assistant master at Cheltenham College—and his saintly wife Frances Owen.[5] They began a mission in Rutland Street, known at the time as 'the worst street in the town—neglected by the clergy and shunned by the police'. They opened first a coffee tavern with a view to reducing the prevalent drunkenness, and later on an industrial school for boys which for a short time was regarded as the Cheltenham College Mission. Miss Beale took a great interest in this work; after the untimely death of Frances Owen a window to her memory was placed in the Ladies' College. James Owen served the town in many ways—as a co-opted member of the Borough Education Committee, and in political work in support of the Liberal de Ferrières. The *Gloucestershire Echo* recorded his death in 1907:

> He was especially attracted to movements having as their object the social uplifting of the working classes. . . . The condition of the Lower High Street and the streets adjacent was early a source of concern to him, as it is to most newcomers to the town, who cannot fail to be struck by the sharp contrasts between wealth and poverty in our midst. . . . He started a successful Mission in Rutland Street where he effected results in a part of the town that had hitherto been deemed to be hopeless.

Perhaps the greatest indictment of the apathy towards the contemporary poverty and vice in Cheltenham came from that great pioneer of women's rights, Josephine Mary Butler, whose husband was for eight years the Vice-Principal at Cheltenham College. It was not, however, until they had moved to Liverpool that Mrs. Butler took up the great work of her life—the campaign against the Contagious Diseases Act for the compulsory registration of prostitutes. The repeal of this Act in 1886 was very largely due to her efforts. In 1902 Mrs. Butler, then a widow, returned for a short time to Cheltenham. In one of her letters she described the town as she saw it in that year.

> There are low class brothels too, well known to the police, and slums which would be a disgrace to London or New York; 12 or 13 of a family in one room, grown ups and children; girls of fifteen carrying their own babies in their arms like bundles of rags, and openly confessing themselves to be the mothers. . . . It is not all this

which grieves me so much as the ignorance of it in the Christians—
these correct Evangelical Protestants. They don't *want* to know of it;
and not a hand is moved or a voice raised except by one humble
minister of Lady Huntingdon's Chapel, and perhaps a poor woman
or two. . . . Oh, the Churches . . . in this correctly Evangelical
Cheltenham, they are all so *comfortable*—so properly Evangelical
that they catch you up if you pronounce a single word which is not
pure low Church shibboleth.[6]

Many changes have taken place since these harsh words
were written. Nearly all the slum areas have been cleared and
poverty is no longer a major cause of immorality in the town.
Many of the basements where the domestic servants sweated
have been converted into garden flats or garages or condemned
as unfit for habitation, and the race of domestic servants has
almost disappeared. Most of the noble mansions have also been
converted into flats or offices or hotels, or demolished, and their
spacious gardens sold for building development. New means
of livelihood have come into existence with the growth of industry during the last quarter of a century. The lateness of this
industrial development saved Cheltenham from the miseries
of the early factory system and from the ugly sprawl of building which so frequently accompanied it. In this connexion the
town owes a very great debt to Sir George Dowty by whose
genius and enterprise the firm of Dowty Equipment Ltd. with
its subsidiaries in many parts of the Commonwealth was built
up. For nearly thirty years he has not only provided employment for large numbers of men and women under what have
been generally admitted to be very good conditions, but he
has shown that industry can flourish without destroying the
beauty of an old town. The original and parent factory of his
organization is still located in the garden of Arle Court—at
least three miles from the town centre, and by strange chance
on the boundary of the medieval hundred of Cheltenham near
what was once the little manor of Redgrove. The present Arle
Court on the Gloucester Road was built by Thomas Packer
Butt in 1834, and when the original Elizabethan house in Arle
was demolished in 1880, much of its panelling and a fine oak
staircase were transferred to the new building. This was
acquired by the firm of Dowty Equipment Ltd. in 1935 and

is now the headquarters of the recently formed Dowty Group, with its far-reaching international interests. No history of Cheltenham would be complete without an acknowledgement of the pioneer work of Sir George Dowty in its industrial development.

At least one other Cheltenham firm, that of Messrs. H. H. Martyn & Co., has achieved a world-wide reputation. Incorporated in 1900 and reorganized in 1932 as part of the Maple Martyn Organization, it has become famous for skilled craftsmanship in wood and metalwork, in carving and sculpture, and in ferrous and non-ferrous foundry castings. Some of its work may be seen in the staircases of the liner *Canberra*; it has also been responsible for part of the interior work in the Guildhall; and for the Speaker's chair, the Despatch Boxes, and other interior work in the House of Commons.

Despite this industrial development the town has retained much of its appeal for visitors, although the waters of the Spa are no longer the main attraction. Many of the Americans who were stationed in the Western area in the last war have returned from time to time. The festivals of Modern Music and Literature, for which the Regency background and the brilliantly coloured gardens are such an admirable setting, have brought many distinguished men and women, both as guests and performers. The Cheltenham Races at Prestbury Park, the National Hunt Meeting, and the Cheltenham Gold Cup have an international fame which would have delighted Colonel Berkeley and the royal dukes of his time.

The Borough Council has so far been successful in maintaining the Regency character of the centre of the town, but it is faced with difficulty in its attempts to preserve the best of the Regency property at a time when the demand for new building sites is so urgent. Large and well-planned new housing estates have been developed, and the population has reached the figure which under favourable auspices could qualify it for the status of a County Borough.

The present Borough, which now includes the new estates of Hester's Way and St. Mark's together with parts of Leckhampton and Charlton Kings,[7] is very largely identical with the old medieval hundred of Cheltenham. It seems far removed from the little borough which has been the subject of this book. The ancient borough, however, remains as the nucleus of the present town. The old Mill Pond may still be seen on the banks of the Chelt, not far from the centre of the town. In the church-yard, which lies a few yards behind the busiest part of the High Street with its long lines of traffic, are the nameless graves of the earlier inhabitants, and in the church itself are the memorials of those who served its interests through the centuries. In recent times the stone heads of those old opponents the Baron de Ferrières and W. H. Gwinnett have been placed on the outer walls, and the lovely medieval tracery of windows in the chancel and other parts of the church have been filled with modern stained glass in memory of James Tynte Agg-Gardner, William Nash Skillicorne, and the Winterbotham family. The nineteenth-century memorials bear witness to those who fought for the Empire from Canada and the West Indies to Cawnpore. Mural tablets erected in the preceding century recall the memory of the Dutton family, the De la Beres, and of the early builders of the Spa—Henry Skillicorne and Thomas Hughes. In the seventeenth century the sad memorial of Dr. English to his wife marks the bitter religious differences of the Civil War. Moving back yet another century the Greville Brass in the chancel commemorates the great family of the Grevilles at old Arle Court, while the empty medieval tombs of the nameless canons of Cirencester Abbey remind us that for nearly four hundred years the great abbey owned and maintained, rebuilt and repaired the church—back to Norman times.

By great good fortune this church has through the centuries escaped the vandalism of Tudor reformers, of Cromwellian soldiers, and nineteenth-century clergy and patrons, and thus within its ancient walls—so near to the busy heart of the modern town—past and present still meet.

NOTES

CHAPTER I

1 1 For a summary of the authorities for local barrows, see Nicholas Thomas, *A Guide to Prehistoric England* (1960), pp. 114–24. Finds from Belas Knap, Cleeve Hill, and Leckhampton are in the Cheltenham Museum. The Birdlip Mirror is in the Gloucester Museum.

3 2 *TBGAS*, vol. lxviii, pp. 14–21.

3 3 A. H. Smith, *English Place-Name Elements* (1956), Part I, p. 88. The same author, in *Place-Names of Gloucestershire* (1964), p. 103, gives the alternative explanation of 'Celta's water-meadow'.

3 4 H. P. R. Finberg, *Early Charters of the West Midlands* (1961), p. 81.

3 5 Collingwood and Myres, *Roman Britain and the English Settlements* (1943), pp. 409–10; F. M. Stenton, *Anglo-Saxon England*, pp. 45–47.

4 6 Birch (editor), *Cartularium Saxonicum*, p. 309.

6 7 Quoted in Freeman's *Norman Conquest* from Chron. Petrib.

7 8 Quoted in C. S. Taylor's *Domesday Survey of Gloucestershire* (1889), p. 165.

7 9 V. H. Galbraith, *The Making of Domesday Book* (1955), p. 64.

8 10 *TBGAS*, F. B. Welch, vol. liv, p. 145. The separate Manor of Ashley, part of Charlton Kings, was carved out of the Manor of Cheltenham and given to Walter de Ashley by Milo of Gloucester in the reign of Stephen.

10 11 F. W. Maitland, *Domesday and Beyond*, pp. 39–40. See also Frank Barlow, *The Feudal Kingdom of England* (1955), p. 120.

11 12 R. Lennard, *Rural England, 1086–1135* (1959), p. 376; *VCH Gloucestershire*, Vol. II, p. 82.

11 13 St. Clair Baddeley's *History of Cirencester* (1924), p. 96, gives a transcript of this charter (1133), which is now considered suspect because it refers to Pope Innocent II as though he were dead, whereas his death did not occur until 1143. There seems, however, 'no reason to doubt the essential genuineness of Henry I's grant' (C. D. Ross). It was confirmed by Henry II and again by Edward III; and by Pope Celestine III, by Pope Innocent III, and by his legate Pandulf.

11 14 See Chapter VII for an account of the *True Survey of the Cheltenham Rectory*—1632 (GCL 6107).

CHAPTER II

13 1 *TBGAS*, vol. xii, p. 288.

13 2 Ibid., vol. liv, p. 57; vol. lvii, p. 54.

14 3 *Landboc sive Registrum Monasterii de Winchelcumba,* introduction by D. Royce, p. 17.

14 4 Ibid., p. 18.

14 5 *Rotuli Chartarum,* vol. i, *John,* pp. 53 and 61.

15 6 F. W. Maitland, *Pleas of the Crown* (1884).

16 7 'In accordance with the famous rule enforced by William the Conqueror, the hundred in which a foreigner was slain was fined if the slayer was not produced. In some way or other the doctrine became established that everyone was deemed a foreigner unless his Englishry was proved' (Maitland).

16 8 An example of a criminal refusing to plead. It is not clear what happened in this case, but later for such a refusal an accused man might be pressed to death. Cf. Chapter IX.

17 9 *Cal. Pat. Rolls,* 1225–32, pp. 63 and 325.

17 10 Cf. Chapter III.

18 11 *Cal. Charter Rolls,* vol. i, p. 218.

18 12 *Cal. Pat. Rolls,* 1232–47, p. 445; *Cal. Close Rolls,* 1242–7, p. 545.

19 13 *L'Abbaye Bénédictine de Fécamp* (1959), vol. i, p. 128, which includes an article by Marjorie Chibnall on Fécamp and England.

19 14 *Cal. Charter Rolls,* vol. i, pp. 321–2.

20 15 *Cal. Pat. Rolls,* 1247–58, p. 18.

21 16 For a most clear and vivid account, see Helen Cam, *The Hundred and the Hundred Rolls* (1930).

21 17 PRO, S.C. 5/Glouc. No. 7.

22 18 *Placita quo Warranto,* p. 257; for Cirencester, p. 244.

22 19 *Cal. Pat. Rolls,* 1364–7, p. 219.

22 20 *Cal. Pat. Rolls,* 1343–5, p. 553.

22 21 *Cal. Pat. Rolls,* 1381–5, p. 325.

23 22 E. F. Jacobs, *England in the Fifteenth Century* (1960), pp. 469, 484.

23 23 G. J. Aungier, *History of Syon Monastery* (1840), in which the text of the charters mentioned are printed from *Cal. Charter Rolls,* vol. v, p. 473, and vol. vi, pp. 91–94 and 206–7.

CHAPTER III

25 1 In this chapter where the phrase 'lord of the manor' is used, the manor includes the whole hundred of Cheltenham. The main sources are the Cheltenham Court Rolls (PRO, S.C. 2/175/25–27 and L.R. 3/21/2): the Ministers' Accounts (PRO, S.C. 6/851–3; 194–204; 1177–1210): the Rentals and Surveys (PRO, S.C. 11/216–227).

26 2 Helen Cam, *The Hundred and the Hundred Rolls,* chap. x.

28 3 In the early *Rentals and Surveys* the greater number of free tenants held a burgage in the borough and were probably the tradesmen and craftsmen of their period.

28 4 S.C. 2/175/25 m. 3 and m. 4.

29 5 *Gloucestershire Studies,* edited by H. P. R. Finberg, p. 67. He

quotes from J. F. Willard's *Taxation Boroughs and Parliamentary Boroughs* in *Historical Essays in Honour of James Tait.*

29   6 PRO, E 112/16/198.

30   7 S.C. 2/175/25 m. 6.

31   8 S.C. 2/175/25 m. 9.

31   9 S.C. 2/175/27 m. 7.

31   10 S.C. 2/175/25 m. 7.

32   11 S.C. 2/175/25 m. 5.

32   12 S.C 2/175/25 m. 9.

32   13 Ibid.

33   14 H. S. Bennett, *Life on the English Manor* (O.U.P.), p. 249, 'The Abbot of Burton told his serfs they owned nothing but their bellies'.

33   15 S.C. 2/175/25/3; 175/26/5.

33   16 GRO, D 855, M. 68. For further reference, PRO, *Cheltenham Rentals and Survey Rolls* (Rolls 216–27). It should be noted that 359 tenancies do not necessarily mean 359 tenants, since some of the holdings were owned by the same tenants.

36   17 S.C. 6/851/22; 851/24.

36   18 S.C. 2/175/26/7 and 7d.

36   19 *Calendar of Miscellaneous Inquisitions*, vol. i, p. 566.

36   20 S.C. 6/852/10.

37   21 Ibid.

38   22 S.C. 6/852/5; 851/24 m. 3.

38   23 S.C. 6/853/2.

38   24 S.C. 6/852/3 (for further details of Oakley Woods, 852/5, 8, 24, 25).

39   25 S.C. 6/852/8.

39   26 *Cal. Pat. Rolls*, 1381–5, p. 325.

39   27 S.C. 6/852/7; 10 and 11. The original spelling of this letter has been retained. In most other quotations it has been modernized for the convenience of the reader.

41   28 Details of administration are given in Eileen Power's *English Nunneries*, and G. J. Aungier's *History of Syon*, op. cit.

41   29 S.C. 6/853/10.

41   30 S.C. 6/852/25.

42   31 S.C. 6/853/9 and 10.

42   32 S.C. 6/851/22 and 23; 852/10; 852/25; 853/5.

43   33 S.C. 6/852/7.

43   34 S.C. 2/175/27. Collumstrete was the medieval name of the present Church Road in Leckhampton.

43   35 S.C. 2/175/27 m. 12.

44   36 S.C. 2/175/27 m. 6.

45   37 GRO, D 1224.

45   38 *TBGAS*, vol. xxxvi, p. 288. Article on Arle Court by Anne Mannooch Welch.

46   39 'Bailiff of the Liberty of Cheltenham has imprisoned John Good

PAGE

in the prison of Cheltenham because in the Consistory Court at Gloucester he was adjudged husband of Julia Stout and refused to agree. Later the Prior of Worcester writes ordering his liberation from prison since he is willing to make satisfaction to God and the Church and will marry the said Julia—security being given for the performance of his promise.' GCL, *Hockaday Extracts*, 147.

47   40 *VCH*, p. 82.

47   41 Cartulary of Cirencester Abbey, Gloucestershire, edited by C. D. Ross (1964).

47   42 *Valor Ecclesiasticus.*

48   43 GCL, *Hockaday Extracts*, 147. The wills of Walter French, Thomas Machyn, William Greville, and many others are included in these extracts from the records of the Consistory Court.

CHAPTER IV

50   1 G. J. Aungier, *History of Syon.*

50   2 Ibid.

51   3 *TBGAS*, vol. xlix. Baskerville. 'The dispossessed Religious of Gloucestershire,' p. 63.

51   4 John Sawyer, *Cheltenham Parish Church* (1903), pp. 120–121.

52   5 GCL, Ref. 6106. Copy of *Grant of Ch. Rectory* (1612).

52   6 *Hockaday Extracts*, 147.

53   7 *TBGAS*, vol. 8, p. 229.

54   8 *VCH*, p. 24.

54   9 *TBGAS*, vol. lvi, p. 329; vol. xlvi, p. 325.

55   10 CPL, Trinder's *Reprint of Grant* (1852); GRO, photo-copy of original deed.

56   11 GRO, VE 2/1, *Cheltenham Vestry Records.*

57   12 Goding, p. 165.

58   13 *Hockaday Extracts*, 147.

59   14 *TBGAS*, vol. v, pp. 222–37.

60   15 *Hockaday MSS.*, 52. Certificate for State of Clergy (1593), as required from the bishops by Archbishop Whitgift.

CHAPTER V

62   1 GRO, Ch. Ct. Bks., D 855/M 1–110.

62   2 In a deed of 1695 (mentioned by Probert) there is a reference to a tenement in the Street, adjoining on the west the Booth Hall or the prison, and on the east, land 'which extendeth itself from the tenement to a great stone there pitched upright in the said street'. This land would be across the opening to the present Colonnade, and the great stone—almost certainly the remains of the High Cross—would be near this opening.

63   3 The Booth Hall and the prison immediately behind it were pulled down as a result of the Act of Parliament (1786).

PAGE

63 4 See Goding, p. 254. A petition to the lord of the manor to assign a place for a new Market-house *on or near* the site of the former house was made in 1654.

63 5 GRO, D 855/M 1, 1 July 1556. 'Edward Bendlow received of the Lord's Surveyor a grant of the reversion of the Court House, with close annexed and certain other demesne lands for a term of years. Fine £4.'

63 6 Goding (p. 184) says that this church house was pulled down in 1813.

66 7 GRO, D 855/M 68, ff. 21–35.

69 8 PRO, Vanderzee/E/159/398 Recorda Hilary 32 Eliz. No. 273. See Goding, p. 67, for a transcript.

70 9 PRO, E 112/16/198.

72 10 BM Add. MS. 6027, pp. 24–25.

72 11 GRO, D 855/M 9, f. 35.

73 12 *TBGAS*, vol. i, p. 61.

76 13 For an explanation of the duties of this office, see G. E. Aylmer, *The King's Servants* (Kegan Paul), p. 93; for the life of John Packer, *Historical Manuscript Commission*, 11th Report, Appendix, pt. vi (1887), p. 174. Burke in the *General Armory* (1884) wrongly assumes that John Packer of Alston and John Packer of Groomsbridge (Clerk of the Privy Seal) were the same person.

CHAPTER VI

77 1 GRO, D 855/M 7. Copy of Norden's Survey.

78 2 W. B. Willcox, *Gloucestershire: A Study in Local Government* (1935).

80 3 GRO, D 855/M 68, ff. 21–35.

82 4 C. V. Wedgwood, *The King's Peace* (1955).

84 5 GRO, D 855/M 68, ff. 36–38. Copy of Deed of Gift (1616).

84 6 BM Add. MS. 6027, ff. 24–25.

88 7 *Visitation of the County of Gloucestershire* (1623).

88 8 Since many of the names are repeated several times it is impossible to be sure of this.

90 9 GRO, D 855/M 68, ff. 10–20.

CHAPTER VII

92 1 GRO, D 855/M 68, ff. 4–8. The text of the Act is printed by Goding, p. 51.

92 2 Money rendered in lieu of services in harvest time.

94 3 H. P. R. Finberg, *Gloucestershire Studies* (1957). Article by R. H. Hilton on 'Winchcombe Abbey and the Manor of Sherborne', pp. 111–12.

94 4 Lord Sherborne, *Memoirs of the Dutton Family*, p. 103. (Privately printed 1899.)

PAGE

95 5 GCL. Copy of the *Grant of the Rectory of Cheltenham and Charlton Kings to Baptist Hicks* (1612).

95 6 GCL, 6107. *True Survey of the Cheltenham Rectory* (1632).

96 7 GRO, D 855/M 68, ff. 10–20.

100 8 Pitt bought the Impropriate Rectory of Cheltenham for £11,470, but this did not include that of Charlton Kings.

100 9 *Walker Revised*, A. G. Matthews, O.U.P. (1948).

100 10 Ibid., p. 7.

101 11 *Memoirs of the Dutton Family*, p. 148.

CHAPTER VIII

102 1 W. B. Willcox, *Gloucestershire*, p. 117, quoted from State Papers 16/33/59.

102 2 *Memoirs of the Dutton Family*.

102 3 *VCH*, p. 36.

104 4 Goding, p. 218, quoted from 'A True and Exact Relation of the Marchings of the Two Regiments of the Train Bands of the City of London', Henry Foster.

104 5 It has been generally assumed that the area stretching from the present St. James's station to the north-east corner of Imperial Square, which was then open fields, was the scene of fighting, since a number of uncoffined skeletons have been found there in conjunction with weapons and coins of the period. Similar skeletons were found in the High Street, but unfortunately neither these nor the weapons have survived (Goding, p. 214).

105 6 *Memoirs of the Dutton Family*.

105 7 Ibid., p. xi.

106 8 Ibid., p. 123.

107 9 *TBGAS*, vol. xlvii, article on Henry Norwood by J. H. Trye, p. 113. Also article by Fairfax Harrison in the *Virginia Magazine of History and Biography*, vol. xxxiii, Jan. 1925.

107 10 GRO D 855/M 68, f. 44.

109 11 *Walker Revised*, op. cit.

109 12 *Hockaday Extracts*, 147, 148—BM Add. MS. 15670–1.

109 13 *Hockaday Collections* 66, Parliamentary Survey of Church Livings.

CHAPTER IX

110 1 Thomas Fuller, *History of the Worthies of England* (1662).

110 2 Willcox, op. cit., quoted from S.P. 14/180/79, p. 159.

110 3 St. Clair Baddeley, *A Cotswold Shrine* (1908), p. 147.

111 4 C. M. MacInnes, *The Early English Tobacco Trade* (1926), pp. 86–89.

111 5 Willcox, p. 159.

112 6 Quoted in full by Goding, p. 227.

113 7 MacInnes, p. 104. Letter from John Beaman, quoted from Cal. State Papers (Domestic), 31 July 1658.

PAGE

114 8 Ibid., p. 112.

114 9 Ibid.

115 10 Goding, p. 245.

115 11 CPL, 63 E 708. P 4. This is probably a copy of the original record.

117 12 GRO, D 1949/M 7.

118 13 Under the Highways Act (1555).

118 14 GCL, *Law Journal* (1861–2).

120 15 *Baptist Magazine*, 18 Oct. 1818.

120 16 GRO, D1340/82.

122 17 Sir Robert Atkyns, *History of Gloucestershire* (1712).

122 18 GRO, D 855/M 12.

122 19 CPL, C. A. Probert, *Footnotes on the History of Cheltenham*.

123 20 *Hearth Tax*, photo-copy GRO, D 83.

123 21 GRO, D 855/M 9.

CHAPTER X

124 1 Moreau, *Tour to Cheltenham Spa* (1783), p. 42.

124 2 William Mason who owned the Bayshill property purchased the Well in 1718—Ridley's *Cheltenham Guide* (1781). For wills of the Mason and Skillicorne families see GRO, D 2010.

126 3 Goding, p. 249.

126 4 This was pulled down in 1860 to make way for the predecessor of the present St. Matthew's Church.

127 5 Now Pittville Street.

127 6 GCL, 'Early History of Methodism in Cheltenham' (*Proceedings of the Wesley Historical Society*, vol. xii).

131 7 CPL, *Memoirs of a Blunderhead* (1783).

131 8 At the south-east corner of the present Rodney Road.

132 9 CPL, J. Ridley, *Cheltenham Guide* (1781), p. 85.

132 10 Hugh Hughes, Perpetual Curate-in-Charge (1778–89). Francis Close who held the same office in the nineteenth century always signed the Vestry Book as minister.

134 11 CPL, Leslie Bayley, *Life of Thomas Hughes* (1952), p. 4.

134 12 On the east corner of Cambray and the High Street.

135 13 These rooms were replaced in 1816 by larger rooms which in turn were taken down to make way for Lloyds Bank (1881).

CHAPTER XI

139 1 *Gentleman's Magazine*, 1788. The royal visit to Cheltenham was fully described in various issues for July and August. Goding, p. 299, gives the relevant passages from the *Morning Post* (18 July 1788) and from Moreau's *Guide* (1806 edition).

CHAPTER XII

144   1 T. D. Fosbroke, *Account of Cheltenham* (1826), p. 25.
144   2 The Great House.
146   3 S. Y. Griffith, *Historical Description of Cheltenham* (1826), p. 27.
146   4 *Rural Economy.*
147   5 Two 'Railway Inns' derive their name from their position on this old track.
148   6 Near the site of the present Gordon Lamp.
148   7 This was moved in 1837 to make way for the present Queen's Hotel and was rebuilt at the back of the Fountain in the Promenade, where it remained until the Regal Cinema displaced it.
149   8 S. Y. Griffith, *Historical Description of Cheltenham* (1826), p. 30.
151   9 *Glos. Notes and Queries*, vol. iii, p. 443.
152 10 GRO, D 181.
154 11 The Cold Bath was near the Chelt, between St. George's Road and St. James's station. It was traditionally a Roman bath, but there is no evidence that this was so.
155 12 GRO, Q/RI 40.

CHAPTER XIII

160   1 GRO, D 149/X 5.
160   2 From Mrs. Neville, in the possession of R. C. Alcock, Esq. (Wagers Court, Charlton Kings), with whose permission this quotation is given.
162   3 Thomas Moore, *Life and Letters of Lord Byron* (1847).
164   4 Thomas Campbell, *Life of Sara Siddons.*
165   5 The original house is still standing and was known as the Basket Shop.
167   6 CPL, C. A. Probert, *A Cheltenham Bi-centenary* (1913).
169   7 T. Baron, *Life of Dr. Jenner* (1824); also *At Cheltenham Spa*, p. 97.

CHAPTER XIV

176   1 G. A. Williams, *Guide Book to Cheltenham* (1826), p. 29.
176   2 CPL, *The English Spy* (1826), p. 246.
178   3 H. Davies, *Cheltenham Past and Present* (1843), p. 187.
178   4 *Country Life* (7 Jan. 1926).
179   5 An article by Sir Hugh Casson in the *Geographical Magazine* (7 Feb. 1943) gives this point of view.
180   6 GRO, D 2010, *Skillicorne Papers.*
182   7 On the site of the present Lloyds Bank at the corner of Rodney Road and the High Street.
182   8 CPL, L. Bayley, *Robert Hughes* (1952), p. 7.
183   9 The arches stretched across the present Bennington Street.
184 10 H. Davies, *The Stranger's Guide to Cheltenham* (1834).
185 11 *Cheltenham Looker-on*, 1 July 1916.

PAGE

CHAPTER XV

186   1   CPL, *Cheltenham Mail-bag* (1828), p. 11.
189   2   *Jane Austen's Letters*, Chapman, O.U.P., reprinted 1959, pp. 132–3.
191   3   S. Y. Griffith, *Historical Description of Cheltenham* (1826), p. 63.
192   4   H. Davies, *Stranger's guide through Cheltenham* (1843) p. 81.
193   5   Quoted by Humphris and Willoughby, *At Cheltenham Spa* (1928), p. 263.
195   6   Catharine Sinclair, *Hill and Valley* (1838).
199   7   *The Examiner*, 1876. 25 Feb. 1873.
200   8   'Pen Pictures of Popular English Preachers', p. 261, quoted by G. Berwick, 'Close of Cheltenham' (unpublished typescript in CPL.)
204   9   Humphris and Willoughby, *At Cheltenham Spa* (1928) p. 253.
204   10   Ibid., p. 259.
204   11   Diaries and papers in the possession of G. Whinyates, Esq.
205   12   Goding, p. 381.
206   13   CPL, Alfred Miles, 'History of Cheltenham', vol. i, p. 232 (unpublished MSS).
207   14   CPL, 63 G 328.
208   15   *Cheltenham Chronicle*, 10 Aug. 1832.
209   16   Goding, p. 38.

CHAPTER XVI

211   1   CPL, Rowe's *Guide to Cheltenham* (1844), p. 13.
212   2   G. A. Hainton and A. Platts, *Education in Gloucestershire* (1954), p. 61.
212   3   Ibid., p. 55.
212   4   C. A. Probert, *A Cheltenham Bi-centenary* (1913).
213   5   W. E. Beck, *The Cheltenham Training Colleges* (1947); Godens, p. 152.
215   6   Alfred Harper (editor), *Cheltenham Grammar School* (1856), p.124.
216   7   A. K. Clarke, *The History of Cheltenham Ladies' College* (1953). p. 29.
218   8   Stopford Brooke, *Life and Letters of Frederick Robertson* (1887). pp. 81, 102.
219   9   G. Berwick, op. cit.
222   10   Joseph McCabe, *Life and Letters of George Jacob Holyoake* (1908).
224   11   C. A. Cardew, *Echoes and Reminiscences of Medical Practitioners of the 19th Century* (Ed. J. Burrow), p. 28.
228   12   Miles, vol. v, p. 196; *Cheltenham Graphic*, 15 Jan. 1927.
228   13   E. Humphris, *Adam Lindsay Gordon* (1933), p. 7.
229   14   Humphris and Willoughby, *At Cheltenham Spa* (1928), p. 283.
230   15   Dorothea Beale, *Cheltenham Ladies' College* (1903), p. 25.
230   16   Hallam Tennyson, *Life of Lord Tennyson* (1912), p. 219.

PAGE

230 17 A. N. L. Munby, *The Family Affairs of Sir Thomas Phillipps* (1952), pp. 91–92.

CHAPTER XVII

233 1 E. T. MacDermot, *History of the Great Western Railway* (1927), pp. 26, 162.
233 2 H. E. Branch, *Cheltenham in the Nineteenth Century* (1900), p. 22.
235 3 Miles, *History of Cheltenham*, vol. v, p. 172.
236 4 GRO, Q/AP 23, Petition from St. Peter's Parish.
237 5 *Cheltenham Journal*, 7 Nov. 1854.
240 6 Sometimes known as Fauconberg Lodge or House and as Bayshill Lodge.
241 7 A. K. Clarke, *History of the Cheltenham Ladies' College* (1953), p. 62.

CHAPTER XVIII

243 1 Probably the Old Town Hall in Regent Street—see Rayner Winterbotham's speech in 1847.
244 2 Sir James Agg-Gardner, *Some Parliamentary Recollections* (1927), pp. 36–38, quoted by kind permission of Messrs. Ed. J. Burrow & Co.
245 3 *Cheltenham Journal*, 25 Jan. 1841.
247 4 Stated in a letter from James Fallon included in Berkeley Letters (GRO, D 1291).
247 5 *Cheltenham Examiner*, 23 Aug. and 29 Nov. 1848.
248 6 Ibid., 15 Dec. 1847.
250 7 *Looker-On*, Nov. 1847.
251 8 GRO, D 1685, 7 Feb. 1850. See Chapter XXII.
252 9 Earl of Bessborough, *Lady Charlotte Guest* (1952).
253 10 Alfred Miles, *History of Cheltenham*, vol. 9, p. 154.
254 11 *Cheltenham Journal*, 15 July 1865.
255 12 *Cheltenham Examiner*, 12 May 1866.
255 13 GRO, D 1291.
255 14 Ibid.

CHAPTER XIX

258 1 GRO, P 78 VE 2/1.
260 2 This is marked on a plan dated 1775, and is located near the present Calcutta Inn. (Photo-copy GRO, QS/RE 1776A.
261 3 The appointment was sometimes made directly—sometimes it was confirmed—by the J.P.s (B. and S. Webb, *Story of the King's Highway*, 1920, pp. 14–26).
261 4 S. and B. Webb, *Story of the King's Highway*, p. 215–22.
264 5 The original water-colour by John Nattes is in the Cheltenham Art Gallery collection.
268 6 This box is still in the possession of the Cheltenham Borough Council.

PAGE

270 7 See *Cheltenham Chronicle*, 24 Jan. 1811, for a description of the fall of the Market-house. 'Thursday the old Market House which has long been in a state of dilapidation, fell with a tremendous crash. . . .' There is a reference in the Commissioners' Minutes (1811) to compensation paid for loss sustained by the fall of the old Market-house and two years later to the removal of the stone steps.

CHAPTER XX

275 1 The information for this chapter has been taken mainly from the *Cheltenham Vestry Records*, GRO, P78/VE 2/1.

280 2 *Glos. Notes and Queries*, vol. iii, p. 246.

280 3 R. A. Lewis, *Edwin Chadwick and the Public Health Movement*.

285 4 S. and B. Webb, *The Parish and the County*, in their series on Local Government (1906).

287 5 GRO, GR/CH.

289 6 Goding, p. 245.

290 7 The others were Thomas Jones—builder and churchwarden; William Gyde—grocer; William Jenkins—yeoman; John Gaskins—inn-holder; John Morris—yeoman; and Dr. Newell, Dr. Minster, Baynham Jones, Esq., Thomas Smith, Esq.—described as principal inhabitants of the town.

292 8 Goding (p. 406) prints a copy of the terrier.

296 9 CPL, Alfred Harper, *Cheltenham Grammar School* (1856), p. 28.

296 10 *Looker-On*, June 1859, p. 28.

CHAPTER XXI

This chapter is based almost entirely on the Commissioners' Reports for the years mentioned and on material from contemporary newspapers.

301 1 Present Henrietta Street.

307 2 The regulations were made under the Quarantine Act (1802) which enabled local boards to establish hospitals and remove nuisances at the expense of the Poor Law Authorities.

309 3 These included all male adult ratepayers.

CHAPTER XXII

314 1 Goding, p. 553.

315 2 *Cheltenham Examiner*, 5 Apr. 1841.

319 3 Letters from Chief Constable's Office (GRO, Q/AP 4).

319 4 Under the Highways Act (1835).

320 5 Set up under the Poor Law Amendment Act (1834), with sanitary powers extended by later Acts.

320 6 Formerly Gallows Lane—now Hales Road.

PAGE

323 7 *Cheltenham Examiner*, 11 Oct. 1848.

323 8 Ibid., 28 Feb. 1849.

324 9 CPL, 'Report by Edward Cresy to General Board of Health . . . an enquiry . . . into the sanitary conditions of Cheltenham' (1849).

CHAPTER XXIII

330 1 *Cheltenham Examiner*, 23 Feb. 1853.

330 2 Quoted by Goding, p. 599.

331 3 CPL, *Enquiry into position of Cheltenham Copyholders* (1863).

332 4 This right was granted in a clause inserted by the House of Lords in the Copyhold Enfranchisement Act (1852) at the instigation of Earl Fitzhardinge (Colonel Berkeley).

CHAPTER XXIV

339 1 Full reports of the Commissioners' meetings were now published in the local newspapers. For early procedure and the appointment of the first officials, see the *Examiner*, weekly issues, 3 June– 7 July 1852.

340 2 *Cheltenham Free Press*, 5 Feb. 1853.

340 3 *Cheltenham Examiner*, 7 Sept. 1853.

344 4 Special Supplement issued by the *Examiner*, 26 Sept. 1855.

346 5 *Cheltenham Journal*, 3 Nov. 1860.

347 6 *Cheltenham Examiner*, 24 June 1874.

348 7 Ibid., 8 May 1872.

349 8 Ibid., 7 July 1874.

349 9 Supplement issued by the *Examiner*, Oct. 1875.

352 10 *Examiner*, 29 Mar. 1876.

354 11 A. C. Fox-Davies, *The Book of Public Arms* (1915).

POSTSCRIPT

355 1 Miles, vol. vi, p. 275.

355 2 *Examiner*, 15 Nov. 1876.

358 3 Catalogue of Permanent Collection of the Cheltenham Art Gallery.

361 4 G. Seaver, *Edward Wilson of the Antarctic* (1933), p. 291.

363 5 CPL, A. S. Owen, *James Owen*, p. 34.

363 6 A. S. G. Butler, *Portrait of Josephine Butler* (1953), p. 210, quoted by kind permission of Messrs. Faber and Faber.

365 7 Estimated population, 74, 910 (med. 1964)

365 8 Parts of Leckhampton and of Charlton Kings were taken in 1893, and of Up Hatherley and of Prestbury in 1935.

INDEX

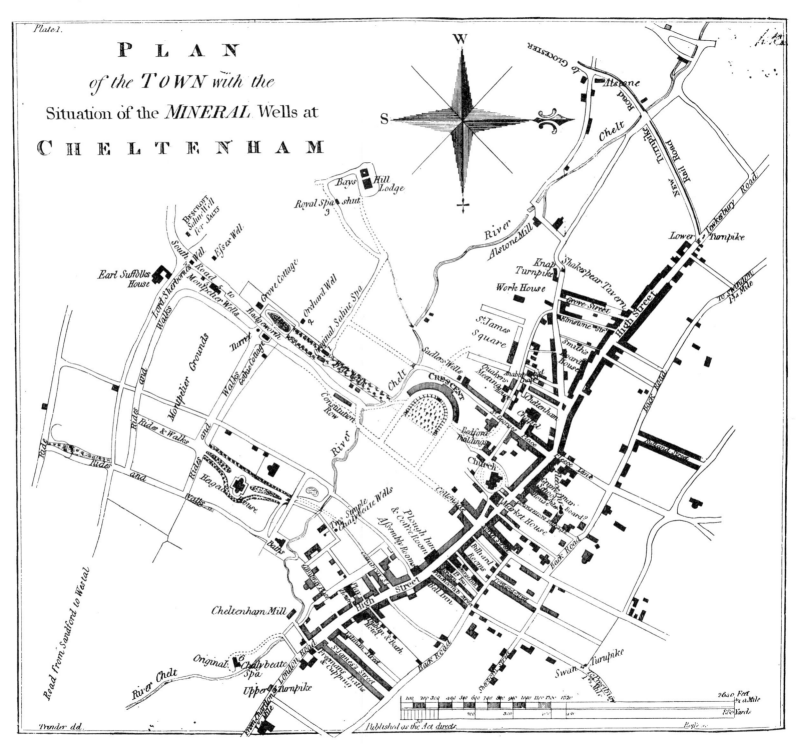

CHELTENHAM: Daniel TRINDER, from *A Treatise on Cheltenham Waters and Bilious Diseases*, by Thomas Jameson, 1809 (9″ × 5″)